THE INTERNATIONALISATION OF ANTITRUST POLICY

The internationalisation of antitrust policy is a topic of great contemporary significance and debate. Dr Dabbah provides an inquiry that is at once clearly stated, original and empirical, setting out the relevant issues in the context of law, economics and politics. He draws on the decisional practice of antitrust authorities, actions and statements of political bodies, as well as the decisions of law courts. Providing a detailed examination of the experiences of the European Community and the United States, Dr Dabbah includes a comprehensive examination of central concepts and ideas related to antitrust law and practice. The book concludes by looking forward to potential developments in the landscape, and suggests a new approach to the internationalisation of antitrust policy. This will be of interest to antitrust officials, as well as international organisations, members of the business community, academics, researchers and policy-makers who are involved in antitrust law and policy.

MAHER M. DABBAH is Lecturer in Competition Law at Queen Mary, University of London, and is a Barrister in England and Wales. He is also Visiting Professor of Competition Law in the College of Management, Academic Division, Israel. He acts as a consultant to several corporations and international organisations and is involved in the training of lawyers, economists, judges and government officials from many countries in the area of antitrust law.

THE
INTERNATIONALISATION OF
ANTITRUST POLICY

MAHER M. DABBAH

*Lecturer in Competition Law at Queen Mary, University of London
and barrister of the Middle Temple.*

CAMBRIDGE
UNIVERSITY PRESS

PUBLISHED BY THE PRESS SYNDICATE OF THE UNIVERSITY OF CAMBRIDGE
The Pitt Building, Trumpington Street, Cambridge, United Kingdom

CAMBRIDGE UNIVERSITY PRESS
The Edinburgh Building, Cambridge, CB2 2RU, UK
40 West 20th Street, New York, NY 10011–4211, USA
477 Williamstown Road, Port Melbourne, VIC 3207, Australia
Ruiz de Alarcón 13, 28014 Madrid, Spain
Dock House, The Waterfront, Cape Town 8001, South Africa

http://www.cambridge.org

First published 2003
Reprinted 2005

Printed in the United Kingdom at the University Press, Cambridge

Typeface Adobe Minion 10.5/13.5 pt.   *System* LATEX 2$_\varepsilon$ [TB]

A catalogue record for this book is available from the British Library

ISBN 0 521 82079 0 hardback

To my parents

CONTENTS

Preface   *page* x
Table of reports   xii
Table of cases   xv
List of abbreviations   xx

1   **Introduction**   1
    General   1
    Similarities and differences   2
    The scope of the book   4
    The nature of the book   6
    The examples of internationalisation   9
    Some reflection on terminology   10
    Globalisation and its implications for antitrust policy   12
    The structure of the book   15

2   **Refining some concepts and ideas**   17
    The concept of competition   17
    Some historical perspectives of a particular idea and
        political philosophy   28
    Market definition   35
    Conclusion   44

3   **Antitrust law: goals and political perspective**   46
    Antitrust law: concept, framework and goals   46
    A political perspective of antitrust law   58
    Competition advocacy   63
    Conclusion   68

4   **The use of discretion**   70
    A framework   71

Identifying instances of discretion   72
Dealing with discretion   76
Some implications of the analysis   83
Conclusion   85

5 **EC antitrust policy**   **86**
Some introductory issues   86
Institutional framework   91
The relationship between EC and domestic antitrust laws   95
The significance and influence of EC antitrust law beyond
    the single market   112
Implications of the analysis   134
Conclusion   138

6 **Sovereignty**   **139**
The conceptual framework of sovereignty   140
Sovereignty under public international law   144
Sovereignty and the internationalisation of antitrust
    policy   149
The emerging order   154
Conclusion   158

7 **Extraterritoriality**   **159**
The question of jurisdiction   159
Some fundamental issues   164
Developments in the USA and the EC   167
Responses to extraterritoriality   187
Some reflections   191
Dealing with extraterritoriality and its conflicts   196
Conclusion   204

8 **Antitrust and trade policies**   **206**
Overview   206
The different restraints   209
The perspectives of antitrust and trade policies   215
The different approaches   216
Market access principle   227
Developments of some interest   234
Implications of the analysis   237
Conclusion   246

9 **Past, present and future: a comparative analysis** **247**
Some important past developments 247
Institutional framework 250
From present to the future 257
Political power and perspectives of countries, firms
and consumer interests 266
Model systems of antitrust 273
The EC–US conflict 277
Convergence and harmonisation 280
Substantive issues 283
Reflections and summary 284

10 **Conclusions: the way forward** **287**

Bibliography 295
Index 315
List of websites 321

PREFACE

The publication of the book comes at a time when enormous and significant developments are taking place in the area of internationalisation of antitrust policy worldwide. Only a month ago, the first annual conference of the young International Competition Network (ICN) was held. The events leading to the birth of the Network in general and the organisation of that conference in particular, along with the conference proceedings and outcomes, have served as a timely reminder of the fact that the internationalisation of antitrust policy is a topic of great contemporary significance and debate. Outside the ICN, extremely important work in the area continues to evolve and take shape, notably within the Organisation for Economic Cooperation and Development (OECD), the United Nations Conference on Trade and Development (UNCTAD) and the World Trade Organization (WTO). Of these important fora, the WTO has been receiving particular attention. The success of the WTO's 4th Ministerial Conference and the preparations already underway for the 5th Ministerial Conference, show not only the importance and need for addressing international antitrust issues effectively but also the important role which the WTO can play in this regard – something which should be encouraged and welcomed.

A decade ago it was extremely rare for antitrust conferences and events to include a mention of the internationalisation of antitrust policy. It is very interesting and remarkable how things have changed in a relatively short period of time. Nowadays it is quite rare for such conferences and events not to include such a mention. Indeed, this development is all the more remarkable in light of the phenomenal increase in the importance and geographical scope of antitrust law itself during the last twenty years or so.

In writing this book I aimed to produce a volume that would be of help and value for officials of antitrust authorities, international organisations dealing with antitrust and international trade issues, the business community, antitrust lawyers including academics and researchers, economists, political scientists and policy-makers interested in antitrust law and policy. Most of the ideas in the book come from my teaching experience and my work as a consultant to several companies and international organisations as well as from being involved in the training of government officials, economists, lawyers and judges from many countries in the area of antitrust law.

Every book has a story, and the present book is no exception. The idea of writing on the internationalisation of antitrust policy took shape several years ago in the land of 'antitrust'. Soon afterwards that idea was turned into a doctoral thesis, of which the present book is a revision and expansion and which I prepared at King's College, London under the supervision of Professor Richard Whish. As the first person to graduate with a PhD under Richard's supervision, I feel I have particularly benefited from his rich experience and knowledge. It was also a great experience for me to teach with Richard the LLM EC Competition Law course at King's College, London for a period of four years. Warm thanks are due to him for all the help and support he often generously offered. I am so fortunate to have such a great colleague and friend.

In addition, I would like to express my appreciation to Dr Tamar Gidron, The Markeys, Professor Steve Anderman, Professor Peter Muchlinski, Professor Eleanor Fox, Christopher Brown, David Bailey and my former research assistant at King's College, London, Monica Chowdry. I also would like to thank the very able and helpful staff at Cambridge University Press. In particular, I would like to express my warm gratitude to Ms Finola O'Sullivan. My thanks also go to my brothers and sisters for their love and support.

Finally, my greatest debt is to my wonderful and great parents, to whom I dedicate this book.

I have aimed to state the law as it stood on 1 November 2002.

Maher Dabbah
Queen Mary, University of London

TABLE OF REPORTS

American Bar Association (ABA)

Private Anti-Competitive Practices as Market Access Barriers (2000)

The Internationalization of Competition Law Rules: Coordination and Convergence (1999)

US Department of Justice

International Competition Policy Advisory Committee Report (ICPAC) (2000)

Antitrust Guidelines for International Operations, United States Department of Justice, Antitrust Division (1995)

Antitrust Guidelines for International Operations, United States Department of Justice, Antitrust Division (1988)

European Commission

Green Paper on Merger Review (2001)

The Enlargement Negotiations after Helsinki MEMO/00/6 (2000)

White Paper on the Modernisation of the Rules Implementing Articles 85 and 86 of the EC Treaty (1999)

European Parliament Resolution on the Commission's 28th Report on Competition Policy (1998) Commission Report (1999)

28th Report on Competition Policy (1998)

Competition Policy in the New Trade Order: Strengthening International Co-operation and Rules COM (95) 359, Report of Group of Experts

25th Report on Competition Policy (1995)

White Paper on the Preparation of the Associated Countries of Central and Eastern Europe for Integration into the Internal Market (1995)

23rd Report on Competition Policy (1993)

15th Report on Competition Policy (1985)
Cockfield White Paper on the Completion of the Internal Market (1985)
13th Report on Competition Policy (1983)
11th Report on Competition Policy (1981)
9th Report on Competition Policy (1979)

Organisation for Economic Cooperation and Development (OECD)

Coherence between Trade and Competition Policy (2000)
Consistencies and Inconsistencies between Trade and Competition Policies (1999)
Trade and Competition Policy for Tomorrow (1999)
Trade and Competition: Exploring the Way Forward (1999)
Positive Comity and Related Benefits (1999)
Recommendation Concerning Hard-Core Cartels (1998)
Antitrust and Market Access (1996)
Revised Recommendations Concerning Co-operation between Member Countries on Anticompetitive Practices Affecting International Trade (1995)
New Dimensions of Market Access in Globalizing World Economy (1995)
Convergence of Competition Policies (1994)
Trade and Competition Policies (1993)
Recommendation for Co-operation between Member Countries in Areas of Potential Conflict between Competition and Trade Policies (1986)
Competition Policy in the OECD Countries (1986)
Competition and Trade Policy: Their Interaction (1984)
Restrictive Business Practices of Multinational Enterprises (1977)

International Chamber of Commerce (ICC)

Competition and Trade in the Global Arena: an International Business Perspective (1998)

World Bank

Linking Competition and Trade Policies in Central and East European Countries, Policy Research Working Paper 1346 (1994)

United Nations Conference on Trade and Development (UNCTAD)

Set of Multilaterally Agreed Principles and Rules for the Control of Restrictive Business Practices (1981)

World Trade Organization (WTO)

Annual Report (1998)
Annual Report (1997)
Annual Report (1996)

TABLE OF CASES

EC Cases

A Ahlström Osukeyhtiö *v.* Commission (Wood Pulp): C-89/85, 104/85,
114/85 (1988), ECJ   *page* 120, 160, 176, 178, 183
Aérospatiale/Alenia/De Havilland (EC Commission Decision)
(1991)   90
Airtours plc *v.* Commission: T-342/99 (2002), CFI   82
Alcatel/Newbridge Networks (EC Commission Decision)
(2000)   42
Alcoa/Reynolds (1999) (EC Commission Decision)   115
Alfa Romeo (EC Commission Decision) (1984)   74
Aluminium Imports from Eastern Europe (EC Commission Decision)
(1985)   183
Aniline Dyes Cartel (EC Commission Decision) (1969)   176
AOL/Time Warner (EC Commission Decision) (2001)   42
Automec srl *v.* Commission: T-24/90 (1992), CFI   73
BASF AG *v.* Commission: T-79/89, 84–86/89, 91–92/89, 94/89, 96/89,
98/89, 102/89, 104/89 (1992)   81
Belgische Radio en Televisie et al. *v.* SV SABAM and NV Fonier:
C-127/73 (1974), ECJ   96
Boeing/McDonnell Douglas (EC Commission Decision)
(1997)   113, 270
British Airways/British Caledonian (EC Commission Decision)
(1988)   74
British Leyland (EC Commission Decision) (1984)   74
British Sugar/Berisford (EC Commission Decision) (1982)   74
CVC/Lenzing (2001) (EC Commission Decision)   115
Compaq/HP (2001) (EC Commission Decision)   115

Continental Can Co. Inc., Re (EC Commission Decision)
  (1972)   80
Costa *v*. ENEL: C-6/64 (1964), ECJ   88
Demirel *v*. Stadt Schwäbisch Gmünd: C-12/86 (1987), ECJ   125
Demo-Studio Schmidt *v*. Commission: 210/81(1983), ECJ   73, 80
Establissements Consten SARL and Grundig-Verkaufs-GmbH *v*.
  Commission: C-56, 58/64) (1966), ECJ   80
European Night Services *v*. Commission: T-374–5, 388/94 (1998),
  CFI   81–82
Exxon/Mobil (EC Commission Decision) (1994)   115, 270
Ford/VW (EC Commission Decision) (1993)   90
Förenings Sparbanken/SEB (EC Commission Decision) (2001)   44
Gencor *v*. Commission: T-102/96 (1999), CFI   177–79, 185
General Electric/Honeywell International (EC Commission Decision)
  (2001): T-209/01, 210/01 judgment pending, CFI   115, 116, 179–81,
                                                                185
Grosfillex-Fillistorf (EC Commission Decision) (1964)   176
IBM *v*. Commission: C-60/81, 190/81 (1981), ECJ   183
ICI Ltd. *v*. Commission (Cases 48/69) [1972] ECR 619   188
Irish Sugar *v*. Commission: T-228/97 (1999), CFI   124
LdPE (EC Commission Decision) (1990)   177
MCIWorldcom/Sprint (EC Commission Decision) (2000)   113, 114, 198
Minnesota Mining and Manufacturing/Quante (EC Commission
  Decision) (2000)   42
NV Algemene Transporten Expeditie Onderneming van Gend en
  Loos *v*. Nederlandse Administratie der Belastingen: C-26/62
  (1963), ECJ   88, 94
PVC (EC Commission Decision) (1990)   81, 177
Radio Telefis Eireann *v*. Commission: T-69/89 (1991), CFI   82
Remia BV *v*. Commission: C-42/84 (1985), ECJ   80
S. A. Hercules Chemicals NV *v*. Commission: T-7/89 (1991),
  CFI   82
Schibsted Multimedia AS/Telenor Nextel AS/Telia AB
  (EC Commission Decision) (1999)   41
Schneider Electric *v*. Commission: T-77/02 (2002), CFI   82
Shell/Montedison (EC Commission Decision) (1994)   270
Società Italiana Vetro *v*. Commission: T-68, 77, 78/89 (1992),
  CFI   81

Sonera Systems/ICL/Invia/Data-info/JV (EC Commission Decision)
(2000) 42
Tetra Laval BV *v*. Commission: T-5/02 (2002), CFI 82
Tetra PakRausing SA *v*. Commission: C-333/94 (1996), CFI 124
United Brands *v*. Commission: 27/76 (1978) 38, 39
VBVB *v*. Commission: 43, 63/82 (1984), ECJ 73
Vodafone Airtouch/Mannesmann (EC Commission Decision)
(2000) 42
Volvo/Renault (EC Commission Decision) (2000) 44
Volvo/Scania (EC Commission Decision) (2001) 44
Walt Wilhelm *v*. Bundeskartellamt: C-148/68 (1969), ECJ 95

International Court of Justice Cases

Denmark *v*. Germany (North Sea Continental Shelf) (1968) 160
France *v*. Turkey (S.S. 'Lotus') (1927) 160

UK Cases

British Nylon Spinners Ltd. *v*. ICI (1953) 190
Darcy *v*. Allein (Case of Monopolies) (1602) 32
Dyer's Case (1414) 32
Rio Tinto Zinc *v*. Westinghouse Electric Corp. (1978) 190

US Cases

American Banana Co *v*. United Fruits Co. (1909) 162
Asahi Metal Indus. Co. *v*. Superior Ct. (1987) 173
Baker *v*. Carr 369 US (1962) 193
Broadcast Music, Inc. *v*. CBS (1979) 274
Brooke Group Ltd. *v*. Brown and Williamson Tobacco
Corp. (1993) 273
Caribbean Broad Sys. *v*. Cable and Wireless Plc (1998) 175
Chicago Board of Trade *v*. United States (1918) 273
Doe *v*. United States (1988) 173
Eastern Railroad Presidents Conference *v*. Noerr Motor Freight, Inc.
(1961) 274
Filetech SARL *v*. France Telecom (1997) 175

Hartford Fire Insurance Co. *v.* California (1993)   171, 174, 175 (171–6),
                                                                    185, 195
Hilton *v.* Guyot (1865)   168
Holophane Co. *v.* United States (1956)   192
In re Grand Jury Subpoena Duces Tecum (1947)   188
In re Insurance Antitrust Litigation (1991)   171, 172
In re Uranium Antitrust Litigation: Westinghouse
   Elec. Corp. *v.* Rio Algom Ltd. (1980)   189, 193
Interamerican Refining Corporation *v.* Texaco Maracaibo, Inc.
   (1970)   174
Laker Airways Ltd. *v.* Sabena, Belgian World Airlines (1984)   168, 169,
                                                                         194
Mannington Mills, Inc. *v.* Congoleum Corp. (1979)   169, 174
Metro Indus. Inc. *v.* Sammi Corp. (1996)   175
National Society of Professional Engineers *v.* United States
   (1978)   274
Northern Pacific Railway *v.* United States (1958)   228
NYNEX Corp. *v.* Discon, Inc. (1998)   53
Parker *v.* Brown (1943)   213
The Schooner Channing Betsy (1804)   192
The Schooner Exch. *v.* M'Faddon (1812)   200
Société Nationale Industrielle Aérospatiale *v.* United States
   District Court (1987)   173
Southern Motor Carriers Rate Conference *v.* US (1985)   213
Spectrum Sports, Inc. *v.* McQuillan (1993)   273
Standard Oil Co. *v.* United States (1911)   273
Timberlane Lumber Co. *v.* Bank of America National Trust
   and Savings Association (1984)   171
Timberlane Lumber Co. *v.* Bank of America National Trust
   and Savings Association (1976)   168, 169, 174
Timken Roller Bearing Co. *v.* United States (1951)   192
Trugman-Nash Inc. *v.* New Zealand Dairy Board (1997)   175
Underhill *v.* Hernandez (1897)   199
United Mine Workers *v.* Pennington (1965)   274
United States *v.* Aluminum Co. of America (Alcoa) (1927)   162
United States *v.* Cerestar Bioproducts BV (1998)   175
United States *v.* Heeremac (1997)   175
United States *v.* Hoffmann-La Roche (1997)   175

United States *v.* Imperial Chem. Indus. Ltd. (1951) 190, 192
United States *v.* Minnesota Mining and Mfg. Co. (1950) 192
United States *v.* Nippon Paper Industries Co. (1997) 175
United States *v.* Pilkington plc (1994) 216
United States *v.* Sisal Sales Corporation (1927) 162
United States *v.* Watchmaking of Switzerland Information
    Centre, Inc. (1955) 150, 199
United States *v.* Watchmakers of Switzerland (1962) 174, 192

ABBREVIATIONS

AB	*Antitrust Bulletin*
AER	*American Economic Review*
AJCL	*American Journal of Comparative Law*
AJCorpL	*Australian Journal of Corporate Law*
AJIL	*American Journal of International Law*
ALJ	*Antitrust Law Journal*
AR	*Antitrust Report*
AULR	*American University Law Review*
BJIL	*Brooklyn Journal of International Law*
BL	*Business Lawyer*
BLR	*Brookings Law Review*
BUILJ	*Boston University International Law Journal*
BULR	*Boston University Law Review*
BYBIL	*British Yearbook of International Law*
CFI	*European Court of First Instance*
CILJ	*Cornell International Law Journal*
CJTL	*Columbia Journal of Transnational Law*
CKLR	*Chicago-Kent Law Review*
CLP	*Current Legal Problems*
CLR	*Cardozo Law Review*
CMLR	*Common Market Law Reports*
CMLRev	*Common Market Law Review*
ColLR	*Columbia Law Review*
CorLR	*Cornell Law Review*
CPE	*Constitutional Political Economy*
CUSLJ	*Canada–United-States Law Journal*
CWILJ	*California Western International Law Journal*
CWRJIL	*Case Western Reserve Journal of International Law*
DG COMP	*Directorate of Commission responsible for antitrust policy*

DJILP	*Denver Journal of International Law and Policy*
ECCPNL	*European Community Competition Policy NewsLetter*
ECJ	*European Court of Justice*
ECLR	*European Competition Law Review*
ECMR	*European Community Merger Regulation*
ECoun	*European Counsel*
ECR	*European Court Reports*
EEA	*European Economic Area*
EECR	*East European Constitutional Review*
EFTA	*European Free Trade Association*
EJPR	*European Journal of Political Research*
ELR	*European Law Review*
FBNJ	*Federal Bar News and Journal*
FCLI	*Fordham Corporate Law Institute*
FILJ	*Fordham International Law Journal*
FLR	*Fordham Law Review*
FTC	*Federal Trade Commission*
GCR	*Global Competition Review*
GLJ	*Georgetown Law Journal*
GMLR	*George-Mason University Law Review*
HICLR	*Hastings International and Comparative Law Review*
HILJ	*Harvard International Law Journal*
HLJ	*Hastings Law Journal*
HLR	*Harvard Law Review*
IBL	*International Business Lawyer*
ICJ	*International Court of Justice*
ICLQ	*International and Comparative Law Quarterly*
ICN	*International Competition Network*
ICPAC	*International Competition Policy Advisory Committee*
IICLR	*Industrial International and Comparative Law Review*
IILR	*International Institute Law Review*
IJEL	*Irish Journal of European Law*
IL	*International Lawyer*
ILR	*Israel Law Review*
IO	*International Organization*
ITR	*International Trade Representative*
JCMS	*Journal of Common Market Studies*
JIS	*Journal of International Studies*

JITE	*Journal of Institutional and Theoretical Economy*
JLE	*Journal of Law and Economics*
JMLR	*John Marshall Law Review*
JWTL	*Journal of World Trade Law*
LLR	*Loyola Law Review*
LPIB	*Law and Policy in International Business*
LQR	*Law Quarterly Review*
LS	*Legal Studies*
MarLR	*Marquette Law Review*
MicLR	*Michigan Law Review*
MJGT	*Minnesota Journal of Global Trade*
MJIL	*Michigan Journal of International Law*
MLR	*Modern Law Review*
MNEs	*Multinational Enterprises*
NELR	*New England Law Review*
NILQ	*Northern Ireland Legal Quarterly*
NJILB	*Northwestern Journal of International Law and Business*
NULR	*Northwestern University Law Review*
NYULR	*New York University Law Review*
OECD	*Organisation for Economic Cooperation and Development*
OJ	*Official Journal of the European Community*
ONULR	*Ohio Northern University Law Review*
OREP	*Oxford Review of Economic Policy*
OSLJ	*Ohio State Law Journal*
PCIJ	*Permanent Court of International Justice*
PRLPJ	*Pacific-Rimely Law and Policy Journal*
QJE	*Quarterly Journal of Economics*
RDC	*Recueil des Cours*
RLR	*Rutgers Law Review*
RMCLUE	*Revue du Marché Commun et de l'Union Européene*
SCLR	*Southern California Law Review*
SCR	*Supreme Court Review*
SJIL	*Stanford Journal of International Law*
SJILC	*Syracuse Journal of International Law and Commerce*
SRICL	*Swiss Review of International Competition Law*
SSNIP	*Small but Significant Non-transitory Increase in Price*
STLJ	*Suffolk Transnational Law Journal*
TL	*Transnational Lawyer*

TLR	*Texas Law Review*
UCDLR	*University of California, Davis Law Review*
UCinLR	*University of Cincinnati Law Review*
UCLF	*University of Chicago Legal Forum*
UCLR	*University of Chicago Law Review*
UFLR	*University of Florida Law Review*
UNCTAD	*United Nations Conference on Trade and Development*
UPitLR	*University of Pittsburgh Law Review*
UPJIBL	*University of Pennsylvania Journal of International Business Law*
UPJIEL	*University of Pennsylvania Journal of International Economic Law*
UPLR	*University of Pennsylvania Law Review*
VanLR	*Vanderbilt Law Review*
VilLR	*Villanova Law Review*
VirLR	*Virginia Law Review*
VJIL	*Virginia Journal of International Law*
VJTL	*Vanderbilt Journal of Transnational Law*
WC	*World Competition*
WLR	*Wayne Law Review*
WTO	*World Trade Organization*
YEL	*Yearbook of European Law*
YJIL	*Yale Journal of International Law*
YLJ	*Yale Law Journal*

1

Introduction

General

The twentieth century witnessed a heated debate between capitalism and communism over the desirability of competition in the marketplace. Until the last quarter of that century there was a tendency in many parts of the world to favour a tradition of exerting strict control over the planning and management of domestic economies. As the end of the century approached, however, the scene began to change dramatically with a move on the part of many countries from monopolisation to demonopolisation and from state control and planning to liberalisation and privatisation. This important development has enormously contributed to the growing recognition that, on the whole, competition can be regarded as an effective tool for enhancing innovation, furthering economic growth and safeguarding the welfare and social development of countries. Remarkably, the debate seems to have settled in favour of the market mechanism, and this has enhanced the desirability of competition.

The growing recognition of the value of competition has been accompanied by a relentless process of globalisation and a sharp increase in the removal of hindrances to the flows of trade and investment worldwide.[1] It has also been accompanied by a considerable increase in the number of countries, which – particularly over the last two decades – have come to recognise not only the desirability of competition but also the need to protect it.[2] The law used to protect competition is commonly referred to as 'antitrust law', or 'competition law'.[3] Today, nearly 100 jurisdictions have

---

[1] See A. Fiebig, 'A Role for the WTO in International Merger Control' (2000) 20 *Northwestern Journal of International Law and Business* 233, 235. See also pp. 12–15 below for a discussion on globalisation and its implications for antitrust policy.

[2] See M. Palim, 'The World Wide Growth of Competition Law: an Empirical Analysis' (1998) 43 *Antitrust Bulletin* 105.

[3] 'Antitrust law' is the term used in the United States (USA). The term 'Competition law' is a synonym used more commonly outside the USA. The term 'antitrust law', unlike the concept

adopted some form of antitrust law and at least thirty others are in the process of developing antitrust legislation.[4] This impressive geographical expansion of the law has not been confined to certain countries or economies; it will, if anything, increase in the years ahead.

Similarities and differences

Most of the world's systems of antitrust share many common features. These include prohibitions on certain horizontal agreements between firms (such as cartels aiming at market-sharing, price-fixing and limiting production etc.), certain vertical restraints and abuses of market power by powerful firms. In more than half of those systems, there is a mechanism for the control of mergers.

In addition to these similarities, there are also many differences. These differences will be examined in detail in later chapters of the book; however, it would be useful at this stage to give an account of some of these differences. The first difference to be mentioned concerns the lack of consensus with respect to the meaning that should be given to terms such as 'competition' and 'anti-competitive'. As will become apparent during the course of the discussion, it is not clear whether countries agree on how these concepts should be defined and understood. Secondly, there is a debate regarding whether competition particularly needs antitrust law at all and whether it can be protected using other types of law and policy. In some countries the laws are referred to as laws against 'restrictive trade practices'. These laws may be more concerned with regulating how large firms use their market muscle than with removing hindrances to free market competition.[5] In other countries the laws are called the laws against unfair competition; and there is a third, but not a final, category of countries where the law is

---

of 'competition', encounters hardly any previous usage in the English language. See D. Gerber, *Law and Competition in Twentieth Century Europe* (Oxford University Press, Oxford, 1998), p. 4, analysing the translation of the term into other languages.

[4] See D. Valentine, 'Antitrust in a Global High Tech-Economy', paper delivered before the American Bar Association of the District of Columbia at the 8th National Forum for Women Corporate Counsel 30 April 1999, available at http://www.ftc.gov/speeches/other/dvatspeech.htm. Also, see W. Rowley and N. Campbell, 'Multi-Jurisdictional Merger Review – Is It Time for a Common Form Filing Treaty?' in *Policy Directions for Global Merger Review*, a special report by the Global Forum for Competition and Trade Policy (1999).

[5] Report of the American Bar Association Sections of Antitrust Law and International Law and Practice on *The Internationalization of Competition Law Rules: Coordination and Convergence*, ABA, December 1999.

called the antitrust or competition and fair trading law. A highly interesting and important question, which will be considered at some stage in the discussion, is whether these laws actually mean and aim to address the same thing. Thirdly, there are differences regarding the antitrust law traditions of countries and the degree of seriousness with which they enforce their antitrust laws. Certain countries may not be keen on enforcing their antitrust laws, whether seriously or at all, if or when foreign firms may be the beneficiaries of enforcement actions. On the other hand, lax antitrust enforcement by countries causes uncertainty and creates incentives for firms to treat these countries as 'antitrust havens', a situation that is likely to lead to distortions of competition in the countries concerned and may even extend beyond domestic boundaries.[6] At the moment, not all countries where antitrust law has been adopted, enjoy a tradition of vigorous enforcement of the law. Some countries have a tradition of separation of antitrust law enforcement and decision-making from politics, but others do not. Some countries have a tradition of state control and planning, which in some cases has been disintegrating, and others have a strong tradition of liberalisation and privatisation. Fourthly, there is no agreement on the proper goals of antitrust law. The possibilities range from economic to social to political goals.[7] Fifthly, there is lack of agreement regarding the right institutional approach to protect competition. In some jurisdictions it is done administratively, whilst in others it is done judicially.[8] Finally, countries differ with regard to the way transnational antitrust issues should be handled. At one end of the spectrum, some countries are 'unilateralist' in their approach and thinking. What this means is that, quite frequently, they are willing to export their domestic antitrust laws into other jurisdictions, a factor which, as will be seen, can be problematic.[9] At the other end of the spectrum, other countries seem to believe that there is scope for creating some common order within antitrust law and policy by adopting a 'bilateral',[10] a 'regional',

---

[6] D. Gerber, 'Afterword: Antitrust and American Business Abroad Revisited' (2000) 20 *Northwestern Journal of International Law and Business* 307, 312. See further chs. 7 and 8.

[7] See pp. 49–57 below.

[8] See J. Griffin, 'What Business People Want from a World Antitrust Code' (1999) 34 *New England Law Review* 39, 44; C. Bellamy, 'Some Reflections on Competition Law in the Global Market' (1999) 34 *New England Law Review* 15, 18–19.

[9] See chs. 7 and 9.

[10] 'Bilateral' is used in this context to refer to the conclusion of bilateral agreements between countries, in particular between their domestic antitrust authorities. See for example the agreement entered into between the European Community (EC) and the USA on 23 September 1991, OJ 1995 No. L95/45 as corrected by OJ 1995 No. L131/38, discussed at pp. 112–16 below.

a 'pluralist' or even proposing a 'global' approach when addressing such issues. Between these two ends, some countries have opted for a mixture of these approaches.

These differences, as well as those which will become apparent in the discussion, are important and therefore cannot be ignored. The differences have been widened by the fact that in some jurisdictions, notably the USA and the EC, antitrust law is well developed and the policies underlying it are in a constant state of change and evolution, whilst in other jurisdictions antitrust law is just seeing the light of the day.[11]

The scope of the book

Generally, a position of difference is not particularly healthy. In antitrust policy there is strong evidence that would support this.[12] In this regard a move from a position of difference to a position of similarity is indeed desirable, but surely one that gives rise to a challenge. This is a challenge which is currently facing antitrust communities in many jurisdictions; and those who have realised the existence of this challenge and the need to move closer to a position of similarity have been seeking ways to 'internationalise' antitrust policy. However, even here differences have surfaced regarding how the 'internationalisation' should be viewed.[13] As a result, different examples of internationalisation seem to have emerged. These examples will be considered in the fifth part of the chapter.

The aim of the present book is to give a serious and fresh consideration of the process of internationalisation of antitrust policy. It inquires into the nature of this process, whether it is a matter of law or politics (or both), and the direction in which this process should be focused. The need for examining the internationalisation of antitrust policy arises not only because of the differences alluded to above but also in the light of several problems that seem to require attention. These problems can be summarised as follows. Domestic antitrust laws have their bounds and limits and because of this they are unable to address international restraints effectively. In light of the relentless process of globalisation, antitrust authorities seem to lack vision when the antitrust issues facing them transcend their domestic

[11] See W. Hannay, 'Transnational Competition Law Aspects of Mergers and Acquisitions' (2000) 20 *Northwestern Journal of International Law and Business* 287.
[12] See ch. 7.   [13] See above.

boundaries. It seems that countries are becoming less representative of firms that have their business offices registered within their boundaries but that manufacture, distribute and sell their products in global markets. This factor is all the more important to consider given that gradually norms and expectations have developed around antitrust policy and have increased in importance and in geographical scope.[14] On the other hand, the antitrust laws of some countries have a wide reach and this means that these laws may end up being used to regulate individuals, firms and transactions in other countries. There is solid evidence to support the view that antitrust policy enforcement by a score of domestic antitrust authorities in the world has become extraterritorial over the years.[15] Although there is merit in the claim that international restraints should not go unpunished, it is doubtful that this development should be regarded as acceptable when such enforcement would interfere with the prerogatives and orders of other countries. Furthermore, the application of the antitrust laws of different countries in the same situation can trigger conflicts between those countries. Apart from the damage that may be caused to the relationship between the countries themselves, conflicting results are damaging to firms, who are normally anxious about the application of more than one domestic antitrust law to their transactions. Firms, quite legitimately so, are concerned about the costs in time and money incurred when their operations and transactions are subjected to review by several domestic antitrust authorities. In addition to such costs, conflicting results can drag firms into diplomatic disputes between countries. The present book will seek to argue that in practical terms all of the points just made show that antitrust authorities in the world have to seek effective ways to overcome jurisdictional hurdles inherent in the territorial nature of antitrust enforcement jurisdiction.

The strategy adopted in this book has three different aims. The first aim, the basic aim on which all else depends, is to expand the way into the jungle of internationalisation of antitrust policy. The second is to open up issues in the discourse between law, economics and politics in this highly important

---

[14] Other reasons include the shortcomings of both bilateral agreements between antitrust authorities and the convergence of antitrust laws of different countries in addressing international antitrust issues. See chs. 7 and 8. See also E. Fox, 'Global Problems in a World of National Law' (1999) 34 *New England Law Review* 11, 11–12, Fiebig, 'International', 233; P. Muchlinski, *Multinational Enterprises and the Law* (Blackwell, Oxford, 1995), p. 384.

[15] See ch. 7 for an examination of the doctrine of extraterritoriality.

and topical area that seem susceptible to further research and thinking. Finally, the third is to formulate an approach and to try to lay down some foundations on which the present book, as well as future study in this area, whether academic or otherwise, can be constructed.

The nature of the book

In examining the process of internationalisation, first the limits of antitrust law have to be defined. It seems sensible to start with some basic concepts and to examine the point and goals of the law. It would be a fruitless exercise to discuss the internationalisation of antitrust policy without having first enquired into the *raison d'être* and aims of the law. This, in turn, entails a further inquiry into how its doctrines have evolved and the nature of its ultimate impact upon public and private power, the structure and function of institutions and markets and the economic freedom of the individual.[16] This in itself is an inquiry into another thread of antitrust (in addition to law and economics): the role and influence of politics and the relevance of the principles of liberal democracy.[17] The significance of this thread can be illustrated in the following manner. Generally, political ideology and initiative serve as the basis for enacting different antitrust laws in different countries.[18] This is based on the view that underlying the concept of antitrust is a serious concern about excessive economic power, and a general awareness that the principles of liberal democracy may be undermined if market *economic democracy* is not afforded adequate protection.[19] As

---

[16] R. Bork, *The Antitrust Paradox* (Basic Books, New York, 1978), p. 3.

[17] Political influence and the principles of liberal democracy, as referred to in the present work, are not identical. Although the principles of liberal democracy bear strong links to several issues with respect to the internationalisation of antitrust policy, there remain other important issues that should be examined within a different framework. The question of sovereignty is an example in point. As chapter 6 shows, several threads related to that question seem to have a wider implication that need to be evaluated within a wider framework than that of the principles of liberal democracy.

[18] Some commentators have argued that the enactment of antitrust law is a political act, and, as such, political factors should be given paramount consideration. See C. Ehlermann and L. Laudati (eds.), *European Competition Law Annual 1997: Objectives of Competition Policy* (Hart Publishing, Oxford, 1998), p. 58.

[19] It is important to emphasise that the present discussion is more concerned with economic democracy than political democracy. For some interesting discussion of the latter concept, see G. Amato, *Antitrust and the Bounds of Power* (Hart Publishing, Oxford, 1997), p. 96; H. Thorelli, *The Federal Antitrust Policy: Origination of an Antitrust Tradition* (Johns Hopkin Press, Baltimore, 1954); E. Fox, 'The Modernization of Antitrust: a New Equilibrium' (1981) 66

political ideology is crucial in the adoption of antitrust law in different jurisdictions, it is essential when examining the internationalisation of antitrust policy to consider issues inherent in such ideology. In particular, it is necessary to be aware that the regulation of competition and enforcement of antitrust law by administrative institutions can involve bureaucratic politics and bureaucratic decision-making. To an extent, the merits of antitrust law enforcement, whether national or regional (such as the case with the European Community),[20] carry implications of political directions ordered by administrative and political institutions. The present book will aim to develop this proposition by demonstrating that the internationalisation of antitrust policy is subject to political influence. So far, there has been little exposition in the literature of the actual or potential importance of politics in this area. As the following chapter will seek to show, one of the contributing factors towards this seems to be that economists chose first to determine to what extent economics, not politics, was a systematic force in antitrust law enforcement. As the discussion in that chapter shows, there is no doubt that one must appreciate the importance of economic analysis in antitrust law and policy. Equally, however, one ought to be aware of the importance of politics and the need to understand its influence on antitrust policy in general and the internationalisation thereof in particular.

The nature of this inquiry opens up the need for new insights from various disciplines, including political science. These insights are valuable in order to understand the internationalisation of antitrust policy and complement its rules, normative principles and guiding policies. It seems that lawyers and political scientists have a great deal of mutual interest in the internationalisation of antitrust policy, which could be realised by constructing an adequate dialogue between the two disciplines.[21] For this reason, the author encourages the adoption of an interdisciplinary approach to any study on the internationalisation of antitrust policy. What one must remain aware of is that institutions have an important role to play in antitrust

---

Cornell Law Review 1140; E. Sullivan (ed.), *The Political Economy of the Sherman Act* (Oxford University Press, Oxford, 1991); D. Millon 'The Sherman Act and the Balance of Power' (1988) 61 *Southern California Law Review* 1219.

[20] See ch. 5.

[21] On constructing dialogues between different disciplines, see generally J. Weiler, 'Community, Member States and European Integration: Is the Law Relevant?' (1982) 21 *Journal of Common Market Studies* 39; R. Pryce, *The Politics of the European Community* (Butterworths, London, 1973).

policy and that the internationalisation of antitrust policy makes the case for considering institutional dimensions particularly pressing. It is advisable to adopt an interdisciplinary approach because of the particular emphasis that should be placed on the importance of institutional dimensions and politics, including the way in which policy processes complement the law in this area. Thus, it is important for any study on this topic to be receptive to insights regarding the choice of methodology within political science and political regulation. This emphasis reflects the need to develop an interdisciplinary approach to the topic and the sense of importance of institutional endowments and their relevance to the internationalisation of antitrust policy.[22]

Generally, it seems that political scientists themselves have been very slow to undertake systematic work on antitrust policy, leaving this area to lawyers and economists.[23] There may be more than one explanation for this. One explanation may be that as antitrust law and policy and their analysis have been dominated by economists, this seems to have made it virtually impossible for political scientists to enter the area. Another, perhaps less convincing, explanation may be that there has been little interest on the part of political scientists to undertake any work in this important area of law and policy. Whichever of these two explanations one may find plausible, it seems very likely that lawyers and economists will eventually need to concede the importance of politics and of institutions; although it is very possible that in the short term, at least, their focus will remain on analysing legal principles, economic models and individual cases in the abstract and without any reference to, or recognition of, political acceptability or political bargaining.[24] Despite such timidity on the part of lawyers, economists and political scientists to give sufficient attention and recognition to the situation just described, it is almost beyond doubt that

[22] See M. Staniland, *What Is Political Economy?: a Study of Social Theory and Underdevelopment* (Yale University Press, New Haven, 1985); D. North, *Institutions, Institutional Change and Economic Performance* (Cambridge University Press, Cambridge, 1990); M. Granovetter, 'Economic Action and Social Structure: the Problem of Embeddedness' in M. Granovetter and R. Swedberg (eds.), *The Sociology of Economic Life* (Westview Press, Boulder, 1992).

[23] C. Doern and S. Wilks (eds.), *Comparative Competition Policy* (Oxford University Press, Oxford, 1996), p. 4.

[24] *Ibid.*, at pp. 4–5. The authors argue that their assertion is not intended to be dismissive of law and economics disciplines, or to imply that academic lawyers or economists invariably overlook political factors. They merely (and it seems rightly) emphasise 'a systematic bias and an understandable, if regrettable, narrowness of viewpoint' on the part of either discipline.

awareness of institutional and political dimensions can vastly contribute to understanding the internationalisation of antitrust policy.

The examples of internationalisation

The point was made above that in seeking to internationalise antitrust policy, differences have surfaced with regard to the way 'internationalisation' in the present context should be viewed. The result is that several examples of internationalisation have emerged which may conveniently be split into four categories. First, there is the idea of bilateral co-operation between different antitrust authorities around the world. Bilateral co-operation revolves around the enforcement of the domestic antitrust laws of the countries concerned. It generally takes the form of formal agreements between the domestic antitrust authorities of those countries which normally include, *inter alia*, provisions on information-sharing and comity.[25] Secondly, there is the idea that domestic antitrust laws can converge towards some common points and standards.[26] The basic idea here is to harmonise the different antitrust laws of different countries. The third example involves creating a detailed international antitrust code to be adopted by countries.[27] A fourth example of internationalisation focuses on establishing an international system of antitrust within a framework of autonomous international institutions.[28] Entrenched in this example is the idea that countries would apply the principles emerging from the system under the auspices of an independent antitrust authority. The system would also provide for a minimalist procedure with a mechanism to resolve disputes among participating countries. Arguably, this example is the most central, but certainly the most ambitious, of all four. It may be appropriate to note in passing that this list of examples is not exhaustive; it is very possible that more examples will come to light. However, these are the four main, principal and important examples which have emerged over the years.

---

[25] See for example the EC–US agreement (23 September 1991) OJ 1995 No. L95/45 as corrected by OJ 1995 No. L131/38, discussed at pp. 112–16 below. Other bilateral agreements also have been entered into by different countries, including Canada, Australia and New Zealand. See chs. 7 and 8 for a discussion on these agreements.

[26] See ch. 5.   [27] See pp. 283–4 below.

[28] See the proposal put by the 'Wise Men Group', a group of experts commissioned by K. van Miert, former Commissioner for antitrust policy in the EC, 'Competition Policy in the New Trade Order: Strengthening International Co-operation and Rules' COM (95) No. 359. The proposal is discussed in ch. 5.

Some reflection on terminology

At this stage, a comment on the employment of terminology in the book would be appropriate. There are three important terms which merit specific mention. These are 'system of antitrust', an 'international system of antitrust' and 'the internationalisation of antitrust policy'. Other important terms and concepts will be mentioned and examined as and when they crop up in the discussion.

System of antitrust

Quite frequently reference will be made to a 'system of antitrust'. It is essential to explain this concept, which it is submitted, includes at least three different components.[29] The concept is suitable to accommodate the three components concerned. The 'system', in this sense, functions as an operative whole, combining the interaction of its ideas and the factors influencing its operation. It is believed that a special relationship exists between the three components concerned, which will be explored at different levels in the book. The book will draw on the knowledge and insights of the disciplines to which these components belong in order to build an analytical framework in which they could be interwoven and therefore complement and enrich one another.

The first component to be mentioned is the concept of competition itself, which is entrenched in economics. The following chapter will demonstrate how the economic philosophy of competition has become its dominant intellectual discourse.[30] Antitrust policy has developed as such that no study of antitrust law and policy which lacks appreciation for the role that competition plays within the market economy can be justifiable, indeed possible. As Dewey, in a characteristically trenchant style, remarked: before deciding what antitrust law ought to be, it is necessary to understand what the process of competition is really like.[31] Secondly, there is antitrust law which

---

[29] See M. Dabbah, 'Measuring the Success of a System of Competition Law: a Preliminary View' (2000) 21 *European Competition Law Review* 369, 370–1.

    Note the employment of the concept by other writers. For example, Gerber uses the concept system to analyse how institutions interact with norms in relation to the protection of competition. According to Gerber, the concept thus becomes more specific and functional, and more analytically valuable, because it focuses on the characteristics and consequences of those interactions. Gerber, *Competition*.

[30] See Amato, *Power*.

[31] D. Dewey, 'The Economic Theory of Antitrust: Science or Religion?' (1964) 50 *Virginia Law Review* 413, 414.

concerns applying a body of legal rules and standards to deal with market imperfections and restoring desirable competitive conditions in the market. The third component is antitrust policy,[32] which is anchored in politics. This deals with public authorities' intervention beyond certain market imperfections, such as market failures.[33] Market failure, in this context, connotes the existence of circumstances in which private forces in the market fail to sustain 'desirable activities' or to estop 'undesirable activities'. The corollary of this provides that sovereign countries are responsible for the formulation of different public policies, and public institutions possess *discretion* to ensure their implementation in practice. In Bork's view, antitrust policy exemplifies one of the most elaborate deployments of governmental force in areas of life still thought primarily committed to private choice and initiative.[34] These thoughts to one side, it is essential to realise that the term 'antitrust policy', like the term 'antitrust law' and the concept of 'competition', has been given different interpretations in different jurisdictions and in different contexts, and that this may present a difficulty in the internationalisation of antitrust policy.

International system of antitrust

In the present book, a distinction is made between a 'system of antitrust' and an 'international system of antitrust'. The latter will – if and when established – inevitably be hybrid in nature. What this means is that the system is to be constructed not only on the basis of ideas originating at the national level, but also on the basis of understanding international politics and international economic issues. Constructing the system will also involve some appropriate recourse to principles of public international law. Finally, to avoid any likely confusion of terminology between this system and other systems (national/regional) of antitrust, the former will be referred to uniformly throughout this book as an international system of antitrust.

The internationalisation of antitrust policy

In addition to highlighting the dividing line between a 'system of antitrust' and an 'international system of antitrust', another distinction needs to be

---

[32] See WTO Annual Report 1997, p. 34.
[33] See F. Bator, 'The Autonomy of Market Failure' (1958) 72 *Quarterly Journal of Economics* 351.
[34] Bork, *Paradox*, p. 3.

made between the latter and 'the internationalisation of antitrust policy'. It is argued that an international system of antitrust can ultimately be constructed through the process of 'internationalisation'. It is important to understand this sequence as the process of internationalisation seeks to deal with issues which seem to be vital in order to construct this system. The term 'internationalisation' is employed in this book, not only to highlight the need to accommodate the various national interests and decision processes into how international institutions are designed and politically justified, but also to refer to the actual penetration of international pressures into the concrete functioning of domestic institutions. These thoughts show that the process of internationalisation functions as a 'double-edge sword'. More importantly, they also result in legal, as well as political, implications for the internationalisation of antitrust policy. These implications will be explained and analysed in the different chapters of the book.

Globalisation and its implications for antitrust policy

In the preceding discussion, reference was made more than once to the concept of 'globalisation'. It may be helpful at this point to explain the use of the concept in the present book and more importantly demonstrate its implications for the place of antitrust policy in a global economy. It is beyond the scope of the book to engage in a detailed discussion on whether globalisation in itself is a good or bad thing; this is a highly debatable issue. There is certainly an argument that globalisation would be considered a good thing in so far as it leads to improvement in economic conditions and standards within different countries, especially developing ones. There would be little sense in attacking or opposing globalisation if consumers worldwide (in both developed and developing countries) were able to enjoy better quality of products and services, more choice and lower prices. In this way, globalisation can have positive effects, which must be welcomed, encouraged and supported. Having said that, there is also a counter argument that globalisation is not a virtue. There is a certain degree of scepticism over globalisation in many quarters. Different groups, including some consumer groups, anti-capitalist groups and developing countries have come to regard globalisation as a process used by developed countries and their firms to impose their standards on these groups and to suppress and constrain their freedom. In this case, and if indeed there is truth behind this, there is hardly any legitimacy in pursuing or supporting globalisation. This important issue raises an extremely interesting and relevant question as far as antitrust policy is concerned, namely how antitrust authorities can ensure that the global integration of markets leads to and maintains competitive outcomes, thus making globalisation both economically more efficient and socially more acceptable. It is believed that antitrust policy – and specifically international co-operation on antitrust policy – has an important role to play if resentment against globalisation and a protectionist backlash are to be avoided.

The important debate on the pros and cons of globalisation to one side, there is a need to be aware that globalisation, like free trade and open competition, is not irresistibly a natural phenomenon. It is a process that follows from political choices. The amount and level, as in fact the actual existence, of globalisation is the product of political decisions and policy formulations adopted by governments which have come to reflect a newer, late 1990s, approach to markets and state regulation. This approach stands in complete contrast to the approach largely witnessed in the years preceding the last two decades or so of the twentieth century. The opening paragraph of the present chapter demonstrated quite succinctly how the global economy witnessed dramatic changes in a remarkably short period of time, including the reduction and elimination of state control and monopolisation; favouring the market mechanism; and opening domestic markets to foreign trade and investment.

Whether one agrees or disagrees with globalisation, it is of significant importance to realise that the concept is susceptible to different meanings, depending on the context in which it is used and the way in which it is understood. For this reason, the concept may not be easy to define. In fact, there is not a single universal definition of globalisation; and probably one should not attempt to argue the case for such a definition. It may be more sensible to identify or describe the concept according to the situation at hand. In the present context, the concept is employed to refer to market globalisation, which has been particularly fostered by advances in technology and the elimination of barriers hindering the flows of trade and investment worldwide.[35]

As a result of globalisation, the number of antitrust policy matters that transcend national boundaries has been increasing. The sequence in this

---

[35] See generally M. Walters, *Globalization* (Routledge, New York, 1995); J. Dunning, *The Globalization of Business: the Challenges of the 1990s* (Routledge, New York, 1993).

regard is an easy one to follow. As markets and competition become in-creasingly international, so do restrictive and anti-competitive practices by firms. These practices may occur in different fields, including air or sea transport, software products, drugs and telecommunications; and they may be in a variety of forms such as export cartels, international cartels and conspiracies, abuse of market dominance and mergers. The economic effects of these practices can easily pierce national boundaries; and are not constrained by the latter. For example, a number of firms may collude on a product market that extends beyond national boundaries. The col-lusive behaviour in this case will have an effect throughout that market. Similarly, a single firm which enjoys dominance in the manufacture and distribution of its products or the provision of its services throughout the world may be able to achieve the same result unilaterally. The same is also true with regard to international mergers which produce effects in more than one country and which normally require the approval of several do-mestic antitrust authorities before they can be implemented. The antitrust law practice and literature are full of examples covering such, or similar, scenarios.

In all of the above scenarios, anti-competitive and restrictive practices affect the interests of consumers on the relevant market and,[36] as a con-sequence, the country and communities of which they are part. It should therefore be clear why domestic antitrust authorities would want to regulate such practices; though it is clear that legal and political hurdles affecting their endeavour may arise along the way. Practices of this nature lead to transfer of wealth from consumers to producers; and in an international context the transfer of wealth will be from consumers in one country to producers in another. Regardless whether one or more domestic antitrust authorities are able to intervene in this situation; whether they will inter-vene; and how they will do so, it is beyond doubt that such situations give rise to fundamental legal, economic and political problems with which the internationalisation of antitrust is concerned.

It can be seen therefore that globalisation has very significant implica-tions for antitrust policy in the global economy. Globalisation has made it almost inevitable to change antitrust law and policy. In this regard, the internationalisation of antitrust policy is a response to market globalisa-tion. It is necessary therefore to examine antitrust policy and its place in the

---

[36] See ch. 2 for discussion on the meaning of the relevant market.

global economy and to enquire into what steps, if any, should be followed and in what direction.

The structure of the book

The book is structured as follows. Chapter 2 refines some concepts and ideas that are important to understand, including the concept of competition. Chapter 3 examines the goals of antitrust law and its political perception. Chapter 4 considers the use of discretion by antitrust authorities and how this affects the internationalisation of antitrust policy. It will be argued that this use of discretion can lead to similar antitrust laws in different jurisdictions being radically different in their enforcement – a situation that often leads to divergence in the legal standards between those jurisdictions. Chapter 5 examines the antitrust experience of the EC – focusing on both the internal and external developments of the experience. Chapters 6 and 7 examine the doctrine of sovereignty and extraterritoriality respectively. Chapter 8 deals with the relationship between antitrust and trade policies. Chapter 9 gives an account of the past, present and future of the internationalisation of antitrust policy from a comparative perspective. It examines, *inter alia*, the perspectives of countries, international organisations, the business community and the consumer on the internationalisation of antitrust policy. Finally, chapter 10 concludes.

* * *

This book is essentially an examination of the internationalisation of antitrust policy, with a special reference to the law, economics and politics thereof, as evidenced in the actions and statements of antitrust authorities, political bodies and decisions of law courts. To a great extent, the book can be seen as an original and empirical inquiry. The theory presented in the book is general, in the sense that it is not tied to any particular jurisdiction, but seeks to give an explanatory and a clarifying account of the internationalisation of antitrust policy.

The book begins with refining some central concepts and ideas, including the concept of competition and antitrust law as well as an examination of the goals of the latter. This is a central theme in the discussion, which illustrates the need to build bridges between different disciplines with respect to the internationalisation of antitrust policy. This theme also contributes to understanding the process of internationalisation and complements its underlying rules, principles and guiding policies.

The book concludes by reviewing the landscape of the international-isation of antitrust policy and asking what further developments can be expected to appear on the horizon. The recommended approach in the book has much to commend it in a world of relentless globalisation, where conflicts between different countries and between countries and multina-tional firms may make legal and political decisions regarding the process of internationalisation more central.

2

Refining some concepts and ideas

This chapter gives a broad account of some central concepts and ideas. It has already been said in the course of the previous chapter that an examination of such concepts and ideas is absolutely vital to understanding the internationalisation of antitrust policy. Such an examination will, *inter alia*, enhance one's awareness of fundamental theories including economic ones, which are essential – as a first step – for a proper evaluation of any antitrust policy debate. The purpose of the chapter is to ensure that such an important first step is taken.

The chapter is divided into four parts. The first part discusses the concept and idea of competition and its economic understanding. The second part provides a historical perspective of a particular political idea and political philosophy about antitrust law. The third part discusses the important issue of market definition before the fourth part gives a brief conclusion.

The concept of competition

The meaning of competition

It is desirable to clarify the meaning of competition at the outset, in order to facilitate a better understanding of its economic implications. *The Oxford English Dictionary* defines the term in the following way:

> 1. a. The action of endeavouring to gain what another endeavours to gain at the same time; the striving of two or more for the same object;
> b. Rivalry in the market, striving for custom between those who have the same commodities to dispose of . . .[1]

---

[1] (Oxford University Press, Oxford, 1989), pp. 604–5. The author's choice of dictionary should not be seen as capricious. It was chosen because of the speciality of definition. Compare with *Johnson's Dictionary of the English Language* and the *Concise Oxford Dictionary*.

As far as academic definitions of the concept are concerned, they do not seem to be identical.[2] Some scholars have defined competition in terms of a struggle or contention for superiority, and in the commercial world in terms of striving for the custom and business of persons in the marketplace.[3] Other scholars have viewed competition in terms of a relationship that exists among any number of firms engaged in selling goods or services of the same type at the same time to an identifiable group of persons.[4]

From the above definitions, it can be gleaned that the term competition refers to:

1. The existence of both a process and a relationship;
2. In a commercial sense, a close association with the concept of marketplace;
3. Having some aim or purpose.

Whichever of the above definitions one finds oneself feeling most comfortable using, at its heart competition connotes the existence of a process of rivalry between firms which, in the pursuit of self-interest, endeavour to win custom in the market.[5] It is essential to note that competition is more than a relationship between firms in the marketplace. It is more appropriate perhaps to think of competition in terms of a process. This is because, although in a wide sense competition concerns a relationship that exists between firms, the term 'relationship' is normally used to describe different situations. In the field of antitrust policy, these situations may range from a vertical agreement between a supplier and a buyer, to a position of collective dominance held by more than one firm to another of cartel agreement.

---

[2] For an account of the 'different meanings' of competition, see R. Bork, *The Antitrust Paradox: a Policy at War with Itself* (Basic Books, New York, 1978), pp. 58–61; *White Motor Co. v. US* 372 US 253 (1963).

[3] See R. Whish, *Competition Law* (4th edn, Butterworths, London, 2001).

[4] See D. Goyder, *EC Competition Law* (4th edn, Oxford University Press, Oxford, 2002).

[5] Note in this regard how economists and lawyers view competition. Economists for example equate competition with impersonal price-making, the most impersonal being the 'purest', whereas lawyers tend to view competition as rivalry among firms to sell goods or services. Despite these differences in the thinking of economists and lawyers, however, both disciplines would view competition as a dialogue of challenge and response – a sequence of moves and responses between competing firms. See J. Clark, *Competition as a Dynamic Process* (Brookings Institution, Washington, 1961), pp. 14–15; E. Mason, 'Monopoly in Law and Economics' (1937) 47 *Yale Law Journal* 34.

Hence it is this author's view that, though in the wide sense competition concerns a relationship, it is more appropriate to employ a term that would connote the existence of a process, since the term 'relationship' falls short of offering a specific definition. More importantly, however, one ought to appreciate that competition is structured first and foremost on the freedom to compete.[6] It is the flywheel of a free economy, the very expression of its spirit and both the cause and the result of its successful operation.[7] Because competition in the commercial world is concerned with the marketplace, it seems to be evolutionary in substance and dynamic in form.[8] The truth behind such a statement can be deduced from the way competition has evolved into a 'world', 'universal' or 'global' concept. As we shall see, international organisations, such as the World Trade Organization, have adopted the concept as an article of faith. In this way, competition has been associated with the process of market globalisation and liberation.

The function of competition

The definition of competition should be distinguished from the function that it is supposed to perform in the marketplace.[9] The function of competition can be illustrated by explaining two notions of competition. First, there is customary competition, which is seen as a dominant dynamic element and a regulatory mechanism within the free-market system. Its function within Smith's 'invisible hand' of the market mechanism is to co-ordinate market deals and transactions. Secondly, there is dynamic competition. This notion of competition involves the idea of achieving an optimal degree of innovation and the diffusion of new technological advances over time. Such an emphasis on the aim of overall economic efficiency has come

---

[6] It has been argued that liberty of action ought not to be subjected to political influence. In some cases it is directed not restrained. Freedom, on the other hand, is not to be construed as liberty to cause harm or detriment. See H. Lutz, *American Legal Writing during the Founding Era* (Liberty Press, London, 1983); M. Charleston, *Rudiments of Law and Governments Deducted from the Law of Nature* (Library of Congress, Washington, 1783).

[7] See S. Khemani, 'Competition Policy: an Engine for Growth' (1997) 1 *Global Competition Review* 20, 23.

[8] See WTO Annual Report 1997, ch. 4; E. Fox, 'Competition Law and the Agenda for the WTO: Forging the Links of Competition and Trade' (1995) 4 *Pacific-Rimely Law and Policy Journal* 1; E. Fox, 'Toward World Antitrust and Market Access' (1997) 91 *American Journal of International Law* 1.

[9] See generally Whish, *Competition*, ch. 1.

to be known as the 'total welfare approach'.[10] According to dynamic competition, competition is a continuing process, based on market innovation, in which competitive advantages accruing, for example, from current
market oligopolies or positions of market dominance are the outcome of
past efficiencies and are readily available to be made use of by the firms
concerned.[11] In this sense, theorists of dynamic competition are far less
concerned about economic power and an unbalanced market structure
than scholars of customary competition.

These notions of competition aside, today it is generally thought that
competition is desirable.[12] The previous chapter explained how the ideological debate between capitalism and communism has settled in favour
of relying on markets to deliver better outcomes than state control, planning and monopolisation. This growing recognition of the reliability of
markets – at the heart of which lies the process of competition – has been
popular in particular among economists, who have always argued in favour
of the desirability of competition.[13] Some economists have advocated that a
successful market economy depends on the existence of competition in the
market and an effective antitrust policy. It seems that this increase of popularity has been triggered by the fact that generally monopoly does seem to
lead to poor quality, restriction in output and harm to consumers. Moreover, since competition offers the consumer a greater degree of protection
and choice, and since no suggestion that innovation is only possible in the
case of monopoly can be sustained, it is very understandable why competition has been popular amongst economists.[14] In addition, as the discussion

[10] See P. Crampton, 'Alternative Approaches to Competition Law: Consumer's Surplus, Total
Welfare and Non-Efficiency Goals' (1994) 17 *World Competition* 55, 55–86. World Trade
Organization Annual Report (1997), pp. 39–40.
    This notion of competition can be contrasted with competition in a static sense, which
connotes the existence of optimal allocation in resources in order to meet the demand side in
the market, incurring the lowest possible cost at any given point in time.
[11] See P. Auerbach, *Competition: the Economics of Industrial Change* (Blackwell, Oxford, 1988),
pp. 22–7. See, however, the views of Schumpeter who emphasised the so-called creative gale
of destruction, which shows that competition is not a given virtue as such. J. Schumpeter,
Capitalism, Socialism and Democracy (Allen and Unwin, London, 1976).
[12] Whish, *Competition*, p. 11.
[13] F. McChesney, 'In Search of the Public Interest Model of Antitrust' in F. McChesney and
W. Shughart (eds.), *The Causes and Consequences of Antitrust: the Public Choice Perspective*
(Chicago University Press, Chicago, 1995), pp. 25–32.
[14] D. Hay, 'The Assessment: Competition Policy' (1993) 9/2 *Oxford Review of Economic Policy* 1.
This approach can be contrasted with certain twentieth-century alternative economic thoughts,
which seem to be competition-sceptics. These argue that competition considerations are not

in chapter 9 will seek to demonstrate, antitrust policy has an important role to play in developed as well as developing countries, both in creating and promoting a competitive environment and in building and ensuring public support for a general pro-competitive policy stance by different countries.

For the discipline of economics, economic efficiency and the maximisation of consumer welfare are the underlying aims of antitrust law. Leading US antitrust figures, such as Bork, for example, have argued that in the USA the only legitimate goal of antitrust law is the maximisation of consumer welfare and therefore competition, for the purposes of antitrust analysis, must be understood as a term of art signifying any state of affairs in which consumer welfare cannot be increased by judicial decision-making.[15] Bork has also argued that when it enacted the Sherman Act 1890, US Congress intended the courts to take into account when deciding antitrust cases only that value which has come to be known today as consumer welfare. To put this point another way, according to Bork, the policy the courts were intended to apply was the maximisation of wealth or consumer want satisfaction. This, in Bork's opinion, requires courts to distinguish between agreements or activities that increase wealth through efficiency and those that decrease it through restriction of output.[16]

Traditionally, economic theory has presupposed that goods and services will be produced in the most efficient manner under circumstances of 'perfect competition'.[17] This means that in circumstances of perfect competition consumer welfare is maximised.[18] It is important in this context to be clear about the meaning of the concept 'consumer welfare'. When consumer welfare is maximised this means that economic efficiency – both allocative and productive – will be achieved, with the result that the wealth of society

---

the only co-ordinating force within liberal markets, and that their dominance of the intellectual discourse of antitrust *is over developed*. They also contend that co-ordination of private economic behaviour is also possible via other terminals such as social collusion, the creation of collectivist norms, decisions and hierarchy and the virtues of social responsibility. See Auerbach, *Competition*, ch. 2; G. Hodgson, *Economics and Institutions* (Polity, Cambridge, 1988).

[15] See Bork, *Paradox*, p. 51.

[16] See R. Bork, 'Legislative Intent and the Policy of the Sherman Act' (1966) 9 *Journal of Law and Economics* 7.

[17] See R. Lipsey and K. Chrystal, *An Introduction to Positive Economics* (Oxford University Press, Oxford, 1995); O. Williamson, *Antitrust Economics* (Blackwell, Oxford, 1987).

[18] See R. Lipsey and K. Chrystal, *Principles of Economic Law* (Oxford University Press, Oxford, 1999); F. Scherer and D. Ross, *Industrial Market Structure and Economic Performance* (Houghton Mifflin, Boston, 1990).

overall will be maximised. To understand this idea it is important to discuss these two forms of efficiency.

Allocative efficiency

Allocative efficiency (also known as Pareto efficiency) occurs in a situation where the marginal cost (the cost of producing an additional unit of output) and the marginal revenue (the price that the producer would obtain for a unit of production) coincide. Where this occurs, it is supposed that allocative efficiency will be achieved since consumers are able to obtain the product or service they desire at the price they are willing to pay. At the same time the producer is able to continue his production without incurring a loss.

Productive efficiency

This form of efficiency is thought to occur in a situation where a producer is able to produce goods and services at the lowest cost possible. In this situation, the wealth of society will be expended at the lowest possible level. The producer will not be inclined to raise his prices above cost. The reason is that if he does it is very likely that his customers will look for somewhere else cheaper to obtain their requirements. If he sells above cost he might also attract other competitors into his market. Nor will such a producer reduce his prices below cost because this means that he would be making no profit. The almost inevitable, and according to economists desirable, result in this situation is that the cost of producing a unit of output and the price of that unit will coincide.

The (im)possibility of perfect competition

The idea behind the economic approach and understanding of perfect competition is intended to provide a simple test, which would be cognisable for most laymen.[19] In particular, the rules of 'perfect competition' are intended to be quite simple to apply. If the only goal of antitrust law was the maximisation of consumer welfare by achieving allocative and productive efficiencies, there would have been little difficulty in formulating legal rules and applying these rules. There would of course always be the problem that such a policy would be essentially economic and that it would not be easy

---

[19] See Scherer and Ross, *Industrial*, chs. 1 and 2; D. Swann, *Competition and Consumer Protection* (Penguin, Harmondsworth, 1979), ch. 3; Williamson, *Antitrust*.

to ask lawyers to leave their own discipline and step into the discipline of economics, but at least it would be possible to proceed by reference to a common objective.

Attractive as this simplicity may be, several claims can still be advanced against this economic approach. The theory of conventional economic analysis suffers from ambiguity of definition and narrowness of viewpoint. For example, Bork – who, as said above, has argued that the dominant goal of antitrust law is the maximisation of consumer welfare – appeared to have recognised that US Congress intended to implement a broader spectrum of values than the neoclassical concept of consumer welfare in the enforcement of antitrust law.[20] In all events, it will be seen, in due course,[21] that economic efficiency and consumer welfare are far from being the only, or even dominant, goals of antitrust law.[22] At a more general level, economists do not seem to be able to craft viable rules suitable for the economic efficiency implications of particular market behaviour and structure.[23] At one end of the spectrum, there is the view that elements of market behaviour and structure may encompass the variability of firms, technological advances, commercial planning, strategies and markets; all of which make it difficult in practice to devise suitable rules to address such issues. At the other end of the spectrum stands the fact that different economic approaches speak of identical issues differently.[24] Further, economists should be encouraged

---

[20] See R. Bork, 'The Role of the Courts in Applying Economics' (1985) 54 *Antitrust Law Journal* 2, 24.

[21] See pp. 52–4, below.

[22] The academic criticism of this goal is extensive. See P. Carstensen, 'Antitrust Law and the Paradigm of Industrial Organization' (1983) 16 *University of California, Davis Law Review* 487; E. Fox, 'The Modernization of Antitrust: a New Equilibrium' (1981) 66 *Cornell Law Review* 1140; E. Fox, 'The Politics of Law and Economics in Judicial Decision Making: Antitrust as a Window' (1986) 61 *New York University Law Review* 554; R. Lande, 'Wealth Transfers as the Original and Primary Concern of Antitrust: the Efficiency Interpretations Challenged' (1982) 34 *Hastings Law Journal* 65; J. May, 'Antitrust Practices in the Formative Era: the Constitutional and Conceptual Reach of State Antitrust Laws, 1880–1918' (1987) 135 *University of Pennsylvania Law Review* 495; L. Orland, 'The Paradox in Bork's Antitrust Paradox' (1987) 9 *Cardozo Law Review* 115; R. Pitofsky, 'The Political Content of Antitrust' (1979) 127 *University of Pennsylvania Law Review* 1051; F. Rowe, 'The Decline of Antitrust and the Dilution of Models: the Faustian Pact of Law and Economics' (1984) 72 *Georgetown Law Journal* 1511; L. Schwartz, ' "Justice" and Other Non-Economic Goals of Antitrust' (1979) 127 *University of Pennsylvania Law Review* 1076; J. Flynn, 'Antitrust Jurisprudence: a Symposium on the Economic, Political and Social Goals of Antitrust Policy' (1977) 125 *University of Pennsylvania Law Review* 1182.

[23] Hay, 'Assessment', 6–12.

[24] Williamson, *Antitrust*, p. 315; Also on this issue, as far as industrial economists are concerned, see D. D. Hay 'Competition Policy' (1986) 2 *Oxford Review of Economic Policy* 1.

not to stray into imaginary domains about markets which enjoy 'perfect competition'. This state of competition does not seem to be attainable.[25] Markets are disorganised in substance, complex in structure, and are far from being capable of generating any strains of 'perfect competition'.

Other claims which can be advanced against the economic approach of perfect competition are based on the fact that the aggregation of the theory of 'contestable markets' and the intellectual influence of Chicago School theories have, to a certain extent, undermined the conventional view on the desirability of competition.[26] The theory of contestable markets is one which has been advocated by some economists in recent years.[27] What this theory says is that an optimal allocation of resources will be ensured provided that the market in question is contestable. Contestable in this sense means that a firm will be able to enter the market without incurring sunk costs (which the firm will not be able to recover once it has ceased to operate at a future date) and exit from the market without incurring cost. In other words, for a market to be contestable, there must be a realistic likeliness that potential competitors can easily enter the market and begin to compete when market conditions, including imperfections, provide the opportunity to do so. The Chicago School of thought, on the other hand, has been particularly prominent in supplying a great deal of the existing US antitrust ideology. The School's 'successful' life span covers the last two decades.[28] Unlike neoclassicism theory, it advocates a more relaxed approach to antitrust policy.

In reality, the discipline of economics is subject to a pragmatic pressure to attack the most serious market failures, to construct principles of reasonable behaviour and ultimately to pursue a goal of 'workable competition'.[29] The concept of 'workable competition' encompasses an idea that is different from a theory (it is generally wider). It operates like a norm that changes according to variation in economic theorem and the conditions

---

[25] See Whish, *Competition*, pp. 4–6.

[26] T. Bailey, 'Contestability and the Design of Regulatory and Antitrust Policy' (1981) 71 *American Economic Review* 178.

[27] See W. Baumol, J. Panzar and D. Willig, *Contestable Markets and the Theory of Industry Structure* (Harcourt Brace Jovanovich, New York, 1988).

[28] See the review of the School's theoretical influence in W. Shughart, 'Be True to Your School: Chicago's Contradictory Views of Antitrust and Regulation' in McChesney and Shughart, *Causes*, pp. 323–40.

[29] Scherer and Ross, *Industrial*; D. Clark, 'Towards a Concept of Workable Competition' (1940) 30 *American Economic Review* 241; D. Sosnick 'A Critique of Concepts of Workable Competition' (1958) 72 *Quarterly Journal of Economics* 380.

and structure of the market, such as shifts in the behaviour of firms, the attitude of public institutions, causes and effects of market globalisation and evolution in technological advances.

More recent American radical theorising, however, transcends this position towards applying a new 'public-choice' approach. Some scholars, for instance, have crafted a strategic path hoping to return the attention of antitrust scholars to first principles, forcing them to consider seriously whether competition or antitrust policy has any legitimate place in a market-based economy. The 'public-choice' approach is interesting because of its views on the importance and role of countries and institutional dimensions, domestic and international.[30]

Competition and contextual economics

Awareness of fundamental economic theories is an essential step in evaluating various antitrust policy debates. It is obvious that competition is concerned with the marketplace and for this reason economic analysis is vital for the formulation of policy decisions which are reasonable and which would help in applying the law in a sensible way. Frequent and infrequent changes in antitrust policy alike have a great impact on the discipline of economics.[31] Thus, an examination of the internationalisation of antitrust policy requires some appreciation and evaluation of economics theories and doctrines.[32] This point is of particular importance in the light of the argument that payments and concessions between countries are quite inevitable in the internationalisation of antitrust policy. This has been advocated, in particular, by economists who have examined the economic incentives of countries and business firms behind the process of internationalisation.

It was said in the previous chapter that the present view adopted of the internationalisation of antitrust policy requires various disciplines to be in harmony with one another. Just as the disciplines of law and political science must bear in mind various economic interpretations, so too economists should be encouraged to remain aware of policy designs offered by political scientists. According to some commentators, the appropriate

---

[30] See further ch. 9.
[31] See D. Neven, R. Nuttall and P. Seabright, *Merger in Daylight* (Centre for Economic Research, London, 1993), ch. 2; J. Bishop and M. Kay, *European Mergers and Merger Policy* (Oxford University Press, Oxford, 1993).
[32] See for example A. Guzman, 'Is International Antitrust Possible?' (1998) 73 *New York University Law Review* 1501, 1505.

design of policy is crucial to the successful operation of antitrust policy.[33] Other commentators have even argued that economic factors have always played an important role on the international plane and that events in the final years of the twentieth century forced different interests to concentrate their attention on the inevitable tensions and continuing interactions between economics and politics.[34]

Competition, economists and policy consideration

Normally, when public policy considerations are injected in the marketplace, analytical dilemmas appear.[35] It is difficult to decipher which of the public policies should be called antitrust policy when the majority of such policies are actually or symbolically capable of affecting the process of competition in the market. There is a query as to whether it should be industrial policy, trade policy, consumer protection policy, other types of social policy or only public policy, which should expressly be named antitrust policy.[36] A simple survey of the situation in various countries by an antitrust law enthusiast would reveal that in some countries the policy is called antitrust policy, but in others it is part of the industrial, trade or even the consumer protection policy of the country. As a result of globalisation, the distinction between these policies has become a fine one. Perhaps the way to reconcile such differences in position is to accept that antitrust policy potentially has very wide scope, encompassing all policies that affect the conditions of competition.[37] Accepting or rejecting such a way for reconciliation is a central point to any examination of the internationalisation of antitrust policy, which will be considered in more detail in later chapters.[38]

Leaving the dilemma of searching for the appropriate form of public policy to one side, the issue of public intervention in order to regulate economic behaviour is itself, prima facie, a source of difficulty. This is an issue to which

---

[33] Hay, 'Assessment', 12.

[34] See R. Gilpin, *Political Economy of International Relations* (Princeton University Press, Princeton, Guilford, 1987), p. 3; M. Porter, *The Competitive Advantage of Nations* (Macmillan, London, 1989); K. Ohmae, *The Borderless World: Power and Strategy in the Interlinked Economy* (Harper-Collins, London, 1994).

[35] See G. Amato, *Antitrust and the Bounds of Power* (Hart Publishing, Oxford, 1997), p. 2.

[36] See ch. 3.

[37] D. Fidler, 'Competition Law and International Relations' (1992) 41 *International and Comparative Law Quarterly* 563, 564.

[38] See for example ch. 8 which includes a very comprehensive account on the relationship between antitrust and trade policies.

the discussion will return in the following chapter.[39] For present purposes, however, it is interesting to observe in this regard the paradox of mainstream economics theorists where, on the one hand, they discourage public regulation of industrial policy but, on the other hand, they are less sceptical as far as public regulation of antitrust policy is concerned. As early as the 1930s, during the time of economic depression in the USA, some of the first Chicago School scholars called for an outright dismantling of gigantic firms and persistent prosecution of firms which conspired or colluded with the aim to fix prices, share markets and limit output. Those scholars argued that antitrust law must prohibit and the government must effectively prevent firms or groups of firms from acquiring substantial market power, regardless of how that power may appear to be exercised. The scholars argued that the Federal Trade Commission – one of the authorities responsible for antitrust policy in the USA – must become the most powerful of all government bodies. This call is quite interesting, and ironic, since it is open for argument that the economic depression during that period may actually have been caused by antitrust law enforcement.[40]

From a critical stance, and in the light of the above analysis, it seems that there is lack of consensus, including amongst economists, on how competition should be viewed, and whether it can be seen to offer a reliable explanation of the behaviour of firms in the market. Economists for example disagree over the nature and extent of competition that should be encouraged. But despite this lack of consensus there seems to be a recognition that competition is needed to deliver the benefits available from the market. Hence, it is desirable to encourage competition and adopt law(s) to protect it.[41]

The means and end debate

The final issue to be considered in this part is the evergreen debate about whether competition is an end in itself or a means for attaining some other objective. The answer to this question does not seem to be particularly easy. Nor has the debate been definitely settled in favour of a particular view. One view – which seems to be the more acceptable one – is that competition

---

[39] See pp. 58–63 below.

[40] H. Simons, *A Positive Program for Laissez Faire: Some Proposals for a Liberal Economic Policy* (Chicago University Press, Chicago, 1934), p. 43.

[41] C. Doern and S. Wilks, (eds.) *Comparative Competition Policy* (Oxford University Press, Oxford, 1996), p. 1.

is a means to achieve economic prosperity and ensure economic fairness in the marketplace.[42] Competition, therefore, is not an ultimate goal in itself, but rather an instrument to enhance the welfare of people and ensure a proper functioning of markets. Protecting competition through law and policy would make little sense if it were not believed that competition would help to achieve such goals.[43] The other less acceptable view seems to be that competition is an end in itself. This view might be justified with reference to US antitrust law, for example, in the case where the Jeffersonian or atomistic competition is simply pursued to the end of having many small, independent businesses. Indeed, this was a motivation behind the Celler-Kaufer Act (1950) when US Congress amended the merger provisions of the Clayton Act (1914). It could be argued, however, that this can be reduced to an argument that competition is a means to achieve some other purpose, since in this case it is striving for perfect competition and thus maximising consumer welfare. Equally though this idea of having a thriving small business culture seems to be an end in itself.

Some historical perspectives of a particular idea and political philosophy

The historical perspective of antitrust law sheds light on how it has developed and informs how it will continue to evolve. This part will explore the historical background and development of antitrust law in several jurisdictions. The author's choice of jurisdictions should not be seen as capricious; it was made on the basis that these jurisdictions offer extremely valuable insights into the historical origins of antitrust law. The discussion, however, will be in outline only. Details of useful literature will be provided where appropriate.

Austria

Starting the present discussion on historical perspective with Austria is more than adopting an alphabetical order in an examination of this important

---

[42] This seems to be the prevailing view, according to many scholars. See C. Bellamy, 'Some Reflections on Competition Law in the Global Market' (1999) 34 *New England Law Review* 15, 16; C. Ehlermann and L. Laudati (eds.), *European Competition Law Annual 1997: Objectives of Competition Policy* (Hart Publishing, Oxford, 1998), pp. 123–4.

[43] See pp. 46–8 below.

issue. The ideas which emerged from the Austrian antitrust law experience during the nineteenth century were crucial in supporting the creation of antitrust law culture in Europe as a whole. Austria had already identified antitrust concerns and attempted to address them even before the debates which led to the adoption of the first antitrust legislation in Europe and in other parts of the world took place.

The increase in the popularity of competition in Austrian society became obvious in the middle of the nineteenth century. During that time, the liberals in Austria acquired political power following years of aristocratic leadership. This increase in popularity was paralleled by events, which led to the creation of the first parliamentary democracy in Austria. However, soon this popularity was challenged and eventually vanished with the economic depression, which hit Austria in 1873 and which lasted for several years. This sharp turn of events discredited the idea of competition and turned it into an evil force. The support for unhindered and free competition was converted into suspicion of its forces and ultimately resulted in support for monopolisation and state intervention, control and planning in the marketplace.

In the last quarter of the nineteenth century, the scene began to witness the creation of cartels, which escalated in both number and power at the time. The first industries to witness cartelisation were the main ones, such as coal and steel. But this activity soon spread to other areas in the final years of that century. During that period, cartels were viewed as a natural and inevitable stage in the development of capitalism rather than a problem that needed to be combated.

As the twentieth century approached, there was a change of attitude towards viewing cartels. This was promoted in part by the changing values and change in the political climate. Cartels came to be seen as a means by which big businesses were able to exploit and hurt the public at large. With this new awareness coming to light, political and intellectual movements developed which began to call for dealing with cartels by enacting an appropriate and effective legislation for fighting such harmful practices;[44] although the question of how and whether this was at all possible was largely unanswered. The effect of cartels was very uncomfortable and many of the elections at town/city, regional and national levels in Austria at that time

---

[44] At that time there was already legislation dealing with cartels in Austria but that legislation was not effective.

were fought on the issue of cartels. Some commentators have argued that
the new attitude towards cartels provided the seeds for the development of
antitrust law in Austria and for antitrust law tradition in Europe.[45]

EC

Chapter 5 will examine the EC antitrust experience at great length. Hence,
the present section will provide only a brief outline of the historical origins
of the experience.

It is widely recognised that antitrust policy arose in the EC as a result of
political and economic necessity.[46] Judge Bellamy, a former Member of the
European Court of First Instance, argued that the purpose behind including
antitrust rules in the Treaty of Rome 1957 was to support the political idea
behind the Treaty, namely to establish not only a single market but also
ultimately 'an ever closer union among the peoples of Europe'.[47]

The antitrust rules included in the EC Treaty pursue 'multi-purpose'
objectives.[48] The rules are contained in chapter 1 of Part III of the EC Treaty.
The chapter in turn contains 9 Articles, Articles 81–89. In addition to these
Articles there are important additional provisions and instruments which
are of supreme importance in EC antitrust law. These include Article 2
which contains the objectives of the EC Treaty, Article 3 which deals with
the activities of the Treaty, in particular Article 3(g) which expressly refers to
'a system ensuring that competition in the internal market is not distorted',
and Regulation 4064/89, the Merger Regulation, which deals with mergers
and which was introduced only in 1989 – some thirty-two years following
the signing of the Treaty of Rome.

Germany

German law traditionally draws a distinction between behaviour and prac-
tices constituting unfair competition and others in restraint of competition.
This distinction is reflected in two main Acts: the Act against Restraints of
Competition (*Gesetz gegen Wettbewerbsbeschränkungen*) which is called the

---

[45] Gerber, *Competition*, p. 43.
[46] See Goyder, *EC Competition*, ch. 3; A. Neale and D. Goyder, *The Antitrust Laws of the United States of America: a Study of Competition Enforced by Law* (Cambridge University Press, Cambridge, 1980), p. 439; Amato, *Power*, p. 2.
[47] Bellamy, 'Reflections', 16.   [48] *Ibid.*, 15–17.

Antitrust Act and the Act against Unfair Competition (*Gesetz gegen den unlauteren Wettbewerb*). Generally, the aim of the Antitrust Act is to preserve freedom of competition by maintaining competitive market structures and the aim of the Unfair Competition Act is to prohibit unethical business practices. The Acts are not mutually exclusive and the same business practice may be caught within the net of both. For example, an abuse of a dominant position may be deemed to be both restrictive and unfair and hence fall within the scope of both instruments.

The law on competitive restraints has evolved separately and independently of the law on unfair competition. The Unfair Competition Act was enacted in 1909. At that time, the German legal system included no legislative provisions on restraints of competition; until that time the freedom to trade was regarded as having been incorporated into the Trade Act (*Gewerbeordnung*) of 1867 and competitors were entitled to enter into cartel agreements regulating production and distribution. It was considered such agreements might even be in the public interest. After 1897, the German economy witnessed a growth of cartelisation at an unprecedented rate. The civil code (*Bürgerliches Gesetzbuch*) of 1900 and its provisions on violations of public policy did little to restrain business practices involving restrictions of competition. During the years of 1914–18, the cartelisation of the German economy was intensified. In 1923 the Act against Abuses of Market Dominating Positions (*Verordnung gegen Mißbrauch wirtschaftlicher Machtstellungen*) was adopted. This law was the first legislation on restraints of competition and granted the government certain powers to intervene against abuses of market dominance and cartels jeopardising the economy or impairing the public interest. However, the Government never forcefully exercised these powers. Finally, during the Hitler years, 1933–45, the most dramatic events took place and the German economy was gradually becoming a fully planned and controlled economy.

There was no breakthrough in the system until after the Second World War, when in 1947 the United States Military Government introduced the Decartelisation and Deconcentration Laws. Equivalent laws soon followed by the British and French Military Governments. Together these laws represented the first modern antitrust legislation in Germany. But it was not until 1958, after a decade of public discussion and debate, that political compromise was reached which permitted the passage of the Antitrust Act. The Antitrust Act, however, did not remain unchanged. It was amended on several occasions to broaden its scope of application.

The introduction of the first modern antitrust legislation in Germany coincided with the foundation of the Ordo-liberal Antitrust School. The School was motivated by a variety of political objectives; among these were objectives such as the dispersal of economic power so as to prevent a recurrence of collusion and conspiracies among cartelised industries and a totalitarian government in Germany. The views of the School were given a lot of support because of the pre-war and war experience. They also prompted the inclusion of far-reaching substantive and procedural constitutional guarantees of individual economic freedoms and property rights into the German Basic Law of 1949. These guarantees were explicitly based on the political premise that all human and basic rights served the purpose of protecting the 'dignity of man'.

UK

The general antithesis towards monopoly and restrictive business practices in the UK is a very old one.[49] As early as 1602, in the case of *Darcy*,[50] the common law of England consolidated its stance towards monopoly. In that case, the King's Bench Division held that monopoly leads to poor quality, harms consumers and restricts competition.[51] In the centuries that followed, this common law view had a far-reaching effect both within the UK and abroad. For example, the view was mentioned in the debates leading to the enactment of the Sherman Act 1890 in the USA, during which Congressman Sherman argued that Congress was setting forth 'the rule of common law, which prevails in England and in this country'.[52]

During the twentieth century in particular the UK system of antitrust developed into a very complex system. Simplification of the system has however been attempted, and to a certain extent achieved. Some significant and radical changes have taken place since the UK acceded to the EC in 1973. Of particular importance to mention is the Competition Act 1998. As a result of enacting this new law, the old formalistic system of restrictive trade practices was abandoned. The Act, which is modelled on Articles 81

---

[49] See *Dyer's* Case (1414) *YB* 11 Hen 5 of 5, 26.
[50] *Darcy* v. *Allein* (Case of Monopolies) (1602), 77 *Eng. Rep.* 1260. (KB 1602).   [51] *Ibid.*, 1262–3.
[52] 20 CONG. REC. 1167 (1889). This statement has led some scholars to believe that the Sherman Act has a transatlantic origin, if not quite a global one. See for example Bellamy, 'Reflections'; R. Posner, *Antitrust Law: an Economic Perspective* (University of Chicago Press, Chicago, 1976), pp. 22–3.

and 82 of the Treaty of Rome, received the Royal Assent on 9 November 1998: the main provisions have been in force since 1 March 2000. The Act has introduced a radical reform of UK antitrust law. Recently, further significant reforms of the UK system of antitrust were introduced.[53]

USA

An understanding of US antitrust law demands an inquiry into its roots, which extend to the nineteenth century. That century witnessed a wide spread of anti-competitive practices in many US industries. Notable in this regard is the situation in the transportation of goods sector, which was dominated by railroad companies, which used to charge excessive and disproportionate prices. These prices were excessive because they exceeded what the customers of those companies could charge for their produce, and disproportionate because the prices did not correspond to the value of the service the companies rendered.

Anti-competitive practices maximised the personal profit of their creators while being detrimental to the public interest. The trend during the nineteenth century was to form trusts, which were orchestrated by influential figures such as John Rockefeller. Trusts were operated by a body of trustees, who had legal control over them and who held stocks in competing firms and who as a result were able to manage the affairs of the industry concerned. Being in such a powerful position, the trustees were able to eliminate competition between the firms they were running. It was against such injurious and uncomfortable practices that the term 'antitrust' was created and the main legislation on the subject matter, the Sherman Act 1890, was passed.[54] Under the new Act it was illegal to enter into contracts in restraint of trade or to monopolise, or attempt to monopolise, a market. The Act had been inspired not only on the grounds of economic efficiency but also by the fight against trusts and by Jefferson's democratic ideal of a society of equal and independent citizens, subject only to democratically legitimate power. The Act was an improvement on the common law because it enabled a public authority to take action against firms guilty of behaving

---

[53] See the Enterprise Act (2002).
[54] One must bear in mind that it was to break up the Standard Oil and US Steel monopolies that the various US antitrust laws were passed. For a good account of the political perspective of the Sherman Act and other US antitrust laws see E. Kintner, *An Antitrust Primer* (Macmillan, London, 1973), pp. 16–26.

anti-competitively while also enabling anyone injured by that behaviour to bring an action against such firms. The Act was expected to be very effective in fighting anti-competitive practices. In reality, however, the Act did not live up to such expectation. The years following the enactment of the Act witnessed distinguished prominence of antitrust law. Indeed one cannot help notice the similarity with the Austrian experience at around the same time, especially since the 1912 US presidential election was fought mainly on the antitrust issue. Several important changes occurred in the US antitrust law scene during the twentieth century, including the enactment in 1914 of the Clayton Act and the Federal Trade Commission Act. By virtue of the former Act particular practices, such as price discrimination and some mergers between firms, were rendered unlawful. The latter Act on the other hand created the Federal Trade Commission, which was assigned specific responsibility for antitrust policy.

Over the years, the US antitrust experience has developed into one of the most mature experiences in the world. For this reason acquiring some awareness of this experience of antitrust would be invaluable especially in the context of a debate on the internationalisation of antitrust policy. Most commercial phenomena that cause antitrust problems have, at some stage, been considered by US courts and antitrust authorities. Such phenomena have also been the subject of extensive comments by US scholars and academics. The end result has been an abundance of case law and literature, which have been extremely valuable in understanding and furthering different antitrust debates. Furthermore, economic analysis has also become influential in US antitrust law recently. The present chapter has already demonstrated how an appreciation and understanding of economic doctrines and theories is an extremely essential component for antitrust lawyers to understand. The US antitrust experience has been invaluable in demonstrating that antitrust law does not exist in a vacuum. The experience shows that antitrust law is an aspect of the social and economic policy of the system to which it belongs, and as such it reflects the tensions and the preoccupations of that system at any time. These two ideas will be spelled out in detail in the following part as well as in the following chapter.

Comment

From the above discussion, the following conclusion can quite easily be gleaned: The historical perspective of the antitrust law in all the jurisdictions we examined has its own political idea and philosophy. In the light of this fact, it seems that Austrian, German, EC, UK and US antitrust law, all originated from a particular political idea or a political philosophy. This indicates a fundamental point about antitrust law: that it is extremely difficult to separate antitrust law from the political and historical framework in which it is set up.

Market definition

The first part of the chapter demonstrated quite vividly the increased economic approach to antitrust policy over the years, especially during the last quarter of the twentieth century. This increase has had many important consequences. One of these consequences has been placing the important issue of market definition at the centre of the process of application of the antitrust laws of many jurisdictions. The aim of this part is to demonstrate the relevance of the issue of market definition to the internationalisation of antitrust policy. Before we do so, however, it is important first to understand some basics about market definition.

The purpose of market definition

Antitrust law is concerned with problems which may result from a firm or firms possessing market power. Market power does not exist in a vacuum but in relation to a market, and as will be seen below, the relevant market. This is an idea which may not be very difficult to understand in theory. In practice, however, the task of market definition – meaning the means by which the relevant market is delimited – can be a very complicated and daunting one.

  Given the importance of the use of market definition in measuring economic strength, it is hardly surprising that market definition has come to occupy a central stage in antitrust law analysis. Defining the relevant market makes it possible to identify situations giving rise to antitrust concerns and measure the market power of a firm or firms; it makes it possible to identify and learn about the actual competitors and the market shares of such firm(s). It is truly the case that the antitrust laws of many jurisdictions cannot be infringed unless firms have some degree of market power. Therefore, the application of the rules also requires a proper market definition.

The increasing significance of market definition

It should not be difficult to conclude from the above that market definition is not an end in itself but rather a means to an end; nevertheless it is worth emphasising this. The need to define the relevant market, and the method and approach for doing so, have been parts of the antitrust policy of some jurisdictions from its inception. In the EC, for example, defining the relevant market has always been a necessary step in the application of central provisions in the EC antitrust law chapter, in particular Articles 81 and 82 EC.

Over the years, there has been a progressive adoption of a more so-phisticated economic approach in the application of antitrust law by many antitrust authorities around the world. As a result of this important devel-opment, the significance of market definition has increased at a phenomenal rate. To take the example of the EC, prior to 1989 the European Commis-sion was called upon to define the relevant market in twenty or thirty cases per year, since that year the Commission has had to define the relevant market in over one hundred cases per year; the significance of the year 1989 is that it was the year in which Regulation 4064/89, the Merger Regula-tion, was adopted. Following the adoption of the Merger Regulation, the Commission was forced to develop a more methodical approach to market definition. Indeed, it would be very fair to say that most of the expertise of the Commission in market definition over the last thirteen or so years has been derived in the area of merger control. In light of the radical and significant changes in the EC system of antitrust law which have occurred in the last ten years and others which are in contemplation, the significance of market definition can only increase in the future.[55]

The increased relevance of the notion of market power and, therefore, the use of market definition as a tool to identify it, have meant that all those whom antitrust law affects or who have to deal with antitrust law have to familiarise themselves with the exercise. This includes firms, their advisors and antitrust authorities. But antitrust authorities have come to carry an additional responsibility, namely to provide a clarification of their policy and approach to market definition. As we shall see, this in a way

---

[55] See for example the increased economic approach adopted by the European Commission in many Regulations, such as Regulation 2790/99 OJ 1999 No. L336/21. This approach is bound to increase in scope to cover other areas in the future. See for example the Commission's recent evaluation report on EC Regulation 240/96, in the area of transfer of technology (December, 2001). The Report is available at http://www.europa.eu.int/comm/competition/index_en.html.

is part of the competition advocacy task of antitrust authorities.[56] The US antitrust authorities and the European Commission have been among the first to accept and bear this additional responsibility. For example, in October 1997, the Commission adopted its Notice, which is essentially a set of guidelines, on the definition of the relevant market for the purposes of EC antitrust law.[57] This document, despite lacking the binding force of the law, is of considerable importance, in that it has rendered public the procedures that the Commission follows and the criteria and evidence on which it relies when approaching the issue of market definition. The Notice also increased the transparency of the Commission's practice and policy and reduced compliance costs for firms. The provision of clear guidance is particularly relevant in light of the ongoing modernisation programme of EC antitrust rules, which increases the need for firms to become self-reliant and to self-assess their compliance with EC antitrust rules.[58]

Basic principles on market definition

Among the dimensions of market definition are the relevant product market dimension and the relevant geographic market dimension.[59] These are the most important dimensions and it is to these dimensions that the discussion now turns.

Relevant product market definition

Generally, the definition of the relevant product market is carried out using a classical 'constraints' approach. In essence this approach rests on the notion that there are three main sources of competitive constraint upon the exercise of market power by firms: demand substitutability, supply substitutability and potential competition. These concepts will be explained in the discussion that follows.

Demand substitutability Demand substitutability concerns a determination of the range of products (B, C and D) readily available in the geographic area or in an alternative area to which consumers or users of product A can actually switch should the price of the latter increase.

---

[56] See ch. 3.   [57] OJ 1997 No. C372/5.   [58] See ch. 5.

[59] Other dimensions also exist. For example, the temporal market, which shows that in some cases it is important to take into account a particular time or season of the year when deciding whether products can serve as substitute for one another.

In order to measure demand substitution, a hypothetical test, commonly known as SSNIP (Small but Significant Non-Transitory Increase in Price) test, is used. This test, which is in operation in several jurisdictions around the world, derives its origins from the US system of antitrust. The question that this test poses is whether the customers of a particular firm would switch to readily available substitutes in response to an hypothetical, small (in the range 5 per cent to 10 per cent), permanent and relative increase in price of the product(s) under consideration. If customers would so switch, these available substitutes are included in the relevant product market. The SSNIP test helps to identify a set of products small enough to allow permanent increases in relative prices that would be profitable. This set of products is what is commonly referred to as a relevant product market for the purposes of antitrust law.[60]

Price, however, is not the only factor that may be taken into account in examining demand substitutability. Factors such as the physical characteristics of a product and its intended use as well as customer habits and preferences can also be relevant.[61] The aim in taking these factors into account is to consider what similarities, if any, may exist between a particular product and its 'actual' or 'potential' substitutes.

Supply substitutability   Supply substitutability entails identifying firms who are able to switch production to the relevant products as a response to a price increase. It is always considered after demand substitutability. Supply substitutability should only be taken into account when the switch in production will occur within a period that does not imply a significant adjustment of existing assets of the firm. In practice, this means within a short period of time.

---

[60] The SSNIP test is not free from limitations. One such limitation is the cellophane fallacy-type of situation, where a monopolist sets prices at such a level that any further increase would be unprofitable. The application of the SSNIP test in such a case would look as if the theoretical price increase was not profitable and, hence, would lead to overly wide markets being defined and to market shares that understate the firm's real market power. This is a limitation, however, which at least some antitrust authorities take into account when defining the relevant market in an antitrust case. See for example the European Commission Notice on Market Definition.

[61] See for example how in the context of EC antitrust law, while the European Commission emphasised price when defining the relevant market, the European Court of Justice has focused more on the physical characteristics of the products and intended use. See, for example, the case of Case 27/76 *United Brands* v. *Commission* [1978] ECR 207; [1978] 1 CMLR 429.

Potential competition   The third element, potential competition, is not taken into account at the market definition stage. Instead, competitive constraints coming from potential competition will be assessed at a later stage of the process to identify market power: the stage of measuring market power. The idea of potential competition here, although important, is beyond the scope of the present discussion.

Relevant geographic market definition

The relevant geographic market comprises the area in which the firms concerned are involved in the supply and demand of the relevant products or services, in which the conditions of competition are sufficiently homogeneous, and which can be distinguished from neighbouring geographic areas because, in particular, conditions of competition are appreciably different in those areas.[62] In identifying this area, the SSNIP test may be used. Essentially, what the test seeks to answer in this context is whether the customers of a particular firm would switch to readily available substitutes or firms located elsewhere in response to a hypothetical, small (in the range of 5–10 per cent), permanent and relative increase in price of the product(s) under consideration. If the answer to the question is in the positive, these areas will be included in the relevant geographic market.

The SSNIP test, however, may not be fully decisive in this context and for this reason looking at additional elements may be helpful and relevant in identifying an area where conditions of competition are sufficiently homogeneous. Factors like past evidence of diversion of orders to other areas, the examination of the customers' current geographic pattern of purchases and trade flows are, of course, very relevant. In addition, the nature of demand for the relevant product may in itself determine the scope of the geographical market. Factors such as national preferences or preferences for national brands, language, culture and life style, and the need for a local presence are all important factors in defining the appropriate relevant geographic market. Furthermore, barriers and switching costs for firms located in other areas may also be taken into account. Perhaps the clearest obstacle for a customer to divert its orders to other areas is the impact of transport costs and transport restrictions arising from provisions of national legislation or from the nature of the relevant products. The physical geographic

---

[62] See *United Brands v. Commission, ibid.* Also, the European Commission's Notice on market definition.

characteristics of some countries or regions can have a serious impact on transport costs and hence on the scope of the geographic market. On the other hand, the existence or absence of regulatory barriers (for example, those arising from public procurement, price regulations, quotas and tariffs limiting trade or production, technical standards, legal monopolies, requirements for administrative authorisations, or other regulations) is very important for geographic market definition.[63]

Geographic market definition would vary according to the relevant geographical location. For example, one can imagine that in the EC, which is a community of independent countries, the exercise would be far more complex than, for instance, in a single country, where issues such as market integration, cultural/linguistic differences, regulatory barriers or national preferences are not relevant as in the case of the EC. Unlike the case with the EC, these differences do not prevent the antitrust authority, and where relevant the courts, of a single country from reaching the conclusion that markets are local. On the contrary, there are many examples of cases where very narrow geographic markets were defined. In the USA, for example, in some cases the relevant geographic market was defined as the metropolitan areas of one or two states.[64]

Market definition in practice

In practice, the starting hypothesis for an antitrust authority's analysis in a particular case is the market definition provided by the parties to the case. For example, in the case of the EC, a substantial part of a document called Form A/B (the notification form under Article 81 EC) and Form CO (the notification form for mergers under Regulation 4064/89 EC) is devoted to market definition issues. The European Commission asks and expects the firms concerned to define the relevant product and geographic markets and to provide very detailed additional information to allow it to examine the definition given by the parties.

---

[63] See, for instance, the two decisions adopted in 2001 against Deutsche Post by the European Commission where the scope of the markets was defined as national because entry was impossible in view of the existence of exclusive rights or fiscal monopolies. See Cases COMP/36.915 and COMP/35.141 OJ 2001 No. L125/27.

[64] See for example the case of *Dairy Farmers of America – Sodiaal*, in (2001) 1 Trade Cases 73, 136; the market was defined as the sales of branded stick and branded whipped butter in the Philadelphia and New York metropolitan areas.

REFINING SOME CONCEPTS AND IDEAS

In addition to the information provided by the parties, an antitrust authority may seek to rely on market studies carried out by independent bodies, such as consumer associations and consultant firms, as well as seek the views of customers and competitors of the parties. Both customers and competitors receive from an antitrust authority requests for information, sometimes very detailed, so as to assist the antitrust authority in defining both product and geographic markets. Of course, competitors might sometimes be tempted to influence the antitrust authority in one or another direction and normally, but not necessarily always, antitrust authorities are aware of that. Some antitrust authorities, such as the European Commission, the US Department of Justice or Federal Trade Commission have enough experience to be able to distinguish between objective facts and subjective opinions and are therefore not unduly influenced in their assessments. Antitrust authorities in other jurisdictions, especially in developing countries, on the other hand, do not necessarily enjoy the same, or similar, experience; in addition such authorities are generally constrained by many factors such as lack of resources and expertise. As a result, their ability to distinguish between objective facts and subjective opinions is hindered if not rendered virtually non-existent.

In some cases the parties, as well as competitors or customers, support their views with econometric analyses that try to show whether correlation exists between the prices of different products or that try to estimate cross-elasticity between different products. If data is abundant and reliable (which is normally the case for mass consumer goods) these studies can contribute positively to an antitrust authority's own analysis. They do not substitute, however, other more traditional aspects of the analysis.

On the basis of all this information, an antitrust authority should usually be in a position to establish the relevant markets concerned or, at least, the few alternative possible relevant markets. In fact, in view of the limited resources of most if not all antitrust authorities in the world, antitrust authorities define markets only when strictly necessary. In EC merger control, for instance, if none of the conceivable alternative market definitions for the operation in question give rise to antitrust concerns, the European Commission normally leaves the question of market definition open.[65]

---

[65] See for example *Schibsted Multimedia AS/Telenor Nextel AS/Telia AB* [1999] 4 CMLR 216. The Commission has left the definition of the relevant market open in over 70 per cent of its merger control cases.

Market definition and the internationalisation of antitrust law

Market definition – in both the product and geographic sense – occupies an extremely significant position in the internationalisation of antitrust policy. As we saw in the previous chapter, there has been an increase in economic activity worldwide, with the result that many markets have become global. The opening up to competition of markets resulting from the lowering of trade barriers, liberalisation and harmonisation (in some parts of the world) will normally lead to widening of the scope of markets at some point in time. A good example of how the scope of the market has become wider with time is furnished by the telecommunications industry, both with regard to equipment and services in the industry. The telecommunications market is one that traditionally was defined as national. However, following intense liberalisation of the industry, many of its sectors are being assessed on the basis of markets that extend beyond the borders of a single country, to a whole region, such as the EC, and even the world.[66] Generally, it seems that antitrust authorities – at least in some important parts of the world – are willing to accept such expansive definitions of the relevant market whenever the introduction of new technology or services provides customers with an effective opportunity to obtain such services and benefits in an area which transcends national boundaries.[67]

The widening of the definition of markets in such a manner is not special however to fast developing and technological sectors such as the telecommunications industry. Even more traditional industries, such as steel tubes and power cables, have come to witness a widening of market definition. Some ten years ago markets in both of these sectors were defined as national. Today, however – and following a concentrated process of liberalisation – markets in such sectors are increasingly being defined wider than this.

The foregoing discussion has attempted to show that lower trade barriers and liberalisation affect the exercise of market definition. The flip side of the same coin is that market definition can have a direct effect on the process

---

[66] See Case COMP/M.2056 *Sonera Systems/ICL/Invia/Data-info/JV* OJ 2000 No. C322/09; Case COMP/M.1880 *Minnesota Mining and Manufacturing/Quante* OJ 2000 No. C255/08; Case COMP/M.1908 *Alcatel/Newbridge Networks* OJ 2000 No. C169/04.
[67] Examples include Case COMP/M.1845 *AOL/Time Warner* OJ 2001 No. L268/28; Case COMP/M.1795 *Vodafone Airtouch/Mannesmann* OJ 2000 No. C141/07.

of globalisation. For example, if the tendency of antitrust authorities is to opt for wide market definition – meaning one that would extend beyond national boundaries – then such a tendency is likely to support the process of globalisation. The way in which this can happen is quite simple to explain: such support can be achieved through the SSNIP test. Furthermore, the tendency of antitrust authorities to opt for wide market definitions can also have a direct effect in other contexts, which may relate to the process of globalisation. This concerns the furthering of economic or even political goals of communities. For example, in the EC an increase in definition of markets as EC-wide by the European Commission will help further the goal of establishing a single market, which has always been a dominant goal in the EC.[68] Indeed, such an increase can already be observed in the case law of the European Commission; which perhaps is an indication that sooner or later the single market objective will become a reality.

Having explored the relationship between market definition and the process of globalisation, the discussion now turns to consider the question of whether opting for defining the relevant market narrowly, as opposed to widely, may adversely affect the interests of small countries and their firms in a globalised economy. This is an extremely important question and looking at it in the present context is not a mere academic indulgence. The situation which this question concerns can be best explained using a simple example. Suppose that two firms in a small country wish to merge together. An antitrust authority which has jurisdiction to clear or block the merger defines a national market in that country and thus it prevents the two firms from merging because they would quickly create a dominant position in the relevant market or because the merger is likely to substantially lessen competition. Regardless of whether or not the decision is correct on the application of the law, a potential criticism of the decision of the antitrust authority in this case would be that such market definition would prevent the firms from reaching the dimension necessary to compete in markets transcending the national boundaries of the country concerned. It could be argued that this is a valid criticism especially when one bears in mind that in large countries a similar situation would not arise since there firms would be able to reach such dimension without reaching a level where antitrust concerns might arise. This criticism was launched on more than

---

[68] See ch. 5.

one occasion by some small Member States of the EC, such as Sweden, which claimed that the European Commission's practice on geographic market definition, especially in merger cases, was open to question since it could discriminate against them.[69] Despite the validity of the criticism however, there is no sufficient evidence to support the argument that a narrow market definition erects a Chinese wall in the face of firms from small countries wishing to compete in global markets. Domestic firms which are prevented from merging together may have the possibility open to them of merging with firms located in other countries.[70] Of course it is essential to be aware that this may not necessarily be a real possibility. Such cross-border merger may still face the same fate as intra-country merger. But even if the alternative merger option is not available, firms always have the possibility for internal growth open to them. A firm can become dominant on national markets and place itself in a good position to compete on global markets through legitimate means, such as those of price reduction and improving the quality of its products and services so as to make them very competitive.

Conclusion

There are three main conclusions to be drawn from the discussion in this chapter. First, awareness of fundamental economic theories is essential to evaluate various antitrust policy debates. In particular, awareness of international economic issues is important to understand the internationalisation of antitrust policy. However, economic theories do not seem to be consistent concerning how competition should be conceptualised, whether it merits protection, and if so how it should be protected. Secondly, it would be beneficial if economists were encouraged to consider policy designs offered by other disciplines, especially those offered by political scientists. It is believed that this would enhance consistency with regard to defining

---

[69] See Case COMP/M.1672 *Volvo/Scania* OJ 2001 No. L143/74; Case COMP/M.2380 *Förenings Sparbanken/SEB* OJ 2001 No. C273/04 (the merger was abandoned by the parties following its notification to the European Commission).

[70] See for example Case COMP/M.1980 *Volvo/Renault* OJ 2000 No. C301/07 on the one hand and the strategic partnership established by Scania and Volkswagen on the other, following the prohibition of the merger between Volvo and Scania by the European Commission (COMP/M. 1672 15 March 2000).

competition and its role in the global economy. Thirdly, the above brief historical perspective begs the question of whether constructing a 'global framework' within antitrust policy is possible when the antitrust laws of countries do not share the same, or similar, historical origins and goals. This, in turn, relates to the overarching point and goals of antitrust law, which are considered in the following chapter.

3

Antitrust law: goals and political perspective

This chapter examines three important issues. The first issue, examined in the first part, is the point and goals of antitrust law, which has always been a subject of heated debate, whether at national, regional or international level.[1] The second issue, examined in the second part, is the political perspective of antitrust law, which is a difficult issue as it requires antitrust lawyers to step outside their own discipline. The third issue, examined in the third part, is concerned with competition advocacy, which has come to assume a very significant value and relevance in the field of antitrust policy. The conclusion of the chapter is contained in the fourth part.

Antitrust law: concept, framework and goals

This part begins with considering antitrust law as a concept, then examines its framework of operation, objective and purpose and finally prepares the stage for a nexus to be established with the discussion on the political perspective of antitrust law.

The concept of antitrust law

Antitrust law, the 'law' used as an expression of the idea of competition, is generally negative and prohibitory in both nature and wording.[2] This is obvious since antitrust law does not directly encourage competition, but rather seeks – through the employment of legal systems – to

---

[1] See remarks by F. Jenny in C. Ehlermann and L. Laudati (eds.), *European Competition Law Annual 1997: Objectives of Competition Policy* (Hart Publishing, Oxford, 1998), p. 3.
[2] See H. First, 'Antitrust Law' in A. Morrison (ed.), *Fundamentals of American Law* (Oxford University Press, Oxford, 1996); R. Bork, *The Antitrust Paradox: a Policy at War with Itself* (Basic Books, New York, 1978), p. 70.

prevent any form of anti-competitive behaviour in the market.[3] In the EC, for example, Article 81(1) EC reads: 'The following shall be prohibited as incompatible with the common market: all agreements between undertakings, decisions by association of undertakings and concerted practices.' In a similar manner, s. 1 of the Sherman Act 1890 in the USA declares: 'Every contract, combination in the form of trust or otherwise, or conspiracy, in restraint of trade or commerce...' In neither provision is there any mention of 'encouraging competition' or of 'compelling' firms to compete.

The fact that law is used to protect competition has raised some difficult questions, especially since over the years the idea of competition has adapted to evolving intellectual influences as well as legal and political changes. There is a considerable disagreement with regard to whether antitrust law should be concerned with regulating uses of power by large firms than with the removal of hindrances to free competition; whether it protects competitors or the process of competition; and whether it is more concerned with the interests of consumers than the interests of producers. Differences between countries around the world also exist with regard to the type of procedures and enforcement mechanism that should be relied on to enforce antitrust law.

Quite interestingly, the point of using antitrust law to protect competition has been questioned. Some commentators have argued that enacting antitrust law does not guarantee competition will ensue and that competition can exist without having antitrust law. This argument is supported with reference to the high degree of competitiveness enjoyed by countries such as Japan, Singapore and Taiwan in the international arena.[4] Those who have advocated this view have put forward two reasons why such countries nevertheless consider and adopt some form of antitrust law: first, because they are forced, due to market globalisation, to address the issue of competitiveness. Secondly, it is thought that such countries turn to antitrust law in order to ensure that powerful domestic firms do not replace former state monopolies.[5]

---

[3] This definition corresponds to other definitions employed by different writers. See D. Fidler, 'Competition Law and International Relations' (1992) 41 *International and Comparative Law Quarterly* 563, 564.

[4] See ch. 9.   [5] See generally Ehlermann and Laudati, *European*, pp. 150–1.

In spite of this view, it was said in the previous chapter that competition needs law as a form of expression. In particular, there is a need to protect competition by antitrust law in order to guarantee the benefits of the market. Furthermore, some of the very reasons given in support of the view expressed above – that certain countries adopt antitrust laws because they are forced to – can be used to support a different view, namely that antitrust policy is an essential part of the efforts by developing countries and countries with economies in transition to restructure their domestic economies and integrate them fully in the global economy in order to be able to exploit new opportunities to compete. In order to receive their fair share of the benefits accruing from globalisation, an increasing number of such countries adopt economic reform packages which liberalise industries, lead to privatisation and help those countries adopt antitrust laws and policies. In this sense it would appear therefore that certain countries, at least, introduce antitrust laws in their domestic legal systems as a matter of choice and as part of a general aim on the part of those countries to become competitive in a globalised economy.

Framework of antitrust law

The means through which antitrust law protects competition centres mainly around addressing the following concerns. First, to ensure that firms do not harm, prevent or distort competition through collusion with their actual or potential competitors. To this end, horizontal agreements between independent firms, such as agreements on price-fixing, market-sharing or other important aspects of the firms' competitive interaction, are generally prohibited. Other types of agreements, for example agreements between firms at different levels in the economy – vertical agreements between supplier and distributor – are less likely to harm competition. But they may bear certain anti-competitive behaviour, particularly in economies in transition or developing ones. Hence, they may also be addressed under antitrust law. Secondly, a firm or firms that enjoy a position of economic strength may be able to harm competition individually or collectively. Against this, it is generally accepted that when a firm wins the competitive struggle lawfully it should not be punished for its superior performance. However, there is no reason to believe that this means that economic strength may be employed by the dominant firm or firms for example to prevent or restrict competition from existing or potential competitors. Hence, economic dominance is subject to carefully crafted provisions in antitrust law. Thirdly, firms might elect to merge in order to become more efficient, something which will improve market conditions and structures, thus generating greater benefit to consumers. But some mergers may have anti-competitive effects, intended to reduce or lessen competition in the market and to artificially create or strengthen a dominant position not based on superior economic performance.[6] The creation of a merger may well lead to a decrease in the number of competitors in the market, thus affording surviving firms the opportunity readily to co-ordinate their activities. Antitrust laws in about seventy of the world's systems of antitrust therefore include provisions to deal with such mergers.

The goals of antitrust law

Writing in 1978, Bork emphasised that determining what the goals of antitrust law are is a precondition to rationalising antitrust policy and building a body of coherent rules.[7] If this is so – which on the basis of the data available seems to be the case – then it becomes essential to search for the goals of antitrust law; however, this is a task which is not particularly easy. The debate on the goals of antitrust law is an evergreen 'old' debate, which seems to stretch from the birth of the concept of antitrust law to the present time. Looking at the nature of antitrust law would reveal the difficulty of this task. The nature of antitrust law continues to be quite fluid, and its identity in general remains to some extent veiled.[8] This is evident from the academic literature in recent years. Some scholars, for example, have referred to the situation in Europe to show that there is little awareness, including on the part of antitrust law specialists, of how European systems of antitrust law have developed, why they were created and the extent to which the systems have achieved their intended goals.[9] However, even if one is to ignore the lack of awareness of the nature of antitrust law, there is no consensus on the issue of goals. Several goals have been claimed in the

---

[6] For an analysis of this concept of economic performance see M. Dabbah, 'Conduct, Dominance and Abuse in "Market Relationships": Analysis of Some Conceptual Issues under Article 82 EC' (2000) 21 *European Competition Law Review* 45.

[7] Bork, *Paradox*, p. 50.

[8] R. Bork, *The Tempting of America* (Sinclair-Stevenson, London, 1990), pp. 331–3.

[9] D. Gerber, *Law and Competition in Twentieth Century Europe* (Oxford University Press, Oxford, 1998), p. 2.

name of antitrust law. It seems that the possibilities range from economic
to social to political goals. In the USA, the idea that the purpose of antitrust
law is to enhance economic efficiency and maximise consumer welfare has
been dominant. Some would argue that the aim of antitrust law is to protect
small or medium firms.[10] Or perhaps its purpose is to prevent the emergence of private monopolies, which is capable of harming producers and
consumers and ultimately threatening democratic society itself. In Eastern
Europe, South America and several other parts of the world, antitrust law
is seen as a means of facilitating the move from monopolisation to demonopolisation and from state control and planning to liberalisation and
privatisation.[11] In the EC, as will be seen in chapter 5, antitrust law has one
important objective, namely furthering market integration. In light of this
therefore it would appear that searching for the goals of antitrust law is a
task fraught with difficulty.

The lack of clear consensus on goals may not generally matter very much
to the extent that it is thought that on the one hand competition is 'good'
and on that basis it should be encouraged and on the other anti-competitive
restraints are 'bad' and on that basis they ought to be condemned.[12] However, not all countries believe that competition is good, and even in some
of those countries where a system of antitrust has been introduced, competition and antitrust law and policy do not seem to be taken seriously. More
importantly, having consensus in respect of the goals of antitrust law does
matter when one is faced with the internationalisation of antitrust policy;
although at the moment it seems that antitrust scholars are divided on this
point. It has been argued that those who are in favour of internationalisation tend to believe that consensus on the issue of the goals does not present
a problem, while those sceptical about internationalisation tend to believe
that lack of consensus on the issue is a real problem.[13] While this author
would caution against aligning one's view on the issue of consensus on goals
with the pro- or anti-internationalisation view, it would be safe to believe

---

[10] C. Bellamy, 'Some Reflections on Competition Law in the Global Market' (1999) 34 *New England Law Review* 15, 17.

[11] See ch. 9.

[12] C. Doern and S. Wilks, *Comparative Competition Policy* (Oxford University Press, Oxford, 1996), p. 1.

[13] See E. Fox, 'Competition Policy Objectives in the Context of Multilateral Competition Code' in Ehlermann and Laudati, *European*, p. 135. Nevertheless, it should not be thought that it is not possible to favour internationalisation whilst at the same time regard the issue of goals as one demanding careful attention.

that it is eventually vital to address the issue of lack of consensus on goals in the context of the internationalisation of antitrust policy. On the basis of this, any attempt to create a 'global standard' within antitrust law and policy could be doomed to failure unless there is such consensus.[14] For this reason, it is essential to initially consider the issue of the goals of antitrust law.

Antitrust law: legislative intent and the dynamics of the law

Before studying the different goals of antitrust law it is important to make a few general comments on the legislative intent behind its enactment. It is important to remain vigilant that the search for the goals of antitrust law is not confined strictly to the search of legislative intent behind its formulation. One ought to realise too that the law has, or is, capable of having wider, as well as other, overriding goals. For this reason, a heavy emphasis amongst lawyers on the legislative intent of antitrust law could lead to a great narrowness of viewpoint.[15]

The issue of legislative intent is pertinent for discovering the motivation behind the enactment of a particular antitrust law by a group of legislators at a particular time. It is crucial to remember this because antitrust law does not stand in isolation but rather stands within a wider framework (identified in the first chapter as 'system').[16] This means that antitrust law belongs to an order, where different disciplines, factors and interests are interwoven which all evolve constantly, and all according to changes related to the relevant time period.[17] Even within the same jurisdiction, changes may occur over time. These include changes in the mix of goals of antitrust law, the extent to which public intervention is acceptable and generally assumptions about the marketplace. One must not lose sight of the fact that market conditions are not static, rather may be influenced by various currents and so the understanding of antitrust law changes accordingly.[18]

---

[14] See WTO Annual Report 1997, ch. 4.

[15] J. Flynn, 'The Reagan Administration's Antitrust Policy, "Original Intent" and the Legislative History of the Sherman Act' (1988) 83 *Antitrust Bulletin* 259, 263.

[16] See ch. 1. See also ch. 5 which contains an examination of EC antitrust law, including Article 3(g) EC. That Article provides that the EC shall have as its task the establishment of a '*system* ensuring that competition in the Common Market is not distorted*' (emphasis added).

[17] Report of the American Bar Association Sections of Antitrust Law and International Law and Practice on *The Internationalization of Competition Law Rules: Coordination and Convergence*, December 1999, note 23.

[18] R. Whish, *Competition Law* (4th edn, Butterworths, London, 2001), p. 16.

Thus, placing a particular emphasis on legislative intent would lead to overlooking the importance of the issue of goals.

Identifying the goals of antitrust law

The first thing to be said is that within a particular antitrust law, different provisions may aim to achieve different goals which may all fall along a spectrum of different policies.[19] Hence, it is advisable to analyse the various provisions of a particular antitrust law in terms of the policies underlying them.

Many goals have been advocated under antitrust law, but no exhaustive list may be drawn up, nor is the fact that a particular goal appears on the list indicative that such a goal is conclusive. Several categories of goals – as referred to in statements of political institutions, antitrust authorities, court decisions and the work of academics and practitioners – may be identified. For the sake of convenience, it is proposed that those goals be classified into three broad categories: economic, social and political.

Economic goals   The first category includes goals that concern issues of economic efficiency, the promotion of trade, facilitating economic liberalisation (including privatisation) and enhancing the development of a market economy.[20] The previous chapter discussed the general assumption among economists that enhancing economic efficiency in order to achieve lower prices, increase choice, and improve product quality for the benefit of the consumer is the primary purpose of antitrust law. As may be recalled, the conclusion of the chapter was that that the claims made by various schools of thought in economics are not decisive on the issue of goals. It is important to remind oneself of that conclusion.

---

[19] See WTO Annual Report 1997, p. 39. Also, see Bellamy, 'Reflections', 18, where the author speaks of antitrust law being placed in 'a broader social compact'.

[20] The literature here is abundant. See E. Fox and E. Sullivan, 'Antitrust–Retrospective and Prospective: Where Are We Coming from? Where Are We Going?' (1987) 62 *New York University Law Review* 936; K. Elzinga, 'The Goals of Antitrust: Other Than Competition and Efficiency, What Else Counts?'; E. Sullivan, 'Economics and More Humanistic Disciplines: What Are the Sources of Wisdom for Antitrust?' (1977) 125 *University of Pennsylvania Law Review* 1191 and 1214 respectively; J. Brodley, 'The Economic Goals of Antitrust: Efficiency, Consumer Welfare, and Technological Progress' (1987) 62 *New York University Law Review* 1020. These articles, with no exception, attempt to show that economic efficiency should not be considered as the only goal of antitrust law.

Social goals   The second category deals with consumer protection other than in the above-mentioned technical sense of economic efficiency. This covers the idea of safeguarding the consumer from undue exercise of market power and the dispersion of socio-economic power of large firms, safeguarding the opportunities and interests of small and medium-size firms, the protection of democratic values and principles, the protection of 'public interest' and ensuring market fairness and equity.[21] Underlying this antipathy towards the risks of private power are the principles of justice and economic equity in a market democracy. Former US President Franklin Roosevelt once warned that the liberty of democracy can be threatened if the people tolerate the growth of private power to a point where it becomes stronger than their democratic state itself.[22]

Broader political goals   The third category relates to wider overriding political aims, such as those relating to the process of integration in communities based on economic unions and free trade areas. The justification for including this third category is grounded on the recognition of these goals in some jurisdictions;[23] and by the fact that antitrust law is related to experience.[24] As will become apparent in light of the discussion in chapter 5, the situation in the EC furnishes an example of these two points.[25] Therefore, when examining antitrust law, one ought not to generalise about the classification of goals. The manner in which antitrust law is interpreted and

---

[21] G. Amato, *Antitrust and the Bounds of Power* (Hart Publishing, Oxford, 1997), pp. 2–3. A more practical explanation of this point can be found in Whish, *Competition*, p. 13.

[22] Franklin D. Roosevelt Library, New York, File 277. Some writers in the USA, especially those who were not convinced by Bork's arguments, saw wealth distribution as being the primary value and goal underlying the legislative history of the Sherman Act 1890. See R. Lande, 'Wealth Transfers as the Original and Primary Concern of Antitrust: the Efficiency Interpretations Challenged' (1982) 34 *Hastings Law Journal*, 65.

It has been argued, however, that principles of fairness and equity normally advantage inefficient firms and disadvantage the most efficient ones. See F. Easterbrook, 'The Limits of Antitrust' (1984) 63 *Texas Law Review* 1; T Briggs, R. Pogue, E. Recheteller and R. Whiting, 'Interview with James Miller Chairman of FTC'. Furthermore, there seems to be some indication that these principles have ceased to be taken into account under US antitrust law. See *NYNEX Corp. v. Discon, Inc.* 119 S. Ct. 493 (1998).

[23] See M. Dabbah, 'The Internationalisation of EC Competition Policy' in I. Akopova, M. Bothe, M. Dabbah, L. Entin and S. Vodolgin (eds.), *The Russian Federation and European Law* (Hopma, Moscow, 2001).

[24] See M. Lerner (ed.), *The Mind and Faith of Justice Holmes: His Speeches, Essays, Letters, and Judicial Opinion* (Random House, New York, 1943), pp. 51–4.

[25] In the case of the EC, antitrust law is recognised as an important tool in achieving the goal of market integration. See ch. 5.

applied in different jurisdictions demonstrates that there are many situations in which it can be used, other than the above-mentioned categories of economic and social goals.[26] These situations can relate to specific sectors in the national economy,[27] or even interstate sectors such as the EC.[28]

Some comments on the classification of goals

These categories, including the various aims therein, are somewhat in competition with each other.[29] It has been said that it is hard to expect such diverse 'types of interests' to be consistent with one another.[30] It appears that diversity on the issue of goals may affect the internationalisation of antitrust policy. Internationalising antitrust policy is a matter that is bound to require a great deal of consensus between countries. A lack of agreement on the issue of goals may, as opposed to helping build this consensus, lead to significant hurdles in achieving it. But even if countries were to agree and accept that antitrust law has a variety of goals, there would be the difficulty of ascertaining which of these goals should be pursued in order to construct a global order within antitrust law and policy.[31]

Recent views within the WTO seem to indicate that these concerns should not be particularly problematic because there may be convergence in the goals of antitrust law towards certain 'core' principles. According to these views, convergence is to be expected, as countries increasingly look to one another for lessons and, as an increasing number of countries seek to become partners in the global trading system. Such an approach is in use already, albeit in a limited form, in certain jurisdictions and international organisations.[32]

---

[26] For a good comparative study see *Competition Policy in the OECD Countries* (OECD, Paris, 1986).

[27] For example, to deal with particular national issues such as economic developments, financial probity and unemployment.

[28] See C. Ehlermann, 'The Contribution of the EC Competition Policy to the Single Market' (1992) 29 *Common Market Law Review* 257.

[29] See E. Petersmann, 'Legal, Economic and Political Objectives of National and International Competition Policies: Constitutional Functions of WTO "Linking Principles for Trade and Competition"' (1999) 34 *New England Law Review* 145, 155.

[30] WTO Annual Report 1997, p. 39.   [31] See chs. 8 and 9.

[32] See, for example, the work of the OECD Committee on Competition Law and Policy, 'Interim Report on Convergence of Competition Policies' (OECD, Paris, 1994); US Federal Trade Commission, 'Anticipating the 21st Century: Competition Policy in the New High-Tech Global Marketplace' (FTC, Washington, 1996). Several countries have adopted a 'core' objective approach, including Canada (Canadian Competition Act (1986)); more information can be found on the Canada Competition Bureau's website http://www.strategis.ic.gc.ca/competition,

The difficulty associated with a convergence approach, however, is that it may not be possible to succeed in making these goals coincide.[33] It could be argued convergence is not possible when different goals are claimed in the name of antitrust law and when antitrust policy is dynamic and constantly evolving. For example, how can one arrive at the 'core' of antitrust law's purpose by convergence of goals covering economic efficiency (economics) and others dealing with generic concepts such as fairness and justice (law)? The fear is that certain goals, not to mention the fact that they are adopted by strong countries, will prevail over other goals; those 'other goals' may, of course, be advocated by weaker countries.[34] For example, in developed countries, a primary goal of antitrust law is to enhance an efficient allocation of resources and maximise consumer welfare in the traditional economic sense. In contrast, developing countries tend to have a broader goal for antitrust law, namely building a market economy and securing the political acceptance necessary for this. In this case if convergence is to be pursued, it might lead to benefiting some countries at the expense of others – a factor which may minimise the prospects of success in internationalising antitrust policy; although the opposite of this view has been argued by some countries with strong systems of antitrust. For example, in the USA the view has been expressed that the internationalisation of antitrust policy, in general, and the convergence of goals in particular, will lead to a lowest common denominator, whereby countries with strong systems of antitrust will be forced to accept weaker goals advocated by other countries with weaker systems of antitrust.[35]

Even if convergence is both possible and effective and an agreement on the goals of antitrust law amongst different systems of antitrust may be reached, there can still be great disparity between countries regarding the means of convergence and regarding how the means to achieve these goals is

---

and Norway (see the Konkurransetilsynet's website, http://www.konkurransetilsynet.no). This issue is covered in the United Nations Conference on Trade and Development (UNCTAD), 'Draft Commentaries to Possible Elements for Articles of a Model Law of Laws' (UNCTAD, Geneva, 1995). Chapter 5 contains some useful discussion of this issue in relation to the EC.

[33] See M. Azcuenaga, 'The Evolution of International Competition Policy: a FTC Perspective' (1992) *Fordham Corporate Law Institute* 1, 13.

[34] See A. Guzman, 'Is International Antitrust Possible?' (1998) 73 *New York University Law Review* 1501, 1505.

[35] Ehlermann and Laudati, *European*, p. 35. See remarks by J. Klein, *ibid.*, pp. 247–60. See further ch. 9.

perceived.[36] This can be illustrated by the way in which different countries consider antitrust policy should be enforced.

Assume that country A, country B and country C share identical goals for antitrust law. A fundamental cause of divergence in antitrust policy between them would be that the means of achieving those goals may be differently conceived by each country. This divergence of perception may be attributed to lack of agreement between the countries over the optimal means of achieving identical goals which is generally caused by differences in the circumstances prevalent in each country. For example, culture may affect the optimal means of achieving a particular goal and thus, the choice of antitrust law and policy.[37] This is reflected by the fact that antitrust law tradition may differ from one jurisdiction to the next. A central feature of the EC antitrust law tradition has been the idea that antitrust law is special and that using law to protect competition moves outside the discipline of law. In light of this view, EC antitrust law is a new type of law, which deals with problems for which traditional legal mechanisms are not suitable, and thus it requires correspondingly non-traditional methods and procedures. This contrasts sharply with the approach of US antitrust law, which relies primarily on traditional legal forms and institutions in protecting competition.[38] It is therefore important to realise that there is no single coherent policy which binds the antitrust laws of more than one jurisdiction together. Neither antitrust law nor antitrust policy exists in the abstract. Different systems of antitrust reflect different concerns, values and possibly goals. As was noted in chapter 1, antitrust law has now been adopted in almost 100 countries, whose economies and economic development may be very different. It would be quite unrealistic to imagine that each system will be concerned with, and pursuing, identical goals.[39]

In addition to these differences, there are other ones which could be mentioned, in particular those which relate to factors such as the size of the country. Such factors may also affect the choice of antitrust law and policy. For example, a relatively small economy may choose to accept an efficiency defence in its system of antitrust when clearing merger transactions with anti-competitive effect, whereas a larger economy may choose not to opt

---

[36] See pp. 2–4 above.
[37] See L. Haucher and M. Moran, *Capitalism, Culture and Economic Regulation* (Oxford University Press, Oxford, 1989), p. 3.
[38] Gerber, *Competition*, p. 12.   [39] See WTO Annual Report 1997, p. 34.

for such a defence. Hence such structural differences as well as differences in substantive law between countries may lead them to diverge with respect to the goals of antitrust law.[40]

Antitrust law is interdisciplinary in nature

A final point to make about the concept and function of antitrust law is one that has lacked recognition in the literature, namely that antitrust law is interdisciplinary in nature. There is sufficient evidence to support this view. In light of the discussion in the previous chapter, it should be apparent that the fathers of the concept of antitrust law in most parts of the world were politicians, not commercial lawyers or even economists.[41] This is of course very interesting given the prominent role that lawyers and economists have come to play in formulating and applying the law. In light of the involvement of the lawyer, the economist and the politician, antitrust law appears to be a special type of law.[42] One can also add that the idea of competition itself and its protection is special in nature. This is a position which one probably would not wish to criticise. On the contrary, the involvement of various disciplines in antitrust law and policy and their development should be welcomed. It is believed that this is necessary for an effective operation of a system of antitrust law. So far, in systems of antitrust of many countries the application of antitrust law and policy has been based primarily on the skills of lawyers and economists, who have been dominant in the field. These skills are vital for an effective and successful enforcement of antitrust law and policy. However, one ought to remember that the administration of antitrust policy also involves the exercise of bureaucratic politics. There is ample evidence that seems to indicate that the priorities and importance attached to the enforcement of antitrust law and policy is dependent on political choices made by ministers and officials acting in a variety of capacities. An adequate understanding of antitrust law and policy therefore requires insights from political science and public administration to complement the legal and the economic perspectives. It is regretted that this 'third intellectual strand' within antitrust law and policy remains little systematically analysed.[43] The members of one discipline, it is argued, seem to be able to offer only half answers, and possibly even less, to questions arising under antitrust law and its enforcement. Hence, one ought

---

[40] See further ch. 9.   [41] Amato, *Power*, p. 2.
[42] See generally Gerber, *Competition*.   [43] Doern and Wilks, *Comparative*, pp. 3–4.

to appreciate that complementary insights offered by other disciplines should be sought – provided, of course, that an interest in full answers is expressed.

A political perspective of antitrust law

The heart of the matter

A fundamental point about antitrust law, which is common to most if not all jurisdictions, is how it is seen as a response to an important problem of democracy.[44] Some commentators have sought to explain that this point concerns how private power may be employed to infringe not only the freedom of other individuals, but also the balance of public decisions which may become vulnerable in the face of such power.[45] According to Amato, on the basis of the principles of liberal democracy, this problem is twofold and constitutes a real dilemma:

> Citizens have the right to have their freedoms acknowledged and to exercise them; but just because they are freedoms they must never become coercion, an imposition on others. Power in liberal democratic societies is, in the public sphere, recognized only in those who hold it legitimately on the basis of law, while in the private sphere, it does not go beyond the limited prerogatives allotted within the firm to its owner. Beyond these limits, private power in a liberal democracy ... is in principle seen to be abusive, and must be limited so that no one can take decisions that produce effects on others without their assent being given.
>
> On the basis of the same principles, the power of government exists specifically to guarantee against the emergence of phenomena of that sort ... But this, which is its task, is also its limitation: abuses forbidden for individuals are not allowed for rulers either. Here is then the dilemma.
>
> In a democratic society, then there are two bounds that should never be crossed: one beyond which the unlegitimated power of individuals arises, the other beyond which legitimate public power becomes illegitimate. Where do these bounds lie? This is the real nub of the dilemma.[46]

---

[44] See generally E. Kintner, *An Antitrust Primer* (Macmillan, London, 1973).

[45] Amato, *Power*, p. 2.

[46] *Ibid.*, p. 3. Reference is made to the principles of liberal democracy because this dilemma really has its roots entrenched there. See J. Locke, *Two Treatises of Government* (Cambridge University Press, Cambridge, 1988), p. 118.

Applying this analysis in the present context, it seems that there is an apparent inconsistency between two perspectives on the role of competition and antitrust law. The idea of competition is rooted in the freedom of firms to carry out their business in a manner and ways they consider best suited to further their personal interest.[47] However, antitrust law can limit this freedom. At first sight, this limitation seems to be inconsistent with the idea of competition, its dynamic and democratic values. This apparent inconsistency results in a balance being struck between two sets of considerations and interests associated with them. One is concerned with the interests of those whose freedom is limited by the law, which is a short-term consideration. This consideration is normally prevalent in jurisdictions where public authorities are hostile to dominant firms and assume that such firms have, and will use their, economic dominance to harm small competitors. The other relates to the interests of those whose freedom is, or may be, limited by the actions of others, in the case of anti-competitive practices of firms. This is a long-term consideration because it takes into account the consequences for those whose freedom would be limited over time, should the law fail to address the limitation on their freedom or the source of harm to their interests.[48] To put this point another way, the balance is essentially between the bounds of public power and private power and the relationship between these two forces. As a corollary of this, the question arises whether the market can be relied on to address competition concerns and to provide for itself in the long term, or whether there is a need for public intervention to address such concerns in the short term.

Who makes decisions?

The apparent inconsistency described above reveals an interesting aspect of antitrust law, that the law is about who should hold power over making various types of decisions that affect the market and its functioning.[49] Two independent views can be put forward in this context. One view might be that each firm should have the right to decide and formulate its own policy in the hope that self-interest and the public interest will somehow coincide. On the other hand it might be thought that public authorities should take a more interventionist approach into the marketplace. An example of the

---

[47] See pp. 17–18 above.   [48] Gerber, *Competition*, p. 9.
[49] Whish, *Competition*, p. 15; WTO Annual Report 1996.

THE INTERNATIONALISATION OF ANTITRUST POLICY

latter approach is furnished by the way in which the European Commission for many years applied Article 81(1) EC – by historically opting for a wide view of practices falling within the Article and then exempting certain agreements under Article 81(3) – an approach that has come to be relaxed in recent years.[50]

The issue of decision-making – or more commonly, the making of important commercial decisions – is central to the debate on the process of internationalisation of antitrust policy. Its relevance resides in the query of whether countries or business firms should be the key player in this process.[51] In turn, this query leads to another on whether entrusting decision-making to one side as opposed to the other affects the process. Normally, the internationalisation of antitrust policy is debated from the perspective of countries, who are viewed as the sole and major players in the process, since they hold the final say on whether to support the process. Recently, however, some recognition has emerged that the internationalisation needs to be considered at least from a shared perspective.[52] The other point of view in question is that of the business community. The justification for this view seems to relate to the fact that the internationalisation of antitrust policy is in part a response to the globalisation of markets – which is a direct result of the operation of business firms in markets beyond national boundaries – and so the needs and the role of business firms should be considered within the process.[53] This is an issue which will be discussed in more detail in chapters 6 and 9.

Public intervention

In regulating the conditions of competition in the market, the 'invisible hand' of competition may, at times, be replaced with the more visible hand of public institutions.[54] Whilst it is understandable that this is inevitable in

---

[50] See for example the less formalistic and more economic approach, which has been adopted by the Commission under important instruments such as EC Regulation 2790/99. See further ch. 5.
[51] Gerber, *Competition*, p. 15. See chs. 6 and 9.
[52] See E. Fox, 'Global Problems in a World of National Law' (1999) 34 *New England Law Review* 11, 11–13; J. Griffin, 'What Business People Want from a World Antitrust Code' (1999) 34 *New England Law Review* 39.
[53] See R. Weintraub, 'Globalization Effect on Antitrust Law' (1999) 34 *New England Law Review* 27.
[54] Whish, *Competition*, p. 15; E. Fox, 'The Politics of Law and Economics in Judicial Decision Making: Antitrust as a Window' (1986) 61 *New York University Law Review* 444, 554.

some cases, especially to address anti-competitive behaviour in the market, it seems that public intervention can generate some uncertain implications. These uncertain implications are a source of difficulty in the internationalisation of antitrust policy. First, the aforementioned opposing perspectives of antitrust law can exist in two different jurisdictions. For example, this seems to be the case with the EC and the USA. Secondly, the perspective within one jurisdiction may change over time.[55] In the USA, for example, it would appear that a change in administration in Washington can impact on such views, with regard to the application and enforcement of US antitrust law. If one traces these uncertain implications to their origin, it becomes apparent that the reason different perspectives on antitrust policy exist, arises from the way antitrust law is applied by public institutions. Leading officials in former US administrations expressed some very strong views over the functioning of US antitrust authorities, such as the Federal Trade Commission, describing the officials in those authorities as individuals who are hostile to the business system, to free trade, and who sit down and invent theories that justify more meddling and interference in the economy and the marketplace.[56] Therefore, there is an important issue in the relationship between the law, as it appears in statute, and the way it is applied by institutions in practice. This relationship has been examined by a few scholars, who have explained that in this relationship antitrust law, as it appears in the statute, defines and configures power relationships, and, in turn, public institutions manipulate the statute and its interpretation in order to achieve institutional, other political and even personal goals.[57]

In light of the discussion thus far, this adequately shows that antitrust law may be, and actually is, subject to political influence. The politics of a system of antitrust is apparent from the manner in which antitrust authorities apply their domestic antitrust law, whether in the way the goals of antitrust law receive legal expressions in the statutes or in their guidelines and policy statements based on these statutes. Some commentators have observed that three modes of such political expression exist: the goals of the core antitrust policy areas; the extent and nature of non-antitrust

---

[55] See also Kintner, *Antitrust*, pp. 228–32.

[56] See remarks of D. Stockman, former Director of Office Management and Budget and a leading official in the Reagan Administration in *Chicago Tribune*, at A-1, cols. 2–3, 23 February 1981.

[57] See D. Gerber, 'The Transformation of European Community Competition Law' (1994) 35 *Harvard International Law Journal* 97, 100; D. Tarullo, 'Norms and Institutions in Global Competition Policy' (2000) 94 *American Journal of International Law* 478.

policy goals that are allowed by statute to be considered in decision-making; and exemption provisions.[58] These expressions vary from one jurisdiction to the next, which, in turn, affects the internationalisation of antitrust policy.[59]

There are several points that illustrate how politics and its influence are apparent in the field of antitrust policy which can also provide a subtle ground for scrutinising the law and politics of the internationalisation of antitrust policy. The first point arises from the manner in which the application of antitrust law is handled and the way antitrust cases are decided. It seems that potentially there is a very long distance between antitrust law and policy and their outcomes. An antitrust case may begin with a complaint to an antitrust authority which may be followed with an investigation by the latter. The investigation may then lead the antitrust authority to warn the defendant firm(s) and in some cases perhaps this will trigger an enforcement, which in turn may bring the case before the court for a final ruling.[60]

The second point is the issue of independence of antitrust authorities. As different players and interests are involved in antitrust law and policy, there is a possibility that antitrust authorities become subject to political pressures. Voices in some quarters have argued that distancing antitrust authorities from these pressures is favourable from a legal standpoint.[61] It has been said that it is important to ensure that decisions regarding the investigation and prosecution of particular cases are consistent with consideration of 'natural justice' or procedural fairness. There is no doubt that injecting more considerations of fairness and justice will reduce the influence of politics. This can have a positive impact on the issue of making important commercial decisions in the market. Ensuring an adequate degree of independence can also help to ensure the administration of antitrust law and policy leads to a sensible body of case law and rules emerging. Distancing antitrust enforcement from political pressures also seems to be desirable from the point of view of institutional structure. The idea here is to foster the political independence of antitrust authorities, establish the

---

[58] See Doern and Wilks, *Comparative*, p. 15.   [59] See ch. 4.
[60] Doern and Wilks, *Comparative*, p. 14.
[61] See A. Krueger, 'The Political Economy of Rent-Seeking Society' (1974) 64 *American Economic Review* 291; J. Buchanan, 'Rent Seeking and Profit Seeking' in J. Buchanan, R. Tollison and G. Tullock (eds.), *Toward a Theory of the Rent Seeking Society* (Texas A and M University, Houston Texas, 1980); WTO Annual Report 1997.

standing of foreign firms in domestic systems of antitrust and introduce non-discrimination principles.[62]

The third issue relates to the question of whether antitrust law aims to protect competition or competitors, which directly arises from the issue of purpose and goals. Some commentators have argued that this question may lead the antitrust community down dangerous paths – as has happened in the EC – with the emergence of two different groups: one that believes the purpose of EC antitrust law, in particular Article 81 EC, is to protect the freedom of firms to sell goods and provide services, and another that believes that the aim of the law is to protect the process of competition.[63] Other views, however, have been less concerned about this question. It has been argued that the direct objective of antitrust law is to protect the process of competition, even though economic conditions differ from one country to the next and even if the impediments to competition and the measures to cure those impediments also differ.[64]

Competition advocacy

The view, as stated above, that antitrust law is directed towards dealing with private restrictive business practices designed to reduce consumer welfare and result in inefficient use of resources would bring one close to assuming that such practices constitute the only source of harm to competition. However, under no circumstances should this be seen as a valid assumption, since harm to competition can also result from the way various public policies are implemented and institutional arrangements are designed.[65] Indeed, private restrictive business practices are often facilitated by various government interventions in the marketplace. One country, for example, may grant legal monopoly to its firms; it may limit in other ways the number

---

[62] Ehlermann and Laudati, *European*, p. 140. See also R. Posner, 'The Federal Trade Commission' (1969) 46 *Chicago-Kent Law Review* 48, 54. Posner noted that the politicisation of antitrust law at the US Federal Trade Commission was due to its dependence on Congress. Note also the old proposal in the EC to establish an independent non-political antitrust authority in order to separate political regulatory powers from decisional ones. See C. Ehlermann, 'Reflections on a European Cartel Office' (1995) 32 *Common Market Law Review* 471; A. Pera and M. Todino, 'Enforcement of EC Competition Rules: a Need for Reform?' (1996) *Fordham Corporate Law Institute* 125. See further chs. 9 and 10.

[63] Ehlermann and Laudati, *European*, p. 12.   [64] *Ibid.*, p. 21.

[65] To support the above discussion on the desirability of the involvement of various disciplines in antitrust law and policy, this is one instance in which the expertise of political scientists would be needed.

of competitors in the market; or it may introduce unduly restrictive rules and regulations. For this reason, the question arises whether the mandate of an antitrust authority should extend beyond mere enforcement of antitrust law.

Embarking on competition advocacy

There is a great deal of merit in the view that antitrust authorities must take part in the formulation of economic policies of countries, especially those which may adversely affect competitive market structures, business conduct and economic performance. To this end, an antitrust authority must act like a competition advocate, a role through which it can particularly encourage government policies that would reduce barriers to entry, enhance deregulation and promote trade liberalisation. As a corollary, an antitrust authority will be able to minimise unnecessary government intervention in the marketplace, something which is regarded as highly desirable for an antitrust authority to do.

Is competition advocacy necessary?

Competition advocacy should enable an antitrust authority to have a greater say on how various public policies should be shaped, as well as affording it the opportunity in some cases to propose different alternatives that would be less detrimental to economic efficiency and consumer welfare. In this regard, competition advocacy can become a safety valve in a system of antitrust law that would ensure against not only anti-competitive practices, but also lobbying and economic rent-seeking behaviour by various interest groups, which seem to be common in the field of antitrust policy. Of course, the desirability of these ends cannot be denied, since they are bound to help achieve greater accountability and transparency in economic decision-making mechanisms and promote sound economic management and business principles in both public and private spheres.[66]

Competition advocacy and enforcement of antitrust law

Certain links seem to exist between competition advocacy and enforcement of antitrust law. This is most particularly so in developing economies or

---

[66] See Doern and Wilks, *Competition*, pp. 334–7.

those in transition. Such economies normally feature markets which in their early stages of development tend to be concentrated and sometimes dominated by one or a few large firms that may engage in anti-competitive behaviour or in extensive lobbying practices. The aim of competition advocacy in this instance is to promote conditions that will translate into more competition in the market without a direct intervention on the part of an antitrust authority or the government generally. The role of an antitrust authority as a competition advocate in these situations can be contrasted with that of antitrust authorities around the world which subject firms in the market to close and continuous supervision. It is simply argued that the latter approach is not entirely satisfactory since it is more resource-intensive, and the justification for it is hardly compelling because it means that antitrust authorities in those countries would be reverting to broad government intervention in the marketplace.[67]

Competition advocacy exists in several jurisdictions in the world. Looking at the examples furnished by those jurisdictions, it would be possible to conclude that competition advocacy can be based on both explicit (statutory) and implied (informal) grounds. In some jurisdictions antitrust authorities enjoy a certain mandate to submit their views on specific matters to the relevant ministry or regulatory agency.[68] In other jurisdictions, the legislation may be silent on the role of the antitrust authority under such circumstances. In such a case, and provided that an antitrust authority is not prohibited under some legislation from participating, it should – through its law enforcement role – actively seek opportunities to make the case for competition in the public forum. Systems of antitrust in France, Germany, the EC and the USA furnish a good example in this regard.[69] Undoubtedly, the benefits which active competition advocacy generates to the economy and to consumers can be guaranteed to be significant, or

---

[67] An interesting discussion of this issue has come from G. Amato, contrasting the position of the USA with that of the EC. See Amato, *Power*, p. 112.

[68] These countries include Canada, Italy, the Republic of Korea, Russia and South Africa. See B. Doern, 'Canadian Competition Policy Institutions and Decision Processes' in Doern and Wilks, *Competition*, pp. 71–7.

[69] See R. Sturm, 'The German Cartel Office in Hostile Environment' and G. Peters, 'United States Policy Institutions: Structural Constraints and Opportunities' in B. Doern and S. Wilks, *Competition*, pp. 187–96 and 42–9 respectively. In the USA, a Competition and Consumer Advocacy programme was adopted by the Federal Trade Commission. See Celnicker, 'The Federal Trade Commission's Competition and Consumer Advocacy Programme' (1988–9) 33 *Saint Louis University Law Journal* 379.

at least as substantial as those accruing from more traditional antitrust enforcement.

A wider role for competition advocacy can be found in the public sphere. The successful establishment of a market economy requires the fostering of a competition culture. Both consumers and the business community need to be educated on the values of antitrust law and policy and on how these will benefit them. An antitrust authority has an important role to fulfil in this educational process. In several jurisdictions the public does not have sufficient experience with antitrust law policy or an appreciation of the desirability and benefits which enhanced competition could bring them.[70] To an extent, however, this may be understandable, since the first experience the public may have with free markets is likely to be negative, not positive. In planned economies or those in transition, the liberalisation of markets often is accompanied by disruption, misallocation and inefficient use of resources, unemployment and a high increase in prices of goods, especially in those which were formerly controlled economies. Under these circumstances, competition advocacy can be particularly helpful, but the task of an antitrust authority in building public support for antitrust policy is especially challenging. Much here can depend on the conditions of competition in the market and the role of an antitrust authority in the formulation of wider economic policies of the country, since the economic environment in which firms operate is conditioned by many economic policies, and the degree of competition in an economy can be strengthened or weakened according to the way in which these policies are developed and applied.

Establishing public awareness of Antitrust policy

Beyond engaging in the formulation and shaping of public policies, an antitrust authority should seek to establish awareness and support for antitrust law and policy among consumers and the business community, a task that may be particularly demanding. This is especially so in developing economies. Hence, it may be appropriate to warn that the present section is more relevant to developing economies as opposed to developed ones.

---

[70] Israel can be mentioned as an example here. The author's strong familiarity with the Israeli system of antitrust law has brought him to observe the obvious lack of information amongst Israeli citizens and businesses on the desirability and benefits of competition.

To ensure a greater degree of transparency and accountability, and to embark on a true educative process, an antitrust authority should, where possible, bridge any existing gap between the work it conducts and the public. To this end, it is recommended that an antitrust authority seek to conduct its work openly in public. The author admits of course that this proposition is subject to significant limitations, since in the investigation of most antitrust law cases an antitrust authority is subject to a strict require-ment of confidentiality relating to the handling of information obtained during the course of investigation.[71] To the extent possible, however, an antitrust authority should attempt to make information about its work publicly available. This can be done by ensuring that enforcement deci-sions are regularly published in bulletins, newsletters and perhaps on the Internet, so that interested parties (other public bodies, regional authorities, business associations and the firms concerned) who are affected by antitrust enforcement can be made aware of their rights and obligations. Additional effective educational tools for making the public more aware of antitrust policy can include publicising summaries of decisions in antitrust cases in the media, press conferences and press releases. Another more technically difficult tool is the formulation of guidelines on specific areas of antitrust law and policy. This tool has been employed by antitrust authorities in several jurisdictions,[72] especially in the area of merger control.[73] The value of these guidelines, especially for firms who wish to observe the law, can be appreciated in the light of the fact that the language of antitrust law in most jurisdictions is sparse and general.[74]

Another way in which an antitrust authority can bring its work closer to the public is through organising antitrust law and policy workshops, confer-ences and seminars to promote an understanding of the role of competition and to show how its enforcement activities further such goals.[75] Through

---

[71] See, for example, Regulation 17/62 OJ 1962 No. 204/62 under EC antitrust law. See ch. 5.

[72] See, for example, the Notice on Defining the Relevant Market, OJ 1997 No. C-372/5, discussed in ch. 2.

[73] The European Commission, for example, has introduced various and important notices which have proved to be very useful for firms and their advisors. See, for example, the Notice on the Concept of a Concentration, adopted under Regulation 4064/89 OJ 1998 No. C 66/1.

[74] See Bork, *Paradox*.

[75] Several domestic competition authorities and other organisations dealing with antitrust law and policy have over the years engaged in such programmes. The US Department of Justice and the German Antitrust Authority are worth mentioning because of their efforts in hosting several meetings attended by officials of antitrust authorities from around the world. Also, the

such forums, an antitrust authority will be able to demonstrate how competition benefits competitors, customers and consumers; how it will help ensure the supply of goods and services at the lowest possible price and highest possible quality; how producers in competitive markets are forced to respond to demands of their consumers; and how competition results in the most efficient allocation of market resources. Antitrust law enforcement will thus be enhanced when an antitrust authority is successful in making the members in its community understand and support the concepts of competition and antitrust law and policy. Such members are not confined to the business community and consumers. They may well include antitrust lawyers, academics with expertise in business and economics, bodies and associations acting for consumers and other interest groups and politicians interested in market economics.

Summary

From the above, it can be argued that competition advocacy seems to be a more effective means to ensure that the law is understood and observed than antitrust law enforcement. Nevertheless, experience of different jurisdictions in the area of antitrust law and policy demonstrates that antitrust law enforcement has been an effective tool for fostering competition, breaking down barriers to entry, increasing economic efficiency and protecting consumer welfare. Holding traditional antitrust law enforcement like an article of faith should not necessarily mean however that competition advocacy will be relegated to a marginal role. At all events, competition advocacy can enlarge the benefits that may accrue from antitrust law enforcement. Hence, competition advocacy can be seen to be complementary to antitrust law enforcement – if not necessarily an alternative.

Conclusion

There are three main conclusions to be drawn from the preceding discussion. First, a discussion on the point and goals of antitrust law is central to the internationalisation of antitrust policy, which confirms the

European Commission has been very active in holding various events for these purposes. It regularly holds antitrust law days and public hearings to which it invites members of the public, firms, consumer organisations and academics.

presumption made at the beginning of the chapter. Secondly, the discussion of goals opens up scope for demonstrating that it is difficult to separate antitrust law from a political perception at any one time. The politics of antitrust law in general, and the internationalisation of antitrust policy in particular, become visible in several ways. A common factor to these ways is the manner in which public institutions give legal expression to the goals of antitrust law, whether in statutes, or in the way they interpret, apply and enforce these instruments. The third conclusion is that it is imperative to consider the issue of public intervention in the market. This, in turn, raises questions of institutional approaches and arrangements, which are examined in the following chapter.

4

The use of discretion

Antitrust authorities and public authorities more generally enjoy discretion in the way they may regulate conditions of competition in the market, and in the way they implement and enforce antitrust policy. The use of discretion is quite common to most legal systems in the world. Some commentators have argued that various policies and their instruments should be viewed within a framework to be wielded by administrative institutions with a high level of discretion.[1] In the field of antitrust policy, the fact that antitrust law tends normally to be vague in terminology makes the use of discretion by antitrust authorities quite inevitable. However, this use of discretion can be an issue of concern in antitrust policy, in general, and in the internationalisation thereof, in particular. The concern in this instance mainly arises from the way in which similar antitrust laws in different jurisdictions may be radically different when enforced – a situation that often leads to a divergence in the legal standards amongst those jurisdictions.[2] This divergence in some cases, may be facilitated by natural factors, such as culture, experience and other structural issues, which are special to those jurisdictions individually;[3] although, in other cases, the divergence can be the pure result of the use of discretion by antitrust authorities. Hence, it is important to inquire to what extent this use of discretion, in general, and the resulting divergence, in particular, affect the internationalisation of antitrust policy. Apart from having such an effect, it seems that divergence between different systems of antitrust is also problematic when it comes to comparing these systems.[4]

---

[1] See K. Davis, *Discretionary Justice* (Louisiana State University Press, Louisiana, 1969), pp. 216–17.
[2] A. Guzman, 'Is International Antitrust Possible?' (1998) 73 *New York University Law Review* 1501, 1545.
[3] See L. Haucher and M. Moran, *Capitalism, Culture and Economic Regulation* (Oxford University Press, Oxford, 1989), p. 3. Also, see pp. 56–7 above.
[4] See C. Doern and S. Wilks, *Comparative Competition Policy* (Oxford University Press, Oxford, 1996), p. 20.

This chapter examines the use of discretion by antitrust authorities, an issue hardly explored in antitrust law literature, and its relation to the internationalisation of antitrust policy. As part of the analytical exercise, the chapter considers questions of institutional approaches, political factors and policy designs. The chapter is structured as follows. The first part attempts an explanation of what discretion really is and compares it with rule-making. The second part then identifies several cases in which the use of discretion can be an issue of concern. This is followed by the third part which proposes some solutions to deal with cases where the use of discretion can be problematic. The fourth part spells out the implications of the present analysis, before the fifth part offers a conclusion.

A framework

Explaining discretion

In the present context, it is essential to be aware that discretion is not the same as competence, which is recognised globally as the legal power of an authority to act. When antitrust authorities make use of discretion, all limits, whether effective or otherwise, which act as a constraint on their exercise of power leave them in a position to choose from a variety of options concerning whether to act or not in a particular case. Some components of this statement require an explanation. Discretion is not confined to what is authorised or what is legal but includes all that which is within the effective limits on the power of antitrust authorities. There are numerous cases in which discretion may be seen as illegal or at least of questionable legality. In addition, cases involving a choice by antitrust authorities to take no action are definitely included. Looking at the decisional practice of most, if not all, antitrust authorities in the world would reveal that decisions by those authorities not to act outnumber those in which action is taken. Some examples of inaction decisions can be found in the way antitrust authorities select cases for investigation, open proceedings and formulate decisions in those cases. In the last example, discretion is exercised not merely in the adoption of final decisions, but also when antitrust authorities adopt interim decisions; again, the practice of antitrust authorities is rich with evidence pointing to the fact that interim decisions outnumber final ones.[5]

---

[5] The truth behind this can be seen in the case of the EC. See, for example, the European Commission 21st Report on Competition Policy 1991.

Finally, it is worth noting that the use of discretion by antitrust authorities is not special to decisions dealing with the substance of antitrust cases but covers those dealing with procedure, enforcement and other non-substantive matters.

Discretion vis-à-vis *rule-making*

To gain a better understanding of what discretion really is, it should be compared with a rule-making approach. It would be wrong to think that rule-making only connotes a process through which rules are made. Rule-making has a wider meaning than that, referring to the means and methods through which the necessary facts and information, which would enable those responsible to determine what kind of rules should be formulated, can be gathered. According to this approach, those who exercise authority must conform strictly to the rules. The expositors of the rules are the courts, which perform their duties within the rigorous confines of written norms. Along with administrative and bureaucratic institutions, they only have the power to interpret and apply, and not alter, those rules.[6] This view of institutions and their role is based on considerations of fairness and protection against abuse(s) of public power. It insists on enhancing the equal treatment of all by eliminating the effects of personal inclination in the decision-making process. By requiring conformity with stated rules,[7] it ensures – as a result of having legal certainty – that natural and legal persons will be able to plan their conduct in accordance with predictable outcomes.

Identifying instances of discretion

The purpose of this part of the chapter is to give an account, albeit brief, of instances in the practice of antitrust authorities which highlight the existence of use of discretion. Normally, this use of discretion is apparent in the following situations:

---

[6] F. Hayek, *The Road to Serfdom* (Chicago University Press, Chicago, 1944), pp. 72–3. Also, see report of the Franks Committee on Administrative Tribunals in the UK, Cmnd 218 (1957), p. 6.

[7] As Duguit observed, 'no organ of the state may render an individual decision which would not conform to a general rule previously stated'. L. Duguit, *Traité de droit constitutionnel* (Ancienne Librairie Fontemong, Paris, 1927), p. 681.

Case selection and initiation of proceeding

Antitrust authorities generally enjoy a wide discretion in their choice of cases for investigation. A good example is provided by the practice of the European Commission. The Commission has a wide discretion in deciding whether or not to open proceedings. This has been confirmed not only by the Commission itself, but also by the EC courts.[8]

Adoption of binding decisions

Caution is necessary when discussing the use of discretion by antitrust authorities in the outcome of antitrust proceedings. This is because not all antitrust authorities in the world enjoy the necessary competence to formulate legal propositions – in the form of binding decisions on firms – when they apply their domestic antitrust laws. This can be illustrated with reference to the situation in the USA and the EC. The US system of antitrust is one in which litigation in courts occupies a central place. US antitrust law – despite the influence of authorities, such as the Department of Justice and the Federal Trade Commission – is largely judge-made law. In the EC, on the other hand, the primary decisions are taken first by the European Commission, which is mainly an administrative body. Judicial review of these decisions however is available at the level of the European Court of First Instance (CFI), whose judgments are in turn subject to appeal to the European Court of Justice (ECJ).[9]

However, those antitrust authorities which are able to issue binding decisions on firms enjoy wide discretion. On this view, some antitrust authorities enjoy more discretion than others, in terms of their ability to formulate binding decisions in antitrust cases. This means that the use of discretion can vary from one antitrust authority to the next, a situation that can impact on the internationalisation of antitrust policy.

---

[8] See Commission 14th Report on Competition Policy 1984, in which the Commission referred at p. 119 to the judgment of the ECJ in Joined Cases 43 and 63/82 *VBVB* v. *Commission* [1984] ECR 19; [1985] 1 CMLR 27. Also, see the Opinion of Advocate General Rozès in Case 210/81 *Demo-Studio Schmidt* v. *Commission* [1983] ECR 3045, 3070; [1984] 1 CMLR 63. The most important case on this issue, however, is Case T-24/90 *Automec srl* v. *Commission* [1992] ECR II-2223; [1992] 5 CMLR 431.

[9] C. Bellamy, 'Some Reflections on Competition Law in the Global Market' (1999) 34 *New England Law Review* 15, 18.

Informal and interim settlements

Not every investigation initiated by an antitrust authority results in a final binding decision. More often, an antitrust authority reaches more informal or interim settlements with firms rather than final decisions. An antitrust authority normally enjoys wide discretion in reaching these settlements.[10] There is no doubt that it would be sensible to encourage the practice of settlements because they can save time and money and at the same time they can offer faster relief to a complainant to an antitrust authority, and the public from restrictive effects of anti-competitive behaviour. Despite the practicalities of these settlements, there seems to be some concern however regarding the way these settlements are reached. Some commentators exemplified this concern with reference to the practice of the European Commission, arguing that when the Commission reaches settlements with firms it is in fact shaping its policy without any of the procedural safeguards provided by an administrative proceeding. As a result, it has been argued that the Commission's practices and decision-making must be sufficiently transparent so as to remain subject to public and judicial supervision.[11] In light of this comment, it is important that the settlement practice of antitrust authorities should be monitored. Once a proceeding is commenced, antitrust authorities should not be at liberty to ignore any existing minimum procedural safeguards simply by embarking on a course towards settlement.[12] Observing minimum procedural safeguards is expected to enhance the rights of

---

[10] A good example is furnished by the settlements that the European Commission reached with *Fiat and Alfa Romeo* (See (1984) 17 EC Bull. No. 11, p. 24) and with *British Leyland* (OJ 1984 No. L207/11). In the first case, a settlement between the Commission and the parties was reached when Fiat and Alfa agreed to instruct their dealers to refrain from promoting the purchase of right-hand-drive cars on the Continent which were sold at lower prices than those in the UK. In the second case, a binding decision and a fine was imposed by the Commission on *British Leyland*, even though the latter made similar commitments to those of *Fiat and Alfa Romeo*.

A similar claim can be made about the position adopted by the Commission in merger cases. Compare, for example, *British Airways/British Caledonian* (noted in Commission 18th Report on Competition Policy 1988, p. 81) and *British Sugar/Berisford* (noted in Commission 12th Report on Competition Policy 1982, p. 104) with *Electrolux/Zanussi* and *Philips/Grundig*, which were completed without any intervention on the part of the Commission.

[11] I. Van Bael, 'Insufficient Judicial Control of EC Competition Law Enforcement' (1992) *Fordham Corporate Law Institute* 733, 735.

[12] Some help can be found here by looking at the US Antitrust Procedures and Penalties Act 1974, which provides an adequate framework for ensuring transparency and judicial control of the settlement practices of the US antitrust authorities.

firms, the propriety and credibility of antitrust authorities, as well as reduce the risks of uncertainty, inconsistency and unjust results.

Exemptions

The issue of exemptions in antitrust policy is problematic. For example, where antitrust law cases involve two or more jurisdictions, the antitrust authority in one jurisdiction may tend to grant an exemption to harmful activities by its own domestic firms on grounds of industrial policy or the authority in question may believe that these activities do not raise any concerns for its domestic market. However, these activities may be harmful to the conditions of competition, and to firms in the other jurisdictions concerned. For example, these activities may impede the access of foreign firms to the domestic market.[13] The fact that an exemption for the source of harm may be defended by the exempting jurisdiction on the basis that no prescriptive law applies at all, can lead to conflicts between the antitrust authorities concerned.[14] Furthermore, an antitrust authority which enjoys the competence to grant exemptions to firms from antitrust law necessarily enjoys wide discretion.

Differences in procedure

A comment on the fact that systems of antitrust in the world differ on procedure would provide an invaluable insight. There are several reasons why procedural differences have to be examined within the internationalisation of antitrust policy. The fact that in some jurisdictions the competence to grant exemptions is not always conferred upon antitrust authorities, but rather is the prerogative of the judiciary and the legislature – as is the case in the USA[15] – means that divergence in the legal standards between different

---

[13] The issue of market access is examined in ch. 8.

[14] See E. Fox, 'Toward World Antitrust and Market Access' (1997) 91 *American Journal of International Law* 1.

[15] The Department of Justice and the Federal Trade Commission are not authorised under US antitrust laws to issue exemptions from the statutory prohibitions. However, this does not mean that exemptions are non-existent under US antitrust law. Congress has occasionally introduced exemptions, for example in relation to export cartels under the Webb-Pomerane Act 1918, railroad cartels, mergers deemed in the 'public interest' and certain shipping cartels. For a good discussion of these exemptions see J. Griffin, 'United States Antitrust Laws and Transnational Transactions: an Introduction' (1987) 21 *International Lawyer* 307, 314–17.

jurisdictions is inevitable. For example, in the EC system of antitrust an investigation is initially opened by the European Commission which may lead to a prohibition, and then a grant of an administrative exemption, a practice that has given rise to a great deal of criticism.[16] In some cases, the Commission's decisions may be reviewed by the CFI, and an appeal can even bring the case before the ECJ. The EC jurisdiction is really an inquisitorial jurisdiction. It is not an adversarial jurisdiction. The ECJ in antitrust cases decides on the need to call witnesses, cross-examines them and decides on the need to appoint an expert to make a report. This contrasts with the more adversarial US system, where the Department of Justice and the Federal Trade Commission bring an action before the courts. Deciding an antitrust case under the US system involves judges, a jury (in criminal cases), a sworn testimony, interrogations, discovery and cross-examination.

Finally, it ought to be acknowledged that procedures used in the relevant system of antitrust greatly influence substantive law developments. Therefore, it is important to examine the issue of procedure, in particular whether courts or administrative authorities should decide on antitrust cases in an international context.

Dealing with discretion

The possible ways

It should not be thought in the light of the discussion in the previous part that the use of discretion is undesirable. Nor should it be assumed that the use of discretion by antitrust authorities is untrammelled under all circumstances. As a matter of fact, that discussion shows that there are instances in which the discretion of antitrust authorities may be quite constrained. The use of discretion by antitrust authorities, like the use of discretion by administrative authorities in general, is not fixed but rather lies along a sliding scale, where in every instance something needs to be done.

Whether the use of discretion by antitrust authorities is wide or narrow depends on the way in which each country's system of antitrust functions, on how antitrust policy and its role is conceived in the relevant system. As domestic antitrust authorities differ in their use of autonomy, the chapter

---

[16] See ch. 5.

proposes that in all cases activities should normally take one of three forms: confining, structuring and checking discretion.[17] By confining, it is meant to establish outer boundaries and keeping discretion within them. The ideal, of course, is to put all necessary discretion within the boundaries, and to put all unnecessary discretion outside the boundaries, by drawing dividing, bright lines. Structuring includes encouraging antitrust authorities to develop plans, policy statements and rules, as well as open rules and open precedents. Finally, checking refers to judicial supervision and review. These three different alternatives will now be examined in turn.

Confining discretion

Discussing constraints on discretion involves an attempt to answer questions such as whether the use of discretion by antitrust authorities should be uncontrolled. It is proposed here that this use of discretion should be confined.[18] The vague nature of antitrust law often means that discretion is delegated to antitrust authorities. The law often fixes certain limitations but leaves the ambit of discretion relatively open. By and large, it can be argued that the legislature usually does about as much as it reasonably can do in specifying the limits on delegated discretion. However, it may be deficient in providing further clarification. This is particularly the case where experience is needed to provide a foundation for this clarification. In such an instance, the legislature is almost deficient in correcting the assumption of discretion by antitrust authorities due to pressures on its time and its inability to draft for every contingency arising in relation to competition.

Structuring discretion

Since there is little scope for legislative intervention in order to confine the use of discretion, developing standards by antitrust authorities, and then, as circumstances permit, confining their own discretion through principles and rules is more promising.[19] This movement from vague standards to

---

[17] The terms were borrowed from Davis, *Justice*.

[18] Note the relevance of this issue in the context of centralisation/decentralisation in the EC system of antitrust, where much of the recent 'modernisation' debate, namely making Article 81(3) EC directly applicable, has been about confining the use of discretion under this provision. See further ch. 5.

[19] A 'rule' is a specified proposition of law, a 'principle' is less specific and broader and a 'standard' is still less specific and often rather vague. See generally R. Dworkin. *Law's Empire* (Harvard University Press, Cambridge, Mass., 1986).

unambiguous standards, broad principles and rules can be accomplished by policy statements. It can also be accomplished by adjudicatory opinions or by the exercise of rule-making power. A considerable part of the task of antitrust authorities should be devoted to facilitating compliance with the antitrust law by helping firms to understand it. Not only judicial policy, but also administrative policy must be developed by precedent and on publicly stated grounds. Only in this way can the law be clarified sensibly. Firms have the right to know what kind of behaviour would lead to prohibitions under the relevant antitrust law. Publishing policy statements by antitrust authorities and relying on a rule-making approach should help in developing a consistent antitrust policy.[20]

A more diligent use of antitrust authorities' rule-making power is a far more promising means of structuring the use of discretion than urging the legislature to enact more meaningful standards. This is not because clarification of law by antitrust authorities is preferable to clarification by the legislature; since the opposite is often true. The reason that the former clarification is more promising is that the legislature may not be expected to provide the needed clarification. Legislators know their own limitations, they know they are ill-equipped to plan detailed programmes for a policy that changes rapidly, all in relation to time, and they recognise that antitrust authorities are better equipped because they can work continuously for long periods in specific areas.

Thus, the hope lies in the clarification of vague statutory standards.[21] The typical failure in a system of antitrust, which is correctable, is not legislative delegation of broad discretion with vague standards; but the procrastination of antitrust authorities in resorting to their rule-making power to replace vagueness with clarity. All concerned – business firms, legislators and the courts – should urge antitrust authorities to consider and adopt earlier and more diligent use of their rule-making power.

However, the typical tendency of antitrust authorities to refrain from resorting to their rule-making power may be understandable. Waiting for a case to arise, then clarifying only to the extent necessary to decide the case, and then waiting for the next case, is one way to construct antitrust

---

[20] See M. Dabbah, 'Measuring the Success of a System of Competition Law: a Preliminary View' (2000) 21 *European Competition Law Review* 369, where it is argued that 'competition advocacy' is one of the factors that ought to be used to measure the success of a system of antitrust. See also ch. 3 for a detailed discussion on the concept.

[21] See further ch. 5.

principles.[22] In some circumstances, the slow process of making law only through adjudication is a necessity, for antitrust authorities may really be unable to decide more than one case at a time. Moreover, sometimes even when they can do more, they properly eschew early rule-making. Developing antitrust law through adjudication is a sound and necessary process; the majority of antitrust law in most jurisdictions is the product of this process.

Despite this fact, the argument can be advanced that antitrust authorities, by and large, have fallen into habits of unnecessarily delaying the use of their rule-making power. They often hold back even when their understanding suffices for useful clarification through rule-making – for reasons of resources or perhaps priorities in handling their investigations. When antitrust authorities do so, the likelihood that they will make use of discretion will be quite high. This is a point which requires considerable thought and academic comment.[23]

Checking discretion

The use of discretion by antitrust authorities needs a framework of judicial control, in order to distinguish between guided and unguided use of discretion. This discussion may be made more concrete by reference to the situation in the EC.

The European Court of Justice (ECJ) The ECJ enjoys wide powers under EC law, including the power to review decisions by the Commission.[24] However, the ECJ has not always been in favour of exercising this power, especially in cases where the Commission has utilised its discretion – including those cases involving wide discretion. This attitude of the ECJ can be identified in the light of several of its major judgments. In the early case of *Consten and Grundig*, the ECJ considered that:

> The exercise of the Commission's powers necessarily implies complex evaluations on economic matters. A judicial review of these evaluations must take account of their nature by confining itself to an examination of the relevance of the facts and of the legal consequences which the Commission

---

[22] See Report of the American Bar Association Sections of Antitrust Law and International Law and Practice on *The Internationalization of Competition Law Rules: Coordination and Convergence*, December 1999, p. 26.

[23] A more detailed examination of these issues somewhere else led the present author to this exact conclusion. See Dabbah, 'Measuring'.

[24] See Article 230 EC.

deduces therefrom. Their review must in the first place be carried out in respect of the reasons given for the decisions which must set out the facts and considerations on which the said evaluations are based.[25]

Twenty years later, the ECJ came to a similar conclusion, noting that the Commission based its decision on an assessment of complex economic situations. In the case of *Remia BV* v. *Commission*[26] the ECJ held that it must limit its review of such an assessment to verifying whether the relevant procedural rules have been complied with, whether the facts on which the choice is based have been accurately stated and whether there has been a manifest error of assessment or abuse of powers.

It is obvious from these two judgments that the ECJ is reluctant to second-guess the decisions of the Commission, unless there is a clear abuse of power.[27] This attitude of the ECJ is controversial. The mere fact that the Commission has not committed any grave error in adopting its decisions in antitrust cases should not necessarily mean that it has properly discharged its obligation of ensuring a proper application of EC antitrust rules. The discretion enjoyed by the Commission cannot and should not veil the requirement to produce informative decisions. It is advisable that the rule remains '*in dubio pro reo*' instead of '*in dubio pro Commissione*'.[28]

Some writers, however, seem less concerned about this attitude of the ECJ. It has been said that as the executive arm of the EC, it is sensible that the Commission is enabled to establish its own role as principal guardian of EC antitrust law, expand its geographical reach and conduct itself in any manner that enhances its international legal personality and recognition.[29]

The need for increased judicial monitoring is particularly important when set against the backdrop of the Commission's decision-making process.[30] Whilst in principle decisions in antitrust cases are supposed to

---

[25] Joined Cases 56 and 58/64 *Establissements Consten SARL and Grundig-Verkaufs-GmbH* v. *Commission* [1966] ECR 299, 347; [1966] CMLR 418.

[26] See Case 42/84 *Remia BV* v. *Commission* [1985] ECR 2545; [1987] 1 CMLR 1.

[27] See M. Mendes, *Antitrust in a World of Interrelated Economies: the Interplay between Antitrust and Trade Policies in the US and the EEC* (Editions de l'Université de Bruxelles, Brussels, 1991), p. 82.

[28] See opinion of Advocate General Rozès in Case 210/81 *Demo-Studio Schmidt* v. *Commission* [1983] ECR 3045, at 3070; [1984] 1 CMLR 63.

[29] See J. Friedberg, 'The Convergence of Law in an Era of Political Integration: the *Wood Pulp* Case and *Alcoa* Effects Doctrine' (1991) 52 *University of Pittsburgh Law Review* 289, 322–3. See also the view expressed by Hawk in favour of this situation of a 'highly centralized system' which he contrasted with 'the Byzantine proliferation of statutes and enforcement authorities in the US', quoted in Mendes, *Antitrust*, p. 82.

[30] See, for example, *Re Continental Can Co. Inc.* [1972] CMLR 690.

be reached by the full Commission – as a collegial body – in practice most of these decisions are reached through the so-called 'written procedure', and not after a debate involving the entire Commission. Under this procedure, a draft decision is distributed amongst all directorates-general in the Commission. A decision is considered to be adopted unless objections are submitted within a time limit – normally less than a week. This actual state of affairs reiterates that the power to make decisions rests with those officials of the Commission who handle the cases. The Commission acts as prosecutor, judge and possibly jury. On the basis of this situation, the ECJ's reluctance to perform more intervention in the practice of the Commission and its decisions means that the use of discretion by the Commission can go uncontrolled.[31]

The Court of First Instance (CFI)   Establishing the CFI in 1989 marked the creation of a specialist court, and antitrust policy falls within the CFI's competence. The Commission's decisions can be subject to judicial review by the CFI, whose judgments, in turn, are subject to appeal to the ECJ.

Since its foundation, the CFI has produced several judgments, which make it difficult to discern the direction in which its jurisprudence has been moving. Nevertheless, it has produced some good judgments which show that the use of discretion by the Commission is being subjected to close scrutiny. In *Italian Flat Glass*, for example, the CFI held that the Commission should bear the burden of proof in antitrust cases and that this required standard is not satisfied by the Commission merely 'recycling' the facts of the case.[32] A similar attitude by the CFI can be seen from its decision in *PVC*, where the CFI lamented the sloppy decision-making process of the Commission.[33]

In *European Night Services* v. *Commission*,[34] the CFI annulled the Commission decision, emphasising the obligation on the Commission to set out

---

[31] The position of the EC can be contrasted with that of Germany where the Kammergericht does not hesitate to review the discretionary findings of the Bundeskartellamt. This situation is remarkable since the Bundeskartellamt is a specialist body, whereas the Commission is a political institution. Of course, the discretionary findings of the Bundeskartellamt cannot be equated with those of the Commission, which is responsible for a wider variety of policies and concerns. For a general discussion on the German system of antitrust see D. Gerber, *Law and Competition in Twentieth Century Europe* (Oxford University Press, Oxford, 1998), pp. 276–306.

[32] Joined Cases T-68, 77 and 78/89 *Società Italiana Vetro* v. *Commission* [1992] ECR II-1403; [1992] 5 CMLR 302.

[33] Joined Cases T-79/89, T-84–86/89, T-91–92/89, T-94/89, T-96/89, T-98/89, T-102/89 and T-104/89 *BASF AG* v. *Commission* [1992] ECR II-315; [1992] 4 CMLR 357.

[34] Cases T-374–5 and 388/94 [1998] ECR II-3141; [1998] CMLR 718.

the facts in individual cases and considerations having decisive importance in the context of its decisions. The CFI stated that while the Commission was not required to discuss the issues of law and facts and the considerations which led it to adopt its decision, it is required under the EC Treaty to make clear to the CFI and the firms concerned the circumstances under which it has applied EC antitrust rules. Thus, when a Commission decision applying EC antitrust law lacks important analytical data – which is vital to the application of EC antitrust provisions and to enable the CFI to establish whether an appreciable effect on competition exists – such as reference to market shares of the firms concerned, the Commission is not entitled to remedy such defect by adducing for the first time before the CFI such data.[35]

Against these good judgments, however, stands a line of cases in which the CFI has not been inclined to interfere with the use of wide discretion by the Commission, especially with regards to the imposition of fines and mitigating circumstances.[36] This attitude by the CFI may seem quite surprising in the light of purpose for which the CFI was established. Some commentators have argued that the very creation of the CFI as a court of both first and last instance for the examination of facts in cases brought before it is an invitation to undertake an intensive review in order to ascertain whether the evidence on which the Commission relies in adopting a contested decision is sound. Despite this view, however, there is no reason to believe that the EC system of antitrust suffers from lack of effective judicial control at least at the level of the CFI. Looking at the area of merger control, for example, since EC Regulation 4064/89, the Merger Regulation, came into force in 1990, only fifteen mergers – which represent less than 1 per cent of all notified cases to the Commission during this period – were prohibited by the European Commission. Of these fifteen decisions by the Commission, about half came before either the CFI or the European Court of Justice. In three of those cases, the CFI annulled the decision of the Commission and the latter's decisional practice was subjected to strong scrutiny and criticism.[37] Thus it seems that there is sufficient evidence to

---

[35] Recently the CFI annulled the Commission decision in the case of *Airtours* because the CFI believed that the Commission did not supply sufficient evidence in support of its decision. See Case T-342/99 *Airtours plc* v. *Commission* (6 June 2002).

[36] See Case T-7/89 *S. A. Hercules Chemicals NV* v. *Commission* [1991] ECR II-1711; [1992] CMLR 84; Case T-69/89 *Radio Telefis Eireann* v. *Commission* [1991] ECR II-485; [1991] 4 CMLR 586; see the opinion of Advocate General Vesterdorf, at 125.

[37] See the CFI judgments in Case T-342/99 *Airtours plc* v. *Commission* (6 June 2002), Case T-77/02 *Schneider Electric* v. *Commission* (22 October 2002) and Case T-5/02 *Tetra Laval BV* v. *Commission* (25 October 2002).

support the view that, on balance and bearing in mind that exceptions can be found, there seems to be effective judicial control in the EC system of antitrust.

Some implications of the analysis

A matter of choice

The adoption of a particular institutional approach by antitrust authorities is essentially a matter of choice. The idea inherent in this kind of choice should be considered in light of the reasons for which the approach is adopted. Indeed, those reasons depend on the category of goals that are advocated in the relevant system of antitrust. Consequently, the category of goals impacts on the type of institutional approach. This means that divergence in the goals between different systems of antitrust can lead to differences in institutional approaches between those systems, which inexorably affects the internationalisation of antitrust policy.[38]

Political factors and policy considerations versus legal rules

It is also apparent from the above discussion that one of the main questions regarding the internationalisation of antitrust policy concerns whether judges or administrators will decide antitrust cases in a global context. This question corresponds to two different perspectives about the role of law courts and antitrust authorities which have to be taken into account. On the one hand, if antitrust policy is regarded as being subject to political influence, the resulting internationalisation thereof is likely to be seen as a matter of debate on the use of discretion by administrative and bureaucratic institutions. If, on the other hand, political influence is ruled out, because, for example, one understands antitrust law as a means of protecting and maintaining a valued social good, the internationalisation of antitrust policy is likely to be seen as a matter of debate on legal rights, judicial analysis, and judicial decision-making. In this instance, the influence of political factors and policy considerations would be decreased.[39]

---

[38] The implications here can be seen in light of the fact that different countries, including developed and developing countries, do not agree on what the goals of antitrust law are or ought to be. See ch. 3.

[39] See further ch. 3.

Further issues

The internationalisation of antitrust policy has been advocated partly as a response to market globalisation – a phenomenon that makes it clear that markets have become wider than countries and that antitrust law matters frequently transcend national boundaries.[40] In this situation, domestic antitrust rules may not be suitable for regulating conditions of competition in those markets in general, and for addressing matters such as international jurisdiction, in particular. On this view, there seems to be a clear absence of adequate rules in this situation. Clearly, this is a situation in which the law ends.

In this situation, antitrust authorities have several options open to them.[41] These options include, but are not limited to, relying on extraterritorial application of domestic antitrust laws, reverting to co-operation agreements which may exist between the authorities concerned etc. In all options, the use of discretion will begin. Antitrust authorities are largely concerned with applying the law, with making discretionary determinations, and with various mixtures of law, discretion and politics. As a matter of fact, they are much more occupied with discretion than with law. It would be appropriate to remind the reader that when the use of discretion begins, choices will naturally present themselves to officials working in antitrust authorities. The choices may be between beneficence and tyranny,[42] justice and injustice, reasonableness and arbitrariness. Yet no official of these authorities would admit that where law ends beneficence, injustice, tyranny or arbitrariness begins. On the contrary, they would have everyone believe that where law ends, wise and just use of discretion begins.

Lastly, one has to appreciate the significance of two different points. First, the use of discretion is related to the question of who should hold the locus of power in a system of antitrust. This is so, since the question is, how interventionist should public power be in the process of competition? Linked to this question is the understanding that a system of antitrust will usually function on the assumption that public power has the final say in any antitrust-related matter. As the discussion in the previous chapter demonstrated, the question in particular, is whether the internationalisation of antitrust policy should be arrived at with public initiative (countries

---

[40] See chs. 1 and 3.   [41] See further chs. 7 and 8.
[42] W. Pitt's words, 'where law ends tyranny begins' are engraved in stone on the Department of Justice Building in Washington D.C.

being the main actors and decision-makers) or private initiative (the market and business firms deciding for themselves). Arguably, the implications of having countries as the primary actors in this matter are far-reaching and would carry with them a great impact on the entire process of internationalisation. One direct consequence would be that this process would be made subject to more political influence.[43] The second point is that the fact that the use of discretion varies among different systems of antitrust affects the internationalisation of antitrust policy. These points are important because apart from anything else, they present an analytical challenge, which extends to issues of political bargaining and political acceptability possessed by the different players concerned.[44]

Conclusion

It is obvious from the above discussion that antitrust authorities make use of discretion, which in some cases may be wide. This use of discretion affects the internationalisation of antitrust policy, especially since it often leads to divergence in the legal standards amongst different systems of antitrust. As we saw above, something must be done to deal with the use of discretion, particularly in cases where the use of discretion is wide. This can take the form of confining, structuring or checking discretion.

Confining discretion is a particularly good option to pursue, since it has the advantage of encouraging antitrust authorities to enhance the coherence of their decisional practice and to develop antitrust policy in a steady and sensible way. Not only would this lead to greater certainty in the practice of antitrust authorities, but also would make it more reliable for firms who often are in need of such certainty in their handling of market operations. The net result would be that the internationalisation of antitrust policy – leading to the creation of an international system of antitrust – would be more achievable.

Confining discretion can also be supplemented with checking discretion. This is also desirable, since it would encourage antitrust authorities to keep within the confines of their discretion as well as afford firms the opportunity to bring actions against antitrust authorities in order to ensure that their interests and rights are adequately protected.

---

[43] See ch. 9.   [44] See further ch. 9 for a detailed account of the players concerned.

5

EC antitrust policy

This chapter examines the antitrust experience of the European Community (EC). Several features of this experience make it suitable for providing some insights into the law, economics and politics of the internationalisation of antitrust policy. In particular, this experience furnishes an example of a successful system of antitrust operating beyond national boundaries, which is supported by a rich background, especially on the relationship between law and politics.[1] Other important features also exist. These will be alluded to later in the discussion.

The chapter is structured as follows. The first part gives an account of some important introductory issues. The second part describes the role of the European Commission, the European Court of Justice (ECJ) and the national courts of Member States in EC antitrust policy. The third part examines the relationship between EC and domestic antitrust laws, followed by the fourth part, giving an account of the importance and the influence of EC antitrust law beyond the single market. The fifth part spells out the implications of the present analysis. Finally, the sixth part gives a conclusion.

Some introductory issues

The special characteristics of EC antitrust law

EC antitrust law is thought to be a unique type of law.[2] This uniqueness arises from several facts. EC antitrust law is enforced in a special context, namely the goal of market integration and therefore it has a market-integrating aspect.[3] In this context, the law belongs to a wider system,

---

[1] See generally D. Gerber, *Law and Competition in Twentieth Century Europe* (Oxford University Press, Oxford, 1998), pp. 417–36.

[2] *Ibid.*

[3] See Articles 2 and 3 EC. These provisions will be discussed below. See p. 89 below.

designed to eliminate barriers between countries and enhance the creation of a single market.[4] During the past forty-five years or so, the law has come to be widely recognised as fundamental to furthering this single market goal,[5] initially in the form of the Common Market and later to establish the Internal Market.[6] Attaining this goal required not only eliminating restraints imposed by Member States, but also ensuring that those restraints would not be replaced by private restraints resulting from the behaviour of private firms, because both were considered capable of harming this goal. For this reason, and others, antitrust law was introduced to address such concerns[7] and this has contributed towards antitrust law becoming of central importance in the EC.[8] Another point that can be made in relation to the uniqueness of EC antitrust law and which arises from the previous one, is that associating antitrust law with the single-market integration goal has meant that the law has developed in many ways that depart from the 'traditional' approach, which can be observed in systems of antitrust in other jurisdictions. This has meant that EC antitrust law was not adopted solely to enhance efficiency and ensure consumer welfare, but also to serve as a 'tool' to achieve a wider political goal.[9] Thus, the law has a variety of goals. EC antitrust law reflects a European regulatory approach. Further, and more importantly for the purposes of the present examination of the internationalisation of antitrust policy, the EC constituted a 'new legal order of international law'. This view derives some force from the words of the ECJ in its groundbreaking judgment of *Van Gend en Loos*, where it firmly heralded that for the benefit of such new legal order of international law the

---

[4] See Report of American Bar Association on Private Anti-Competitive Practices as Market Access Barriers, January 2000.

[5] Many commentators share the view that antitrust policy is regarded as the most fundamental and successful of EC policies. See L. McGowan and S. Wilks, 'The First Supranational Policy in the European Union: Competition Policy' (1995) 28 *European Journal of Political Research* 141.

[6] See B. Hawk, 'Antitrust in the EEC – the First Decade' (1972) 41 *Fordham Law Review* 229, 231; U. Kitzinger, *The Politics and Economics of European Integration: Britain, Europe, and the United States* (Basic Books, New York, 1963), pp. 22–58; the Commission 23rd Report on Competition Policy 1993, p. 88. Similar aspirations can also be found in the Cockfield White Paper on the Completion of the Internal Market COM (85) 310, 7, para. 14.

[7] See the discussion on the EC antitrust chapter, pp. 88–9 below.

[8] See P. Massey, 'Reform of EC Competition Law: Substance, Procedure and Institutions' (1996) *Fordham Corporate Law Institute* 91.

[9] See M. Mendes, *Antitrust in a World of Interrelated Economies: the Interplay between Antitrust and Trade Policies in the US and the EEC* (Editions de l'Université de Bruxelles, Brussels, 1991), p. 74.

Member States of the EC have limited their sovereign rights, albeit within limited fields, and the subjects of this legal order comprise not only Member States but also their nationals.[10] Adopting and using antitrust law in this legal order supplies an example of the internationalisation of antitrust policy. Consequently, it is helpful to draw on the successes or failures of the antitrust experience of this new legal order.

The EC antitrust chapter

The antitrust rules of the EC appear in Chapter 1 of Part III of the EC Treaty. The Chapter consists of 9 Articles, Articles 81–89 EC. There are important antitrust instruments which fall outside the Chapter, mainly in the form of Regulations; among these are Regulation 17/62 EC and Regulation 4064/89 EC, the Merger Regulation.

Within Chapter 1, two Articles deserve a special mention. The first is Article 81 EC which in paragraph 1 prohibits agreements, decisions by associations of undertakings[11] and concerted practices which restrict competition and which affect trade between Member States. By virtue of Article 81(2) EC, any agreement, decision or concerted practice which is caught by paragraph 1 of the Article is declared void; however, the prohibition may be declared inapplicable in the case of agreements or practices which satisfy the requirements of the third paragraph of the Article. Article 82 EC, on the other hand, is directed towards any abuse by one or more undertakings of a dominant position in the Common Market or a substantial part of it which

---

[10] Case 26/62, *NV Algemene Transporten Expeditie Onderneming van Gend en Loos* v. *Nederlandse Administratie der Belastingen* [1963] ECR 1.

    The question of legal personality and nature of the EC has also been considered on other occasions by the European Court of Justice. The following characteristics of the legal order established by the EC have been emphasised by the ECJ. By contrast with ordinary international treaties, the EC created its own legal system which became an integral part of the legal systems of the Member States. By creating a Community of unlimited duration, having its own institutions, its own legal capacity and capacity of representation on the international plane and real powers stemming from a limitation of sovereignty or a transfer of powers, the Member States have limited their sovereign rights. This limitation of Member States sovereignty is permanent. Case 6/64 *Costa* v. *ENEL* [1964] ECR 585, p. 593. See how this view of the ECJ corresponds to EC legislation. Article 281 EC states that the EC has legal personality, and Article 312 EC states that it has concluded for unlimited duration.

[11] The concept of 'undertaking' includes all persons, natural and legal, engaged in a commercial activity. The present chapter will continue to use the concept of 'firm' however to mean an undertaking within the EC context.

may affect trade between Member States. Finally, the Merger Regulation applies to concentrations, meaning mergers, between firms.

The above rules, however, should not be read and understood on their own, but rather in conjunction with three important Articles in the EC Treaty. These are Articles 2, 3 and 4 EC. Article 2 EC is a very important provision which merits full recital here. The Article reads as follows:

> The Community shall have as its task, by establishing a common market and an economic and monetary union and by implementing the common policies or activities referred to in Articles 3 and 4, to promote throughout the Community a harmonious, balanced and sustainable development of economic activities, a high level of employment and of social protection, equality between men and women, sustainable and non-inflationary growth, a high degree of competitiveness and convergence of economic performance, a high level of protection and improvement of the quality of the environment, the raising of the standard of living and quality of life, and economic and social cohesion among Member States.

These objectives are followed by Article 3 EC, which contains the activities of the Community. Of particular relevance is paragraph (g) of the Article which expressly refers to 'a system ensuring that competition in the internal market is not distorted'. Article 4 EC in its turn provides that the activities of the Community and of Member States shall be conducted in accordance with the principle of an open market economy with free competition.

The nature of EC antitrust law

It was seen in chapter 2 that EC antitrust law, like the antitrust laws of many countries, was desired neither by lawyers nor by economists, but by politicians and by 'scholars attentive to the pillars of the democratic systems, who saw it as an answer (if not indeed "the" answer) to a crucial problem of democracy'.[12] The involvement of these factors in the creation, and arguably the development, of EC antitrust law supports the view expressed in previous chapters: that it is difficult to divorce antitrust law from a particular political idea at a particular point in time.[13] Furthermore, it supports the view that a study on antitrust law and policy, including one dealing with the

---

[12] G. Amato, *Antitrust and the Bounds of Power* (Hart Publishing, Oxford, 1997), p. 2.
[13] See pp. 34–5 above.

internationalisation thereof, ought to be approached in an *interdisciplinary* manner.[14] In the case of the EC, this is obvious from the fact that the creation and development of EC antitrust law is as much about politics as law and economics.[15]

There are two additional comments that are worth making in respect of the nature of EC antitrust law and experience. First, despite the fact that the wording of the antitrust provisions in the EC Treaty has not changed for over forty-five years, the policies underlying these provisions have changed according to changes in time and political thinking. These changes reflect the political nature of EC antitrust policy, especially at the level of EC bureaucratic politics. As was seen in the previous chapter, the political nature of EC antitrust policy is quite obvious from the adoption of decisions in some antitrust cases,[16] where compromises may be reached between antitrust policy and other types of policies, often industrial policy, within the European Commission.[17]

The second comment relates to another made in the introduction to the book,[18] that one of the aims of this author is to examine whether the nature of the internationalisation of antitrust policy is a matter of 'law' or 'politics' (or both). In this regard, considering EC antitrust law experience is crucial because it can provide a subtle ground for this examination. An illustration of this point ensues from EC antitrust law at its inception:

> German participants tended to see the competition law as fundamentally 'juridical' – legal norms that had to be interpreted and applied according to judicial methods. At the very least, the decade-long controversy over the introduction of a German competition law conditioned German participants to think of Community competition as 'law'.

---

[14] See pp. 57–8 above. Also, see M. Dabbah, 'Measuring the Success of a System of Competition Law: a Preliminary View' (2000) 21 *European Competition Law Review* 369, 371.

[15] Amato, *Power*, p. 2.

[16] See further ch. 4 for a discussion on the use of discretion by the Commission, as an example of the political nature of EC antitrust policy.

[17] I. Maher, 'Alignment of Competition Laws in the European Community' (1996) 16 *Yearbook of European Law* 223, 229.

Former Commissioner K. van Miert once said, antitrust policy 'is politics'; quoted in C. Doern and S. Wilks, *Comparative Competition Policy* (Oxford University Press, Oxford, 1996), p. 254. For an illustration of the kind of compromises in question in the Commission decisional practice, see *Aérospatiale / Alenia / De Havilland* (Case IV/M.053) OJ 1991 No. L334/42; [1992] 4 CMLR M2; *Ford/VW* OJ 1993 No. L20/14; [1993] 5 CMLR 617.

[18] At pp. 4–5 above.

Decision-makers from other Member States were often inclined to view Articles 85 (now 81) and 86 (now 82) not as 'enforceable law', but rather as programmatic statements of policy intended to guide administrative decision-making of the Commission. Thus the French, for example, tended to see competition law in political and policy terms, preferring to base decisions on the evaluation by Community officials of the needs of the Community and its Member States. They were steeped in the values and methods of *dirigisme* and *planification* which tended to view competition law in that light.[19]

The conclusion to be drawn from the above is that EC antitrust experience provides significant insights into the legal and political dimensions of the internationalisation of antitrust policy that can and need to be explained. The EC system of antitrust has developed enormously over the years. However, as will be seen, it has the potential to develop further.

Institutional framework

The EC Treaty established new autonomous institutions in order to interpret, apply and enforce EC law.[20] Two EC institutions, namely the ECJ and the Commission, came to play a central role in interpreting and enforcing EC antitrust law.[21] Much of the meaning of EC antitrust law has been provided by these two institutions. As a result, they also provoked the most controversy surrounding its application.[22]

The Commission

The use of law to protect competition in the EC meant the law had to be separated from domestic attributes, since the aim was to deal with private

---

[19] Gerber, *Competition*, p. 346 (footnotes omitted).
   This, in turn, raises the issue of the seriousness of antitrust law beyond national boundaries. Initially, some Member States believed that EC law, in general, and EC antitrust law, in particular, could be enforced seriously under such circumstances, whilst others held a completely opposite view.

[20] Article 7 EC.

[21] Not, however, the role of the Court of First Instance (CFI), examined at pp. 81–3 above.

[22] For example, the employment of Article 82 EC by the Commission and the ECJ has made it difficult to decipher the aims of the provision. See M. Dabbah, 'Conduct, Dominance and Abuse in "Market Relationship": Analysis of Some Conceptual Issues under Article 82 EC' (2000) 21 *European Competition Law Review* 45; V. Korah, 'Tetra Pak II – Lack of Reasoning in Court's Judgment' (1997) 18 *European Competition Law Review* 98.

anti-competitive economic activities beyond national boundaries. According to some commentators, marginalising the role of Member States in this case and centralising a new supranational institution was necessary for establishing a 'culture of competition' because EC antitrust rules were novel and almost revolutionary.[23] From the beginning, the rules required fundamental changes in deeply ingrained habits of thought and patterns of economic conduct. There was very little trust within the Commission of the business community, lawyers and judges in Member States applying the rules either correctly or even in good faith.[24] Other reasons for centralising a new institution in EC antitrust policy can also be identified. These relate to the fact that the Commission had experienced legal and economic experts, which made it a more suitable institution and more qualified to decide cases with legal, economic and political significance. On the other hand, the decision of the founding Member States to hand over responsibilities to the Commission was the result of the economic growth which the EC witnessed in the first fifteen years, which corresponded to the exact aim of the Treaty as expressed in Article 2 EC. This view is in line with the Commission's own view on the matter. Recently, the Commission has emphasised that in the early years antitrust policy was not a widely known phenomenon throughout the EC. According to the Commission, centralised enforcement of EC antitrust rules was the only appropriate system at the time when the interpretation of EC antitrust law, in particular, Article 81(3) EC, was still uncertain and when the EC's main objective was to further the goal of market integration. As a centralised institution, the Commission believes that it was enabled to establish uniform application of EC antitrust rules throughout the Member States, promote market integration by preventing the erection of private barriers and create a body of rules acceptable to all Member States and the industry as fundamental to the proper functioning of the single market.[25] This process of institutional centralisation was initiated by Regulation 17/62 EC, a measure that proved

---

[23] I. Forrester and C. Norall, 'The Laicization of Community Law: Self-Help and the Rule of Reason: How Competition Law Is and Could Be Applied' (1984) 21 *Common Market Law Review* 11, 13.

[24] See M. Hutchings and M. Levitt, 'Concurrent Jurisdiction' (1994) 15 *European Competition Law Review* 123; M. Reynolds and P. Mansfield, 'Complaining to the Commission' (1997) 2 *European Counsel* 34.

[25] See the Commission White Paper on *The Modernisation of the Rules Implementing Articles 85 and 86 of the EC Treaty*, 28 April 1999, para. 4.

to be very difficult to draft.[26] The powers of the Commission are rooted in this Regulation, which specifically defines the role of the Commission in EC antitrust policy.[27]

The Court of Justice

The ECJ is a strong self-made intellectual leader in EC law in general, and in EC antitrust law in particular. This leadership is partly the result of the ECJ's own conception of its role, partly due to the state of political sclerosis from which the EC suffered from the late-1960s to the early-1980s and partly due to the teleological vision which the ECJ had of the EC and antitrust law.[28]

The ECJ has developed EC antitrust law mainly through advancing the propositions it created over the first two decades following 1957. A major tool in achieving this has been the ECJ's unique interpretative method, namely teleological reasoning.[29] Through this type of reasoning the ECJ considered EC antitrust law within a specific context: the goal of single market integration. The ECJ viewed the availability of a centralised institution – the Commission – to achieve this goal as necessary. To this end, it was willing to interpret EC antitrust law in a specific way in order to enhance the powers of the Commission and place it at the centre *vis-à-vis* Member States and their domestic antitrust authorities. According to some writers, in doing so, the ECJ provided the Commission with 'windows of opportunity' where the ECJ would look beyond the facts of a particular case, confirming its willingness to support particular policy developments of antitrust law by the Commission.[30] By contributing towards the expansion of the

---

[26] OJ 1962 204. See V. Korah, *An Introductory Guide to EC Competition Law and Practice* (Sweet & Maxwell, London, 1994); A. Deringer, 'The Distribution of Powers in the Enforcement of the Rules of Competition and the Rome Treaty' (1963) 1 *Common Market Law Review* 30.

[27] Note, however, the existence of Regulation 4064/89 EC, which upon its enactment rendered Regulation 17/62 inapplicable to mergers. Further discussion on Regulation 17/62 can be found at pp. 109–12 below.

[28] D. Gerber, 'The Transformation of European Community Competition Law' (1994) 35 *Harvard International Law Journal* 97, 127–30.

[29] See generally J. Bengoetxea, *The Legal Reasoning of the European Court of Justice* (Oxford University Press, Oxford, 1993); B. Van der Esch, 'The Principles of Interpretation Applied by the Court of Justice of the European Communities and Their Relevance for the Scope of the EEC Competition Rules' (1991) *Fordham Corporate Law Institute* 223, 225–34; M. Dabbah, 'The Dilemma of Keck – the Nature of the Ruling and the Ramifications of the Judgment' (1999) 8 *Irish Journal of European Law* 84.

[30] See D. Goyder, *EC Competition Law* (4th edn, Oxford University Press, Oxford, 2002), pp. 578–82.

prerogatives of the Commission, the ECJ has strengthened EC antitrust law.

The significance of the ECJ cannot be understated. In centralising the Commission in antitrust policy, it can be said that the ECJ adopted a political role. This becomes clear when one considers this issue within a wider framework covering EC law in its entirety, where the ECJ seems to have played a major role in the push towards market integration.[31] Extending the scope of antitrust law towards a wider political goal, such as market integration, can mean that the act of doing so is political.[32] In light of this, the ECJ seems to have widely assumed a policy-making role. Secondly, the ECJ has played a substantial role in establishing a system of antitrust beyond national boundaries. This fact has some implications for the subject-matter of this book because the internationalisation of antitrust policy involves a question of what role the judiciary would play in this process and ultimately in an international system of antitrust.[33]

Domestic courts

It is important to mention that EC antitrust rules, save for Article 81(3) EC, are directly applicable. This means that they become part of the legal system of the Member States without this being conditional upon any action taken by the Member States. The rules are also directly effective, meaning that they may be invoked by individuals, whether as claimant or defendant, in the domestic courts of the Member States.[34] In this way, domestic courts have a very important role to play in applying EC antitrust rules. As will be seen, this role has increased over the years and is expected to be enhanced when the Commission's modernisation programme is finally accomplished.[35]

It is worth mentioning an important provision in the EC Treaty, namely Article 234 EC, which gives the domestic courts of Member States the chance to enter into a dialogue with the ECJ, subject to limitations, on all aspects of EC law. This provision has been very useful in the context of EC antitrust law not only in starting and developing this dialogue but also in getting domestic courts to become more engaged in the application of the antitrust

---

[31] See P. Craig and G. De Burca, *EU Law* (3rd edn, Oxford University Press, Oxford, 1998), p. 88.

[32] See A. Green, *Political Integration by Jurisprudence: the Work of the Court of Justice of the European Communities in European Political Integration* (Sijthoff, Leiden, 1969).

   The flip-side of this argument is that a political topic has been 'judicialised'. This would, of course, raise the question whether this is desirable or inevitable. See the discussion in chs. 4 and 7 on the desirability of judicial control.

[33] See p. 83 above and ch. 10.   [34] See the case of *Van Gend en Loos*.   [35] See pp. 109–12 below.

rules of the EC. Under the provision, a domestic court can ask the ECJ to give an interpretative ruling in relation to a matter of EC antitrust law that has arisen in the course of proceedings before the domestic court. Whenever this request is made, the ECJ aims to avoid ruling on questions of fact, which fall within the jurisdiction of the domestic court. The function of the ECJ is rather to lay down, in the abstract, the principles of EC antitrust law to be applied to the case in question.

The relationship between EC and domestic antitrust laws

The issue of influence

The relationship between EC and domestic antitrust laws is normally examined from legal and economic perspectives.[36] In the present book, however, this relationship is examined from a political perspective as it is believed that the relationship concerns political factors as much as legal and economic ones. The need to consider how EC antitrust law influences domestic antitrust laws is of particular significance for several reasons. One reason that stands out at this stage, relates to the fact that not all Member States had systems of antitrust upon their accession to the EC.[37] In this regard, it is important to consider the role played by the EC system of antitrust in constructing domestic systems of antitrust.

The first twenty-five years: characterising the relationship

During the first twenty-five years of the EC, the relationship between EC and domestic antitrust laws stood exclusively on a jurisdictional competence criterion.[38] The applicability of the criterion was determined according to a 'two-barrier theory' – introduced by the ECJ early in its jurisprudence.[39] This theory, which defined the respective areas – EC and domestic – of

---

[36] See Massey, 'Reform', 117–21; J. Temple Lang, 'European Community Constitutional Law and the Enforcement of Community Antitrust Law' (1993) *Fordham Corporate Law Institute* 525.

[37] One such Member State is Italy. See M. Siragusa and G. Scassellati-Sforztine, 'Italian and EC Competition Law: a New Relationship – Reciprocal Exclusivity and Common Principles' (1993) 29 *Common Market Law Review* 93; F. Romani, 'The New Italian Antitrust Law' (1991) *Fordham Corporate Law Institute* 479; B. Cova and F. Fine, 'The New Italian Antitrust Act *vis-à-vis* EC Competition Law' (1991) 12 *European Competition Law Review* 20. Also, see the Italian antitrust authority's website http://www.agcm.it.

[38] C. Kirchner, 'Competence Catalogues and the Principle of Subsidiarity in a European Constitution' (1997) 8 *Constitutional Political Economy* 71.

[39] Case C-148/68 *Walt Wilhelm v. Bundeskartellamt* [1969] ECR 1.

competence, modelled the basic components of the relationship between both sets of laws. It provided that EC antitrust law was applicable wherever there was an effect on interstate trade.[40] Member States were free, however, to apply their domestic antitrust laws to conduct affecting conditions of competition within their individual territories, provided that such action did not conflict with EC antitrust law.

The fact that during this period both laws were applied within two separate spheres of competence did not, however, exclude the possibility of co-ordination amongst these spheres.[41] Yet there was no indication of a strong motive to co-ordinate. This lack of motive can be attributed to several factors, the most important of which was the existence then of certain limitations on the competence of domestic courts to enforce antitrust law generally.[42] Domestic systems of antitrust functioned almost exclusively on the basis of enforcement by administrative institutions.[43] For this reason, those who wished to complain about anti-competitive restraints had little motive to turn to the judiciary to seek a remedy for injury sustained by them as a result of such restraints. They found it easier, less expensive and less uncertain instead to commence legal actions before their domestic antitrust authorities or complain to the Commission.[44] Added to this inclination is the fact that the way in which EC antitrust law was supposed to be applied in domestic courts was highly unclear.[45]

---

[40] See J. Faull, 'Effect on Trade between Member States and Community: Member States Jurisdiction' (1989) Fordham Corporate Law Institute 485.

[41] In the early-1970s, it was clear that domestic courts could apply most of EC antitrust law. See Case 127/73 Belgische Radio en Televisie et al. v. SV SABAM and NV Fonier [1974] ECR 51, para. 16 and 17; [1974] 2 CMLR 238.

[42] See J. Bourgeois, 'EC Competition Law and Member States Courts' (1993) 17 Fordham International Law Journal 331; Forrester and Norall, 'Laicization'.

[43] Also, it was obvious that anti-competitive activities of firms could affect markets in more than one Member State. Hence, it was not possible for domestic courts to regulate such activities when they affected markets beyond national boundaries.

[44] See R. Whish, 'Enforcement of EC Competition law in the Domestic Courts of Member States' (1994) 15 European Competition Law Review 60, 61–2; L. Hiljemark, 'Enforcement of EC Competition Law in National Courts – the Perspective of Judicial Protection' (1997) 17 Yearbook of European Law 83.

[45] See D. Hall, 'Enforcement of EC Competition Law by National Courts' in P. Slot and A. McDonnell (eds.), Procedure and Enforcement in EC and US Competition Law (Sweet & Maxwell, London, 1993), p. 42; L. Rittler, D. Braun and F. Rawlinson, EEC Competition Law – a Practitioner's Guide (Kluwer, Deventor, 1991), p. 718; G. Cumming, 'Assessors, Judicial Notice and Domestic Enforcement of Articles 85 and 86' (1997) 18 European Competition Law Review 370; C. Kerse, EC Antitrust Procedure (Sweet & Maxwell, London, 1994), pp. 81–2; C. Kerse, 'The Complainant in Competition Cases: a Progress Report' (1997) 34 Common Market Law Review 230; I. Van Bael, 'The Role of National Courts' (1994) 15 European Competition Law Review 6.

Other factors leading to a lack of motive for co-ordination between the two spheres related to the fact that under the centralisation system (discussed below) domestic courts were only authorised to apply certain, but not all, parts of EC antitrust law. For example, they were not authorised to issue individual exemptions under Article 81(3) EC, since Regulation 17/62 reserved this power for the Commission's exercise only.[46] This limitation on the ability of domestic courts to apply EC antitrust law in its entirety also discouraged complainants from seeking to enforce EC antitrust law, in particular Article 81 EC, in domestic courts,[47] whilst encouraging them to stay proceedings and seek an exemption from the Commission as a defensive tactic.

These limitations on the competence and jurisdiction of domestic courts did not mean that co-ordination between EC and domestic spheres of competence was not possible through other channels. One option was for domestic antitrust authorities to enforce EC antitrust law.[48] However, the fact that domestic antitrust authorities also lacked competence to grant exemptions under Article 81(3) EC,[49] combined with some of them lacking even authority under their domestic laws to apply EC antitrust law in the first place, meant that this option was even less popular than the courts' option.

The second twenty-five years: the centralisation and decentralisation debate

The relationship between EC and domestic antitrust laws, including the division between their respective spheres of competence, received little attention in the period between 1957 and the early-1980s, whether in the legal literature or on the agenda of the Commission officials.[50] On the basis of this situation, there was hardly any consideration of whether a

---

[46] See Article 9 of the Regulation.
[47] Even if a domestic court found the Article 81 EC prohibition applicable, the defendant firm might be able to convince the Commission to issue an exemption and thus render the legal action meaningless.
[48] Notice on *Co-operation between the Commission and National Competition Authorities in Handling Cases Falling within the Scope of Article 85 and 86 EC*, OJ 1996 No. C262/5, p. 13.
[49] It was obvious that a domestic antitrust authority might expend its resources to bring an action under Article 81(1) EC over which it did not have ultimate control. See M. Fernandez Ordonez, 'Enforcement by National Authority of EC and Member States' Antitrust Law' (1993) *Fordham Corporate Law Institute* 629.
[50] It seems that the reason for this relates to the economic difficulties during that period, with the Oil Shock, as well as political sclerosis at international level generally.

change in the formal relationship was necessary in terms of expanding the co-ordination between EC and domestic spheres of competence.

From the mid-1980s, however, a change of thought regarding this relationship began to appear on the horizon.[51] In particular, the revival of the process of market integration, as marked by the introduction of the Single European Act (SEA) 1986, indicated that it was no longer possible to maintain a formal division of competence. This development brought into the question the criterion of jurisdictional competence as a determining factor in the relationship between EC and domestic antitrust laws. The EC was heading towards a higher degree of integration and this raised the issue of the need for a fundamentally more co-operative and integrated framework for EC law in general, and for EC antitrust law in particular. This spawned the existence of what has materialised as a central debate in EC antitrust law and policy, namely the centralisation/ decentralisation debate.

Centralisation

Centralisation is essentially a centripetal process which, in the early years of the EC, suggested that power should be concentrated at the EC level. Different factors led to this perspective. One motivation was the concern on the part of officials of the Commission at the dawn of the Treaty to pool power in Brussels and marginalise the role of Member States and their domestic antitrust authorities in antitrust policy. Another reason emerged from the goal of single market integration. The common feeling, in the light of this goal, was that EC antitrust law and institutions had to gradually move towards the heart of the antitrust policy scene in the EC. Hence, domestic antitrust laws were pushed to the side and were confined to dealing with antitrust policy issues that raised concerns within their national boundaries.[52]

Decentralisation

Against the above perspective of centralisation stands a centrifugal process that calls for the delegation of authority to the national level. This

---

[51] During this period, there was a change of economic conditions and political consensus within the EC was growing.

[52] This development seems to have been confirmed by introducing the Merger Regulation, Regulation 4064/89 EC in 1989. The Regulation authorised the Merger Task Force of the Commission to take mergers with political, economic and legal significance out of the control of domestic antitrust authorities.

process is known as decentralisation. The process entered the EC antitrust policy scene from the mid-1980s,[53] when the Commission began to properly consider the need to involve domestic courts and domestic antitrust authorities in applying EC antitrust law.[54] Several factors contributed to this trend. Most significantly, it was apparent that the Commission was unable to meet its responsibilities under the system because: first, there was lack of resources, mainly caused by financial and political factors;[55] and secondly, there was the possibility (one may say it was a fact) that the EC in the mid-1980s was going to expand geographically.[56] The case for decentralisation became even more pressing with major events that took place in the late-1980s and early-1990s. These events included the collapse of the Soviet Union in 1989,[57] the signing of the Treaty on European Union (TEU) in 1992[58] and the impending accession of more countries during that period.[59]

---

[53] Prior to this, the Commission was hesitant about decentralisation, because: first, it was thought that it would reduce the capacity of EC institutions to influence the development of an EC system of antitrust; secondly, it would afford Member States the opportunity to use it to further their own objectives and individual interests; and thirdly, it would increase the risk of inconsistencies within the system. See J. Meade, 'Decentralisation in the Implementation of EEC Competition Law – a Challenge for the Lawyers' (1986) 37 *Northern Ireland Law Quarterly*, 101.

[54] See Commission 13th and 15th Reports on Competition Policy 1983 and 1985, paras. 217 and 38 respectively.

[55] See Hiljemark, 'Enforcement', 87.

[56] In 1986 Spain and Portugal acceded to the EC, and the accession of more countries such as Sweden, Finland and Austria was appearing on the horizon. Also, the accession programme included countries which upon acceding to the EC had either no antitrust law or had systems of antitrust at a very early stage of development. This meant that firms and future officials in those countries would have to be informed about antitrust law concepts, and this would cause an increase in both the financial and educational burdens of the Commission.

[57] The changing situation in Central and Eastern Europe meant that the EC had to at least consider the possibility of expanding its membership to include certain Central and Eastern European countries where the concepts of competition and antitrust law were unfamiliar. See pp. 120–30 below.

[58] The TEU introduced the principle of subsidiarity under Article 5 EC, which provides that the EC should not regulate conduct that could be regulated at least as effectively at the national level. The principle of subsidiarity did not require changes in the EC system of antitrust. However, it has played a central role in the relationship between EC and domestic antitrust laws, and in this form it entered the centralisation/decentralisation debate. See B. Francis, 'Subsidiarity and Antitrust: the Enforcement of European Competition Law in the National Courts of Member States' (1995) 27 *Law and Policy in International Business* 247; R. Alford, 'Subsidiarity and Competition: Decentralized Enforcement of EU Competition Laws' (1994) 27 *Cornell International Law Journal* 275; R. Wesseling, 'Subsidiarity in Community Law: Setting the Right Agenda' (1997) 22 *European Law Review* 35.

[59] See note 57 above.

The types and meanings of decentralisation   Three different types of decentralisation with three corresponding meanings can be identified:

The application of EC antitrust law by domestic courts   This variant of decentralisation calls for further involvement of domestic courts in interpreting, applying and enforcing EC antitrust law. The Commission regarded increasing the function of domestic courts as a good way to deal effectively with the problem of its extensive caseload whilst simultaneously fostering awareness of and enhancing compliance with EC antitrust law at the national level. In addition, decentralisation in this manner was also desirable, since no change to the 'two-barrier theory' was necessary, nor would the Commission be forced to loosen its grip on the EC system of antitrust.

   This type of decentralisation became apparent in the early-1990s, with the Commission concentrating its earlier efforts to encourage the bringing of legal actions before domestic courts rather than having complainants go to Brussels to seek a remedy.[60] These efforts were concluded later in a Notice concerning Co-operation between the Commission and Courts of the Member States with Regards to the Application of Articles 85 (now Article 81) and 86 (now Article 82) EC, issued by the Commission in 1993.[61]

   Several purposes seem to underpin the Notice.[62] The Notice highlights both the Commission's efforts to encourage private actions and the importance the Commission attaches to the issue of compliance.[63] It strongly heralds the principle that cases with no particular political, economic or legal significance for the EC should, as a general rule, be handled by domestic courts or antitrust authorities.[64] In order to clarify the role of domestic courts, the Notice offers procedural guidelines for domestic courts to follow in handling the application of EC antitrust law. It specifies the factors that

---

[60] C. Ehlermann, 'The European Community, Its Law and Lawyers' (1992) 29 *Common Market Law Review* 213, 225.

[61] OJ 1993 No. C39/6. Some have argued that the Notice was a reaction on the part of the Commission to a lack of response to the intensification of its earlier efforts. See R. Wesseling, 'The Commission Notices on Decentralisation of EC Antitrust Law: in for a Penny, Not for a Pound' (1997) 18 *European Competition Law Review* 94.

[62] See A. Riley, 'More Radicalism, Please: the Notice on Co-operation between National Courts and the Commission in Applying Articles 85 and 86 of the EEC Treaty' (1993) 14 *European Competition Law Review* 93.

[63] See paras. 15 and 16 of the Notice.

[64] Note that the Notice was issued at virtually the same time as the subsidiarity principle was introduced, and this seemed to suggest that the Commission was here applying the principle within EC antitrust law. See para. 14 of the Notice.

domestic courts should consider when deciding cases and the steps they should take.[65] Essentially, domestic courts are directed under the Notice to base their decisions on EC antitrust law to the extent it is possible for them to predict how the Commission, and possibly EC courts, would decide the antitrust dispute. The Notice recommends that domestic courts take into account, in addition to the judgments of EC courts, the decisional practice of the Commission under the block exemptions. The understanding seems to be that the more legal territory these exemptions cover, the less serious an obstacle it is that domestic courts cannot issue individual exemptions under Article 81(3) EC. The Notice indicates that the Commission will actively use this mechanism as a means of furthering decentralisation.

During the first year of its existence, the Notice triggered some scepticism over whether it would generate a significant increase in the utilisation of domestic courts. This doubt was based on the view that neither the Notice itself nor any other relevant Commission actions at that time influenced or altered the general attitude of firms with regard to the risks and uncertainties attached to legal actions brought before domestic courts.[66] As a matter of fact, this scepticism has continued throughout the Notice's existence. There is no doubt that some hurdles still remain in the face of this type of decentralisation, such as those relating to domestic courts' lack of competence to issue individual exemptions.[67] Despite this scepticism, it can be said that, on the whole, the Notice is a positive step forward in co-ordinating the relationship between the Commission and domestic courts.

The application of Community antitrust law by domestic antitrust authorities   The second variant of decentralisation relates to domestic antitrust authorities directly enforcing EC antitrust law. For many years, there was relatively little incentive on the part of the Commission to advance this variant.[68] Several reasons may be professed for this lack of enthusiasm. For a number of years the Commission viewed this variant of decentralisation as complex and more uncertain than decentralisation via domestic courts. The Commission thought this option would have rendered

---

[65] See paras. 17–32 of the Notice.
[66] See C. Ehlermann, 'Implementation of EC Competition Law by National Antitrust Authorities' (1996) 17 European Competition Law Review 88, 89.
[67] G. Marenco, 'The Uneasy Enforcement of Article 85 EEC as between Community and National Levels' (1993) Fordham Corporate Law Institute 605.
[68] See Temple Lang, 'European', 571–5.

inevitable orchestrating the relationship between domestic antitrust authorities and itself through co-ordination in the decision-making between
officials of those authorities and its own officials. This was seen as risky
because each set of officials enjoys a degree of discretion and each is receptive to policy considerations and responds to pressures of the system
of antitrust within which it operates.[69] Another reason for this lack of
enthusiasm is that domestic antitrust authorities showed little interest in
enforcing EC antitrust law rather than their own domestic antitrust laws.[70]
Furthermore, the fact that most domestic antitrust authorities had limited
resources and experience, coupled with the fact that some Member States,
notably Italy, did not even have systems of antitrust, let alone the fact that
major differences existed between national antitrust laws and EC antitrust
law, contributed to a large extent to this lack of enthusiasm.

Despite this obvious reluctance by the Commission to pursue this variant
of decentralisation, and the equally evident lack of incentive on the part of
domestic antitrust authorities to apply EC antitrust law, the Commission
issued a Notice on Co-operation between the Commission and National
Competition Authorities in Handling Cases Falling within the Scope of
Article 85 (now Article 81) and 86 (now Article 82) EC (the 'Notice') in
1996.[71] The Notice, which indicates the willingness of the Commission to
consider seriously this type of decentralisation, specifically refers to the
principle of subsidiarity – which allocates the competence between the EC
and domestic levels – as a justification for increased transfer of competence,
albeit in a limited manner, to domestic antitrust authorities.[72] The Notice

[69] The Commission also thought that this could impose significant additional costs on the Commission as well as interfere with its capacity to control efforts to protect competition in the
EC.

[70] To a certain extent, this is understandable because they lack competence to issue individual
exemptions under Article 81(3) EC. They are primarily responsible for the development and
enforcement of their own domestic antitrust laws, and their competent performance is likely to
be judged in light of the fulfilment of this task.

[71] OJ 1996 No. C262/5.

[72] In the light of this allocation principle, the competence of the Commission or the relevant
domestic antitrust authority to act is determined by the size and effect of the agreement.
    Regarding cases in which the allocation principle is applicable, the Commission takes the
position that where the main effects of conduct are within one Member State, the domestic
antitrust authority of that state may handle the case. Nevertheless the Commission reserves
the right to take a case where it considers that it has important political, economic or legal
significance – for example, if it raises new points of law or if it involves conduct in which another
Member State has a particular interest. See Commission 25th Report on Competition Policy
1995. This position seems to have been confirmed by the Commission's paper on modernisation.
See pp. 109–12 below.

explains that if, by reason of its scale or effects, the proposed action can best be taken at Community level, it is for the Commission to act. If, on the other hand, the action can be taken satisfactorily at national level, the antitrust authority of the Member State concerned is better placed to act. Whilst clearly of value, this allocation of competence principle – as introduced in the Notice – is limited in terms of its sphere of operation and application, mainly due to the lack of competence of domestic antitrust authorities to grant exemptions under Article 81(3) EC.

The Notice shows that the Commission has come to recognise the importance of co-operation with domestic antitrust authorities. It shows the benefit of such co-operation, especially to avoid duplication of antitrust enforcement.[73] The Notice does not, however, fundamentally change the attitude of domestic policy-makers to think more positively with regard to the process of decentralisation. It is clear, in light of the Notice, that making this type of decentralisation more viable requires further significant steps on the part of the Commission towards consolidating its efforts in this direction; as will be seen below, some steps have already been taken.[74]

Domestic authorities applying their own antitrust laws   A third variant of decentralisation is for domestic antitrust authorities to continue to apply their own domestic antitrust laws, but to do so more increasingly.[75] Naturally, this variant of decentralisation has been little discussed, mainly because the Commission and the antitrust community always used the term 'decentralisation' to mean only the decentralised application of EC antitrust law.[76] Nevertheless, two reasons can be advanced to explain why this variant should also be considered. First, an increase in the application of domestic antitrust laws by antitrust authorities of Member States responds to the values and concerns attached to the principle of subsidiarity. These values and concerns reduce the centralisation of power at EC level and increase the authority of Member States to protect competition, where they can do so, at least as effectively as the Commission. Secondly, to the extent that domestic

---

[73] The Notice aims to avoid the possibility that domestic antitrust authorities will expend effort and resources in cases which the Commission ultimately takes out of their area of competence.

[74] See pp. 109–12 below.

[75] See P. Bos, 'Towards a Clear Distribution of Competence between EC and National Competition Authorities' (1995) 16 *European Competition Law Review* 410.

[76] For example, the Commission's policy has always been to strengthen the role and effectiveness of EC antitrust law, and increased reliance on domestic law is a step in the opposite direction.

antitrust authorities satisfactorily protect competition by relying on domestic antitrust laws, the Commission would accomplish its objectives without drying up its resources any further. Increased reliance on domestic antitrust laws in such cases may also avoid many of the difficulties that arise when the Commission and one or more domestic antitrust authorities apply EC antitrust law.

In spite of the above factors, it can be argued that an increased reliance by domestic authorities on their domestic antitrust laws is controversial. For over fifty-five years the Commission has sought to establish EC antitrust law as the basis of market integration. It seems that an increased reliance on domestic antitrust laws would reverse this process. Such action reduces the superiority and authority of the Commission. Affording domestic antitrust authorities the opportunity to advise the business community, make important commercial decisions and decide on the norms to be followed by firms would challenge the superiority of the Commission. In addition, there appears to be doubts within the Commission about the extent to which domestic antitrust laws may be relied on to protect competition at least as satisfactorily as EC antitrust law. Such doubts may be justified given that restrictions on competition often have cross-border effect. These restrictions might infringe the laws of more than one Member State and thereby create conflicts among Member States as well as costs in both time and resources for both domestic antitrust authorities and the firms involved. A Member State is not necessarily able to address effectively restrictions which have effects in more than one Member State, because it is not guaranteed that it will have unlimited, or even in some cases sufficient, access to information and evidence in other Member States.[77]

It is suggested, however, that the concern triggered by these factors can be eliminated to the extent that domestic antitrust authorities would enforce similar substantive antitrust rules in similar ways. There is no doubt that the closer domestic systems of antitrust are, the easier it should be to develop means of distributing authority between the Community level and the domestic level, especially in difficult cases and those involving regulating evidentiary matters. Furthermore, the more similar these systems are, the more meaningless the distinction between EC and domestic antitrust laws

---

[77] There is also the argument that increased reliance by domestic antitrust authorities on their domestic laws can undermine the supremacy of EC antitrust law and the values of the one-stop shop principle which has been prominent in EC merger control.

becomes. The net result in applying domestic antitrust law by domestic antitrust authorities will be less objectionable.

The convergence of domestic antitrust laws: a closer relationship   The renewed confidence between the mid-1980s and the early-1990s in achieving the goal of single market integration – as evidenced through the introduction of the SEA and the TEU in 1986 and 1992 respectively – opened a new chapter in the EC antitrust policy scene. Since that time, several Member States have either introduced new systems of antitrust similar to the EC model or altered their systems so as to bring them more into line with that model.[78] Interestingly, this recent shift towards greater convergence has been the result of initiatives on the part of certain Member States rather than the result of the decentralisation efforts on the part of the Commission. Accommodating antitrust rules of a similar type to EC antitrust law enabled a Member State to demonstrate its support to some of the founding fathers of the EC, such as France and Germany, who were pursuing further integration. Such a Member State could expect that such support would be appreciated by other supporters of these initiatives. Countries seeking future accession to the EC in the early-1990s, expressed an interest to 'converge' their laws. Sweden, Austria and Finland were in various stages of accession, and by enacting antitrust laws similar to EC antitrust law they could demonstrate their support for the integration efforts of existing

---

[78] In 1998, the UK reformed its antitrust law in this manner. The new law adopted Articles 81 and 82 EC standards. See the Competition Act 1998, which came into force on 1 March 2000. For a good account of the new legislation see B. Rodger and A. MacCulloch, *The UK Competition Act* (Hart Publishing, Oxford, 2000); P. Freeman and R. Whish, *A Guide to the Competition Act 1998* (Butterworths, London, 1999); S. Singleton, *Blackstone's Guide to the Competition Act 1998* (Blackstone, London, 1999). Also, see UK Office of Fair Trading's website: http://www.oft.gov.uk and the UK Competition Commission's website: http://www.competition-commission.org.uk.
    In its 25th Report on Competition Policy 1995, at p. 36 the Commission stated that convergence of domestic antitrust laws has taken place in nine different Member States.
    Whilst the present discussion will not attempt to deal with the situation in individual Member States, it will attempt to offer more than general comments on the relationship between EC and domestic antitrust laws. See the following literature on the situation in individual Member States. P. Wessman, 'Competition Sharpens in Sweden' (1993) 17 *World Competition* 113; J. Ratliff and E. Wright, 'Belgian Competition Law: the Advent of Free Market Principles' (1992) 16 *World Competition* 33; S. Martinzez Lage, 'Significant Developments in Spanish Antitrust Law' (1996) 17 *European Competition Law Review* 194; T. Liakopoulos, 'New Rules on Competition Law in Greece' (1992) 16 *World Competition* 17; K. Stockmann, 'Trends and Developments in European Antitrust Laws' (1991) *Fordham Corporate Law Institute* 441, 448–69. Also, Commission 28th Report on Competition Policy 1998, pp. 329–57.

Member States and of EC institutions. The relevant period also witnessed an intensifying battle for foreign investment among Member States. This development encouraged business firms to follow the domestic legal environment that was not significantly different and was not more stringent than that of the EC. The 'definite' possibility in the early-1990s that certain countries were likely to accede to the EC added more vigour to the views of the business community. Furthermore, the present possibility that in the near future, the EC may have twenty-five Member States, as opposed to fifteen, strengthens such arguments.

Several factors have contributed towards the convergence of domestic antitrust laws. In particular, three main factors are worth mentioning. The first are economic factors. The arguments of business firms in different Member States have emphasised that they and interstate commerce would benefit from operating under uniform antitrust rules in different Member States. Secondly, the willingness on the part of domestic antitrust authorities to learn from each other has increased, especially since the late-1980s. Thirdly, there has been a growing recognition throughout Europe of the value of competition. This can be seen from the way that the market mechanism has become more dominant, which has made it necessary to adopt measures to protect its dynamics and ensure its proper functioning. To some extent, this has provided an ideological shift. It has also reflected a growing awareness of the need for economic reinvigoration throughout Europe and that increased competition was the most likely means of fostering strong and healthy economic environments.

Types of convergence   There have been two different types of convergence. The first is textual convergence,[79] under which there has been an increase in following the framework of Articles 81 and 82 EC. In some cases, some domestic laws, such as the French law,[80] merely followed the basic framework of these provisions, whilst others, such as the Swedish laws, adopted their terminology.[81] The second is institutional and procedural convergence. In

---

[79] H. Ullrich, 'Harmonisation within the European Union' (1996) 17 *European Competition Law Review* 178.

[80] See generally F. Jenny, 'French Competition Law Update: 1987–1994' (1995) *Fordham Corporate Law Institute* 203. For information on the French system of antitrust see the Director-General's website: http://www.finances.gouv.fr/DGCCRF/index-d.htm and the Competition Council's website: http://www.finances.gouv.fr/conseilconcurrence.

[81] See M. Widegren, 'Competition Law in Sweden – a Brief Introduction to the New Legislation' (1995) *Fordham Corporate Law Institute* 241.

this sense, viewing the EC system of antitrust as a model for convergence is more ambitious than its textual counterpart. Nevertheless, general patterns of change at the institutional level have been to move towards more judicial characteristics and institutions that are inclined towards more judicial roles in domestic systems of antitrust. They have adopted roles that involve interpretation, application and enforcement of antitrust provisions at the national level, unlike the administrative control regimes, which previously existed in the Member States concerned. To this end, domestic antitrust authorities have increasingly, for example, been given greater independence from political influence.

Stages of convergence   Convergence mainly involves two stages. The first is the adoption at the national level of similar patterns of convergence towards EC antitrust law. The second stage concerns efforts to co-ordinate EC and domestic systems of antitrust. The developments to which these stages may lead are salient. It can be expected that the interaction between these stages will play a central role in shaping the future relationship between EC and domestic antitrust laws. Further integration within the EC calls for an increasingly integrated system of antitrust. The interaction of the stages of convergence may help to clarify the future dynamics of this system and its different components.[82] This is all the more likely, since it is not clear whether the components – EC and domestic – of the system will operate on a closely integrated basis or whether mere formal jurisdictional rules will link these components together.[83]

It is not difficult to identify the picture that seems to be emerging in the light of this closer relationship between EC and domestic systems of antitrust. The emerging antitrust landscape places the EC system at the heart of the development of antitrust policy and principles in the EC and provides a centre to which domestic systems of antitrust are primarily connected. The 'two-barrier theory' will continue to constitute a key element, as the question of competence to investigate and decide in a particular antitrust law case – the Commission or the relevant domestic antitrust authority – will continue to be a central issue. This is a difficult (and largely political) issue because the Commission's power and authority may be threatened with the involvement of domestic antitrust authorities. This means that political conflicts will be located along decisional edges. Moreover, it is a

---

[82] See generally Maher, 'Alignment'.   [83] See generally Temple Lang, 'European'.

political issue because decision-makers in the EC and in Member States are generally committed to different and sometimes inconsistent policy and personal objectives.

System structure: horizontal and vertical co-operation   Two dimensions are surfacing in the relationship between EC and domestic systems of antitrust. The first may be referred to as 'vertical co-operation'. This dimension includes factors such as the extent to which Commission officials and those in domestic antitrust authorities share common interests and forge institutional means to pursue and protect such interests. Whilst policy-makers at either level share the common goal of protecting the process of competition, they often diverge with regards to the best means of achieving this goal. Also, it is not clear whether their interests coalesce with regard to other goals and values. In this way, establishing a common intellectual and communicative base for pursuing common interests between the EC and domestic systems of antitrust is a difficult project to undertake.

The second dimension may be termed 'horizontal co-operation'. This dimension connotes the prospects of domestic antitrust authorities creating close links between themselves. This depends on the extent to which they perceive common interests. Also, the extent to which they are willing and able to create means to pursue such interests – independently of the 'vertical dimension' – will be another important factor in this regard.

A comment   For many years, there has been little awareness of the importance of these dimensions. This is mainly due to the fact that until recently antitrust law has been examined exclusively from the perspectives of individual – EC or domestic – systems of antitrust. Hence, few, including lawyers, economists and policy-makers, have good knowledge of similar experiences and common and shared problems and solutions between the different systems.[84]

The foregoing discussion demonstrated, however, that this situation has been changing and more attention is being drawn to the importance of these dimensions. Of course it is difficult to predict with sufficient certainty whether this importance will increase, and the degree to which these dimensions may integrate with each other. It is quite likely that this will be influenced by factors that are exogenous to the EC system of antitrust.

---

[84] Gerber, *Competition*, p. 3.

These include factors such as the accession of third countries to the EC.[85] The issue of accession in this regard depends on the countries that will accede, when they will accede and on the type of economic, political and legal traditions that will accompany their accession. These questions are among the ones which will be addressed in the following part of the chapter.

Factors endogenous to the system will also be influential. One important endogenous factor that is likely to prove influential, concerns changes in global economic climate, and how far these do go. Another important factor is how Member States perceive the EC system of antitrust. If the system is viewed as successful and useful, this will create incentives for Member States to move their own systems of antitrust closer to it, which means that the system will be likely to win support, force and influence. This is also likely to be mutually valuable, as the EC and domestic systems will support each other. If, on the other hand, a view to the contrary is held by the Member States, then they will be less likely to take such steps. A major challenge for the Commission is likely to be whether it can manage its relationship with domestic antitrust authorities in a manner which would avoid creating incentives for the latter to define their own interests in opposition to it or to one another. To this end, the effectiveness of the 'vertical dimension' seems to be a key factor in shaping incentives for the 'horizontal dimension'. The issue of perceptions by Member States demands careful examination in order to ensure a comprehensive and reasoned analysis and to avoid politically motivated assumptions, which may be harmful.

The relationship between EC and domestic antitrust laws should be seen to reside at the heart of the goal of market integration. Effective co-ordination between EC and domestic systems of antitrust is likely to foster this goal. This will also enhance the influence of the EC system of antitrust beyond the borders of the EC. Hence, it is important to support the co-ordination efforts in order to avoid any adverse effect on the image of the EC system of antitrust within and outside the EC.

Recent developments

On 28 April 1999, the Commission introduced its White Paper on the Modernisation of the Rules Implementing Articles 85 (now Article 81) and

---

[85] For a discussion on the issue of accession see pp. 120–30 below.

86 (now Article 82) EC (Paper).[86] The Paper presents a fundamental rethink by the Commission on the EC systems of antitrust 'which has worked so well' but which 'is no longer appropriate for the Community of today with 15 Member States, 11 languages and over 350 million inhabitants'.[87] The Commission offers in the Paper some reasons for the proposed revision – albeit in incomplete terms. At paragraph 5 of the Paper, the Commission provides that the reasons for this rethink reside in Regulation 17/62 'and in the external factors to the development of the Community'. Furthermore, at paragraph 10 of the Paper, the Commission explains that the current system is no longer adequate to meet the new challenges facing the EC. The Commission believes that it is essential to adapt the current system in order to remedy the present problem of resources, to relieve business firms from unnecessary costs and bureaucracy, to enable the Commission to pursue more serious antitrust law infringements and to stimulate a simpler and more efficient system of control.

According to the Commission, the time has now come when the responsibility of enforcing EC antitrust law, including a determination of whether the criteria of Article 81(3) EC are satisfied, should be by domestic courts and antitrust authorities. This means that domestic courts and antitrust authorities would be able to apply Article 81 EC in its entirety, rather than just Article 81(1) EC and the provisions of the block exemptions, as now. It therefore proposed that the notification and exemption system in Regulation 17/62 should be abolished and replaced by a Council Regulation, which would render the criteria in Article 81(3) EC directly applicable without a prior decision of the Commission. This proposal would leave the Commission in a position to concentrate its priorities, such as combating cartels with transnational operations and effects. This does not, of course, mean that the Commission would relinquish being the guardian of EC antitrust rules. On the contrary, the Commission makes it clear in the Paper that it will continue to observe how these rules are applied by domestic courts and antitrust authorities. This will involve asserting jurisdiction in particular cases, namely those with legal, economic and political significance for the EC.

The proposals of the Commission are radical, especially the Commission's proposal to abandon its monopoly to grant Article 81(3) EC exemptions. However, for firms and those advising them, ending the notification

---

[86] OJ 1999 No. C132/1; [1999] 5 CMLR 208.   [87] See para. 5 of the Paper.

and authorisation system provides a relief. One of the problems with the current system has been that, for the majority of agreements, obtaining an individual exemption from the Commission required a notification to it. The Commission has suffered for many years from lack of resources and shortage of staff to keep up with the increasing number of notifications and for this reason the system is flawed.[88] The proposals in the Paper have the effect of abandoning the notification procedure completely. Notification will not be possible. Firms will be responsible for making their own assessment of the compatibility of their restrictive practices with EC antitrust law in the light of the relevant legislation and case law.[89]

Abandoning notification will be an issue of particular challenge to firms and their legal advisors. This will help to harmonise the position of the EC on antitrust policy exemptions with that in the USA, where firms have to be more self-reliant – an aspect which may have a direct positive effect on the internationalisation of antitrust policy.[90] It is to be anticipated that this issue, along with many other more detailed points of law and practice, will be debated for a considerable time to come. Recently, a new Council Regulation on the implementation of Articles 81 and 82 EC has been produced.[91] The new Regulation contains very important provisions on the relationship between EC and domestic systems of antitrust. In particular, Article 11 of the Regulation deserves mentioning. According to this provision, which deals with co-operation between the Commission and domestic antitrust authorities and courts, the application of EC antitrust rules will be on the basis of close co-operation between the two sides. The provision also states that domestic antitrust authorities and courts are required to inform the Commission at the outset of any proceedings involving the application of Articles 81 and 82 EC opened by them. Furthermore, domestic antitrust authorities and courts are expected to consult the Commission prior to adopting a decision under these provisions requiring an infringement to be terminated, accepting commitments by firms or withdrawing the benefit of one of the block exemptions. This obligation includes submitting to the Commission no later than one month before a decision is adopted a summary of the case and any related important documents. The Commission also preserves the right to request any other relevant documents. Finally, the provision states that

---

[88] One can of course argue that in spite of this, the system still provided for notification for those who wished to notify.
[89] See para. 77 of the Paper.   [90] See ch. 9.   [91] Regulation 1/2003 OJ 2003 No. L1/1.

where the Commission has decided to initiate proceedings, domestic antitrust authorities will be relieved of their competence to apply Article 81
and 82 EC.

The significance and influence of EC antitrust law beyond the single market

Through its supranational position and international outlook more generally, the Commission has been seeking co-operation with other antitrust
authorities in the world, as well as stretching the influence of EC antitrust
law internationally, by exporting its concepts and ideas. This has been hap-
pening on different fronts, including: first, concluding bilateral agreements
with antitrust authorities in third countries, formalising co-operation in
the enforcement of their antitrust laws; secondly, encapsulating antitrust
rules in the European Economic Agreement (EEA);[92] thirdly, approximat-
ing antitrust laws in Association Agreements between the EC and European
and Baltic countries and in Partnership and Co-operation Agreements with
other countries;[93] and fourthly, proposing international initiatives at a multilateral level.[94]

Bilateral perspective: the EC/US relationship

A framework of co-operation

The co-operative relationship between the EC and the USA in antitrust
policy is governed by the bilateral agreement of 23 September 1991.[95] The

---

[92] See J. Stragier, 'The Competition Rules of the EEA Agreement and Their Implementation' (1993)
14 *European Competition Law Review* 30.

[93] See Commission 25th Report on Competition Policy 1995, para. 221; D. Kennedy and D. Webb,
'The Limits of Integration: Eastern Europe and the European Communities' (1993) 30 *Common
Market Law Review* 1095, 1113.

[94] See pp. 130–2 below.

[95] Initially, a technical deficiency led the ECJ to invalidate the agreement. However, the agreement
was validly adopted in 1995. See OJ 1995 No. L95/45 as corrected by OJ 1995 No. L131/38. See
also Commission 25th Report on Competition Policy 1995, para. 224.
   The literature on the issue of bilateral co-operation between the Commission and the US
antitrust authorities is abundant. See K. van Miert, 'International Cooperation in the Field
of Competition: a View from the EC' (1997) *Fordham Corporate Law Institute* 13, 16–25; J.
Parisi, 'The EC–US Agreement Regarding the Application of Their Competition Laws: Another
Step towards Fostering International Cooperation in Antitrust Enforcement', address before the

agreement provides for co-operation in respect to several aspects of EC and US antitrust laws. In particular, Articles II–V of the agreement are worth mentioning. Article II deals with the need to notify the other party whenever it becomes apparent to one party that its enforcement activities are likely to affect the interests of the former. Article III deals with exchange of information between the parties. Article IV deals with co-ordination of enforcement activities between the parties. Article V deals with the important issue of 'positive comity'.[96] Under this principle, one party to the agreement (known as the requesting party) can ask the other party (known as the requested party) to address anti-competitive behaviour, within the latter's boundaries, which has an effect on the interests of the former.

The agreement has the benefit, including the opportunity, for the parties to exchange views in all cases of mutual interest and, when appropriate, to co-ordinate enforcement activities. Co-operation under the agreement has generally been quite close and productive for the last eleven years.[97] A good example in which co-operation was seen as important is the *CRS/SABRE* case. In this case, the US Department of Justice requested the Commission to investigate activities within the computer reservation system markets (CRS) that were suspected of hindering the ability of US-based CRS firms from competing effectively in certain European markets. A claim was made by SABRE, which is owned by American Airlines, that the anti-competitive behaviour of the three large airline owners of Amadeus on the European side

European Trade Law Association, Brussels, December 1991; D. Ham, 'International Cooperation in the Antitrust Field and in Particular the Agreement between the United States and the Commission of the European Communities' (1992) 30 *Common Market Law Review* 571; J. Griffin, 'EC/US Antitrust Cooperation Agreement: Impact on Transnational Business' (1993) 24 *Law and Policy in International Business* 1051.

[96] See D. Conn, 'Assessing the Impact of Preferential Trade Agreements and New Rules of Origin on the Extraterritorial Application of Antitrust Law to International Mergers' (1993) 93 *Columbia Law Review* 119, 148; C. Ehlermann, 'The International Dimension of Competition Policy' (1994) 17 *Fordham International Law Journal* 833, 836. See further pp. 218–19 below.

[97] In the period from January 1995 to December 1996, for example, there were varying degrees of co-operation in nearly 100 cases. See J. Griffin, 'EC and US Extraterritoriality: Activism and Cooperation' (1994) 17 *Fordham International Law Journal*, 353. Note, however, the *Boeing/McDonnell Douglas* case, which indicates that this has not always been the case. OJ 1997 No. L336/16. Yet, the recent *MCIWorldcom/Sprint* case is a paradigmatic example of the European Commission and the US antitrust authorities working closer than ever before and sharing information constructively. See Commission Press Release, 'Commission Opens Full Investigation into the MCIWorldCom/Sprint Merger', 21 February 2000, available at: http://www.europa.eu.int/comm/competition/index_en.html.

of the Atlantic, the leading CRS, impeded its ability to penetrate markets in Europe.[98]

The US Department of Justice (DoJ) decided to make a positive comity referral on the basis of the co-operation agreement between the EC and the USA. J. Klein, then in charge of the DoJ's Antitrust Division, said that the Commission was in the best position to investigate this conduct because it occurred within the EC and consumers there are the ones who are principally at risk if competition has been distorted.[99] By contrast, A. Schaub, former Director-General of DG COMP within the Commission, believed the case was 'important psychologically'. In its investigation, the Commission treated this as a priority case because it was aware of the fact that how it handles US positive comity referrals will certainly determine largely how the US antitrust authorities will handle its referrals.[100]

In 1997 the Commission began an 'initial inquiry', which lasted for two years. This was followed in March 1999 by a formal proceeding against Air France, one of the three European airline owners of Amadeus named in the US request. The Commission stated, on the basis of its initial inquiry, that Air France had discriminated against SABRE to favour Amadeus.[101]

It remains to be seen, however, whether this particular case will ultimately enhance the confidence of the EC and the USA regarding the effectiveness of the principle of positive comity. Some US legislators have made positive statements regarding these signs of EC responses to US requests for enforcement. Senator H. Kohl of the Antitrust, Business Rights and Competition Sub-committee stated in the wake of the Commission's investigation that it was becoming obvious that the US' most important positive comity agreement, with the EC, was beginning to pay off.[102] However, the more recent

---

[98] It was alleged that the three airline owners in collaboration with their travel providers refused to supply SABRE with the same fare data as they supplied to Amadeus, in addition to denying the former the ability to carry out the various booking and ticketing functions available to the latter.

[99] US Department of Justice Press Release, 'Justice Department Asks European Communities to Investigate Possible Anticompetitive Conduct Affecting U.S. Airlines' computer reservation systems', 28 April 1997. See http://www.usdoj.gov.

[100] Commission Press Release, 'EU Gives Priority to US Airline Reservation Case', 9 September 1997.

[101] European Commission Press Release, 'Commission Opens Procedure Against Air France for Favouring Amadeus Reservation System', 15 March 1999.

[102] See 'Senate Sub-Committee Focuses on International Enforcement, Positive Comity' 76 Antitrust & Trade Reg. Rep. (BNA) 482, 6 May 1999.

The case of MCIWorldcom/Sprint is a very good example of true comity being practised between the USA and the EC.

developments in the relationship between the USA and the EC in the field of antitrust policy have not generated an equally positive attitude on the US side of the Atlantic. In making this statement the author of course has in mind the *GE/Honeywell* decision, which will be discussed in chapter 7. The Commission's decision to block the merger between General Electric and Honeywell International, when the operation was cleared in the USA, was met by heavy and wide criticism in the USA. Despite the conflicting results reached in the case by the Commission and the Department of Justice, co-operation between the two authorities was evident in the case, as it has been in other cases.[103]

Recent developments

In June 1996, and in the wake of successful negotiations with the US authorities, the Commission adopted a proposal to build on the 1991 Agreement. The step to deepen the EC–US relations through another formal agreement was taken in 1998.[104] The new agreement has many advantages. First, it contributes to advancing the principle of positive comity. Secondly, it confirms the efforts of the parties to continue employing the principle. Thirdly, it clarifies the manner in which the principle will be implemented. Further agreements enhancing the level of co-operation between the EC and the USA, as well as between the EC and other countries, are in contemplation,[105] and should be welcomed.

The 1991 and 1998 Agreements have contributed significantly to bringing these two important systems of antitrust closer to each other. Following the agreements, contacts between staff at the Commission and the US Department of Justice and the Federal Trade Commission have become something of a daily routine in the work of the three authorities. These

---

[103] See the closely co-ordinated parallel investigations in cases such as *Exxon/Mobil* (1999) OJ C127/2 (Commission/FTC), *CVC/Lenzing* (2001) OJ C141/13 (Commission/FTC), *Alcoa/Reynolds* (1999) OJ C339/14 (Commission/DoJ) and *Compaq/HP* (2001) OJ C374/68 (Commission/FTC).

[104] OJ 1998 No. L173/26; [1999] 4 CMLR 502.

The agreement creates a presumption that in certain circumstances one party (so-called 'requesting party') will normally defer or suspend its own enforcement activities, where anti-competitive behaviour is occurring principally in and directed principally towards the other party's territory. The proposed positive comity agreement is an important development in this respect, because it represents a commitment on the part of the USA to co-operate with respect to antitrust enforcement rather than seeking to apply its antitrust laws extraterritorially. See ch. 7.

[105] An agreement has also been entered into with Canada. See Co-operation Agreement between Canada, the EC and the ECSC: OJ 1999 No. L175/49; [1999] 5 CMLR 713.

daily contacts have been prominent in the area of merger control. It is this author's view that the advance stage, which the daily co-operation between the EC and USA has reached in the area of merger control, deserves a special emphasis given the fact that both parties apply different procedural and substantive rules. There have of course been divergences in the same case and on the same facts between the three authorities.[106] Remarkably, however, these divergences are rare. Without wishing to express an opinion on which party was wrong and which was right in those rare cases of divergences, it is sufficient to remember that reasonable minds may reach different conclusions on the application of the same law to the same facts using the same body of evidence. In the case of the EC and the USA, at least, as has already been said, different rules are applied by each party.[107] It is therefore understandable that divergences may occur in some cases. What is important, however, is that both parties seem to be committed to fostering a more broadly based transatlantic dialogue on antitrust policy, identifying areas of convergence and seeking to narrow those of divergence. This was the impression given by EC antitrust Commissioner Mario Monti, former Assistant Attorney-General Charles James and the Director of the Federal Trade Commission Tim Morris after their meeting on 24 September 2001; although it ought to be admitted that it is very striking that the USA is committed to expanding and intensifying its bilateral co-operation with the EC in antitrust policy given the Bush Administration's odd policies in other areas such as steel and even others as diverse as the Middle East conflict and the establishment of the International Criminal Court.

The EEA Agreement

Introduction

The Agreement on the European Economic Area (the Agreement) came into force on 1 January 1994. The original contracting parties to the Agreement were the E(E)C, the European Coal and Steel Community and the then twelve EC Member States, on the one hand, and five EFTA Countries, Austria, Finland, Iceland, Norway and Sweden, on the other. Upon the accession of Austria, Finland and Sweden to the EC in 1995, Iceland and

---

[106] See, for example, the case of *GE/Honeywell*, discussed at pp. 179–81 below.
[107] See further chs. 4 and 9.

Norway were left as the only EFTA Countries. The number of EFTA Countries was subsequently increased to three in May 1995 when Liechtenstein
became a party to the Agreement.

The broad objective of the Agreement is to establish a dynamic and homogeneous European Economic Area, based on common rules and equal
conditions of competition. To this end the cornerstone policies and principles of the EC, as well as a wide range of accompanying EC rules and
policies, were incorporated into the Agreement. Among the most important of the policies and principles which have been incorporated are those in
the areas of free movement of goods, persons, services and capital, antitrust,
public procurement, social policy, consumer protection and the environment. Secondary EC legislation in areas covered by the Agreement has also
been incorporated into the Agreement by means of direct references in the
Agreement to such legislation.

Parallel systems

Two independent legal systems have in effect been established following the
signing of the Agreement. First, there is the EEA Agreement which applies
to relations between the EFTA and EC sides as well as between the EFTA
Contracting Countries themselves. Secondly, there is EC law which applies
to the relations between Member States within the EC. This state of affairs
has meant that for the EEA to be viable the two legal systems need to develop
in parallel and be applied and enforced uniformly. To this end, the Agreement provides for decision-making procedures for the integration into the
EEA of new secondary EC legislation and for a surveillance mechanism to
ensure the fulfilment of obligations under the Agreement and a uniform
interpretation and application of its provisions.

Under the Agreement a Joint Committee – which is made of representatives of the contracting parties – was established. This Committee is responsible for the introduction of new rules within the EEA. The surveillance
mechanism, however, is arranged in the form of a two-pillar structure of
independent bodies of the two sides. The implementation and application
of the Agreement within the EC is monitored by the European Commission, whereas the Surveillance Authority is responsible for carrying out the
same task within the EFTA pillar. In order to ensure a uniform surveillance
throughout the EEA, the two bodies are expected to co-operate, exchange
information and consult each other on surveillance policy issues and individual cases.

The two-pillar structure also applies to the judicial control mechanism, with the EFTA Court exercising competences similar to those of the ECJ and the CFI with regard to, *inter alia*, the surveillance procedure regarding the EFTA Countries and appeals concerning decisions taken by the EFTA Surveillance Authority.

The institutions

The EFTA Surveillance Authority   The EFTA Surveillance Authority (the Authority) was established under the Agreement between the EFTA Countries on the Establishment of a Surveillance Authority and a Court of Justice. This agreement, *inter alia*, contains basic provisions on the Authority's structure and lays down its tasks and competences. The Authority is managed by a College of three Members, all of whom are appointed by common accord of the Governments of the EFTA Countries for a period of four years which is renewable. At the head of the Authority stands a President, who is appointed in the same manner, for a period of two years. The Members are completely independent in carrying out their duties. They are supposed not to seek or take instructions from any Government or other body and they are expected to refrain from any action incompatible with their duties. In this sense, the Members are supposed to be individuals whose independence is beyond doubt and which is not vulnerable to any sort of compromise.

The main task of the Authority is to ensure that the EFTA Countries fulfil their obligations under the EEA Agreement. In general terms, this means that the Authority is under a general surveillance obligation, namely to ensure that the provisions of the Agreement, including the protocols and the acts referred to in the Annexes, are properly implemented in the domestic legal orders of the EFTA Countries and that they are correctly applied by their authorities.

In the field of antitrust policy, the Authority has extended competence, including a range of tasks of an administrative character which supplements those vested in the Authority with regard to general surveillance and which fully reflects the extended competences of the European Commission in these fields. These tasks mainly relate to the practices and behaviour of firms in the marketplace. Thus, the Authority is expected to ensure that the antitrust rules of the Agreement are complied with, notably the prohibitions on anti-competitive behaviour and on the abuse of market dominance by firms. To ensure that the Authority is able to carry out such tasks, it possesses similar powers to those enjoyed by the European Commission, namely the power to, *inter alia*, make on-the-spot inspections, impose fines and periodic penalties and, in the case of an infringement, make a decision compelling the firms concerned to bring the infringement to an end.

The EFTA Court   The EFTA Court has jurisdiction with regard to EFTA Countries, which are parties to the EEA Agreement. The Court is mainly competent to deal with infringement actions brought by the EFTA Surveillance Authority against an EFTA Country with regard to the implementation, application or interpretation of an EEA rule. The settlement of disputes between two or more EFTA Countries, hearing appeals concerning decisions taken by the EFTA Surveillance Authority and the giving of advisory opinions to courts in EFTA Countries on the interpretation of EEA rules are also within the general competence of the Court. Thus, the jurisdiction of the Court mainly corresponds to the jurisdiction of the ECJ – as described in the previous chapter and the previous part of the present one.

The EFTA Court consists of three Judges, one nominated by each of the three EFTA Countries. The Judges' appointment is by common accord of the Governments of those countries for a period of six years. The Judges elect their President for a term of three years. In addition to the regular Judges, there is also a system of *ad hoc* judges, the purpose of which is to cater for situations where a regular Judge cannot sit in a particular case. The judgments of the Court – unlike in the case of the ECJ – are delivered on a majority basis. The procedure followed by the Court is laid down in the Statute of the EFTA Court and in its Rules of Procedure.

The antitrust provisions of the EEA Agreement

The antitrust chapter   The EEA Agreement contains several important provisions dealing with antitrust matters which are worth mentioning. Articles 53, 54 and 59 of the EEA Agreement mirror Articles 81, 82 and 86 EC. The control of concentrations, which is modelled on the basis of Regulation 4064/89 EC, is incorporated into Article 57 of the Agreement. By virtue of Article 60 and Annex XIV of the Agreement most of the EC Regulations concerning antitrust law have been incorporated, subject to certain modifications, into the EEA system. Article 61 of the Agreement contains a mirror provision of that found in Article 87 EC.

Comment   It would appear in light of the above that the body of EC law (*acquis communautaire*) was adopted into the EEA Agreement. It seems that this was a response instigated by the Commission to the globalisation of international trade,[108] and the pressure the latter created for increased co-ordination in antitrust policy between different antitrust authorities.[109] In light of this, the antitrust rules contained in the Agreement apply where there is an impact on trade between an EFTA Country and the EC.[110] The Agreement is similar to the EC Treaty in that it does not require signatories to adopt EC antitrust rules into the domestic legal order.

The EEA Agreement provides for consultation procedures between the parties on the antitrust rules therein. These rules, according to the ECJ in its judgment in *Wood Pulp*, could in no way preclude the integral application of EC antitrust law.[111] Since this was also the view expounded by the Commission, it may well be that this explains why the Commission never thought it necessary to invoke these provisions in antitrust cases. This view is reinforced by the 'extra-territoriality' doctrine which was upheld by the ECJ in the same judgment, and which gives the Commission jurisdiction to act under the EC Treaty rules whenever an anti-competitive agreement or another anti-competitive practice, despite originating from outside the EC, is implemented within the EC.[112]

Bilateral agreements within Europe

Several bilateral agreements with Central and Eastern European countries have been entered into by the EC. There are two main types of such agreements: Association Agreements and Partnership and Co-operation Agreements.[113] These agreements exhibit some similarities, but they also

---

[108] See generally T. Jakob, 'EEA and Eastern Europe Agreements with the European Community' (1992) *Fordham Corporate Law Institute* 403; S. Norberg, 'The EEA Agreement: Institutional Solutions for a Dynamic and Homogeneous EEA in the Area of Competition' (1992) *Fordham Corporate Law Institute* 437.

[109] Commission 25th Report on Competition Policy 1995, section V.

[110] See Articles 53–7 of the Agreement. There are clear rules on jurisdiction in the Agreement thus avoiding the possibility of duplication of efforts on the part of both the EEA Authority and the Commission when investigating a case. See J. Stragier, 'The Competition Rules of the EEA Agreement and Their Implementation' (1993) 14 *European Competition Law Review* 30.

[111] [1988] ECR 5193; [1988] 4 CMLR 474.   [112] See ch. 7 on the doctrine of extraterritoriality.

[113] Partnership and Co-operation Agreements were signed with Russia, the Ukraine and Central-Asian Republics. See generally, M. Maresceau and E. Montaguti, 'The Relations between the European Union and Central and Eastern Europe: a Legal Appraisal' (1995) 32 *Common Market Law Review* 1327.

   The discussion will use the Partnership and Co-operation Agreement between the EC and the Russian Federation as an example.

differ in several ways. Unless otherwise stated, the term 'agreements' is used in the following discussion to refer to both Association Agreements and the Partnership and Co-operation Agreement between the EC and the Russian Federation.

Some background

Association Agreements   The general shift by the EC and countries in Central and Eastern Europe to a new form of Association Agreement in the 1990s reflected the unprecedented and profound political and economic transitions experienced by the latter.[114] These Association Agreements signalled a desire on the part of these countries for closer links with the EC, which seems to have been based not only on their geographic proximity, but also on shared values and increasing interdependence between them all.[115] On its part, the EC had already taken decisive steps towards the creation of a system based on democracy and a market-oriented economy, the rule of law and respect for human rights, so for this reason its response was positive.[116] Hence, it was important for the EC to support the political and economic changes in these countries.

---

[114] Initially, there were three separate Association Agreements between the EC, its Member States and, in turn, Hungary (OJ 1992 No. L116/1), Poland (OJ 1992 No. L114/1) and Czechoslovakia (OJ 1992 No. L115/1), which were signed on 16 December 1991. Similar agreements with Romania and Bulgaria, however, were initiated on 17 November and 22 December 1992 respectively. Agreements were also concluded later on with other countries bringing the number of all such agreements to a total of ten. The conclusion of all these agreements was the consequence of the conviction that free trade must go hand in hand with ensuring undistorted competition. See E. Faucompert, J. Konings and H. Vandenbussche, 'The Integration of Central and Eastern Europe in the European Union – Trade and Labour Market Adjustment' (1999) 33 *Journal of World Trade Law* 121, 132–4.

    For an overview of these Association Agreements, see C. Lucron, 'Contenu et portée des accords entre la Communauté et la Hongrie, la Pologne et la Tchécoslovaquie' (1992) 35 *Revue du Marché Commun et de L'Union Européenne* 293. A more up-to-date account of these agreements is available at: http://www.europa.eu.int/comm/dg04/internal/multilateral.htm.

[115] All these Association Agreements have been conceived with a view to substantially contributing to the countries' full integration into the EC, both in economic and political terms. Although the question whether such integration must necessarily lead to future accession to the EC is not answered, such a step seems to be aspired to by all participating countries. For a general discussion, see T. Jakob, 'EEA and Eastern Europe Agreements with the European Community (1992) *Fordham Corporate Law Institute* 403, 429–34; G. Marceau, 'The Full Potential of the Europe Agreements: Trade and Competition Issues: the Case of Poland' (1995) *World Competition* 44.

[116] See generally Commission 9th Report on Competition Policy 1979, p. 9. Also, T. Frazer, 'Competition Policy after 1992: the Next Step' (1990) 53 *Modern Law Review* 609.

The Partnership and Co-operation Agreement (PCA) between the EC and the Russian Federation   The PCA between the EC and the Russian Federation was signed on 14 June 1994. This Agreement follows from an earlier Trade and Co-operation Agreement between the EC and the USSR in 1989, which in less than two years was regarded as unsuitable for developing the relations between the parties. In entering into the PCA, Russia attempted to bring this Agreement closer to the Association Agreements. However, the EC, being concerned about the uncertainties in the transformation process in Russia and grounding its decision on geopolitical considerations, opted for a much looser framework in political, legal and economic terms. Nevertheless, from the perspective of the parties, the Agreement indicated that Russia was no longer a state-trading country but one with an economy in transition.[117] The Preamble to the PCA also referred to a 'political conditionality' clause, declaring that the parties are convinced of the paramount importance that must be accorded to the rule of law and respect for human rights.

The main contents

The agreements are comprehensive. They provide for almost all aspects of economic activity, political dialogue and cultural co-operation in addition to trade, commercial and economic co-operation. The main areas covered by the agreements include political dialogue at the highest level possible, free movement of goods, workers, establishment, services, payments, capital, antitrust and other economic provisions, approximation of laws, economic, cultural and financial co-operation and institutions.

The role of antitrust law in the agreements

Antitrust provisions are prominent features of the agreements. In entering into the agreements, all relevant parties concerned aimed to ensure that competition should not be distorted within the framework of the agreements. Including antitrust provisions in the agreements can be seen as contributing to a number of objectives: establishment of new rules, policies and practices as a basis for closer relations with the EC (in the case of Association Agreements, further integration into the EC). Put differently, the antitrust provisions sought to give an appropriate framework for gradual co-operation with the EC. This power to support co-operation (in the case

---

[117] See generally Maresceau and Montaguti, 'Relations', 1338–43.

of Association Agreements, integration), which is attributed to the antitrust provisions, is not entirely surprising as it has been one of the characteristic features of EC antitrust law. On the basis of EC experience, it is therefore almost logical for the free trade provisions contained in these agreements to be supplemented by antitrust provisions, in order to prevent private trade barriers from distorting harmonious economic relations between the parties.

According to the agreements, restrictions of competition that affect trade between the parties will be assessed by the Commission or by the competent domestic authority of the relevant country, or by both, depending on the circumstances in question. The assessment is to be taken according to rules modelled on the antitrust policy chapter in the EC Treaty. To give practical effect to these general provisions, implementing rules were negotiated in order to ensure effective co-operation between the parties.[118]

Matters requiring specific attention

Including antitrust provisions in the agreements does not of course mean that regulating conditions of competition in cases in which the parties have an interest will be free of difficulty. Three problems may require specific attention:

Jurisdictional overlap   First of all, the legal problems concern the question of how to deal with cases falling within both EC and the relevant country's jurisdiction. Under Article 81 EC, the EC can assert jurisdiction over anti-competitive agreements implemented in the Common Market, in accordance with the *Wood Pulp* doctrine developed by the ECJ.[119] If the *Wood Pulp* condition is satisfied in these cases, EC law would apply. However, since close links between the economies of the EC and the other parties

---

[118] In the case of Association Agreements, the rules necessary to implement the antitrust provisions were agreed to be established by the Association Councils within a period of three years. See, for example, the implementing rules for the application of the antitrust provisions applicable to firms provided for in Arts. 33(1)(i) and (ii) and 33(2) of the EC–Poland Interim Agreement OJ 1996 L208/24. See M. Blässar and J. Stragier, 'Enlargement' (1999) 1 *European Community Competition Policy NewsLetter* 58; T. Vardady, 'The Emergence of Competition Law in (Former) Socialist Countries' (1999) 47 *American Journal of Comparative Law* 229, 251; K. van Miert, 'Competition Policy in Relation to the Central and Eastern European Countries – Achievements and Challenges' (1998) 2 *European Community Competition Policy NewsLetter* 1; Jakob, 'Agreements'.

[119] See p. 120 above.

to the agreements will be established, it is possible that certain practices, within the meaning of Article 81 EC, between firms, will be implemented within the territory of both parties. In this scenario, not only can the EC assert jurisdiction, but also the other party concerned. The question would therefore be how to address problems that might arise when more than one antitrust authority becomes involved and possibly reaches different conclusions. The Associated Countries and Russia, for example, have undertaken to adapt their own antitrust rules to the principles covered by the EC antitrust policy chapter. However, this does not eliminate all the problems of concurrent jurisdiction. For example, there will always be scope for divergence in the way antitrust provisions are enforced by different antitrust authorities – as was demonstrated during the course of the previous chapter.

Issues of jurisdictional overlap may arise in the context of abuse of dominance under Article 82 EC. However, they are likely to be less problematic. Abuse is likely to occur primarily in the market where the firm in question holds a dominant position.[120] In this instance, questions of concurrent jurisdiction might arise less frequently.

Regarding merger control, neither the PCA nor Association Agreements prejudice the exercise by the EC of its powers under the Merger Regulation, Regulation 4064/89 EC. With Russia and the Associated Countries having merger control regimes in their domestic systems, issues of jurisdictional overlap in merger cases are likely to arise.

No assertion of jurisdiction   A situation can be envisaged where neither the EC nor the other party concerned may assert jurisdiction. Decisions will need to be taken on the course of action to be pursued under such circumstances. In this context, an interesting question arises because an anti-competitive agreement between firms may not affect trade between Member States, but affects trade between the EC and the other party. Would the EC be able to deal with such an agreement on the basis of the provisions of the PCA or the Association Agreements? The provisions of the PCA and Association Agreements are not intended to have 'direct effect', and it is doubtful in any case that the provisions of the agreements should have

---

[120] However, note the situation can arise where dominance and abuse can fall within different markets. See C-333/94 *Tetra PakRausing SA* v. *Commission* [1996] ECR I-5951; [1997] 4 CMLR 662; Case T-228/97 *Irish Sugar* v. *Commission* [1999] 5 CMLR 1300.

direct effect.[121] This view flows from a brief consultation of the conditions of direct effect, as laid down in the case of *Van Gend en Loos*, which establishes that for a provision to have direct effect it needs, *inter alia*, to be clear, precise and unconditional. In the case of the agreements, it seems that the requirement of unconditionality, at least, is not satisfied. This is because further implementation measures must still be decided upon. Also, it seems that the requirement of precision is also not met. The agreements do not include an 'Article 81(3) EC' type of provision which means that exemption will be provided by way of interpretation. This in itself perhaps would not necessarily render the EC unable to take action. However, for EC jurisdiction to exist in such cases, it is necessary for it to be instituted by specific executing provisions in the agreements.

Interests of parties It is possible to conceive of cases where only one party has jurisdiction but, nonetheless, important interests of the other party may be involved. In this instance, the purpose of the implementing rules should be to provide the basis for a co-operative and transparent treatment of such cases by the relevant antitrust authorities. Above all, it is essential that the process should be free from complexities. Given inevitable differences between the market conditions of the parties, it can be expected that individual cases will be treated under different legal standards and so different conclusions will be reached. More significantly, a certain amount of co-ordination of action and a readiness to take into account the other parties' interests would be required. Co-operation in this instance could be modelled on the 1986 Organisation for Economic Cooperation and Development (OECD) Recommendation or the present co-operation agreements between the EC and the USA.

The place of secondary legislation

Another salient issue concerns both certain EC secondary legislation (such as block exemption regulations) and its future development. The principles covered by these secondary instruments should apply when it comes to

---

[121] See, for example, Article 63 of the EC–Poland Agreement, in which it is stated that the Association Council may be required 'at a later stage to examine to what extent and under what conditions certain exemption rules may be directly applicable, taking into account the progress made in the integration process between the Community and Poland'.

Having said that, Case 12/86 *Demirel* v. *Stadt Schwäbisch Gmünd* [1987] ECR 3719 seems to suggest that Association Agreements may produce direct effect.

assessing an anti-competitive practice under the agreements. On the other hand, if EC legislation changes in the future, then ways and means should be found to ensure that these developments are also taken into account in interpreting such agreements.

EC interest

In the case of the antitrust provisions under the Association Agreements which follow Articles 81 and 82 EC,[122] each Association Council was supposed to establish rules for the implementation of these provisions by 1 March 1995. The EC was active in providing advice to the Associated Countries on implementation, which is reflected in the similarity, at least prima facie, between the antitrust rules of the EC and the Associated Countries.

In many respects, co-ordination in enforcement of the antitrust policies in the Associated Countries predicated on EC antitrust rules is in the latter's interest. Reliance by the EC on extraterritorial application of its antitrust rules is not guaranteed to be successful.[123] Also, EC firms may be served by strong enforcement of antitrust rules in the Associated Countries, especially in areas of state aid, government monopolies and abuse of dominance.

Approximation of laws

The agreements contain provisions on the approximation of antitrust laws.[124] A distinction can be drawn, however, between the PCA and Association Agreements. In the former, approximation is limited to endeavouring to ensure that legislation is gradually harmonised with EC antitrust law. For

---

[122] For a translation of the statutes and a detailed analysis of the implementation of these provisions see J. Fingleton, E. Fox, D. Neven and P. Seabright, *Competition Policy and the Transformation of Central Europe* (CEPR, London, 1995), ch. 4 and Appendix 2.

[123] For a discussion on the doctrine of extraterritoriality see ch. 7.

[124] See (1996) 1 *Commission Competition Newsletter* 38. Such approximation – which includes existing and future legislation – is considered a major precondition for forging closer links with the EC. The PCA contains a clause in Article 55 stating that Russia will 'endeavour to ensure that [its] legislation shall be gradually made compatible with that of the Community'.

In the case of Association Agreements, approximation of laws was seen as a condition for the countries concerned to integrate into the EC. Whereas Hungary 'shall act to ensure that future legislation is compatible with Community legislation as far as possible', Poland 'shall use its best endeavours to ensure that future legislation is compatible with Community legislation', and the Czech and Slovak Republic, Romania, Bulgaria, Estonia, Latvia, Lithuania and Slovenia, for their part, 'shall endeavour to ensure that [their] legislation will be gradually made compatible with that of the Community'.

Association Agreements, given their image as pre-accession arrangements, the approximation requirement is stronger and has generated national laws broadly aligned with EC antitrust law.

The nature of the approximation requirement is open to some debate.[125] Approximation is a major precondition for closer economic links with the EC, and the countries concerned undertake to ensure all future legislation is compatible with EC antitrust law. This commitment has, in effect, imposed an obligation to simply introduce, *inter alia*, antitrust rules similar to those found in the EC without imposing an alignment obligation, which would go beyond any obligation imposed on existing Member States. In the case of Association Countries, the Commission, in its 1995 White Paper on Preparation of the Associated Countries of Central and Eastern Europe for Integration into the Internal Market of the Union, gave the requirement of approximation a narrow meaning by imposing a requirement on Associated Countries to comply not only with general antitrust principles, but also with the existing case law of the EC.

The EC conception of antitrust is not necessarily ideal for these small, emerging market economies. In a relatively advanced economy, there are often tensions between a strict antitrust policy and accommodation of the rapid structural changes in the economy. Hence, imposing an 'approxima- tion of laws' obligation on these countries leaves very little *discretion* to their governments.[126] In comparison, developed countries have generally, first developed an industrial policy and then modified it in the light of in- ternational agreements. Thus, the inclusion of such a commitment would mean that the policy of these countries will be shaped from the outset by international obligations. It should be pointed out here that whilst devel- oped countries, during times of rapid structural change, modify antitrust policy to facilitate necessary changes, this will not be possible in the case of these economies in transition due to their international obligations.

If accession to the EC is an objective, then approximation of laws at a general level is consistent, even essential, in order to realise that goal. Such approximation of laws is a sensible step because these countries will be able to ensure and protect effective competition by their own means. It is also desirable from the point of view of business firms because this will relieve them from having to deal with totally different systems of antitrust. This has

[125] See Fingleton, Fox, Neven and Seabright, *Competition*, p. 55.
[126] F. Vissi, 'Challenges and Questions around Competition Policy: the Hungarian Experience' (1995) 18 *Fordham International Law Journal* 1230, 1241.

both substantive law and procedural benefits. In this case, parachuting-in laws on the basis of external obligations may not necessarily be objectionable. At the same time, the need for adopting antitrust law within the domestic legal order seems to be important in the context of the new market economies. If the aim of the countries concerned in creating closer co-operation with the EC is to develop market economies, as opposed to seeking future accession to the EC, probably the adoption of rules consistent with the cultural and institutional context of the country concerned is more desirable because they are more readily accepted by those to whom they apply, than parachuting-in laws. In this case, attention to effectiveness is more fundamental than approximation *per se*. The issue of effectiveness and approximation is perhaps more one of timing. The Commission may need to reappraise the importance of detailed convergence to allow for the proper development and absorption of EC antitrust law into the domestic law of such transitional economies. Domestic antitrust authorities and policy-makers in these countries, on the other hand, will need to work out a careful compromise between the current needs of their economies and the aim of closer links with the EC.

At a more general level, the inclusion of such an approximation commitment in the agreements can be seen as part of the regulatory competition between the USA and the EC for influencing the post-Soviet countries of Europe.[127] Approximation makes it easier for EC firms to operate in these countries and will also facilitate fuller co-operation with the EC and, in the case of Association Agreements, further integration with a view to ultimate membership. Nonetheless, it seems that relations with the EC are very much driven by the internal agenda of the EC rather than the needs of these countries to develop.[128] Approximation is required even though EC antitrust law itself is not always the best model. The EC is driven by an integration agenda and yet insists on dealing with these countries one-by-one, rather than collectively, even though arguments in favour of approximation are centred around globalisation and the need for shared responses by domestic antitrust authorities across national boundaries. The Association Agreements, for example, emphasise the existence of conditions which have to be met before membership will be considered. As a result, one may

---

[127] See L. McGowan and S. Wilks, 'The First Supranational Policy on the European Union: Competition Policy' (1995) 28 *European Journal of Political Research* 141, at 144.
[128] See Kennedy and Webb, 'Limits', 1095.

conclude that the postponement of fuller co-operation between Russia and the EC and accession to the EC in respect of Association Agreements is premised not on the inability of the EC to consume goods produced in the East but on the inability of the countries concerned to withstand competition from EC firms. Thus, the approximation requirement may not be solely in the interests of the countries concerned, but also serves the interests of EC firms in general and, those of the EC in particular. Furthermore, the inclusion of this requirement in different forms reflects not only the different stage of development for the economies of the countries concerned, but also the lack of balance in the bargaining positions of the parties.

Recent developments

On 16–17 June 2002, the Commission and the thirteen Candidate Countries held their 8th Annual Conference in Lithuania.[129] The topics considered in the Conference were quite diverse. The main focus was on the progress achieved by the Candidate Countries in the field of antitrust policy over the preceding twelve months and on how the parties can organise their future co-operation. Other topics of discussion included exchange of views on developments in the World Trade Organization and the International Competition Network.[130]

At a more basic level, the Conference has built on the success achieved in the 6th and 7th Annual Conferences. During the 7th Annual Conference, the main theme was the Commission's assessment of the Candidate Countries' enforcement record in antitrust law. This assessment proved very useful in helping countries such as Estonia, Latvia, Lithuania and Slovenia to provisionally close the accession negotiations on the antitrust chapter. The 6th Annual Conference, on the other hand, focused on the importance of full and efficient enforcement of antitrust law. At that conference, the Commission emphasised that establishing effective systems of antitrust in the countries concerned is of central significance to the ongoing accession negotiations. For the Candidate Countries, the Conference signalled that negotiations with the Commission on the EC antitrust policy chapter had

---

[129] These countries are Bulgaria, Cyprus, Czech Republic, Estonia, Hungary, Latvia, Lithuania, Malta, Poland, Romania, Slovak Republic, Slovenia and Turkey. Useful summaries of the various workshops of the Conference are available at: http://www.europa.eu.int/comm/competition.

[130] See ch. 9 for a discussion on these developments.

been opened and full efficient enforcement of antitrust rules was of key importance in these negotiations.

The Annual Conference has come to be regarded as an event of extreme importance in the antitrust law diaries of the Commission and Candidate Countries. In general, it is a policy-oriented event, focused in particular on the development of EC antitrust law and on how to ensure the full and proper enforcement of its rules in Candidate Countries. It has served to demonstrate the necessity of a timely application of EC antitrust law for a successful accession, and has reconfirmed the commitment of the Commission and Candidate Countries to enhancing co-operation in the field of antitrust law. The Conference has also helped the Commission in evaluating the situation in all Candidate Countries, especially those that have been having difficulties in completing their negotiations on the antitrust law chapter with the Commission. The Conference has also served as an appropriate medium for the Commission to convey the message to Candidate Countries that a Candidate Country can be ready for EC membership only if its public authorities and firms have become accustomed to a competition discipline such as that of the EC well prior to accession. As far as the Commission is concerned, each Candidate Country is required to demonstrate that it has the necessary legislative framework in place; it has established the necessary administrative capacity; and it has established a credible enforcement record.

Towards a wider framework of antitrust policy

The Commission's efforts towards creating a wider framework of antitrust policy beyond the EC and Europe have been quite substantial.[131] Various groups in the EC have attempted to tackle this issue. In 1994, for example, the 'Wise Men Group', a group of experts commissioned by Karel van Miert, then Commissioner for antitrust within the Commission, made some interesting proposals in order to strengthen the multilateral framework of antitrust rules and to promote international co-operation in this area. The Group recommended strengthening plurilateral co-operation in response to global competition. It recommended creating a fully-fledged

---

[131] See Commission 25th Report on Competition Policy 1995, section V; Commission 28th Report on Competition Policy 1998, pp. 118–20.

international instrument, including an adequate enforcement structure, a core of common principles and a positive comity provision. The Group also put forward a proposal for a dispute settlement mechanism that could be used to settle disputes between member countries regarding their compliance with rules and principles of the instrument.[132]

Beyond this, the Commission has been particularly active in discussions within the WTO, the OECD, the newly established International Competition Network (ICN) and the United Nations Conference on Trade and Development (UNCTAD), adopting a Code on Restrictive Business Practices.[133] The Commission has been a strong supporter of the Code, and it seems to endorse most of its views. An interesting feature of the Code relates to its terminology, which seems to be closely related to that of EC antitrust law, such as the concepts of 'dominance' and 'abuse'. This, along with the fact that the Code emphasises the importance of institutional dimensions, and the interaction between these and substantive provisions, as is the case with the EC system of antitrust, makes it clear that EC antitrust law has played a central role in the development of this Code.

The Commission's efforts towards internationalisation have been the result of several factors, including those relating to increased globalisation and technical changes and future accession to the EC, as well as the need to build a global order within antitrust policy. These efforts will be examined in more detail in chapters 9 and 10. One important endeavour, however, is worth mentioning at present: The Commission has been very active in making concrete contributions, in terms of offering technical assistance, to countries willing to introduce antitrust laws and policies within their domestic economies. It should not require a great deal of convincing for one to accept that building a system of antitrust, with effective antitrust law and policy and credible and transparent enforcement bodies, is a formidable task. Constructing such a system is integrally linked to broader private sector development strategies. When developing countries and those in transition consider adopting antitrust laws within their domestic legal systems, their main concern normally revolves around the lack of sufficient resources and the necessary expertise.

---

[132] See 'Competition Policy in the New Trade Order: Strengthening International Co-operation and Rules' COM (95) 359, available at: http://www.europa.eu.int.

[133] A detailed examination of the WTO, the OECD, UNCTAD and the ICN can be found in ch. 9.

The European Commission has over the years made it clear that it understands this concern and therefore has expressed a willingness and shown readiness to offer assistance and support in terms of organising and financing important projects in countries and regions interested in adopting antitrust laws and policies. Indeed, this initiative by the Commission should be seen in parallel to similar initiatives by other important antitrust authorities, such as those in the USA and important international organisations, such as UNCTAD. During the last decade or so, the Commission has organised training sessions for antitrust law officials from Candidate Countries for EC accession, Latin and Central America, Africa and the Middle East. Of these projects, it is worth mentioning the co-operation project between the Commission and the Common Market for East and Southern Africa (COMESA). The aim of this project is to develop a regional antitrust policy in Africa and to focus on capacity-building in the enforcement of antitrust policy by antitrust authorities within COMESA. Despite its relatively short life, the project has come to assume great significance. The project is based on the recognition that antitrust policy is one of the trade-related areas of co-operation between the EC and COMESA and a crucial part of the overall integration of COMESA and its welfare-enhancing objective. It is anticipated that the project will increase in significance in the years ahead. As a result of the project, member countries of COMESA should be able to enjoy a greater capacity in formulating antitrust laws. This includes developing clear and transparent antitrust laws, credible institutions with highly developed antitrust expertise and effective enforcement.

The value of EC antitrust law

A final important comment to be made in this part relates to the value of EC antitrust law beyond the single market. EC antitrust law is a useful tool for third countries that aim to introduce or develop a framework for competition in general and, for antitrust law in particular. It has been written:

> European competition law experience is also, however, a valuable source of knowledge and guidance for policy-makers in states that are today trying to develop market economies and forge appropriate legal frameworks for them. Most such countries have competition law systems, but they generally play marginal roles, at least in part because there is little understanding of the dynamics, costs and consequences of such systems. Policy-makers often face

situations that are similar to those faced by Europeans in the recent past, and thus European experience may aid them in identifying and perhaps achieving competition law systems.[134]

The fact that the EC system of antitrust has been successful is a factor that will influence the decision of policy-makers in third countries to use it for insights and guidance when they consider adopting antitrust laws or changing their existing ones. The number of countries that have adopted antitrust laws on the basis of EC antitrust law has increased over the years.[135] As was seen above, some of these countries are already moving towards future accession to the EC, but there are other ones which bear no relation to the EC, whether in geographical or other terms.[136] Such a development highlights an important role for EC antitrust law, and its growing success and influence present an opportunity that the Commission has been keen to exploit in several ways.

However, this is also a challenge for the Commission. Certain countries may not be willing to consult EC antitrust experience for insights and lessons. The USA, for example, has been a forerunner in this respect because the common sentiment on the other side of the Atlantic has always been that such experience has little to offer to a system of antitrust which celebrated its centenary over a decade ago. To a certain extent, this reaction is understandable because the USA has an extremely well-established tradition of antitrust law and policy. However, as will be seen, this reaction has some serious implications for the internationalisation of antitrust policy.[137] The fact that the US system of antitrust is strong, and that US policy-makers are mostly unwilling to consider the EC system of antitrust for guidance on how antitrust policy may be internationalised means that the Commission will find it hard to advocate the development of an international system of antitrust – a proposal the Commission is in favour of – on the basis of the principles and ideas developed in the EC system over the years. It is doubtful whether the USA, and several other countries,[138] will regard the EC system of antitrust – which provides a model of internationalisation of antitrust policy – as a useful example for how to develop a comprehensive

---

[134] Gerber, *Competition*, p. 5.   [135] See pp. 278–9 below.
[136] See the Commission 28th Report on Competition Policy 1998, pp. 116–18. See also ch. 9.
[137] See pp. 277–80 below.
[138] An example is Norway, which has been reluctant to model its antitrust law on that of the EC. See F. Engzelius, 'The Norwegian Competition Act 1983' (1996) 17 *European Competition Law Review* 384.

international system of antitrust. This can be seen from the number of occasions over the years on which the USA rejected proposals put forward by the EC for such a system.[139] This situation has led to a conflict of views between the USA and the EC which seems to constitute a hurdle in the face of internationalisation of antitrust policy. This is an extremely important issue to which the discussion will return in chapter 9.

Implications of the analysis

In spite of the state of stagnation and the divisive conflicts which the EC has suffered at certain stages of its existence,[140] its system of antitrust seems to have been largely successful. The political significance and influence of the system has been as extensive as its economic and legal impact. The success of the system can be looked at from the following angle:

The relationship between EC and domestic antitrust laws

The convergence of domestic antitrust laws seems to carry various implications for the separation between EC and domestic levels. In marking a new departure for the traditional EC/Member State relationship, this convergence has furnished an important example of how EC membership and this 'new legal order of international law' affected the national legal order. This impact can be seen in light of the fact that convergence has even been considered by Member States, which, on more than one occasion, seemed unwilling to shift from their well-established systems of antitrust to the EC model.[141]

Convergence is not necessarily free from difficulties. Even with the existence of a comprehensive textual and procedural harmonisation, there can still be scope for divergence between the EC and Member States on the one hand and among the Member States themselves on the other, in so far as

---

[139] See D. Gerber, 'The US–European Conflict over the Globalisation of Antitrust Law' (1999) 34 *New England Law Review* 123, 130. Also, pp. 258–9 below.

One can also add that the USA does not believe that international antitrust policy should usurp its own. Furthermore the USA seems to be sceptical over how far the EC focuses on competitive impact as opposed to non-economic factors. See further ch. 9.

[140] See generally Craig and De Burca, *EU Law*, pp. 13–14.

[141] A good example is Germany. See P. Norman, 'Bonn Plans Cartel Law Change', *Financial Times*, 28 April 1997; S. Held, 'German Antitrust Law and Policy' (1992) *Fordham Corporate Law Institute* 311; R. Bechtold, 'Antitrust Law in the European Community and Germany – an Uncoordinated Co-Existence?' (1992) *Fordham Corporate Law Institute* 343.

policies underlying EC and domestic antitrust laws may differ.[142] It is true that such disparity may not present a difficulty if there is sufficient flexibility at the national level to accommodate the grounding of EC antitrust law within domestic legal orders and if the antitrust laws – EC and domestic – reflect general underlying principles. Still, divergence may prove problematic where the direct consequence of convergence leads to obfuscation in the relationship between EC and domestic antitrust laws, with the more subtle differences between the two not being considered.

Convergence may increase interest at the domestic level in developments at EC level, which may promote more two-way traffic between them. Moreover, it can be seen as a vote of confidence in the EC system of antitrust. At the same time, responsiveness to domestic legal culture in different Member States will inevitably lead to nationally specific antitrust laws,[143] albeit ones with a common genesis (as a result of convergence).[144] Furthermore, convergence may eventually allow for a better division of competence between EC and national spheres, but in the short term, the problems associated with overlapping jurisdiction and the ensuing legal uncertainties are likely to remain.

An additional comment should be made on the co-ordinating role of the Commission in relation to decentralised enforcement of EC antitrust law. Through this capacity, the Commission will be passively overseeing the way domestic antitrust laws develop. To ensure effective co-ordination, the Commission will need to facilitate informal contacts between domestic antitrust authorities, which will surely increase the importance of EC antitrust law. If this happens, the latter's influence on domestic antitrust laws may lead to increased interest at the national level in the way the former develops.

The voluntary adoption of EC antitrust law norms in the legal systems of Member States can be contrasted with the experience of Central and Eastern European countries, where approximation of laws has been a priority for

---

[142] See B. Bishop and S. Bishop, 'Reforming Competition Policy: Bundeskartellamt – Model or Muddle' (1996) 17 *European Competition Law Review* 207.
   Given that EC antitrust law is shaped by policies underlying it, convergence of domestic antitrust laws within the EC depends not only on formal adoption of text and procedure of EC antitrust law at domestic level, but ultimately on the convergence of those policies. See Maher, 'Alignment'.
[143] The importance of culture has already been spelt out in chs. 3 and 4. See generally Haucher and Moran, *Capitalism*, p. 3.
[144] See J. Jacquemin, 'The International Dimension of European Competition Policy' (1993) 31 *Journal of Common Market Studies* 91.

the Commission. Of course, convergence within the EC cannot be equated with the approximation of laws elsewhere in Europe. It is this angle to which the discussion now turns.

The EC and its agreements with neighbouring countries

Some emphasis was placed above on the Commission's initiatives on a wider level in Europe. These efforts have led to the conclusion of different types of agreements between the Commission and its neighbouring countries. Clearly, the importance of the EC system of antitrust has increased in light of these efforts. As the Commission has linked some of these agreements (Association Agreements) to the objective of future accession to the EC,[145] it has placed itself, and the EC, in a superior bargaining position. Including an approximation of law requirement in those agreements has meant that EC antitrust law is becoming increasingly transposed into different legal systems and traditions. Arguably, this should be seen as one of the main successes of EC antitrust law experience. Accommodating EC-like antitrust law in Central and Eastern European countries seems to indicate that EC antitrust law continues to be of importance in achieving further integration. Thus, the EC is likely to expand in geographic terms, whilst at the same time maintaining the rules and principles on which it was originally based and which have contributed to its development over the last forty-five years or so. This seems to have equipped the Commission with the confidence and experience to advocate EC antitrust thinking beyond all EC and European boundaries.

EC antitrust law on the international plane

It was said above that the EC has been particularly keen to demonstrate its antitrust lessons at a higher level, mainly through participating in multilateral discussions and contributing to the work of international organisations dealing with antitrust policy. However, the EC's success in this instance cannot be equated with that in the context of its relationship with its Member States, nor with that of its efforts at a wider European level.

---

[145] See the Commission's document on 'The Enlargement Negotiations after Helsinki' MEMO/00/6, 6 February 2000.

As far as the international plane is concerned, the EC has been presented with a 'double-edged sword': an opportunity and a challenge regarding its antitrust thinking. At one end of the spectrum, this is an opportunity for the EC to inform the world on how to set up and operate a strong and successful new type of 'international system of antitrust'.[146] With its successes at both EC and European levels, the EC seems to be justified in advocating its views on a blueprint for an international system of antitrust. At the other end of the spectrum, it is a challenge because the EC is competing with countries that have a strong antitrust tradition. A leading example is the USA, which is keen neither on surrendering to international antitrust interventions by international organisations, nor enthusiastic about receiving antitrust lessons from the European side of the Atlantic.

The Commission as a supranational institution

Pushing the discussion to its extremes, it is clear that the Commission – as a supranational institution – has contributed immensely to the success of the EC system of antitrust and its growing influence. In fact, the position of the Commission is rather special. The Commission is an EC institution and in becoming a leading player in the EC system of antitrust, it has confirmed its commitment to shaping this newly created legal order. Yet, the Commission is also an international institution, or a supranational one to say the least. This is not only confirmed by the fact that the EC is 'a new legal order of international law', but more importantly, by how the Commission has developed the EC system of antitrust, both within and outside the boundaries of the EC. In this way, the Commission has evolved into an institution with an international antitrust thinking. Expanding the international reach of EC antitrust law by the Commission, has been encouraged by several commentators.[147] Since an early stage in the development of the EC, the Commission has paid close attention to the relationship between EC and domestic antitrust law. The original goal of the Commission within EC antitrust policy was to strengthen the role of the EC system of antitrust as a whole. Through committing itself to enhancing the system,

---

[146] See Commission 28th Report on Competition Policy 1998, p. 118.
[147] See J. Friedberg, 'The Convergence of Law in an Era of Political Integration: the *Wood Pulp* and *Alcoa* Effects Doctrine' (1991) *University of Pittsburgh Law Review* 289, 322–3.

the Commission has successfully expanded the importance and influence of the system. This success has depended to a large extent on the support the Commission has received from other key EC institutions, such as the courts, the Council and Parliament,[148] and from important domestic forces, such as the sectors of national industry. The future success of the Commission, especially as far as its international antitrust thinking is concerned, will definitely continue to depend on these players. Still its success will also depend on the power of the Member States, which will arise from factors such as the extent to which they seek to co-operate with one another; the extent to which domestic politicians and policy-makers consider antitrust policy is important; and the extent to which officials of domestic antitrust authorities believe they can combat anti-competitive practices as satisfactorily as the directorate-general of antitrust in Brussels.

Conclusion

Looking at the developments of the EC system of antitrust over the last forty-five years, it is clear that it has been successful and its success has immensely contributed towards its current, advanced state. Those developments have been gradual, but also largely unpredictable. The EC antitrust law experience is of significance not only for countries seeking to develop systems of antitrust law, but also for those in favour of furthering the process of internationalisation of antitrust policy.

The degree to which this experience is seen as valuable for these purposes depends on extrinsic as well as intrinsic factors. The former include the willingness of policy-makers in other countries to utilise EC antitrust experience for inspiration. Conversely, intrinsic factors, on the other hand, include how the EC system of antitrust will develop in the light of new acts of accession to the EC and the relationship between the EC and national levels. How these factors will evolve and what kind of forces they will bring with them will undoubtedly shape the Community of today and tomorrow and will impact on the process of internationalisation of antitrust policy.

---

[148] See Parliament resolution on the Commission 28th Report on Competition Policy 1998, Commission Report: SEC 1999-743; Bull. 5–1999, point 1.2.48.

6

Sovereignty

This chapter examines the doctrine of state sovereignty and its significance for the internationalisation of antitrust policy. There is an abundance of literature discussing the doctrine in general and its considerations. However, there is very little said about sovereignty and antitrust policy,[1] and even less on the relationship between sovereignty and the internationalisation of antitrust policy.

It would be desirable to explain at the outset the author's decision to examine the doctrine in the present book and his decision to do so in this chapter in particular. The decision to devote an entire chapter of the book to sovereignty comes in light of the fact that the doctrine – although perhaps not the entire building – is one of the pillars on which the internationalisation of antitrust policy stands. As will become very clear during the course of the chapter, an important question in the process of internationalisation – leading to the creation of an international system of antitrust – is to what extent does the process involve or require relinquishing of sovereignty by countries; and to the extent that such relinquishing is involved or required, to what extent are countries willing to do so. Given the importance of this question and the fact that the doctrine has not, in the context of internationalisation of antitrust policy, been adequately considered in the literature, it becomes imperative to examine the doctrine. Doing so in the present chapter in particular should enhance and keep the

---

[1] See N. Averitt and R. Lande, 'Consumer Sovereignty: a United Theory of Antitrust and Consumer Protection Law' (1997) 65 *Antitrust Law Journal* 713; S. Farmer, 'Altering the Balance between Sovereignty and Competition: the Impact of *Seminole Tribe* on the Antitrust State Action Immunity Doctrine' (1997) 23 *Ohio Northern University Law Review* 1403; S. Farmer, 'Balancing State Sovereignty and Competition: an Analysis of the Impact of *Seminole Tribe* [*Seminole Tribe v. Florida*, 116 S. Ct. 114 (1996)] on the Antitrust State Action Immunity Doctrine' (1997) 42 *Villanova Law Review* 111; J. Griffin, 'When Sovereignties May Collide in the Antitrust Area?' (1994) 20 *Canada–United States Law Journal* 91; S. Snell, 'Controlling Restrictive Business Practices in Global Markets: Reflections on the Concepts of Sovereignty, Fairness and Comity' (1997) 33 *Stanford Journal of International Law* 215.

present discussion flowing in the right direction and at the right speed especially given that the EC antitrust experience was examined in the previous chapter. It will be remembered that establishing the EC involved a degree of limitation of the sovereignty of independent countries – a development that assumes great significance in any debate on EC law in general and EC antitrust law in particular. Furthermore, an examination of sovereignty opens up highly interesting and important issues in relation to the doctrine of extraterritoriality, which will be considered in the next chapter. Hence, the decision to examine sovereignty in the present chapter is both in order and appropriate.

The chapter is structured as follows. The first part examines the conceptual framework of sovereignty. It considers issues such as the legal, social and political roles of sovereignty. The second part considers the place of sovereignty under public international law generally. It analyses questions such as relinquishment and acquisition of sovereignty which are of importance in the internationalisation of antitrust policy. The third and fourth parts deal with the relationship between sovereignty and the internationalisation of antitrust policy and the emerging order in that relationship respectively. Finally, the fifth part offers a conclusion.

The conceptual framework of sovereignty

Rethinking sovereignty

Scholars of public international law have explained that under public international law a country occupies a definite part of the surface of the earth, within which it normally exercises, subject to the limitations imposed by public international law, jurisdiction over persons and things to the exclusion of the jurisdiction of other countries, and that when a country exercises such authority it is said to be 'sovereign' over the territory.[2] It is beyond the scope of this chapter to provide an exhaustive examination of the origin and historical perspective of sovereignty, rather its aim is to examine whether sovereignty plays any role in the world today and if so, how this affects the internationalisation of antitrust policy.

---

[2] J. Brierly, *The Law of Nations* (Oxford University Press, Oxford, 1963), p. 162. See also O. Higgins, 'The Legal Basis of Jurisdiction' in C. Olmstead (ed.), *International Law Association, Extraterritorial Application of Laws and Responses Thereto* (Oxford University Press, Oxford, 1984), p. 5.

Over the years, sovereignty permeated the understanding of national and international relations. It grew in parallel to the evolution of the modern state,[3] and it seems to reflect the evolving relationship between the state and civil society and, to a certain extent, between political authority and the business community.[4] However, sovereignty is not a fact, but rather a concept or a claim concerning the way political power is, or should be, exercised.[5]

Sovereignty has acquired many connotations over the centuries, which have given rise to the confusion surrounding it, in particular its association with national interest, national independence and national security. Other factors have also contributed to this confusion, such as the identification of sovereignty with the ability of countries to impose their will in certain cases, whether on their citizens, foreign nationals or other countries[6] – a point that this and the next chapter shall explain, and raises important questions under public international law in general and, the internationalisation of antitrust policy in particular. In light of this, in addition to the far-reaching transformation of the landscape of antitrust policy witnessed during the last century, especially in recent decades, the existence of such confusion creates a need to rethink the concept and practice of sovereignty.

Types of sovereignty

There are two types of sovereignty. On the one hand, there is 'operational sovereignty' – the power needed to exert supreme legitimate authority. On the other hand, there is 'state sovereignty', which remains the organising

---

[3] J. Anderson (ed.), *The Rise of the Modern State* (Wheatsheaf Books, Brighton, 1986).

[4] R. Ashley, 'Untying the Sovereign State: a Double Reading of the Anarchy Problematique' (1988) 17 *Journal of International Studies* 231; R. Walker, 'Sovereignty, Identity, Community: Reflections on the Horizons of Contemporary Political Practice' in R. Walker and S. Mendlovitz (eds.), *Contending Sovereignties: Redefining Political Community* (Boulder, Co., Lynne Rienner, London, 1990); F. Halliday, 'State and Society in International Relations: a Second Agenda' (1987) 16 *Journal of International Studies* 218; P. Muchlinski, *Multinational Enterprises and the Law* (Blackwell, Oxford, 1995).

[5] F. Hinsley, *Sovereignty* (C. A. Watts, London, 1966), p. 1.

[6] It has been argued that sovereignty should be seen in both positive and negative terms. In positive terms it may be described as the oneness of the legal system within the territory of a country, i.e. that the jurisdiction over the territory is in the hands of one authority, which is supreme. In negative terms sovereignty means a system of law and administration of justice which is free from outside interference. See D. Lasok and J. Bridge, *An Introduction to the Law and Institutions of the European Communities* (Butterworths, London, 1982), p. 262.

principle of international relations. This chapter is concerned with state sovereignty.

The significance of sovereignty

The significance of sovereignty raises difficult questions about its relevance to the internationalisation of antitrust policy. At one end of the spectrum – especially with the emergence of new countries – and for the purposes of the present book the emergence of new systems of antitrust – sovereignty seems to be an ever more important factor in the contemporary world. At the other end of the spectrum, lies the view that with the economic and cultural integration fuelled by the process of globalisation, sovereignty seems to be a less significant factor. An accelerated process of globalisation raises new questions about the practice of state sovereignty.[7]

The roles of sovereignty

The roles of sovereignty on the other hand concern its social, political and legal values. As far as the first two are concerned, it has become arguable that sovereignty serves both as a shield protecting national interests against foreign interference and influences and as a means for combating restraints on individual freedom by the economic power of persons, whether legal or natural ones. Yet, the position is less clear as far as the legal role of sovereignty is concerned. To establish whether sovereignty has a legal role to play or whether it simply exists in the crossroads between law and politics, the content of sovereignty has to be identified. This is an issue which is dealt with below.

In a way, the above discussion shows that there seems to be a paradox surrounding the concept of sovereignty, which has only recently emerged. In the 1970s, sovereignty was seriously questioned when both political scientists and international lawyers mounted a strong challenge from the cornerstone of their disciplines. This is evident from the writings of several scholars who have widely argued that during that period sovereignty was residual.[8] In spite of this, however, the concept of sovereignty remains a

---

[7] J. Rapsenau, 'Muddling, Meddling and Modelling: Alternative Approaches to the Study of World Politics in an Era of Rapid Change' (1979) 8 *Journal of International Studies* 130.

[8] J. Camilleri and J. Falk, *The End of Sovereignty?: the Politics of a Shrinking and Fragmenting World* (Edward Elgar, Aldershot, 1992).

vital issue in the world order. The conclusion to be drawn from this is that the concept may be seen to have been under revision but not yet extinct. Sovereignty is believed to carry an increasingly persuasive force. Indeed, claims to sovereignty have been on the increase. The concept has, moreover, been used as a shield by countries and their communities against domination or control by external influences including for the purposes of protection of national freedom. In this way at least the catchword of sovereignty continues to intoxicate national policies.[9]

Measuring the content of sovereignty

It is doubtful whether many concepts under public international law have been more vehemently debated in legal doctrine than that of sovereignty.[10] In addition, hardly any other concept has been so elastic, so much subject to modifications and consequently so confusing as that of sovereignty. The manifestations of the concept have been numerous. For different writers, sovereignty varies not only according to its alleged content, its legal implications and the prerequisites upon which it may be founded, but also the subject or object of which it is supposed to be an attribute. Diversity has also been a fundamental connotation of sovereignty. All these variations run so closely parallel to the political changes of time that it becomes almost impossible to determine whether the variation is a product of the political change, or vice versa. For these reasons, measuring the content of sovereignty does not seem to be particularly easy.

Some comments

Whichever of the functions described above is attached to the concept of sovereignty, one cannot derive, extract or deduce substantive rules or principles, whether general or specific, from the concept. Prominent scholars such as Kelsen repeatedly emphasised the triviality of this.[11] One can thus conclude that it is an illusion to believe that legal rules can be derived from the concept of sovereignty. It is entirely unjustified to derive any rights

---

[9] C. Jenks, *A New World of Law: a Study of the Creative Imagination in International Law* (Longman, Harlow, 1969), p. 131; W. Friedmann, *The Changing Structure of International Law* (Columbia University Press, New York, 1964), p. 35.

[10] M. Korowicz, 'Some Present Aspects of Sovereignty in International Law' (1961) 102 *Recueil des Cours* 1, 5.

[11] See generally H. Kelsen, *Principles of International Law* (Rinehart & Winton, New York, 1966).

for sovereign countries from the concept of sovereignty. One cannot draw any conclusions from this concept, other than that a sovereign country is a subject of public international law, upon which rights are conferred and obligations imposed. As the discussion below shows, this constitutes a central aspect of the significance of sovereignty within the internationalisation of antitrust policy.

Sovereignty and the framework of ideas which surround it are a dominant feature of contemporary political debate, analysis and policy. There seems to be a sovereignty discourse – a way of thinking about the world in which countries are the principal actors, the repositories of power and the principal objects of interest. Debate about national policies, national competition, national culture and national actors and objectives are a constitutive part of this discourse. Measures that support the state reinforce the sense of national community, advance the national interest and represent actions in which this discourse plays a key explanatory role.

Sovereignty under public international law

Before addressing the significance of sovereignty in the internationalisation of antitrust policy, it is essential to examine the scope of the doctrine under public international law generally. In particular, this part of the chapter looks at the question of the acquisition and relinquishment of sovereignty since this is an issue of central concern for the purposes of the present book.

Who enjoys sovereignty under public international law?

Public international lawyers would agree that sovereignty is attributed to countries in the world community. That much seems clear. Countries are considered to be sovereign according to a formula embedded in public international law.[12] Since only countries can be sovereign, other subjects of public international law, such as international organisations and legal and natural persons, would thus be subordinate. Looking at that formula would reveal the reasons for this.

---

[12] Article I of the Convention on Rights and Duties of States signed at Montevideo 26 December 1933 in force 26 December 1934 provides that: 'The state as a person of international law should possess the following qualifications (a) a permanent population; (b) a defined territory; (c) government; and (d) capacity to enter into relations with the other states.'

Acquisition and relinquishment of sovereignty

In order to know when sovereignty is relinquished or acquired, the relevant formula under public international law must be consulted. The position here is as follows: the assumption is generally made that sovereignty concerns the ability – in the sense of competence or authority – of a country to impose duties and confer rights, and that a country must retain a certain minimum of this power in order to be sovereign. This is the way in which sovereignty is acquired or retained. An issue that is of more importance for the purposes of the present chapter relates to the query of what does it take for countries to relinquish their sovereignty? To illustrate, reference is made to the case of the EC.

Member States of the EC have committed themselves to a legal order of unlimited duration.[13] The different treaties on which the EC, and later the European Union (EU), rest clearly have not led to a loss of the sovereignty of Member States, but a limitation, albeit in certain fields, thereof.[14] Arguably, this can be seen as a loss of sovereignty. However, one could say that Member States have not lost their sovereignty completely, but fetters in some cases, since they can always leave the EC, even if impossible politically.

An interesting question in this regard relates to what would be needed for Member States to relinquish their sovereignty and consequently for the EC as such to become a sovereign (federal) country. Surely, this would not happen with the abolition of the veto power of Member States in one sector. The position is less clear however, once the veto power is abolished in several sectors, in all sectors or even with the establishment of a central government in the EC. Somewhere along this continuum, the point must be reached where Member States are no longer sovereign under public international law. In spite of this, one point is very obvious: through creating a supranational system of antitrust as part of a wider legal order, Member States do not seem to have relinquished their sovereignty. This point has obvious implications for the internationalisation of antitrust policy because it may be possible to argue that creating an international system of antitrust – which as we saw in chapter 1 is the most central and ambitious form of internationalisation of antitrust policy – cannot reasonably be expected to involve a relinquishment of national sovereignty; a limitation thereupon, however, can be legitimately expected.

---

[13] See Article 312 EC.   [14] See ch. 5.

Sovereignty is relative not absolute

The general consensus under public international law is that sovereignty is not absolute. Countries do not enjoy 'unqualified sovereignty'. This means that as long as more than one country exists in the international family, countries cannot have absolute freedom of action individually. The understanding is that absolute sovereignty would conflict with the principles of public international law – a law binding on all countries – and would afford countries the opportunity to ignore the binding force of those principles. Thus, from the perspective of these principles, the sovereignty attributed to countries cannot be of an absolute character – for otherwise there would be a contradiction in terms. In legal terms, the more acceptable view is that sovereignty must be relative: Public international law imposes restrictions on countries; and their rights or freedom are relative to those restrictions.[15]

Relative sovereignty acknowledges the fact that countries are included in a 'web of relationships' which necessarily imposes certain limitations upon their will.[16] These limitations vary of course from time to time, all according to the development – whether in an expanding or retracting direction – of public international law. In this way, it is said that one of the characteristics of sovereign countries as subjects of public international law is that they are immediately subordinated to public international law and, consequently, that there is no other intermediate supranational law governing the state.[17]

Thus, in order to determine whether a country is sovereign under public international law, and therefore subject to it, one must discover the character of the law immediately governing the country, i.e. whether the law is international or otherwise in nature. Here it would be meaningless to apply the definition of public international law as a law binding on sovereign countries. This can be illustrated with reference to the distinction between the EC and the USA. In the EC, Member States are considered

---

[15] See H. Kelsen, 'The Principles of Sovereign Equality of States as a Basis for International Organization' (1944) 53 *Yale Law Journal* 207, 208. See also Kelsen, *Principles*, p. 441.

[16] C. de Visscher, *Théorie et réalité en droit international public* (Paris, 1953); translated into English by P. E. Corbett, *Theory and Reality in Public International Law* (Princeton University Press, Princeton, 1968).

[17] Obviously, the position here is arguable, especially in the case of the EC. Member States of the EC, though subject to international law, are bound by the treaties establishing the EC. The argument can still be made, however, that Member States are still subject to international law, in spite of the existence of the EC.

to be immediately subordinated to public international law, whilst in the USA states are considered to be immediately subordinate to national law, i.e. US law. If an agreement or a treaty concluded between sovereign countries is based on the understanding that one or several of its participants shall surrender some of the qualities which under public international law are considered essential for sovereignty, then the treaty, at least in that respect, is no longer public international law. The several states of the US federal system lost their sovereignty in the public international law sense, the Member States of the EC have not.

Vertical relationship

Regarding the relation between public international law and national law, as opposed to the inter-country relation, there is no minimum competence required of countries in order to be sovereign. In this way, the notion of sovereignty would serve no purpose. As was seen earlier in the present chapter, public international law can restrict the freedom of countries to any extent without reaching a point where the bounds of sovereignty are split. Such a point does not exist. International law may restrict the freedom of countries; it may limit their competence (power) until there remain only minor administrative functions for the country to fulfil and may go even further. Public international law may even imply the abolition of multiple statehood altogether and the creation of a new world state. Obviously, in this case – with the absence of individual sovereign countries – sovereignty is relinquished.

Thus, sovereignty may be relinquished to another country, or group of countries or all other countries, but not to the sphere of public international law. Relinquishment of sovereignty is a horizontal, not vertical, phenomenon. This is not to suggest that international agreements always confer rights and impose duties upon countries co-extensively, or that it is compatible with public international law that a country surrenders its sovereignty by concluding an agreement with other countries, or that customary law, especially if particular in character, cannot have like effects. It is merely suggested that the international law system – in this case an international system of antitrust – may expand its jurisdiction at the expense of the national law systems – in this case domestic systems of antitrust – without infringing the sovereignty of countries, and that this issue lies entirely within the realm of the public international law–national law relationship. In other words, all countries cannot lose their sovereignty, unless a new world state is established which would extinguish the multitude of countries.

Substance of sovereignty

This seemingly obvious conclusion has one further implication. Under public international law, the formula on sovereignty cannot be substance-oriented. The fact that substance cannot constitute the criteria for sovereignty can be explained in the following manner. As was seen above, there is the proposition that an international system may encroach upon national systems without infringing the sovereignty of countries. Public international law may – by regulating and restricting the freedoms of countries – reduce to any extent the domestic sphere, and thus there would be no field that could not be regulated by public international law. As a corollary to this, it is argued that there is the fact that public international law is a flexible legal system in a process of continuous development. It follows therefore that the substance of sovereignty, if there is such a thing, varies with the development of public international law. The substance of sovereignty cannot be static as, in order to establish any kind of substance of sovereignty, one must first analyse the principles of public international law in general. It is the total effect of public international law upon the domestic sphere that determines the boundaries of sovereignty. Sovereignty under public international law as a whole is in a constant state of change and evolution. The substance of sovereignty is viable and cannot be regarded as fixed and definite. It is important to both acknowledge and recognise this conclusion.

Thus, the concept of sovereignty is intimately linked to matters falling within the domestic domain and unregulated by public international law. The formula on sovereignty seems to relate to the possibility of a country independently governing matters in the domestic domain. Or somewhat more concretely: in order to be subject to public international law, a country must be able to independently govern – without the legal authority of another country – those matters which fall within the domestic sphere (and not the international law sphere), that is, it must be sovereign. The scope of the domestic domain can be determined only on the basis of the relation between public international law and national law at a particular moment, and hardly with any precision. For instance, one could say that a country lacks sovereignty on the grounds of that relationship at a particular moment. Since – and this is vital – the substance of sovereignty is viable, there cannot be an international law formula on sovereignty that is substance-oriented, i.e. a formula which prescribes that, in order for a country to be sovereign, it must be able independently to govern certain matters. All that such formulas may predict is that sovereignty has to do with substance within the domestic domain.

Sovereignty and the internationalisation of antitrust policy

Searching for an appropriate nexus

The concept of sovereignty has implications for the creation, operation and enforcement of domestic systems of antitrust. To an extent, the truth behind this statement is not hard to deduce. The idea of protecting competition itself is, in many ways, closely linked to elements of national interest and policy considerations, which themselves are attached to sovereignty. Further, implications can be identified through considering the different dimensions of sovereignty.

The two dimensions of sovereignty

Sovereignty is a bi-dimensional concept, and a full account must be taken of each relevant dimension in order to facilitate an understanding of its relevance to the internationalisation of antitrust policy.

The first dimension: sovereignty from a national perspective

From a national perspective, sovereignty is relevant to the subject-matter of the present book for two reasons. The first concerns the view held by certain countries that a form of internationalisation of antitrust policy – through which autonomous international institutions will be created – amounts to a clear interference with their national sovereignty. One does not need to go further than the position of the USA to be able to see that this is actually the case.[18] The second reason is related to the fact that extraterritorial application of the domestic antitrust laws of one country – an issue examined in the following chapter – may be deemed to encroach upon national sovereignty of other countries. The most frequent argument in the diplomatic protests lodged against reliance by countries – especially

---

[18] See J. Griffin, 'What Business People Want from a World Antitrust Code' (1999) 34 *New England Law Review* 39, 45.

by the USA – on the doctrine of extraterritoriality in antitrust policy has been that the extension of enforcement jurisdiction by those countries over foreign firms in antitrust policy matters transcending national boundaries infringes the sovereignty of other countries. For example, during the US antitrust proceedings against the Swiss Watchmaking Industry, the Swiss Government claimed that the application by the USA of its antitrust law in the case would infringe Swiss sovereignty, violate international law and harm the international relations of the USA.[19] The implications of these reasons prompt a particular need to examine the doctrine of sovereignty and its place from a national perspective under the internationalisation of antitrust policy.

The second dimension: sovereignty from an international perspective

Having outlined the national dimension of sovereignty, the international dimension is examined next. Sovereignty faces certain limitations under the creation of an international system of antitrust. It is legitimate to suggest that a form of internationalisation of antitrust policy – as a result of which autonomous international institutions are established – presupposes some kind of limitation on the sovereignty of individual countries. Support for this suggestion can be sought from the previous chapter, where it was demonstrated how the EC provides a good example of limitations on the sovereignty of individual countries. This, it was argued, is evident from the way the EC has created a 'new legal order of international law'.[20] The following chapter extends the scope of this issue to enforcement powers of countries in antitrust matters which transcend national boundaries. It will be argued in that context that curtailing reliance by individual countries on the doctrine of extraterritoriality can be regarded – albeit indirectly – as a kind of limitation on the sovereignty of the countries concerned. Arguably, reliance on the doctrine of extraterritoriality in the field of antitrust policy seems to be triggered by sovereignty concerns. It would not require a great deal of imagination to picture a situation where certain countries would claim that their aim in enforcing their antitrust laws extraterritorially is based on the need to protect their interests and prerogatives. Not

---

[19] See *United States* v. *Watchmaking of Switzerland Information Centre, Inc.* 133 F. Supp. 40 (SDNY 1955).
[20] See ch. 5.

infrequently such interests and prerogatives have been identified as defences of national sovereignty.[21] Judged properly, such a limitation does not necessarily need to be regarded as either severe or undesirable. It can simply be seen as a necessary concomitant of the creation and/or operation of an international system of antitrust.

Towards an international system of antitrust

The first thing to be said about sovereignty and an international system of antitrust is that one cannot expect the latter to be as far-reaching as either the Constitution of the USA or the treaties establishing the EC, and later the EU. For this reason, it would be an exaggeration in principle to hold that establishing an international system of antitrust would open up a relinquishment/acquisition of sovereignty debate *in absolute terms*. In other words, it would not be possible to argue that under this system, countries would absolutely lose their sovereignty and that whatever autonomous institutions were created under it would become wholly sovereign as a result. Nevertheless, as the above discussion made clear, a limitation on national sovereignty in this respect can be expected.

The existence of an international system of antitrust

It would be a misuse of the concept of sovereignty to maintain that the existence of autonomous institutions in an international system of antitrust, endowed with the competence to bind different countries, is incompatible with the sovereignty of contracting countries under the system. The freedom of action of the contracting countries would certainly not be any more restricted under this system than by, say, the EC. Yet, the difference between these two systems and between this system and all other international systems remains only a quantitative, not a qualitative one, since under any legal order – whether national, regional or international – unlimited freedom of action for countries is impossible.

An international system of antitrust in this case may, as an international order with binding powers, differ from other international systems, but only in the degree of its centralisation. It is not correct, therefore, to say that such a system, owing to its centralised character, should necessarily cause countries to no longer be considered sovereign or for them to be deprived

---

[21] See further ch. 7.

of the power legally to act independently in the international community. Neither does the fact that autonomous institutions exist within the system very much restrict the freedom of action of the contracting countries, nor does the fact that the system is more centralised than other international systems justify the argument that the existence of the system is incompatible with the nature of public international law or the sovereignty of countries. In any event, it is doubtful whether an international system of antitrust would be more centralised than the EC. Yet, in the case of the latter it is difficult to seriously assert that there has been a complete relinquishment of sovereignty.

Transfer of competence

In creating an international system of antitrust, one can expect a transfer of competence bottom-up under the system, from the national level to the international level. Of course, there are difficulties if only some countries, as opposed to all countries, commit themselves to such transfer of competence. For example, this would bring the entire existence of the system into question, in terms of how international this system would be. This issue is dealt with in chapter 9.

The present chapter concentrates on this transfer of competence as opposed to its consequences. In particular, the chapter examines whether sovereignty does or does not presuppose a minimum competence, i.e. whether the sovereignty of a country would be unaffected if that country were to transfer its competence to autonomous institutions in an international system of antitrust. In light of the view that sovereignty within public international law can mean only the legal authority or competence of a country limited and limitable only by public international law, the conclusion can be drawn that establishing an international system of antitrust in the sense of transfer of competence from national to international level should not necessarily amount to an infringement of the sovereignty of countries.

However, creating an international system of antitrust would be problematic if there would be an over-emphasis on the significance of the basis for the specific legal order which the contracting countries establish. If the basis is a treaty, then it will be international law and would remain so, then the parties concluding that treaty will be subordinated to public international law alone – i.e. they will still be sovereign. Quite different is the case where a constitution of a federal country is established by an international treaty. Here national law arises from public international law. In separating treaties and constitutions into strict categories – public international law and national law – the above view that sovereignty may be relinquished only in quantity but not in quality can be upheld – i.e. that under a treaty the freedom of country action may be more or less restricted, without the relinquishment of sovereignty.

Yet, there is a risk of over-formalism in this regard. If country A transfers its legislative competence in antitrust policy to country B, by establishing a framework between them, then from country A's standpoint, it is no longer the treaty implementing the framework that represents the highest level of the legal order, but rather country B's domestic system of antitrust. From the perspective of country B, it has full freedom of action as against country A, wherefore the new framework has become wholly incorporated into country B's sphere of power. Hence, there would be no international system of antitrust in the true sense of the word (denoting an agreement between countries) since the system would extinguish the existence of country A in the world community. Therefore, it is important to distinguish between different systems of antitrust. This is a point that was explained above.[22] A true international system of antitrust would first of all involve more than two different countries, and secondly it would not involve a transfer of competence from one country to another.

Thus, loss of quality as a sovereign country happens as the law created by the system assumes the character of national law because of the centralisation of the order constituted under the system, as in the case of a treaty by which a federal country is established. Regarding the international law status of country A, in the example above, it can be said that the order constituted by the agreement between country A and country B is international only with regard to its creation by a bilateral international agreement, but not regarding its structure. The conclusion then is that countries, in order to be subjects of public international law, must be sovereign within a particular territory, and in order to be sovereign they must enjoy a threshold minimum competence. However, the country's competence must be enjoyed only in a horizontal respect – as against other countries – and not in a vertical respect – as against public international law.

---

[22] See pp. 10–12 above.

The emerging order

Understanding the concept of sovereignty and its place and relevance to the internationalisation of antitrust policy initially requires an examination of the nature and evolution of sovereignty, both at a conceptual framework, and as it emerges in contemporary political practice. Accordingly, the above discussion looked at these basic issues, briefly showing how the modern idea of sovereignty has emerged over the centuries as a particular way of associating the structure of political power with a corresponding structure of territorial space.

Are countries the principal actors?

The theory of sovereignty portrays a world in which supreme power is exerted within a particular territorial boundary. Who or what exerts that power may not be straightforward, but it is usually assumed to be sovereign countries. Consistent with this idea, nation, state and national power are often considered to coincide to form the 'nation-state'. Within its own boundaries a country enjoys supremacy; recognising no higher or superior authority. Beyond the national boundaries are other sovereign countries. In this image of the world, the principal actor is the nation-state. Countries are characterised by their particular national territories, preferences, culture, interest and policy considerations. Associated with that territory are all the people who live within it – including firms operating therein – and who identify themselves as members of the national community.

How has sovereignty evolved?

One may of course anticipate an important conclusion that the theory of sovereignty is limited, either as a description of how the world is, how it is evolving or how it might develop. It is important to observe the ongoing process of relentless globalisation. Not only is the world experiencing progressive integration but, perhaps paradoxically, it is also witnessing a process of progressive decentralisation of power and authority.

The existence of other players

Paradoxically, although the activity of countries has been expanding, their role has increasingly been focused on the central goal of creating a suitable environment for their domestic firms to compete in what have become global markets. In attempting to meet this objective, countries are by no means the only players. International organisations such as the Organisation for Economic Cooperation and Development (OECD) and regional organisations such as the EC play an increasingly complex and vigorous role in cultivating and shaping antitrust law and policy as well as other laws and policies.

In this environment, the discourse of sovereignty may tend to marginalise many questions, which increasingly seem relevant. These include the extent to which one can expect or rely on countries to shape technological change to meet social or national objectives; the extent to which countries can be said to be sovereign over a domain in which technological development is in part drawn from within them and in part required from outside; the extent to which the nation-state can even be said to be setting its own agenda; and the extent to which due to the level of independence between countries this can reasonably be considered possible.

Today's world is one of continuous and fast transition, with major implications for governments, business firms, communities and various other interest groups alike. This has brought about particular challenges, including how the relationship between the different players should be regulated, and whether countries should be considered the principal actors. The answers herein may not be obvious, but clearly any alternative perspective to that depicted by the discourse of sovereignty must be sensitive to the significance of the economic and technological transformations. But the impact of change goes well beyond these factors.

The emergence of business power on the international scene

This section does not examine in detail the relationship between sovereign countries and private business firms, since this is an issue that is carefully covered in later parts of the book.[23] The section merely provides some description of this relationship in the context of the present chapter.[24]

Countries and business firms stand in complete contrast. A country is expected to protect the public interest, and for long it was regarded as the

---

[23] See ch. 9.

[24] A useful discussion of these issues, especially with regard to the previous and contemporary positions, can be found in Muchlinski, *Multinational*, ch. 1.

only device for public participation and control in the shaping of society. Firms, by contrast, exist to promote their self-interests. The interesting developments which emerged during the twentieth century have dictated that the growth of multinational enterprises (MNEs) has been matched by the growth in government regulation of economic activity, including regulation of MNEs outside national boundaries.[25]

The theory and practice of political economy has for many years experienced no major problems with this: if a firm was deemed to limit individual freedom – for example by reverting to practices which would exploit consumers – the country concerned could, and sometimes did, intervene to prevent this. In other words, as communities of countries developed and expanded, the sovereign powers of countries developed and expanded in parallel, and continued to regulate those communities. This has led several scholars to profess the existence of a contrast between the state and the market. Some scholars have argued that underlying the state are the concepts of territory, loyalty, exclusivity and the monopoly of the legitimate use of coercion. Markets, on the other hand, are associated with the concepts of functional integration, conceptual relationships and expanding interdependence with consumers.[26] According to this view, these present fundamentally different ways of ordering human relations, and the tension between them has had a profound impact on the course of modern history and is a crucial problem in the study of political economy.[27]

However, as the economic activity of firms is increasingly becoming more global, this description of the relationship is changing accordingly. It has been argued that for the last three decades there has been an unprecedented transfer of sovereignty from countries to international firms; instead of being pooled (as it were) upwards into inter- or supra-national reservoirs of a consciously political nature (where it should be placed), sovereignty

---

[25] For an account on the definition of the term 'MNEs' see Muchlinski, *Multinational*, pp. 12–15. See also the work of other scholars, who have argued that the fact that the activities of MNEs can be regulated and the fact that this may place them in a weak position promotes rather than excludes adopting a co-operative approach when examining the relationship between countries and MNEs. See J. Stopford and S. Strange, *Rival States, Rival Firms* (Cambridge University Press, Cambridge, 1991).

[26] See the interesting views of J. Jackson about markets and their relationship with countries, noting in particular that 'markets can be very beneficial, and, even when not beneficial, market forces demand respect and can cause great difficulties when not respected'. See J. Jackson, *The Jurisprudence of GATT and the WTO* (Cambridge University Press, Cambridge, 2000), p. 6.

[27] See R. Gilpin, *The Political Economy of International Relations* (Princeton University Press, Princeton, 1987), pp. 10–11.

is seeping away downwards into the invisible tuber system of politically irresponsible business power.[28] Such development seems to have enabled firms involved in international operations to evade or circumvent the laws of countries, and therefore democratic control. With an increased process of globalisation, these firms can employ their personnel and corporate structure to drain know-how away from one country to another in less than it takes to tell a tale. As some commentators have convincingly argued, it is total futility to talk about a 'US firm' or a 'German firm' when the factories of the firm are located in Malaysia, its IT programmes in India and its executives are recruited worldwide.[29] The effect of this situation can, *inter alia*, mean that firms may choose to operate in jurisdictions with lax antitrust law enforcement. Thus, those firms will be able to avoid jurisdictions where antitrust law is strictly or seriously enforced.

International political economy seeks to explain international political-economic relations and how they affect the global systems of production, exchange and distribution. International political economy views the nation-state as the key actor in the global system, and the organiser of the international political order. Countries are treated as the alternative to the market, which in turn is seen as the organiser of economic relations. As the above discussion shows, there seems to be a particular emphasis on this contrast between 'countries' and 'markets'.

However, the concept of countries versus markets is flawed because the market is a structure, not an actor, and hence cannot be considered a counterpart to a country. The appropriate counterpoint is the multinational firms, the key non-country actor dominating both domestic and international markets.

Control by countries of business power led to the latter being used by the former to further many goals and national interests, in particular to extend the jurisdictional reach of domestic antitrust laws beyond territorial limits. As the following chapter demonstrates, the USA in particular practised this method of extraterritoriality.[30]

---

[28] See L. Eden, 'Bringing the Firm Back in: Multinationals in International Political Economy' in L. Eden and E. Potter (eds.), *Multinationals in Global Political Economy* (Macmillan, New York, 1993).

[29] R. Weintraub, 'Globalization Effect on Antitrust Law' (1999) 34 *New England Law Review* 27.

[30] See R. Vernon, *Sovereignty at Bay: the Multinational Spread of US Enterprises* (Longman, London, 1971), pp. 231–47; 'Sovereignty at Bay: Ten Years after' (1981) 35 *International Organization* 517.

Conclusion

This chapter has dealt with the concept of sovereignty, and how it is expressed in current political analysis, its relevance to the internationalisation of antitrust policy and its impact on this process and vice versa.

This sovereignty discourse is of far more than peripheral interest. It is the way in which mainstream discussions of many of the most contentious issues in the world are advanced, arbitrated and resolved. Yet, compared to the authority the concept should exert, its basis and validity have received remarkably little attention. True, there is a body of literature dealing with some aspects of sovereignty – in particular the relation between sovereignty and public international law, and the relationship between sovereign countries and their corresponding national communities. Nevertheless, overarching questions about the enduring value of the concept as a way of explaining how power in the contemporary world is actually exercised, or how change may be achieved, remain outstanding and require urgent attention. The purpose of this chapter was to explore a number of these questions and pave the way for finding answers.

It is clear that any form of internationalisation of antitrust policy, including the creation of an international system of antitrust, will not prevent a country system of antitrust from co-existing. However, it seems that an international system of antitrust may override the construct of sovereignty to the extent necessary to achieve common goals. If there remain additional concerns on the part of countries concerning sovereignty, then such concerns can be alleviated by introducing a principle of subsidiarity. Under this principle, countries can continue to exercise those functions which they can better perform than autonomous institutions within the system.[31]

---

[31] See, for example, Article 5 EC which contains the principle of subsidiarity under EC law. Some discussion on the issue can be found in ch. 5. See further J. Trachtman, 'L'Etat, c'est nous: Sovereignty, Economic Integration and Subsidiarity' (1992) 33 *Harvard International Law Journal* 459, 460.

7

Extraterritoriality

This chapter examines the doctrine of extraterritoriality in antitrust policy and the difficult issues it has triggered over the years. Reference has already been made more than once during the course of the discussion in the previous chapter to the fact that antitrust enforcement by several antitrust authorities around the world has become extraterritorial over the years. In light of this, it should not be difficult to see that an examination of such an activity is of extreme importance in the internationalisation of antitrust policy. The chapter is structured as follows. The first part considers the question of jurisdiction under public international law. The second part evaluates some fundamental issues underlying extraterritoriality. It advocates the view that the difficulties with extraterritoriality reside not only in the conflicts it has caused between countries, but also in the search for a compelling definition of it. The third part gives an account of developments in the USA and the EC in the area. The fourth part deals with the responses of countries which have been generated by reliance on extraterritoriality by other countries. The fifth part provides some reflections on extraterritoriality. It examines, *inter alia*, the role of the judiciary in asserting extraterritorial jurisdiction in antitrust policy. The sixth part examines and offers some proposals on how to avoid or minimise conflicts triggered by extraterritoriality. Finally, the seventh part concludes.

The question of jurisdiction

Traditional principles

It is apparent from the previous chapter that a fundamental attribute of sovereignty resides in the fact that an individual country is competent to enact laws that are binding upon persons as well as regulating conditions within its national boundaries.[1] This fundamental attribute of sovereignty arises from an important principle under public international law, namely the principle of territoriality.[2] On the basis of this principle, a country is able to enact and enforce laws within its boundaries. If a country seeks to assert jurisdiction over acts committed beyond its borders it might infringe the sovereignty of other countries, an action which can amount to a violation of principles of public international law. Yet as public international law developed, it became apparent that exceptions to the principle were inevitable. Several exceptions, therefore, have been introduced where the competence of countries may extend to certain situations beyond their national boundaries.[3] One exception is the nationality principle, which allows a country to assert jurisdiction over its nationals abroad.[4] A second exception is the protective principle of jurisdiction which permits a country to regulate offences abroad targeting its national security such as its political independence or territorial integrity. A third exception relates to the passive personality principle which covers situations in which a country will be able to assert jurisdiction over acts committed beyond national boundaries, that

---

[1] The ability of a country to enact and enforce its laws rests primarily on two grounds. The first is subject-matter jurisdiction, also known as legislative or prescriptive jurisdiction. According to this type of jurisdiction, a country has competence to enact laws, meaning 'to lay down general or individual rules through its legislative, executive and judicial bodies'. The second is enforcement jurisdiction. This type of jurisdiction covers a country's ability to enforce its laws, that is the power of a country to give effect to a general rule or an individual decision by means of substantive implementing measures which may include even coercion by the authorities. See Opinion of Advocate General Darmon in Case 114/85 A. Ahlström Osukeyhtiö v. Commission (Woodpulp) [1988] ECR 5139; [1988] 4 CMLR 901, p. 923.

[2] See P. Brown, 'The Codification of International Law' (1935) 29 American Journal of International Law 25; I. Brownlie, Principles of Public International Law (Oxford University Press, Oxford, 1998); R. Jennings and A. Watts (eds.), Oppenheim's International Law (Longman, London, 1996), vol. I, pp. 456–88; F. Mann, 'The Doctrine of Jurisdiction in International Law' (1964) 111 Recueil des Cours 9; M. Akehurst, 'Jurisdiction in International Law' (1972–3) 46 British Yearbook of International Law 145; D. Rosenthal and W. Knighton, National Laws and International Commerce: the Problem of Extraterritoriality (Routledge, London, 1982); A. Lowe, Extraterritorial Jurisdiction: an Annotated Collection of Legal Materials (Grotius, Cambridge, 1983); C. Olmstead, Extraterritorial Application of the Laws and Responses Thereto (Oxford University Press, Oxford, 1984); B. Hawk, United States, Common Market and International Antitrust (Prentice-Hall Law and Business, New York, 1993).

[3] See P. Muchlinski, Multinational Enterprises and the Law (Blackwell, Oxford, 1995), pp. 124–6 for a discussion on these exceptions, apart from the passive personality principle, in relation to the regulation of multinational enterprises.

[4] Under customary international law, a country is able to enforce its laws against its nationals, even when these laws have some effects beyond national borders. See France v. Turkey ('S.S. Lotus') (1927) PCIJ 9, 19; Denmark v. Germany (North Sea Continental Shelf) (1968) ICJ 3, 44–5.

harm its nationals abroad. A fourth exception is the objective territoriality principle, namely when an act is commenced outside the boundaries of a country but concluded within its territory.[5]

However, beyond the principle of territoriality and its exceptions, the competence of a country to assert jurisdiction over situations outside its territory, especially those involving foreign individuals, becomes highly questionable. In this situation, more than one country may assert jurisdiction, which means that a conflict is likely to arise between those countries. Nevertheless, generally it is thought that as long as a country does not attempt to apply its laws to conduct performed within the territory of another country, a mere assertion of the subject-matter jurisdiction by the former over individuals in the latter may not lead to any conflict between the countries concerned or to a violation of principles of public international law. Should the former seek enforcement though, the possibility of conflict and violation becomes obvious.[6]

Areas of economic law

The above principles of public international law were initially developed in the context of physical conduct – for example, the scenario of the poison where one person in country A sends poison from that country to country B which a person in the latter country consumes and dies as a result – and not in a context of economic conduct – for example, in the case of an agreement between business firms. Whether these principles could be invoked in the latter context was, for some time, considered to be a difficult conundrum. These principles did not seem to be sufficient to address questions of economic conduct, since they emerged with physical conduct in mind. Thus, it was not clear whether an individual country could assert jurisdiction over acts committed beyond its borders on the basis that these acts produced economic effects within its territory.

The 'effects' doctrine

To solve this conundrum, harmful economic effects were considered to be equivalent to effects of physical conduct originating from the territory of

---

[5] International lawyers have frequently cited the example where one person sends poison from one country to another as an adequate illustration.
[6] See Rosenthal and Knighton, *National*.

one country but concluded in another. This shift in position has received recognition, not under public international law, but in the jurisprudence of certain countries.[7] Given the imperative to address such economic harm, some countries adopted an expansive concept of competence. In doing so, they have heavily relied on a doctrine of 'effects', which has served as a basis to the doctrine of extraterritoriality in antitrust policy.

The USA was amongst the first of those countries to recognise the 'effects' doctrine,[8] though it was believed at one point that US antitrust laws did not apply to activities outside the USA.[9] In *United States* v. *Sisal Sales Corporation*, the US Supreme Court allowed jurisdiction over conduct taking place within and outside the borders of the USA.[10] A similar conclusion was reached nearly twenty years later in the famous case of *United States* v. *Aluminum Co. of America (Alcoa)*, in which Judge Learned Hand crafted the proposition that the USA can assert jurisdiction over a cartel agreement concluded outside its territory by foreign firms, with the US firm not being party to the agreement. He stated that:

> It is settled law . . . that any State may impose liabilities, even upon persons not within its allegiance, for conduct outside its borders which has consequences within its boarders which the State reprehends; and these liabilities other States will ordinarily recognize.[11]

Judge Hand reasoned that it was irrelevant under such circumstances that the agreement was of a completely foreign nature. Such an agreement could still be declared unlawful because a country may punish an economically harmful act, which it may reprehend, even if committed by individuals beyond its borders.[12]

---

[7] See D. Gerber, 'The Extraterritorial Application of German Antitrust Law' (1983) 77 *American Journal of International Law* 756, 791–3.
[8] See D. Stroock, L. Stroock and S. Lavan, 'Convergence of Trade Laws and Antitrust Laws: Unilateral Extraterritorial US Antitrust Enforcement – Can It Work to Open Japan's Markets?' in H. Coretesi (ed.), *Unilateral Application of Antitrust and Trade Laws: toward a New Economic Relationship between the United States and Japan* (The Institute, New York, 1994), p. 114.
    The origins of the doctrine of extraterritoriality are illustrated in several antitrust laws in the USA. See the Sherman Act 1890, the Clayton Act 1914, the Federal Trade Commission Act 1914, the Robinson-Patman Act 1936, the Hart-Scott-Rodino Antitrust Improvements Act 1976 and the Wilson Tariff Act 1994.
[9] See *American Banana Co.* v. *United Fruits Co.* 213 US 347 (1909) in which the Supreme Court held that the Sherman Act did not apply to activities outside the USA.
[10] 274 US 268 (1927).   [11] 148 F 2d 416 (2nd Cir., 1945), 444.   [12] *Ibid.*, 443.

A comment

It is important to shed some light on the justification for employing the effects doctrine as a valid basis for asserting jurisdiction over foreign situations. Several factors can be found on which this justification can be based. It is obvious that the territoriality principle falls short of guarding the legitimate interest of a country in areas of economic relations.[13] An individual country which asserts subject-matter jurisdiction in antitrust policy aims to ensure proper protection of its national economic order, and is justified by the fundamental rights of countries to self-determination. In light of the increasing interdependence of countries and the significance of international trade for the welfare of countries, it is difficult to disagree with the logic behind adopting an effects doctrine. Following the territoriality principle in an area of economic law, such as antitrust policy, would place already strong firms in a position to evade all national regulation.[14] It would not be difficult to imagine that strict territoriality may transform countries into antitrust havens in which firms could evade antitrust rules. This may well result in harm to consumers and competitors of those firms. Firms would therefore be able to engage in harmful economic conduct without being subjected to any form of supervision, since their acts would have been committed 'beyond' national boundaries.[15]

Under public international law, an individual country's assertion of jurisdiction needs to satisfy a requirement of a sufficiently close or reasonable link between its territory and the acts taking place beyond national boundaries.[16] Countries cannot assert jurisdiction if the minimum requirement of such national nexus is not met. Since jurisdiction in antitrust cases cannot be asserted without the presence of direct, substantial and foreseeable anti-competitive effects, the effects doctrine can be said to meet this requirement of a reasonable link. In the absence of a definition in international law of direct, substantial and foreseeable effects, individual countries will individually decide on the matter, using a minimum standard of reasonableness. Furthermore, although conflicts between countries over

[13] See D. Turner, 'Application of Competition Laws to Foreign Conduct: Appropriate Resolution of Jurisdictional Issues' (1985) *Fordham Corporate Law Institute* 231, 233.

[14] See D. Gerber, 'Afterword: Antitrust and American Business Abroad Revisited' (2000) 20 *Northwestern Journal of International Law and Business* 307. Also, ch. 1.

[15] T. Dunfee and A. Friedman, 'The Extraterritorial Application of United States Antitrust Laws: a Proposal for an Interim Solution' (1984) 45 *Ohio State Law Journal* 883, 889–90.

[16] See Mann, 'Doctrine'.

the application of extraterritoriality – especially in the case of the US – have arisen in the context of actions brought against foreign firms, many cases do involve domestic firms as well.

In light of the above factors, the effects doctrine can be regarded as a legitimate basis to assert jurisdiction over acts committed abroad, but which adversely impact upon domestic situations *under certain circumstances*. It is essential to limit this proposition to certain circumstances. For example, there is no reason why, in principle, the validity of the effects doctrine should not be questioned, if the country relying on it fails to take into consideration the sovereign interests of other countries. The most effective way of taking account of such interests would be for countries to adhere to the principles of public international law. It seems, therefore, that although the effects doctrine may constitute a legitimate basis for asserting jurisdiction, its assertion is not absolute, i.e. it is subject to certain conditions – imposed under international law – which an asserting country must satisfy.[17] This is particularly so if the aim to minimise or eliminate conflicts arising as a result of extraterritoriality between countries is to be achieved.

Some fundamental issues

Definition

It is desirable to examine whether extraterritoriality is susceptible to some kind of definition, especially since this issue has not received any adequate attention in the literature. The reason for the lack of definition seems to stem from the fact that proposing a compelling and shared definition is difficult, if not impossible. Perhaps the best definition that can be offered, it seems, is that the antitrust laws of a country are extraterritorially applied in a specific case when that case contains 'foreign elements'. Even then, the concept of 'foreign elements' defies a general definition, especially in areas of economic law. For this reason, it is suggested that instead of searching for a definition, one should focus on identifying situations of extraterritoriality. Hence, all that can be supplied are examples: acts wholly or partly performed, contracts wholly or partly concluded etc., beyond the boundaries of a country. Still the term 'beyond' would remain undefined. When, for example, is an act

---

[17] See R. Alford, 'The Extraterritorial Application of Antitrust Laws: the United States and the European Community Approaches' (1992) 33 *Virginia Journal of International Law* 1, 5.

performed beyond those boundaries, in other words in the territories of other countries?

When talking about extraterritoriality in antitrust policy, at least three different situations can be envisaged: first, when antitrust laws of country A are applied by the judiciary and antitrust authorities of country B within the latter's territory; secondly, when these laws are applied by the judiciary and antitrust authorities of country A within country B; thirdly, when the same laws are applied by the judiciary and antitrust authorities of country A within its territory, but somehow affect firms operating in country B.

The specific situation identified in the present discussion is where a country applies its domestic antitrust law(s) to the behaviour and activities of foreign firms taking place beyond national boundaries. Certain parts of this definition merit special emphasis. The ability of a country to control activities of its own firms beyond its own boundaries should be distinguished from its ability to control activities of foreign firms under similar circumstances. Whilst the former seems to be a recognised principle under public international law, the latter does not seem to have equal recognition, and thus it has given rise to classic questions of jurisdiction, which are amongst the most important and intractable conflicts of public international law.[18]

Extraterritoriality and the internationalisation of antitrust policy

There are strong links between extraterritoriality and the internationalisation of antitrust policy. Arguably, relying on extraterritorial application of domestic antitrust laws would reduce the incentives of countries for the internationalisation of antitrust policy in a 'bilateral' or 'pluralist' sense. If, by relying on its own antitrust laws, a country is independently able to control activities beyond its boundaries, then its willingness to co-operate with other countries on the international plane will not be particularly strong, unless it could achieve better results through co-operation.[19] In addition, an increased reliance on the doctrine of extraterritoriality will lead to an increase in conflicts between countries, especially since the number

[18] See A. Lowe, 'The Problems of Extraterritorial Jurisdiction: Economic Sovereignty and the Search for a Solution' (1985) 34 *International and Comparative Law Quarterly* 724, 727.
[19] This point can be illustrated with reference to the USA and its use of its antitrust law in the period between the 1930s and 1950s. As the discussion in ch. 9 will show, the USA, while expressing its views in favour of co-operation, delivered major blows to the efforts of countries at that time to internationalise antitrust policy. See Gerber, 'Afterword', 307–8.

of countries instituting systems of antitrust has been rising.[20] In light of this, a country's extraterritorial application of its antitrust laws would not necessarily be regarded as acceptable to other countries. The reverse is often true. Experience in this area shows that many countries have not been in favour of other countries' reliance on extraterritoriality in antitrust policy.[21] If a country's motive for applying the doctrine is to guard its national sovereignty, then other countries' defiance of such a move, because they view this move as an intrusion into their internal affairs and territorial integrity and thus as a violation of their national sovereignty, should not be regarded as unacceptable.[22] The resulting situation from extraterritorial application of national antitrust laws would be one of national antitrust imperialism in the world, where strong countries would be able to impose their standards on other countries.[23]

Examining extraterritoriality in antitrust policy paves the way to examining the role of the judiciary in the internationalisation of antitrust policy and ultimately in an international system of antitrust.[24] To this end, it is important to evaluate the contribution of the judiciary towards harmonisation of antitrust policy standards on the international plane. At present, however, extraterritorial application of domestic antitrust laws, as sought by antitrust authorities and recognised by the judiciary in certain jurisdictions, conflicts with public international law.[25] Finally, extraterritoriality, both in theory and practice, concerns situations which extend beyond the national level and move more towards the international plane. Therefore, strong links seem to exist between extraterritoriality and the internationalisation of antitrust policy. By way of stating a sub-conclusion, one could argue that an increased reliance on the doctrine of extraterritoriality represents a step

---

[20] See ch. 1.   [21] See pp. 187–91 below.

[22] See Justice Holmes in *American Banana* where he wrote at p. 356 of the judgment that the lawfulness of an act 'must be determined wholly by the law of the country where the act alone is done'. Otherwise, according to Justice Holmes, the assertion of jurisdiction would be unjust and would be an interference with the sovereignty of another country, which the other country 'justly might resent'.

[23] It has been argued that in applying its antitrust law extraterritorially, the USA was, in the view of countries, imposing respect for its antitrust laws on the entire world in order to serve US interests and promote its economic ethics. See D. Rishikesh, 'Extraterritoriality Versus Sovereignty in International Antitrust Jurisdiction' (1991) 14 *World Competition* 33, 36.

[24] This aspect of the debate would also complement the discussion in ch. 4, on the role of law courts.

[25] This view was even correct fifty years ago. See G. Haight, 'International Law and Extraterritorial Application of the Antitrust Laws' (1954) 63 *Yale Law Journal* 639, 640.

in the opposite direction to a groping for a meaningful internationalisation of antitrust policy.

The political dimension

Defining extraterritoriality in terms of situations of foreign developments and occurrence beyond national boundaries would almost bring one close to assuming that conflicts triggered by extraterritoriality may appear to be only a 'dry' debate about jurisdiction and international law. Nevertheless, it will be argued that extraterritoriality lies in the crossroads between law and politics and that the conflicts it has triggered, involve important political questions,[26] such as who can make and enforce rules regulating behaviour of business firms.[27] In other words, the argument will be made that the nature and content of the doctrine is as much political as legal.[28] Consequently, it is necessary to examine the legal and political limits of extraterritoriality.

Developments in the USA and the EC

The USA

After *Alcoa*

The *Alcoa* case gave rise to conflicts between the USA and other countries.[29] Due to the controversy surrounding the case – and in the light of the protests by foreign countries – later formulations of the effects doctrine by US courts

---

[26] H. Maier, 'Extraterritorial Jurisdiction at a Crossroads: an Intersection between Public and Private International Law' (1982) 76 *American Journal of International Law* 280.

[27] See ch. 3.

[28] Several writers have argued – quite incompletely – that the problem of extraterritoriality is one of legal conflict. See generally Rishikesh, 'Extraterritoriality'. Against this, some writers have argued that disputes arising as a result of extraterritoriality are not simply about legal theory; they are equally disputes about the policy objectives the law should serve. See J. Bridge, 'The Law and Politics of United States Foreign Policy Export Controls' (1984) 4 *Legal Studies* 2; Lowe, 'Problems', 724.

[29] See K. Brewster, *Antitrust and American Business Abroad* (McGraw-Hill, New York, 1958), pp. 46–51; W. Fugate, *Foreign Commerce and Antitrust Laws* (Little, Brown, Boston, 1958), pp. 344–6; N. Katzenbach, 'Conflicts on an Unruly Horse: Reciprocal Claims and Tolerance in Interstate and International Law' (1956) 65 *Yale Law Journal* 1087, 1148–9; D. Rosenthal, 'Relationship of US Antitrust Laws to the Formulation of Foreign Economic Policy, Particularly Export and Overseas Investment Policy' (1980) 49 *Antitrust Law Journal* 1189, 1193; Mann, 'Doctrine', 104; J. Sandage, 'Forum Non Conveniens and the Extraterritorial Application of United States Antitrust Laws' (1985) 94 *Yale Law Journal* 1693, 1694.

had to be more carefully worded.[30] To this end, some US courts began to draw on the principle of judicial comity,[31] which seems to follow from the work of a prominent scholar in the late 1950s, in which he advocated a 'jurisdictional rule of reason', which involves a balancing exercise between national and foreign interests in a broad sense.[32] In *Timberlane I*, the US Court of Appeal for the Ninth Circuit stated a number of factors that must be taken into account in this balancing exercise. These include:

> the degree of conflict with foreign law or policy, the nationality or allegiance of the parties and the locations or principal places of business of corporations, the extent to which enforcement by either state can be expected to achieve compliance, the relative significance of effects on the US as compared with those elsewhere, the extent to which there is explicit purpose to harm or affect American commerce, the foreseeability of such effect, and the relative importance to the violations charged of conduct within the US as compared with conduct abroad.[33]

Thus, in opting for a narrower approach,[34] it seems that some US courts have attempted to limit the scope of application of the doctrine by demanding not only the existence of a direct and substantial effect within the USA, but also a balancing of the respective interests of the USA in asserting jurisdiction, and of any other country which might be offended by such assertion.[35]

---

[30] In the case of *Timberlane*, the US Court of Appeal held that the effects doctrine as enunciated in *Alcoa* is 'by itself . . . incomplete because it fails to consider other nations' interests. Nor does it expressly take into account the full nature of the relationship between the actors and this country.' See *Timberlane Lumber Co. v. Bank of America National Trust and Savings Association*, 549 F 2d 597 (9th Cir. 1976), 611–12.

[31] The term 'comity' describes a general principle that a country should take other countries' important interests into account in its law enforcement in return for their doing the same. The US Supreme Court has defined comity as 'the recognition which one nation allows within its territory to the legislative, executive or judicial acts of another nation, having due regard both to international duty and convenience, and to the rights of its own citizens'. See *Hilton v. Guyot*, 159 US 113, 163–4 (1865). See also *Laker Airways Ltd. v. Sabena, Belgian World Airlines*, 731 F 2d 909, at 937(D.C. Cir. 1984), where it was held that 'the central precept of comity teaches that, when possible, the decisions of foreign tribunals should be given effect in domestic courts, since recognition fosters international cooperation and encourages reciprocity, thereby promoting predictability and stability.' See H. Yntema, 'The Comity Doctrine' (1966) 65 *Michigan Law Review* 1.

[32] See Brewster, *Antitrust*.   [33] 549 F 2d 614.

[34] In spite of this narrowing of the scope of the doctrine, however, other countries still held the view that the doctrine offended against common principles of public international law. See generally A. Neale and D. Goyder, *The Antitrust Laws of the United States of America: a Study of Competition Enforced by Law* (Cambridge University Press, Cambridge, 1980).

[35] See E. Fox, 'Extraterritoriality and Antitrust – Is Reasonableness the Answer?' (1986) *Fordham Corporate Law Institute* 49.

The FTAIA approach

In 1982, the USA Congress adopted the Foreign Trade Antitrust Improvements Act (FTAIA) to simplify the appropriate extraterritorial reach of US antitrust laws.[36] To this end, the Act established a uniform test, whereby jurisdiction could only be asserted over conduct that has a 'direct, substantial, and reasonably foreseeable' effect on US domestic or export commerce. The Act seems to be neutral regarding the 'jurisdictional rule of reason' – as adopted in *Timberlane*. This is evident from the legislative history of the Act, where it was stated that prior to its final adoption the bill was intended neither to prevent nor to encourage additional judicial recognition of the special international characteristics of transactions. The bill also provided that it would have no effect on the courts' ability to employ notions of comity or otherwise to take account of the international character of transactions where a court determines that the requirements of subject-matter jurisdiction were met.[37] Nevertheless, the Third Restatement of the Foreign Relations Law 1988 in the US adopted the 'jurisdictional rule of reason' type of approach.[38] The Restatement considered that a balancing approach, derived from the principle of judicial comity, was necessary by virtue of principles of public international law.[39]

Guidelines of enforcement authorities

The US antitrust authorities have not been consistent in their application of the doctrine of extraterritoriality. Some twenty years ago, the Department of Justice stated that the main purpose of extraterritoriality was to protect US export and investment opportunities against private restrictions. It also stated then that its concern was that each US-based firm exporting goods, services or capital should be allowed to compete and not be kept out of foreign markets by some restriction introduced by a stronger or

---

It is arguable, however, whether US courts fully endorsed the idea of reasonableness expressed in the *Timberlane* factors. Compare *Mannington Mills, Inc. v. Congoleum Corp.*, 595 F 2d 1287 (3rd Cir. 1979) (adopting similar factors) with *Laker Airways Ltd. v. Sabena, Belgian World Airlines*, 731 F 2d 909 (D.C. Cir. 1984) (questioning the effectiveness of the factors).

[36] The Act amended the Sherman and the Federal Trade Commission Acts in regards to export commerce and wholly foreign conduct, but not with respect to import commerce.

[37] See H. R. Rep. No. 97–686 (1982), 10.

[38] See D. Murphy, 'Moderating Antitrust Subject Matter Jurisdiction: the Foreign Trade Antitrust Improvements Act and the Restatement of Foreign Relations Law (Revised)' (1986) 54 *University of Cincinnati Law Review* 779.

[39] See in particular sections 402, 403 and 415 of the Restatement. For a good discussion of these provisions see Alford, 'Application', 23–7.

less-principled firm.[40] A few years later, the Department of Justice seems to have abandoned this concern and transposed the consumer welfare objective into its operations within the international sphere. In its reaction to the test of reasonableness, the Department of Justice stated in its 1988 Guidelines that in taking enforcement actions against export restraints that harmed consumers in the USA and its exports, the idea of reasonableness was a matter of 'prosecutorial discretion' rather than law:

> Although the FTAIA [Foreign Trade Antitrust Improvements Act] extends jurisdiction under the Sherman Act to conduct that has a direct, substantial and reasonably foreseeable effect on the export trade or export commerce of a person engaged in such commerce in the United States, the Department is concerned with adverse effects on competition that would harm US consumers by reducing output or raising prices.[41]

Early in the 1990s, this paragraph was repealed. At the time, the Department of Justice explained that US Congress did not intend antitrust law to be limited to cases based on direct harm to consumers, arguing that when both imports and exports are of importance to the US economy, the Department would not limit its concern to competition in only half of US trade. This different line of policy was later inserted into the 1995 Antitrust Enforcement Guidelines for International Operations adopted jointly by the Department of Justice and the Federal Trade Commission which stated that the authorities may, in appropriate cases, take enforcement action against anti-competitive conduct, wherever occurring, that restrains US exports, if: first, the conduct has a direct, substantial and reasonably foreseeable effect on exports of goods or services from the USA, and secondly, the US courts can obtain jurisdiction over persons or firms engaged in such conduct.[42] Along this new line of policy, the authorities agreed to consider legitimate interests of other countries in accordance with the recommendations of the OECD and various bilateral agreements.[43] The Guidelines further explain

---

[40] See Antitrust Guidelines for International Operations, US Department of Justice, Antitrust Division 1988, p. 5.

[41] *Ibid.*, footnote 159. See M. Lao, 'Jurisdictional Reach of the US Antitrust Laws: Yokosuka and Yokota, and "Footnote 159" Scenarios' (1994) 46 *Rutgers Law Review* 821.

[42] *Guidelines* 1995, note 73.

[43] *Ibid.* By way of extension, note 74 of the Guidelines mentions a number of factors which the authorities would take into account when considering the legitimate interests of other countries. These factors have been derived partly from previous international guidelines and partly from the 1991 Co-operation Agreement between the USA and the EC.

that the Department of Justice would take into consideration, as a matter of 'prosecutorial discretion', comity beyond whether there is a conflict with foreign law.[44] The Department of Justice has emphasised that it does not believe that it is the role of the courts to 'second-guess' the antitrust authorities' judgment as to the proper role of comity concerns under such circumstances.[45] Although controversial, such comments seem to make it clear that the USA remains determined to tackle foreign conduct that harms its exports, but would do so only after some account has been taken of any possible reaction by foreign countries to this policy approach.

Hartford Fire[46]

In 1988, several US and UK insurance companies were alleged to have breached the Sherman Act 1890 by entering into agreements to alter certain terms of insurance coverage and not to offer certain types of insurance coverage. In their response to the allegations, the UK-based firms argued that the US courts should not assert jurisdiction over conduct that occurred in another jurisdiction and was lawful there, even if the conduct in question produced effects in the USA.

The district court In its decision, the District Court held that it could assert jurisdiction over the conduct of the UK firms under the Sherman Act 1890 because their decision to refuse to provide reinsurance or retrocessional reinsurance to cover certain types of risks in the USA had a direct effect on the availability of primary insurance in the USA.[47] In dealing with the international comity point, the court, referring to *Timberlane II*,[48] held that extraterritorial assertion of jurisdiction should give way to international comity considerations.

---

[44] The Guidelines provide, at p. 20, that as part of a traditional comity evaluation, the Department of Justice would consider whether one country encourages a certain course of conduct, leaves firms free to choose among different strategies or prohibits some of those strategies. In addition, the Department of Justice would take into account the effect of its enforcement activities on related enforcement activities of a foreign antitrust authority.

[45] Guidelines, pp. 21–22.

[46] Case of *Hartford Fire Insurance Co.* v. *California* 113 S. Ct. 2891 (1993).

[47] *In re Insurance Antitrust Litigation*, 732 F. Supp. 464 (N.D. Cal. 1991), 484.

[48] In *Timberlane II*, the 9th Circuit for the Court of Appeal held that in asserting extraterritorial jurisdiction, a court should examine '(1) the effect or intended effect on the foreign commerce of the United States; (2) the type and magnitude of the alleged illegal behaviour, and (3) the appropriateness of exercising extraterritorial jurisdiction in light of considerations of international comity and fairness.' *Timberlane Lumber Co.* v. *Bank of America National Trust and Savings Association*, 749 F 2d 1378 (9th Cir. 1984), 1382.

The Court of Appeal   Whilst agreeing with the district court on the existence of effects within the USA, the Ninth Circuit for the Court of Appeal reversed the former's ruling with respect to the international comity consideration.[49]

The Supreme Court   The Supreme Court was divided on the issue. By a majority of 5–4, it was held that the Sherman Act 1890 does apply to foreign conduct that was meant to produce and did in fact produce some substantial effect in the USA.[50] Regarding international comity considerations, it was held that there was no need to decide this question, and that in any case, 'international comity would not counsel against exercising jurisdiction in the circumstances alleged', even if asserting jurisdiction over foreign acts usually gives way to international comity considerations.[51]

An important point made in the judgment that is worth mentioning relates to the argument of the UK firms and Government, that the challenged conduct was not contrary to UK law and policy. The court responded to this argument by saying that there was no 'true conflict' between UK and US laws.[52] The court referred to section 415 of the Third Restatement, holding that there cannot be a 'true conflict' if the firm, subject to the laws of two jurisdictions, can comply with both. As there was no 'true conflict' in this case, held the court, there was no need to consider whether a US court should, on the basis of international comity, refrain from asserting jurisdiction.

A comment

The judgment of the Supreme Court raises several questions.[53] The view of the majority that for a 'true conflict' to exist, compliance with US law

---

[49] *In re Insurance Antitrust Litigation*, 938 F 2d 919, 932 (9th Cir. 1991), 934.

[50] 509 US 764 (1993), 796, per Justice Souter.   [51] *Ibid.*, 798.   [52] *Ibid.*, 798–9.

[53] Many of these questions have been noted in the literature on the case. See V. Gupta, 'After *Hartford Fire*: Antitrust and Comity' (1996) 84 *Georgetown Law Journal* 2287; J. Trentor, 'Jurisdiction and the Extraterritorial Application of Antitrust Laws after *Hartford Fire*' (1995) 62 *University of Chicago Law Review* 1583; K. Dam, 'Extraterritoriality in an Age of Globalization: the *Hartford Fire* Case' (1993) *Supreme Court Review* 289; L. Kramer, 'Extraterritorial Application of American Law after the Insurance Antitrust Case: a Reply to Professors Lowenfeld and Trimble' (1995) 89 *American Journal of International Law* 750; P. Trimble, 'The Supreme Court and International Law: the Demise of Restatement Section 403' (1995) 89 *American Journal of International Law* 53; P. Roth, 'Jurisdiction, British Public Policy and the Supreme Court' (1994) 110 *Law Quarterly Review* 194; E. Fox, 'US Law and Global Competition and Trade – Jurisdiction and Comity' (1993) *Antitrust Report* 3; S. Calkins, 'The October 1992 Supreme Court Term and Antitrust: More Objectivity than Ever' (1994) 62 *Antitrust Law Journal* 327, 361–8; Hawk, *United States* (Supp. 1993), p. 148.

should lead to a violation of the law of another country is difficult to accept. Indeed, in the case itself, Justice Scalia, delivering the judgment for the minority, described this view as a 'breathtakingly broad proposition'.[54] One can anticipate that such a view would trigger conflicts between US antitrust law and the legitimate interests of other countries. Moreover, the claim may be made that the judgment seems to have misinterpreted the approach of the Third Restatement. Lowenfeld – the principal author of the part of the Restatement on which the Supreme Court relied in its judgment – has written:

> In determining whether state A exercises jurisdiction over an activity significantly linked to state B, one important question, in my submission, is whether B has a demonstrable system of values and priorities different from those of A that would be impaired by the application of the law of A. I am not suggesting that, if the answer to the question is yes, A must stay its hand. The magnitude of A's interest, the effect of the challenged activity within A, the intention of the actors, and the other factors that I hope will disappear from view remain important. But, conflict is not just about commands: it is also about interests, values and competing priorities. All of these need to be taken into account in arriving at a rational allocation of jurisdiction in a world of nation-states.[55]

By emphasising the need for a 'true conflict', the Supreme Court seems to have departed from previous judgments in which it placed a specific emphasis on the importance of taking into account the interests of foreign countries,[56] as well as on the need to carefully inquire into the reasonableness of the assertion of jurisdiction in antitrust cases.[57] It seems that it would be preferable for the US courts to refrain from asserting jurisdiction over foreign situations if such an assertion were unreasonable. This would be in accordance with the Third Restatement, especially section 403 thereof. In the case, Justice Scalia applied the section and the factors therein to the facts of the case and concluded that these factors went against the application of US law. According to Justice Scalia, the relevant actions took place

---

[54] At 820 of the judgment.

[55] See A. Lowenfeld, 'Conflict, Balancing of Interests and the Exercise of Jurisdiction to Prescribe: Reflections on the Insurance Antitrust Case' (1995) 89 *American Journal of International Law* 42, 51.

[56] See *Doe v. United States*, 487 US 201 (1988), 218; *Société Nationale Industrielle Aérospatiale v. United States District Court*, 482 US 522 (1987), 543–4.

[57] See *Asahi Metal Indus. Co. v. Superior Ct.*, 480 US 102, 115 (1987).

primarily in the UK, and the defendants were UK firms whose principal place of business was outside the USA. He thought it was beyond imagination to consider that an assertion of legislative jurisdiction by the USA would be reasonable, and therefore it was inappropriate to assume, in the absence of statutory indication to the contrary, that Congress had made such an assertion.[58]

The difficult questions which the judgment raises also concern the use of the sovereign compulsion defence.[59] This defence calls for denial of jurisdiction by US courts in cases where an explicit law of another country compels the persons committing the anti-competitive acts – who would face sanctions should they not comply – to do so. This is based on the assertion that sovereignty includes the right of a country to regulate commerce within its boundaries; therefore when such country compels a particular practice, firms there have no choice but to obey. In this way, acts of firms are considered to become effectively acts of the country. In the USA, the Sherman Act 1890 does not confer jurisdiction on US courts over acts of foreign countries. By its terms, it prohibits only anti-competitive practices of natural persons and firms. In the judgment itself the requirement that the challenged conduct be compelled by foreign law appears to confuse the exercise of judicial discretion in the context of international comity with the evidence necessary to establish the affirmative defence of foreign sovereign compulsion. Thus, if the UK firms could have established their challenged conduct was compelled by UK law, they would have been entitled to dismissal pursuant to the foreign sovereign compulsion defence, without the need for any analysis of international comity. The majority opinion in *Hartford Fire* leaves open the question whether international comity could require a US court to consider abstaining from exercising jurisdiction in the absence of a true conflict and, if so, under what circumstances.[60]

The difficulty raised by this issue can also be observed in the post-*Hartford Fire* case law, which is divided on the issue of comity.[61] Some

---

[58] At 819.
[59] See *Interamerican Refining Corporation* v. *Texaco Maracaibo, Inc.*, 307 F. Suppl. (D.Del. 1970); *Mannington Mills Inc.* v. *Congoleum Corp.*, 696 F 2d 1287 (3rd Cir. 1979), 1293; *Timberlane Lumber Co.* v. *Bank of America National Trust and Savings Association*, 549 F 2d 597 (9th Cir. 1976); *United States* v. *Watchmakers of Switzerland* 1963 Trade Cas. (CCH) 70,600 (SDNY 1962). See also J. Leidig, 'The Uncertain Status of the Defence of Foreign Sovereign Compulsion: Two Proposals for Change' (1991) 31 *Virginia Journal of International Law* 321.
[60] J. Griffin, 'Extraterritoriality in US and EU Antitrust Enforcement' (1999) 67 *Antitrust Law Journal* 159, 193.
[61] See Lowenfeld, 'Conflict'.

subsequent cases noted that *Hartford Fire* 'did not question the propriety of the jurisdictional rule of reason or the seven comity factors in *Timberlane I*',[62] and in several cases the courts have struck out claims after finding 'true conflicts' with foreign law,[63] whilst in other cases the courts refused to dismiss claims on the basis of international comity.[64]

Perhaps the most difficult question raised by *Hartford Fire* is where the case has left the US' enthusiasm for extraterritoriality in applying its antitrust laws and the principle of international comity.[65] It has been argued that the case will encourage the US Government, different US states and private claimants to aggressively rely on extraterritoriality. The answer may be found in some subsequent rulings by the US courts. A good exposition is *United States* v. *Nippon Paper Industries Co.*[66] The case involved a Japanese firm, Nippon Paper, charged by the USA with conspiracy to fix prices in the USA contrary to section 1 of the Sherman Act 1890. The District Court dismissed the charge and held that criminal antitrust prosecution could not extend to wholly extraterritorial conduct. On appeal, the First Circuit reversed the District Court decision, holding that the US Government could prosecute Nippon Paper for conspiring to fix prices in the USA. The court stated that there was no compelling reason why principles of comity should exempt Nippon Paper from prosecution. According to the court, a finding in Nippon Paper's favour would encourage firms to use nefarious means to influence markets in the USA, rewarding them for erecting as many territorial firewalls as possible between cause and effect.

It is difficult to estimate the far-reaching effect of *Nippon Paper*, especially since the Supreme Court did not give leave to the defendant firm to appeal. However, it may be appropriate to agree that in the light of the *Hartford Fire* case law[67] in general, and in *Nippon Paper* in particular, US antitrust authorities have continued to be zealous in their reliance on extraterritoriality,

---

[62] *Metro Indus. Inc.* v. *Sammi Corp.*, 82 F 3d 839 (9th Cir. 1996), 846, note 5.
[63] See *Filetech SARL* v. *France Telecom*, 978 F. Supp. 464 (SDNY 1997); *Trugman-Nash Inc.* v. *New Zealand Dairy Board*, 945 F. Supp. 733 (SDNY 1997), 736.
[64] See, for example, *Caribbean Broad Sys.* v. *Cable and Wireless Plc*, 1998–2 Trade Cas (CCH) 72,209 (D.C. Cir. 1998).
[65] See J. Griffin, 'Extraterritorial Application of US Antitrust Law Clarified by United States Supreme Court' (1993) 40 *Federal Bar News and Journal*, 564.
[66] 109 F 3d 1 (1st Cir. 1997), 8–9. For a commentary on the case see A. Gluck, 'Preserving *Per Se*' (1999) 108 *Yale Law Journal* 913.
[67] See *United States* v. *Cerestar Bioproducts BV*, 6 Trade Reg. Rep. (CCH) 45,098 (N.D. Cal. 1998); *United States* v. *Heeremac*, 6 Trade Reg. Rep. (CCH) 45,097 (N.D. Ill. 22 Dec. 1997) (Case Nos. 4323–4); *United States* v. *Hoffmann-La Roche*, 6 Trade Reg. Rep. (CCH) 45,097, Case Nos. 4277–8 (N.D. Cal. 1997).

and comity considerations appear to have had little impact on outcomes in antitrust cases.[68]

The EC

Wood Pulp

The issue of whether EC antitrust law is capable of extraterritorial application arose in the case of *Wood Pulp*.[69] In its decision, the European Commission stated that EC antitrust law does apply extraterritorially where conduct outside the EC produces adverse economic effects within it.[70] The ECJ, on the other hand, declined to address this issue,[71] but held that Article 81(1) EC would apply where a price-fixing agreement is *implemented* within the EC.[72]

After *Wood Pulp*

After *Wood Pulp*, the Commission's decisional practice seems to have been largely based on the implementation doctrine. Two cases can be mentioned

---

[68] See Griffin, 'Extraterritoriality', 168.

[69] [1988] ECR 5193; [1988] 4 CMLR 474. The first occasion on which the Commission considered the question of effects was in 1964. In the case of *Grosfillex*, the Commission stated that the territorial scope of EC antitrust law is determined neither by the domicile of the firm nor by where the agreement is concluded or carried out. On the contrary, the sole and decisive criterion is whether an agreement affects competition within the Common Market or is designed to have this effect. *Grosfillex-Fillistorf* [1964] 3 CMLR 237. See also Commission 11th Report on Competition Policy 1981, referring to *Grosfillex*, where the Commission stated at p. 36 that it was one of the first antitrust authorities to have applied the internal effect theory to foreign firms. See also *Aniline Dyes Cartel* [1969] 8 CMLR D23, at D33.

[70] At pp. 499–500. For a general discussion of these issues see M. Waelbroeck, 'Specific Extraterritorial Applications of Jurisdiction Resulting in Conflict: the European Community Approach' in Olmstead, *Extraterritorial*; L. Whatstein, 'Extraterritorial Application of EU Competition Law – Comments and Reflections' (1992) 26 *Israel Law Review* 195.

[71] See L. Brittan, *Competition Policy and Merger Control in the Single European Market* (Grotius, Cambridge, 1991), pp. 7–9. The ECJ avoided this question earlier in the case of *Dyestuffs*, in which the ECJ declined to accept the suggestion of Advocate General Mayers to adopt the effects doctrine, and instead asserted jurisdiction on the basis of the principle of territoriality, relying on the 'economic entity' doctrine. Cases 48/69 etc. [1972] 3 ECR 619; [1972] CMLR 557. See F. Mann, 'The *Dyestuffs* Case in the Court of Justice of the European Communities' (1973) 22 *International and Comparative Law Quarterly* 35.

[72] In contrast to what was said above about the position of the Commission, it has been argued that the ECJ remains dedicated to 'an objective territoriality principle', which requires that a foreign firm engage in a 'consummating act' within the EC in order to extend jurisdiction and to further the goal of single market integration when dealing with antitrust law cases. See Alford, 'Application', 31–7; J. Griffin, 'EC and US Extraterritoriality: Activism and Cooperation' (1994) 17 *Fordham International Law Journal* 353, 378–9.

as examples to illustrate. In the first case, *PVC*,[73] the Commission based its decision on the doctrine of implementation in asserting jurisdiction over a Norwegian manufacturer of PVC for allegedly participating in a price-fixing cartel. In another case, *LdPE*,[74] the Commission also employed the implementation doctrine to bring an action against several manufacturers of thermoplastic low-density polyethylene for fixing prices and engaging in other forms of collusion. Interestingly, however, the Commission singled out Rapsol, the Spanish firm, because unlike the Austrian, Finnish and Norwegian firms, Rapsol did not implement its agreement in the EC, but rather in Spain, before the latter acceded to the EC. The Commission stated that this fact did not immunise Rapsol from legal action. Thus, according to the Commission, it was entitled to assert jurisdiction to the extent that Rapsol's involvement in the cartel affected competition within the EC.[75] Hence, it may be observed that the Commission seems to have moved beyond the implementation doctrine, in this particular instance, towards an effects doctrine.[76]

Gencor v. Commission   In 1999, the question of extraterritorial application of EC antitrust law was addressed by the European Court of First Instance (CFI) in a case under the Merger Regulation 4064/89 EC, *Gencor v. Commission*.[77] The case concerned a proposal to create a joint venture between Gencor, a firm incorporated in South Africa, and Lonrho, a firm incorporated in the UK. At the relevant time, Gencor was active mainly in the mineral resources and metal sectors. It held a stake of 46.5% in Implats, a firm also incorporated in South Africa, which brought together Gencor's activities in the Platinum Group Metal (PGM) sectors. Lonrho, on the other hand, was active in the mining, metals, agriculture, hotels and general trade sectors. It controlled 73% of Eastern Platinum Ltd. and Western Platinum Ltd. (LPD), both incorporated in South Africa, which brought together Lonrho's activities in the PGM sector. Gencor controlled the remaining 27% of LPD.

---

[73] OJ 1990 No. L74/1; [1990] 4 CMLR 345.   [74] OJ 1989 No. L74/21; [1990] 4 CMLR 382.
[75] *Ibid.*, 409–10.
[76] Quite interestingly, former EC Commissioner for antitrust, K. van Miert, seems to have indicated on several occasions that in asserting jurisdiction in extraterritorial situations the Commission will make use of the 'effects' doctrine. See K. van Miert, 'Analysis and Guidelines on Competition Policy', address at the Royal Institute of International Affairs, London, 11 May 1993; 'Global Forces Affecting Competition Policy in a Post-Recessionary Environment' (1993) 17 *World Competition* 135.
[77] Case T-102/96 [1999] ECR II-753; [1999] 4 CMLR 971.

The proposal was for Gencor and Lonrho to acquire joint control of Implats. As a result of the operation, the shares of Implats were intended to be divided as follows: the public was expected to hold 36%, Gencor 32% and Lonrho 32%. The parties notified their proposed operation to both the South Africa Competition Board and the European Commission. While the former approved the proposed operation, the latter decided to block it because the Commission thought that the operation was incompatible with the Common Market. The European Commission believed that the proposed operation would have created a dominant position as a result of which effective competition would have been significantly impeded in the Common Market.

The case assumed great significance because, *inter alia*, it opened very important questions with regard to the ability of the Commission to assume jurisdiction in the case and because conflicting decisions on the same facts were reached by two different antitrust authorities. The case also witnessed political intervention at a high level by the Government of South Africa in order to persuade the Commission that the operation should be allowed to proceed; although none of the political figures who actually intervened attempted to contest the decision of the Commission.

The parties, in particular Gencor, did not believe that the Commission was entitled to exercise jurisdiction in the case and therefore sought annulment of the decision by the CFI. In its submission before the latter, Gencor tried to argue that the Commission lacked jurisdiction under EC Regulation 4064/89 since the operation was carried out outside the EC. The firm also argued in the alternative that if the Regulation was applicable and the Commission could exercise jurisdiction, this exercise of jurisdiction was unlawful and therefore inapplicable pursuant to Article 241 EC.

However convincing such arguments may appear to be, the CFI refused to accept them and dismissed the application for judicial review of the Commission decision accordingly. The CFI held that the Regulation was applicable to the proposed operation, even if consummated in South Africa, explaining that the jurisdictional criteria of the Regulation were consistent with the judgment in *Wood Pulp*. The Court emphasised that there was no requirement in Article 1 of the Regulation – which deals with the concept of Community dimension, according to which the Commission can assert jurisdiction – that the firms concerned must be incorporated or established in the EC or that the production facilities covered by the operation must be carried out within the EC. On that basis, the Court held that the Commission will have jurisdiction in a case such as the one at hand where the activities of the firm concerned – although carried out outside the EC – have the effect of creating or strengthening a dominant position as a result of which effective competition in the Common Market or in a substantial part of it will be significantly impeded. The CFI also considered that, as a matter of public international law, there could be no objection to the assertion of jurisdiction on the part of the Commission under the Merger Regulation in relation to an operation outside the EC, provided that its effects within the EC would be immediate (meaning in the medium term), substantial and foreseeable. The Court explained at paragraph 90 of the judgment that the application of the Regulation is justified under public international law when it is foreseeable that a proposed concentration will have an immediate and substantial effect in the Community. The CFI also opined at paragraph 98 of the judgment that in the case of an operation or transaction which substantially affects competition within the Common Market by creating a dominant position, the Commission cannot be prevented from asserting jurisdiction over such operation or transaction by reason of the fact that, in a world market, other parts of the world are affected by the operation or transaction.

GE/Honeywell   On 3 July 2001, the European Commission decided to block the proposed merger between the US firms General Electric (GE) and Honeywell International on the ground that this operation would have led to the creation of a dominant position on several markets as a result of the combination of Honeywell's leading positions on these markets with GE's financial strength and vertical integration into aircraft purchasing, financing, leasing and aftermarket services. The Commission held that the merger was incompatible with the Common Market.[78]

The merger, however, was cleared in the USA; and this factor made the case attract an unprecedented level of publicity and interest. Furthermore, the fact that the Commission blocked the merger led to very severe and harsh criticism by the USA of the practices of the European Commission. In particular, the Commission was accused of being concerned with the

---

[78] The parties in the case have launched an appeal against the decision of the Commission. The huge media interest which the decision of the Commission has generated, makes the judgment in the case one to watch out for. See Cases T-209/01 and 210/01 (judgment pending).

interest of competitors as opposed to consumers, a claim the European
Commission has consistently denied.

In substantive terms, the case opened up fresh and serious questions
about the differences in the test in use on either side of the Atlantic when
deciding whether to clear or block a merger. In the USA, the test which is in
use – contained in section 7 of the Clayton Act 1914 – is that of 'substantial
lessening of competition' (SLC). According to this test, a merger will be
prohibited if it will lead to SLC. In the EC, on the other hand, the test in
use is that of creating or strengthening a dominant position as a result of
which competition will be significantly impeded in the Common Market or
in a substantial part of it.[79] The test is commonly referred to as the 'dominance' test. Recently, the European Commission has opened up a debate on
whether the dominance test should be changed to an SLC one.[80] The effect
of changing the test will mean that the same test will be in application on
either side of the Atlantic. It seems that there are strong arguments in favour
and against such a change. Mario Monti, Commissioner for antitrust, has
summarised the arguments of the pro- and anti-change groups which the
Commission has received following the publication of its Green Paper on
Merger Review 2001 in the following manner:

> In the pro-change camp, there [is the argument] that the SLC wording [is]
> better suited to the kind of micro-economic analysis required in merger
> cases, [since it is believed] it avoids... the legal 'strait-jacket' of establishing
> dominance. There are some who are moreover of the view that there are
> potential 'gaps' in the scope of the current test, particularly when it comes to
> situations of collective dominance. Some respondents also point to what they
> see as the risk that a broadening of the concept of dominance in merger cases is
> at the same time broadening the category of companies to whom the 'special'
> rules in Article 82 apply, thereby potentially curtailing their ability to engage
> in certain types of commercial conduct. This concern applies particularly, but
> not exclusively, to collective dominance. They take the view that a separation
> of the dominance concept in the Merger Regulation from that in Article
> 82 may therefore be desirable. Those who oppose change consider that the
> current test is proving to be an effective merger control instrument... Many
> industry respondents are opposed to the idea of change, fearing in particular
> the uncertainty that would result, at least for a transitional period. Some also

---

[79] See Article 2 of EC Regulation 4064/89.
[80] See the *Green Paper on the Review of Regulation 4064/89* (2001), available at http://www.
europa.eu.int/comm/competition/index_en.html.

fear that an SLC standard would give the Commission too broad a margin of discretion, and that it could result in what they fear might be an unacceptably interventionist merger control policy. The Green Paper had also recognised that a change to the test in the Merger Regulation might involve some practical drawbacks. In particular, it was acknowledged that such a change might give rise to a degree of uncertainty or unpredictability about how exactly the new standard would be interpreted, at least for an initial period. After all, a considerable body of precedent (emanating from both the Commission and the Courts) has been built up under the Regulation's dominance test. Another possible complication relates to the fact that many Member States (and many of the Candidate Countries) have aligned their merger control provisions to the dominance test.[81]

The Commission recognised that both sides in the debate – namely those who favour a change from the dominance test to the SLC test and those who oppose such a change – enjoy equal strengths. Therefore, it was absolutely crucial for the Commission to examine carefully the arguments put forward by either side. Following a lengthy examination and significant thinking, and following extensive consultation with the Member States, the Commission's final decision was to maintain the dominance test, albeit with some reformulation in its wording. This reformulation is reflected in a new paragraph in Article 2 in the proposal for a Council Regulation to replace the existing Merger Regulation, Regulation 4064/89. The proposal can be obtained from the Commission's website.

Beyond substantive issues, the decision in *GE/Honeywell* is also important given that it seems to have marked a continuation of the Commission's approach to asserting jurisdiction in merger cases in which none of the firms involved are incorporated or have their production facilities within the EC – as has been witnessed under previous decisions, including *Gencor v. Commission*. For this reason, and others, the decision is a remarkable one. More importantly, it is very arguable that following *GE/Honeywell*, the Commission's understanding of appropriate jurisdiction, especially in light of its decision and the judgment of the CFI in *Gencor v. Commission*, corresponds precisely with the US' understanding of appropriate jurisdiction and with the US' understanding of the effects doctrine.

---

[81] See 'Review of the EC Merger Regulation – Roadmap for the Reform Project', speech given at the Conference on Reform of European Merger Control, British Chamber of Commerce, Brussels, June 2002.

A comment

In the EC, whilst the Commission has shown it is willing to move closer to the position of the USA,[82] the ECJ has revealed a clear reluctance to endorse a US effect-based doctrine. The division between the ECJ and the Commission confirms that the doctrine plays a very weak role within the EC.[83] The delay on the part of the ECJ is susceptible to different explanations. One explanation may be that the delay seems to be related to the ECJ's commitment to the goal of market integration, to which it accords primacy.[84] A second explanation is that the ECJ seems to uphold that US-type solutions are not necessarily sensitive or suitable to conditions within the EC.[85] A third explanation may be that one could argue that the ECJ has not really needed to make a finding on this matter in its case law.

Regarding international comity, the EC seems to generally respect the principle, especially regarding the OECD Recommendations on the matter.[86] Those Recommendations state that member countries recognise the need to give effect to the principles of international law and comity and to use moderation and self-restraint in the interest of co-operation in the fight against anti-competitive practices. As far as the Commission is concerned, it has made clear that the assertion of jurisdiction does not give way to international comity in the application of EC law: first, does not require the firms concerned to act in breach of their domestic laws; or secondly, does not adversely affect the important interests of a third country. In any case, according to the Commission, the interests of third countries must be

[82] See Alford, 'Application', 29; P. Roth (ed.), *Common Market Law of Competition* (5th edn, Sweet & Maxwell, London, 2001); K. Stockman, 'Foreign Application of European Antitrust Laws' (1985) *Fordham Corporate Law Institute* 251, 266; K. Messen, 'Antitrust Jurisdiction under Customary International Law' (1984) 78 *American Journal of International Law* 783, 797; Commission 11th Report on Competition Policy 1981, p. 37; J. Bellis, 'International Trade and the Competition Law of the European Economic Community' (1979) 16 *Common Market Law Review* 647.

Some writers have argued that the Commission has supplemented its integration agenda with the US notion of comity. See B. Pearce, 'The Comity Doctrine as a Barrier to Judicial Jurisdiction: a US–EU Comparison' (1994) 30 *Stanford Journal of International Law* 525, 576.
[83] See A. Himmelfarb, 'International Language of Convergence: Reviving Antitrust Dialogue between the United States and the European Union with a Uniform Understanding of "Extraterritoriality"' (1996) 17 *University of Pennsylvania Journal of International Economic Law* 909, 926–7.
[84] See ch. 5.   [85] See Pearce, 'Comity', 577.
[86] See Revised Recommendations of the OECD Council Concerning Co-operation between Member Countries on Anticompetitive Practices Affecting International Trade, OECD Doc. No. C (95) 130 (Final), 27 July 1995.

so important in order to prevail over the fundamental interest of the EC in maintaining undistorted competition in the latter.[87] Unlike the Commission, the ECJ has offered a limited explanation regarding its position on international comity. Over the years, it has only occasionally touched on the issue. In the case of *IBM*, for example, in response to the argument of IBM that the Commission should have considered international comity before initiating its proceedings and formulating its decisions, the ECJ held that the Commission need not do so.[88] This brevity of the ECJ in dealing with the matter can also be seen in light of *Wood Pulp*. In the judgment, the ECJ devoted only one paragraph to its position regarding the application of international comity, holding that in relation to the argument on disregard of international comity, it was sufficient to observe that it amounted to calling into question the EC's jurisdiction to apply its antitrust rules to conduct such as that which was found to exist in that case and that, as such, that argument had already been rejected.[89]

The USA, on the other hand, has not retreated from its core value of promoting extraterritoriality. For example, in the 1995 Antitrust Enforcement Guidelines for International Operations the US antitrust authorities continued to assert jurisdiction under the effects doctrine in accordance with both *Hartford Fire* and the 'direct, substantial, and reasonably foreseeable effect' test under the FTAIA. On the one hand, there seem to be some signals that the US authorities will seek to co-operate with antitrust authorities in other jurisdictions to address cross-border anti-competitive behaviour.[90] Nevertheless, the 1995 Guidelines make it clear that the possibility of a

---

[87] See *Aluminum Imports from Eastern Europe* OJ 1985 No. L92/1, p. 14. In the case, the Commission seems to have implicitly recognised that in certain cases EC fundamental interest of ensuring undistorted competition has to give way to comity considerations.

L. Brittan stated that the Commission considers itself obliged to have regard to comity when exercising its jurisdiction in antitrust cases involving foreign elements. See Brittan, *Competition*, p. 16.

[88] Cases C-60/81 and 190/81 *IBM* v. *Commission* [1981] ECR 2639, 2655. It has been argued that as the ECJ has never rejected the effects doctrine, the Commission remains able to employ it, and might do so. See remarks by L. Brittan, quoted in W. Collins, 'The Coming of Age of EC Competition Policy' (1992) 17 *Yale Journal of International Law* 249. According to J. Griffin this even suggests that the ECJ considers international comity an issue within the Commission's discretion, at least in facts similar to *Wood Pulp*, i.e. the challenged conduct was not compelled by foreign law as the remedy does not require the firms to act in any way contrary to their national law. See Griffin, 'Activism', 358–9.

[89] See *Woodpulp*, 5344.

[90] See US Department of Justice, press release 'Justice Department Closes Investigation into the Way AC Nielsen Co. Contracts Its Services for Tracking Retail Sales', 3 December 1996.

unilateral action by the US antitrust authorities is not ruled out, especially in cases where foreign countries fail to take action or take only inadequate action to address anti-competitive behaviour of private firms, which the USA condemns within its boundaries.

Several comments are worth making on the scope of the differences and similarities between the developments on either side of the Atlantic. Perhaps the most obvious point of distinction relates to the effects and implementation doctrines.[91] Any practical importance of the distinction between anti-competitive conduct outside the EC 'implemented' within it and the 'effect' of such conduct seems to be limited to a few, rare cases. This preference towards limiting the areas of application of the implementation doctrine has been expressed by some commentators who have argued that it was necessary for the EC to exclude certain antitrust prohibitions from its jurisdictional purview, if the implementation doctrine was to remain consistent with the expressed will of the ECJ to assert jurisdiction on the basis of the territoriality principle.[92] Still, it is not very clear which areas should be included and which should be excluded in this case. It has been recommended that anti-competitive practices, such as refusal to buy from, or supply to, firms established within the EC, should be covered under the implementation doctrine,[93] whilst others have argued that this would stretch the current jurisprudence of the ECJ. A more important issue relates

---

[91] It may be of interest to observe in this regard the view expressed by the US Department of Justice that the 'implementation' test adopted in the ECJ usually produces the same result as the US effects doctrine employed in the United States. See 1995 Antitrust Enforcement Guidelines for International Operations, 20, 589–8.

   Against this, it has been argued that this view cannot be accepted, since the ECJ has consciously rejected the effects doctrine. See P. Torremans, 'Extraterritorial Application of EU and US Competition Law' (1996) 21 *European Law Review* 280; W. van Gerven, 'EC Jurisdiction in Antitrust Matters: the *Wood Pulp* Judgment' (1989) *Fordham Corporate Law Institute* 451, 466–7.

   In practice, the ECJ's notion of 'implementation' will be sufficient to catch most agreements concluded outside the EC which seriously harm competition within it; however, there may be some cases which would not be caught under the 'implementation' doctrine, but would be under the 'effects' doctrine: for example, a refusal by non-EC firms to supply goods or services to EC firms.

[92] Alford, 'Application', 36.

[93] See T. Christoforou and D. Rockwell, 'European Economic Community Law: the Territorial Scope of Application of EEC Antitrust Law' (1989) 30 *Harvard International Law Journal* 195, 204; J. Santos, 'The Territorial Scope of Article 85 of the EEC Treaty' (1989) *Fordham Corporate Law Institute* 571, 575–7.

to how the Commission will act in cases which are not covered under the implementation doctrine. It is of interest to see whether the Commission will remain faithful to the implementation doctrine, whether it will utilise the effects doctrine in those cases or whether it will rely on the positive comity principle as covered in the EC–US bilateral agreement.

The impact of *Hartford Fire, Gencor* v. *Commission* and *GE/Honeywell* is also important. The Supreme Court in *Hartford Fire* adopted a wide formulation of the extraterritorial scope of US antitrust law. It has been argued that in doing so, the Supreme Court has ignored the limits placed on the US' jurisdiction by public international law. Moreover, it has forgone the opportunity to place the US' approach to extraterritoriality upon the same principles as those which underpin other systems of antitrust in the world, in particular the EC system of antitrust as animated by the ECJ's jurisprudence on the topic. It is likely that this will trigger a conflict between the world's two major systems of antitrust.[94] By contrast, *GE/Honeywell* and *Gencor* v. *Commission* seem to have brought the EC position on extraterritoriality closer to that of the USA.

Nevertheless, a mutual liberal extraterritorial application of antitrust law between the USA and the EC does not necessarily mean the elimination of all the difficulties associated with extraterritoriality. Nor does it mean that such a mutually expansive scope for the laws of one jurisdiction will be free of friction. However, taken in parallel with the above description of the extraterritorial reach of US antitrust laws, the ruling by the CFI in *Gencor* v. *Commission* and the decision of the Commission in *GE/Honeywell* make it clear that sooner rather than later, the question of whether antitrust policy should be internationalised leading to the creation of an international system of antitrust – albeit in limited areas, such as mergers – requires attention.[95]

It may be anticipated that differences between the USA and the EC systems of antitrust will impact on the position of the parties, with respect to their relationship. For example, in the bilateral co-operation agreement between the EC and the USA, whilst the comity rights granted in Articles V and VI of the agreement apply to both parties, it seems that the benefits to both parties will be disproportionate in light of the differences in approach to extraterritoriality by the USA and the EC.

---

[94] The issue of conflict between the two systems is discussed at pp. 277–80 below.   [95] See ch. 9.

In sum, it seems that the EC and the USA do not share the same conception of comity principles and extraterritoriality. Moreover, in the USA the position on extraterritoriality does not seem to be entirely consistent, as two different standards have been employed.[96] The first is the common law test of whether, in the light of international comity concerns, jurisdiction should be exercised on the particular facts.[97] The second is the 'direct, substantial, and reasonably foreseeable' test under the FTAIA, under which the position is not clear with regards to whether comity considerations are always taken into account as an adequate substitute for the criteria of 'direct, substantial, and reasonably foreseeable'.[98] These criteria appear to focus exclusively on establishing a sufficiently close link with the USA to justify the assertion of jurisdiction, without reference to international comity.[99] The existence of different tests may cause inconsistency and lack of uniformity in how US antitrust law and policy develop.[100] On the European side of the Atlantic, the Commission seems to be more willing than the ECJ to move closer to the US position on extraterritoriality. However, the ECJ so far seems to have remained committed to territorial requirements, and unwilling to follow the US' version of 'effects' doctrine and comity principles. Such differences in the position of the EC and the USA exemplify the difficulties that are bound to appear in both the interaction between antitrust policy and public international law and in bringing the EC and US systems of antitrust closer together which, in turn, will have a major impact on the internationalisation of antitrust policy.[101]

---

[96] See V. Sharma, 'Approaches to the Issue of Extra-Territorial Jurisdiction' (1995) 5 *Australian Journal of Corporate Law* 45.

[97] See Alford, 'Application', 16.   [98] See Hawk, *United States*, p. 150.

[99] It has been argued that the nature and intensity of the US' interest in regulating extraterritorial conduct cannot alone determine the proper limits on extraterritorial jurisdiction. See 'Predictability and Comity: toward Common Principles of Extra-Territorial Jurisdiction' (1985) 98 *Harvard Law Review* 1310, 1320 (Notes section). See also Messen, 'Antitrust', 784–5, stating that this was exactly the view of the Ninth Circuit in *Timberlane Lumber Co.* v. *Bank of America*, 549 F 2d 597 (9th Cir. 1976), which established that although a country may have jurisdiction whenever a sufficient number of connecting factors are present, it should nevertheless refuse to exercise jurisdiction if the regulatory interests it is pursuing are outweighed by the interests of one or more foreign countries, who are likely to be seriously injured by the assertion of such jurisdiction.

[100] See E. Rholl, 'Inconsistent Application of the Extraterritorial Provisions of the Sherman Act: a Judicial Response Based upon the Much Maligned "Effects" Test' (1990) 73 *Marquette Law Review* 435.

[101] See further ch. 9.

Responses to extraterritoriality

In vigorously pursuing the extraterritorial reach of its antitrust law, the USA seems to have encouraged other jurisdictions to follow suit, by adopting the 'effects' doctrine under their systems of antitrust.[102] However, it has also provoked vehement responses from other countries.[103] Over the years, the number of countries which have resisted the US position on extraterritoriality within antitrust policy has increased piecemeal.[104]

A strong advocate against the US extraterritoriality has been the UK,[105] which has argued on more than one occasion that the US assertions that foreclosure of a foreign market or refusal to adopt US technical standards is sufficient to establish the requisite effect, show US antitrust law being used as a trade policy tool to open markets perceived as closed to US firms. This, according to the UK, is an objectionable and inappropriate use of antitrust law.[106] In the EC, the Commission has noted that the accent on unilateral action by the US authorities under the 1995 Antitrust Enforcement Guidelines for International Operations in fact is contrary to on the one hand the commitment to respect comity principles and on the other hand, the efforts of the US authorities to support international co-operation.[107] For this reason, and bearing in mind the need to respond to such an assertion of extraterritoriality, several methods have been used to resist expansive extraterritoriality, which are three-fold: diplomatic protest, blocking through statutes and blocking through case law.

[102] An OECD Report on 'Restrictive Business Practices of Multinational Enterprises', produced in 1977, concluded at para. 120 that at that time thirteen systems of antitrust had embraced the 'effects' doctrine, although it included in this list the EC system as to which the position is uncertain.
[103] See Sandage, 'Forum', 1693.
[104] See J. Griffin, 'Foreign Governmental Reactions to US Assertion of Extraterritorial Jurisdiction' (1998) 6 *George Mason Law Review* 505. For an account of the position of the Pacific countries *vis-à-vis* US extraterritoriality see S. Chang, 'Extraterritorial Application of US Antitrust Laws to Other Pacific Countries: Proposed Bilateral Agreements for Resolving International Conflicts within the Pacific Community' (1993) 16 *Hastings International and Comparative Law Review* 295.
[105] See Sharma, 'Approaches', 50–2.
[106] Comments of the UK Government on the Antitrust Enforcement Guidelines for International Operations (1995) December 1994. See J. Griffin, 'International Antitrust Guidelines Send Mixed Message of Robust Enforcement and Comity' (1995) 19 *World Competition* 5.
[107] Comments of the European Commission Services February 1995.

Diplomatic protest

Diplomatic protest by foreign governments has been the most immediate reaction to US extraterritorial application of antitrust laws. Over the years, intense diplomatic dialogues, at the highest level, have occurred between Washington and no fewer than twenty other capitals in the world.[108] At the heart of diplomatic protest lies the claim that the extraterritorial application of US antitrust law adversely affects other countries' interests. Nevertheless, it is not clear whether diplomatic protest, and ultimately diplomatic dialogues, can effectively help foreign countries in their international antitrust conflicts with the USA, especially in light of the uncertain position of comity considerations in the latter.

Blocking through legislation

As a result of the unproductive nature of dialogues at the diplomatic level,[109] countries have sometimes felt it necessary to strengthen their domestic legal systems to deal with what they feel is an unacceptable intrusion by the USA into matters within their own jurisdictions.[110] A series of legislation was introduced in several countries to thwart excessive assertions of jurisdiction by the USA. The most common type of legislation countries have equipped themselves with has been blocking statutes.[111] The aim of these statutes

---

[108] See Diplomatic Notes, reprinted in Lowe, *Extraterritorial*; G. Haight, 'Extracts from Some Published Material on Official Protests, Directives, Prohibitions, Comments, etc' in Report of the 51st International Law Association Conference 1964, pp. 565–92; J. Davidow, 'Extraterritorial Antitrust and the Concept of Comity' (1981) 15 *Journal of World Trade Law* 500, 508; M. Weiner, 'Remedies in International Transactions: a Case for Flexibility' (1996) 65 *Antitrust Law Journal* 261.

[109] In some cases diplomatic efforts have been fruitful in the past. See J. Atwood, *Antitrust and American Business Abroad* (McGraw-Hill, New York, 1981), pp. 136–45; M. Sennett and A. Gavil, 'Antitrust Jurisdiction, Extraterritorial Conduct and Interest Balancing' (1985) 19 *International Lawyer*, 1185, 1213–14.

[110] Case 48/69 *ICI Ltd.* v. *Commission* [1972] ECR 619; [1972] CMLR 557.

[111] See the Ontario Business Records Protection Act 1947, enacted as a result of the discovery order in *In re Grand Jury Subpoena Duces Tecum*, 72 F. Supp. 1013 (SDNY 1947), the first of such legislation. See also P. Pettit and C. Styles, 'The International Response to the Extraterritorial Application of United States Antitrust Laws' (1982) 37 *Business Lawyer* 697, 707–14; A. Carroll, 'The Extraterritorial Enforcement of US Antitrust Laws and Retaliatory Legislation in the United Kingdom and Australia' (1984) 13 *Denver Journal of International Law and Policy* 377. For a good overview of these instruments see A. Lowe, 'Blocking Extraterritorial Jurisdiction: the British Protection of Trading Interests Act 1980' (1981) 75 *American Journal of International Law* 257; A. Hermann, *Conflicts of National Laws with International Business Activity: Issues of Extraterritoriality* (Howe Institute, London, 1982), pp. 56–68.

is to prohibit or block the disclosure, copying, inspection or removal of documents located in the territory of the enacting country in compliance with orders of foreign authorities.

The UK has passed two such statutes.[112] The first was the Shipping Contracts and Commercial Documents Act 1964, enacted in reaction to the US investigations of the liner conferences. The second was the Protection of Trading Interests Act 1980 which came to replace the 1964 Act.[113] This statute empowers the Secretary of State to prohibit compliance with foreign measures for regulating or controlling international trade and the supply of any commercial documents or information in response to the requirements of a foreign court. France introduced legislation that made it a criminal offence to communicate documents relating to commercial or technical matters for use in foreign proceedings, except pursuant to treaty or international agreement.[114] Similar statutes have also been introduced in several other countries,[115] especially those with domestic firms involved in the uranium proceedings.[116]

Blocking through case law

Blocking attempts of extraterritoriality through case law is a third method which some countries have employed to resist reliance on extraterritoriality

---

[112] For an overview see M. Novicoff, 'Blocking and Clawing Back in the Name of Public Policy: the United Kingdom's Protection of Private Economic Interests against Adverse Foreign Adjudications' (1985) 7 *Northwestern Journal of International Law and Business* 12.

[113] See A. Huntley, 'The Protection of Trading Interests Act 1980: Some Jurisdictional Aspects of Enforcement of Antitrust Laws' (1981) 30 *International and Comparative Law Quarterly* 213.

[114] See Law No. 80-538 16 July 1980, J.O., p. 1799.

[115] For example, Australia, Canada, South Africa and New Zealand. Some of these countries reinforced their legislation by amending them under the influence of the UK legislation. For example, Australia replaced its previous legislation with the Foreign Proceedings (Excess of Jurisdiction) Act No. 3 of 1984, and so did Canada and South Africa with the passing of the Foreign Extraterritorial Measures Act, S.C. 1984 c. 49 and the Protection of Business Amendment Act No. 71 of 1984 respectively.

See Rosenthal and Knighton, *National*; J. Griffin, 'Possible Resolutions of International Disputes over Enforcement of US Antitrust Law' (1982) 18 *Stanford Journal of International Law* 279; M. Harvers, 'Good Fences Make Good Neighbours: a Discussion of Problems Concerning the Exercise of Jurisdiction' (1983) 17 *International Lawyer* 784; M. Joelson, 'International Antitrust: Problems and Defences' (1983) 15 *Law and Policy in International Business* 1121; D. Sabalot, 'Shortening the Long Arm of American Antitrust Jurisdiction: Extraterritoriality and the Foreign Blocking Statutes' (1982) 28 *Loyola Law Review* 213 (includes table of different states with blocking statutes).

[116] *In re Uranium Antitrust Litigation: Westinghouse Elec. Corp.* v. *Rio Algom Ltd.*, 617 F 2d, 1248 (7th Cir. 1980).

in antitrust policy by the USA. In the UK, the earliest attempt made by domestic courts to prevent the extraterritorial application of US antitrust laws arose in 1952. In *British Nylon Spinners* v. *ICI* the Court of Appeal ordered ICI not to comply with a court order from the USA, requiring ICI to re-assign certain patents to Du Pont.[117] The Court of Appeal disregarded an earlier order by Judge Ryan in *United States* v. *Imperial Chemical Industries* (ICI)[118] to dispose of industrial property abroad because it was said that this constituted an attempt to assert extraterritoriality which UK courts did not recognise.[119] Referring to the statement in Judge Ryan's opinion that it is not an infringement of the authority of a foreign country for a US court to order harmful effects on US trade to be removed,[120] the Master of the Rolls said:

> If by that passage the learned Judge intended to say (as it seems to me that he did) that it was not an intrusion on the authority of a foreign sovereign to make directions addressed to that foreign sovereign or to its courts or to nationals of that foreign power effective to remove (as he said) 'harmful effects on the trade of the United States', I am bound to say that, as at present advised, I find myself unable to agree with it.[121]

More than twenty years later, in *Rio Tinto Zinc* v. *Westinghouse Electric Corp.*[122] a similar antithesis to the US extraterritorial approach was expressed in the House of Lords. Lord Diplock submitted that the use by the US Government of US judiciary as a means to investigate activities of UK firms taking place outside the USA on the basis that those activities infringed US antitrust laws amounted to an unacceptable invasion of the sovereignty of the UK.[123]

A comment

It is this author's view that the USA – and indeed any other country seeking extraterritorial application of its antitrust law – should take the above

---

[117] *British Nylon Spinners Ltd.* v. *ICI* [1953] I Ch. 19. See O. Khan-Freund, 'English Contracts and American Antitrust Law: the *Nylon Patent* Case' (1955) 18 *Modern Law Review* 65.

[118] *United States* v. *ICI*, 100 F. Supp. 504, at 592 (SDNY 1951).   [119] *British Nylon*, at 24.

[120] *United States* v. *ICI*, 105 F. Supp. 215 (SDNY 1951), 229.   [121] *British Nylon*, 24.

[122] [1978] 1 All ER 434.

[123] *Ibid.*, 639. For a good discussion of this case see G. Newman, 'Potential Havens from American Jurisdiction and Discovery Laws in International Antitrust Enforcement' (1981) 33 *University of Florida Law Review* 240. See also the similar view expressed in the same case by Lord Wilberforce, at page 448, that 'it is axiomatic that in antitrust matters the policy of one state may be to defend what is the policy of another state to attack'.

concerns and interests of foreign countries seriously. A decision by the USA to take action under its antitrust laws against anti-competitive acts beyond its national boundaries should be sensitive to any potentially negative consequences, to both relations with other countries under its foreign policy, and its efforts to promote co-operation with antitrust authorities in different jurisdictions.[124] Over the years, however, this sensitivity has not been clearly demonstrated.

A due regard for the sovereignty and independence of other countries in matters relating to their own trade and national interest requires restraint on the part of countries attempting to impose their own laws and methods of regulating economic conditions outside their own territorial boundaries. Whilst countries have an absolute sovereign right to deal with acts committed within their borders which infringe their laws, such a desire to apply their laws beyond their boundaries – and even their absolute belief that their own laws and methods are ideal for all jurisdictions – cannot justify an absolute assertion of extraterritorial jurisdiction over economic activities of foreign firms. President Eisenhower when he considered in his inaugural speech whether the USA should cease attempting to impose its antitrust laws upon other countries famously remarked that in respecting the identity and heritage of each country in the world, the USA should never use its strength to try to impress upon the citizens of other countries its cherished political and economic institutions.

Some reflections

Extraterritoriality as an act of aggression

When country A seeks to extend its jurisdiction over acts in country B to nationals of country B, this will normally be a breach both of the law of the latter and of international comity. Looking closely at this situation, it becomes obvious that, in effect, this is an act of aggression.[125] In antitrust policy and as far as the USA is concerned, this has been an act of

---

[124] See G. Born, 'Recent British Responses to the Extraterritorial Application of United States Law: the *Midland Bank* Decision and Retaliatory Legislation Involving Unitary Taxation' (1985) 26 *Virginia Journal of International Law* 91.

[125] See D. Wood, 'The Impossible Dream: Real International Antitrust' (1992) *University of Chicago Legal Forum* 277, 280–1.

judicial aggression,[126] which seems to contradict a well-established understanding between countries, namely that in the absence of a clear legislative intent to the contrary the courts of one country will apply and
enforce the principles of public international law.[127] One such principle
is that the domestic laws of an individual country cannot extend beyond
its own territories, except so far as regards its own nationals. Countries
should recognise that their jurisdictional competence is governed by this
territoriality principle. US courts, however, through ignorance or disregard
of this principle seem to seek to address the extraterritorial behaviour of
foreign firms over which they have obtained jurisdiction according to US
rules. This is a real judicial obstacle to the internationalisation of antitrust
policy.

The above-mentioned US cases can be relied on in support of this view.
These cases demonstrate a basic misconception regarding the competence
of the courts under public international law, to proceed against foreign
firms under their domestic laws. If a country can assume extraterritorial
jurisdiction over acts by foreign firms because they have 'consequences'
within its territory and because it 'reprehends' such acts, the door will definitely be opened to an almost unlimited extension of this jurisdiction.
Clearly, there is a need to know where to draw the line. Therefore, examining the role of law courts seems to be the logical next step in this
analysis.

The role of law courts

The manner in which the US courts have applied the doctrine of extraterritoriality raises several questions with regard to the role of the judiciary
in the context of extraterritoriality and international comity. It is not clear
whether it is a proper task for the judiciary to decide such issues in this
context.[128] In an area which is the juxtaposition of law and politics, it is

---

[126] See *Timken Roller Bearing Co.* v. *United States*, 341 US 593 (1951); *United States* v. *Minnesota Mining and Mfg. Co.*, 92 F. Supp. 947 (D. Mass. 1950); *United States* v. *Imperial Chem. Indus. Ltd.*, 100 F. Supp. 504 (SDNY 1951); *Holophane Co.* v. *United States*, 352 US 903 (1956); *United States* v. *Watchmakers of Switz. Info. Ctr., Inc.*, 1963 Trade Cas. (CCH) 70,600 (SDNY 1962), order modified, 1965 Trade Cas. (CCH) 71,352 (SDNY 1965).

[127] See *The Schooner Channing Betsy*, 2 Cranch 64, 118 (US 1804).

[128] See J. Stanford, 'The Application of the Sherman Act to Conduct Outside the United States: a View from Abroad' (1978) 11 *Cornell International Law Journal* 195, 213.

doubtful whether judges are in the best position to assess the impact that any decision they make will have on foreign relations.[129] Furthermore, there is always the risk that this would compromise their independence. If the national legislature has not given a clear signal regarding its aim to regulate activities beyond national borders,[130] it is questionable whether courts are justified in interfering.[131]

It seems that in practice, US courts have not been completely objective in their analysis, tending to give more weight to domestic than foreign interests.[132] Arguably, it is difficult to expect domestic courts to arrive at an impartial balance between national interests and those of other countries. The balancing of these interests, as may be observed in the case of the USA, is not confined to the discipline of law as such, but seems to take place within the context of other domains,[133] including international comity. For this reason, the balancing may in some cases be a more political than legal exercise. Some commentators have argued that such balancing of interest by the courts is neither appropriate nor workable because it requires balancing sensitive political and diplomatic concerns traditionally considered

---

[129] See D. Blair, 'The Canadian Experience' and M. Joelson, 'The Department of Justice's Antitrust Guide for International Operations' in J. Griffin (ed.), *Perspectives on the Extraterritorial Application of US Antitrust and Other Laws* (ABA, Section of International Law, New York, 1979). Interestingly, some US courts have shed some doubt on the competence of the courts to handle issues of this nature. See *In re Uranium Antitrust Litigation*, 480 F. Supp. 1138 (N.D. Ill. 1979), at 1148.

[130] It has been argued that if the US Congress has not expressed its views on the matter, US courts in dealing with the extraterritorial scope of US antitrust law should proceed on the presumption that Congress did not intend to violate principles of international law. See generally Trentor, 'Jurisdiction'.

The case of *Baker* v. *Carr*, 369 US 186 (1962), 198–200 seems to establish that a court should refrain from dealing with an action based on a federal statute unless the prohibition constituting the subject-matter of the action has been declared unlawful by Congress. See E. Craig, 'Extraterritorial Application of the Sherman Act: the Search for a Jurisdictional Standard' (1983) 7 *Suffolk Transnational Law Journal* 295.

[131] Lowe, 'Problems', 731. It is interesting to observe the attitude of the US Court of Appeals for the Seventh Circuit in the *Uranium* case, where the court described the foreign countries, despite the encouragement of the US Department of Justice to them to submit their arguments to the US courts, as 'surrogates' for absent defendants, adding that 'shockingly to us, the governments of the defaulters have subserviently presented for them their case against the exercise of jurisdiction'. *In re Uranium Antitrust Litigation*, 1256 (note 116).

[132] See H. Maier, 'Interest Balancing and Extra-Territorial Jurisdiction' (1983) 31 *American Journal of Comparative Law* 579; D. Bowett, 'Jurisdiction: Changing Patterns of Authority over Activities and Resources' (1982) 53 *British Yearbook of International Law* 1.

[133] See generally L. Jaffe, 'Standing to Secure Judicial Review: Public Actions' (1961) 74 *Harvard Law Review* 1265, 1304.

'non-justiciable'.[134] In the absence of herculean detachment, there is in-
evitably a risk of a 'home town' decision merely by virtue of the fact that
US courts have a different perspective from courts in other jurisdictions.[135]
This will inevitably lead to application of the *lex fori*.[136]

Even if courts are able to undertake such an exercise, it seems that resolving such issues should occur using inter-governmental consultation and
negotiation.[137] It is difficult to expect that public international law will apply in an international antitrust issue, which is really a manifestation of
a policy conflict between countries. In such cases, it is more appropriate
to resolve the conflict through means of consultation and negotiation. It
is thought that if the courts in one country seek to resolve the conflict in
favour of that country by invoking domestic antitrust law, this cannot be
considered to be the rule of law but a regrettable support, in judicial guise,
in favour of the principle that economic might is right.[138]

Performing this exercise of extraterritoriality within US courts can also
give rise to uncertainty in law and policy, in general, and for firms, in
particular; and there seems to be an indication that the practice of the courts
in the past has been confusing and contradictory.[139] At the moment, it is
extremely difficult for a foreign firm operating outside the USA to predict
whether any of its conduct may potentially give rise to liability under US
antitrust law.[140] The jurisprudence of US courts in general, and the decision

---

[134] See Sandage, 'Forum', 1700.

[135] See generally Akehurst, 'Jurisdiction', 185–6; Maier, 'Crossroads', 317.

[136] See M. Ehrenzweig, 'The *lex fori* – Basic Rule in the Conflict of Laws' (1960) 58 *Michigan Law Review* 637, 643.

[137] Former Australian Attorney General P. Durack once argued that law courts should not decide on the justification of law and policy in extraterritoriality conflict, stating that in this kind of conflict an important matter is the question of the impact of the conflict upon foreign relations which is not justiciable, as it falls within the realm of diplomatic negotiations. See P. Durack, 'Extraterritorial Application of US Antitrust Law and US Foreign Policy', address before the ABA Section of International Law, 12 August 1981, Library of Congress, File 1055; J. Snyder, 'International Competition: towards a Normative Theory of United States Antitrust Law and Policy' (1985) 3 *Boston University International Law Journal* 257.

[138] Support for this point can be found in the case of *Laker Airways* v. *Sabena*, 731 F 2d 909 (D.C. Cir. 1984).

[139] See J. McNeill, 'Extraterritorial Antitrust Jurisdiction: Continuing the Confusion in Policy, Law, and Jurisdiction' (1998) 28 *California Western International Law Journal* 425; J. Shenefield, 'Extraterritoriality in Antitrust' (1983) 15 *Law and Policy in International Business* 1109; J. Ongman, '"Be No Longer Chaos": Constructing a Normative Theory of the Sherman Act's Extraterritorial Jurisdictional Scope' (1977) 71 *Northwestern University Law Review* 733.

[140] In *Laker Airways*, Laker Airways rejected the jurisdictional rule of reason because it considered US courts ill-equipped to determine whether the vital national interests of the USA or

of the majority in the Supreme Court in *Hartford Fire* in particular, increases this uncertainty.[141]

Against these arguments, however, stand other arguments supporting a judicial involvement in the context of extraterritoriality and comity.[142] In particular, it has been noted that analysing comity considerations is a proper exercise for the courts and that the involvement of foreign elements or foreign relations does not *ipso facto* render the courts incompetent to deal with the matter. It has also been said that it should not be supposed that a case touching or concerning foreign relations lies beyond judicial cognisance.[143]

A comment

In light of the above, it seems to be appropriate to view the problem with extraterritoriality as not solely, or indeed essentially, a legal one. The problem is a national one in the sense that it concerns the relation of one country with other countries. Not infrequently, a country may have a genuine national interest of considerable importance in the continued existence of a cartel or another type of practice,[144] or in some state-owned or other important national firms not having to face large fines, not having to reveal certain information,[145] or not having to comply with a particular kind of remedy order, which may all arise as a result of extraterritorial application of other countries' domestic antitrust laws.[146] The involvement of a substantial national interest in this regard is bound to trigger problems. The fact that a

those of other nations should predominate, arguing, at pp. 949–50, that balancing 'generally incorporate[s] purely political factors which the court is neither qualified to evaluate comparatively nor capable of properly balancing'. See also the view expressed by some commentators that there are serious doubts that courts are an appropriate forum for evaluating conflicting national and foreign interests on a case-by-case basis. See Turner, 'Application', 233.

[141] Also, note the existence of the treble damages remedy increases the dangers in US litigation, hence the enhanced risk for foreign firms. See pp. 201–3 below.

[142] See S. Burr, 'The Application of US Antitrust Law to Foreign Conduct: Has *Hartford Fire* Extinguished Considerations of Comity?' (1994) 15 *University of Pennsylvania Journal of International Business Law* 221.

[143] See *Baker v. Carr*, 369 US 186, 211, at 211–12 (1962).

[144] See D. Rosenthal, 'What Should Be the Agenda of a Presidential Commission to Study the International Application of US Antitrust Law?' (1980) 2 *Northwestern Journal of International Law and Business* 372.

[145] D. Papakrivopoulos, 'The Role of Competition Law as an International Trade Remedy in the Context of the World Trade Organization' (1999) 22 *World Competition* 45, 59.

[146] See generally J. Shenefield, 'Thoughts on Extraterritorial Application of the United States Antitrust Laws' (1983) 52 *Fordham Law Review* 350.

country has the right to protest against the extraterritorial application of the antitrust law of another country would not solve such problems in an effective way. Certain countries have very strong beliefs about what they see as literally being dominated by other countries, and it is irrelevant that this may arise only occasionally. This is a real psychological attitude on the part of certain countries, and this must be recognised as a fact. Thus, genuine conflicts of national economic interests may arise in this context.

Dealing with extraterritoriality and its conflicts

The problem of extraterritoriality cannot be solved merely by jurisdiction or comity rules, whether judicial or of any other type. The problem is far more considerable than that. It seems that an increase in bilateral and multilateral negotiations between countries in antitrust policy is required to resolve these issues.[147] Closer forms of co-operation between countries and their antitrust authorities should be fostered. The situation will only deteriorate if countries continue to exchange court orders and blocking statutes. The amount of animosity and friction produced by this issue can have very serious implications for relations between countries and effective efforts towards co-operation between them in the internationalisation of antitrust policy. This problem needs to be solved in the most effective and expedient way possible.

The most desirable result, it seems, is to avoid extraterritorial application of domestic antitrust laws, provided that less harmful effective means may be found to replace extraterritoriality. In the absence of such effective means, it is suggested that alternative possible means should be found to resolve conflicts inherent in extraterritoriality in antitrust policy.[148]

---

[147] See T. Anderson, 'Extraterritorial Application of National Antitrust Laws: the Need for More Uniform Regulation' (1992) 38 *Wayne Law Review* 1579, 1589–97.

[148] The literature on solutions suggested by scholars is abundant. See Rosenthal and Knighton, *National*; Shenefield, 'Thoughts'; Davidow, 'Extraterritorial'; R. Feinberg, 'Economic Coercion and Economic Sanctions: the Expansion of United States' Extraterritorial Jurisdiction' (1981) 30 *American University Law Review* 323; M. Grippando, 'Declining to Exercise Extraterritorial Jurisdiction on Grounds of International Comity: an Illegitimate Extension of the Judicial Abstention Doctrine' (1983) 23 *Virginia Journal of International Law* 395; B. Grossfeld and P. Rogers, 'A Shared Values Approach to Jurisdictional Conflicts in International Economic Law' (1983) 32 *International and Comparative Law Quarterly* 931; B. Hawk, 'International Antitrust Policy and the 1982 Acts: the Continuing Need for Reassessment' (1982) 51 *Fordham Law Review* 201; J. Mirabito and W. Friedler, 'The Commission on the International Application of the US Antitrust Laws: Pulling in the Reins' (1982) 6 *Suffolk Transnational Law Journal* 1.

Avoiding extraterritoriality

It seems that in most cases extraterritoriality has been employed in order to deal with anti-competitive acts committed beyond national boundaries which foreclose foreign markets.[149] If one proposes the elimination of extraterritoriality, other effective means will have to be proposed to take its place. One alternative means could be to employ trade policy to deal with such market foreclosure stemming from anti-competitive behaviour taking place beyond national boundaries.[150] This suggestion seems to arise from the fact that domestic antitrust law falls short of providing a remedy when more than one jurisdiction is involved in the matter, especially when it comes to collecting information and evidence located in foreign jurisdiction. Added to this fact, not every domestic antitrust authority can be relied upon to take effective action to protect the interests of other countries and their firms.

According to this proposal, since anti-competitive behaviour beyond national boundaries raises barriers to market access, the adequate response should be to adopt an effective trade policy as opposed to antitrust policy instruments. One such instrument would be for domestic trade agencies to undertake empirical analysis and market access evaluation into foreign market restraints. An inquiry of this kind has been suggested by some antitrust law practitioners on the US side of the Atlantic who have argued that such an inquiry would help identify large markets where there are few or no imports, identify where there are no exports from one major country to another and identify where persistent and dramatic price differentials exist between markets.[151]

Although very attractive, such a proposal seems to be problematic in many ways. In addition to the confusion that may be added to the roles of antitrust and trade policy,[152] imbuing trade agencies with the task of

---

[149] See J. Farlow, 'Ego or Equity? Examining United States Extension of the Sherman Act' (1998) 11 *Transnational Lawyer* 175.

[150] Ch. 8 deals with antitrust and trade policies with respect to market access-restraining private anti-competitive behaviour.

[151] See Report of the International Competition Policy Advisory Committee to the US Attorney General and the Assistant Attorney General for Antitrust (ICPAC) (2000), p. 249. Note that a similar proposal seems to have come from some firms. The Eastman Kodak Co. proposed during 1999 that an independent body make a finding that a restrictive practice is taking place on foreign markets and thus constitutes a hindrance to market access; this will then be used as a presumption on the part of antitrust authorities that it is necessary to initiate an enforcement action. See http://www.kodak.com.

[152] See ch. 8.

antitrust policy does not seem to be appropriate. Apart from the lack of expertise of trade agencies in antitrust policy matters, it is likely that this would complicate antitrust policy enforcement and result in uncertainty. On the other hand, whilst it would be appropriate to recommend involving trade and antitrust policy experts in transnational antitrust policy matters,[153] it is less appropriate to suggest the exclusion of the latter. A report prepared by the International Competition Policy Advisory Committee to the US Attorney General and for the Assistant Attorney General for Antitrust (ICPAC) in 2000 argued against applying the trade methodology to practices of firms beyond US borders. ICPAC stated there is a risk that firms operating within the USA and others in foreign markets will be subjected to different standards with the consequence being adverse for the latter. The report also warned of the risk that applying different standards would also trigger parallel actions by other countries, something that US firms are very certain to contest.[154]

Minimising or avoiding conflicts of extraterritoriality

Instead of avoiding extraterritoriality in the manner described above, one may advocate a closer co-operation between countries in order to minimise (or better still avoid) conflicts arising as a result of extraterritoriality. The following discussion sheds some light on several proposals to realise that aim.

Taking account of the ability of foreign antitrust authorities to deal with anti-competitive acts on their territory

An antitrust authority should be encouraged to consider the ability of other antitrust authorities to deal with anti-competitive acts committed beyond its own boundaries and within the latter's jurisdiction, before it should seek extraterritorial enforcement of its own antitrust laws.[155] The authority should examine whether its concerns can be addressed more effectively by its counterparts in other jurisdictions. The above discussion makes it clear that

---

[153] See ch. 10.

[154] See ICPAC (2000), p. 251. See, however, the *MCIWorldcom/Sprint* case for a good example of real co-operation between the USA and the EC, with the USA leaving EC matters to the European Commission to handle, discussed in ch. 5.

[155] See D. Valentine, 'Building a Co-operative Framework for Oversights in Mergers – the Answer to Extraterritoriality Issues in Merger Review' (1998) 6 *George Mason Law Review* 525.

the recent position adopted by the USA has come to mirror such a proposal, albeit to a limited extent.[156] The 1995 Antitrust Enforcement Guidelines for International Operations make it clear that the US authorities *may* consult with interested foreign countries through appropriate diplomatic channels to attempt to eliminate anti-competitive effects in the USA instead of bringing their own enforcement actions.[157]

Extraterritoriality in most exceptional circumstances

A second alternative could be to rely on extraterritoriality only when it is first apparent that there is a link between the anti-competitive behaviour taking place beyond national boundaries and the commerce of a country and the conditions of competition therein and secondly, only in the absence of the ability of other antitrust authorities to deal with the matter themselves.[158] Thus, extraterritorial application of antitrust laws in this instance should be confined to cases in which co-operation with other antitrust authorities is not possible. This would present an improvement on previous positions adopted by the USA under which the USA applied its antitrust laws to foreign activities that had a 'direct, substantial, and foreseeable' anti-competitive effect on its commerce regardless of whether the activities in question were sanctioned by other antitrust authorities or not. As a way of expressing respect for the interests of other countries, US courts, for example, developed several devices to achieve that end. These are the Act of state doctrine, the principle of comity, the sovereign immunity and the foreign sovereign compulsion defence.[159]

---

[156] See C. Lytle, 'A Hegemonic Interpretation of Extraterritorial Jurisdiction in Antitrust: from *American Banana* to *Hartford Fire*' (1997) 24 *Syracuse Journal of International Law and Commerce* 41, 69–72.

[157] See *Guidelines*, p. 21.

[158] See *United States* v. *Watchmaking of Switzerland Information Centre, Inc.* 133 F. Supp. 40 (SDNY 1955).

[159] For a good discussion of these instruments see J. Griffin, 'United States Antitrust Law and Transnational Transactions: an Introduction' (1987) 21 *International Lawyer* 307, 327–33; P. Areeda and L. Kaplow, *Antitrust Analysis: Problems Text, Cases* (Little, Brown, Boston, 1988).

Under the Act of state doctrine, US courts would refrain from questioning the legality of acts adopted by other countries within their jurisdiction. This is because a sovereign country is bound to respect the independence of every other sovereign country and the courts in one country will not sit in judgment on the acts of a government of another country done within its own territory. See *Underhill* v. *Hernandez*, 168 US 250 (1897). See also D. Gill, 'Two Cheers for *Timberlane*' (1980) 10 *Swiss Review of International Competition Law* 7.

Under the sovereign immunity defence, a country should not be made a defendant in US courts with regard to its political activities, as opposed to commercial activities. See *The*

To this, as was said above, US courts added the jurisdictional rule of reason.

However, this proposal has limitations. It is very doubtful whether other countries would accept such a proposal, even in light of the fact that extraterritoriality is being asserted in the most exceptional circumstances. Furthermore, more than one claim can be made against the adequacy of defences such as the foreign compulsion defence. It seems to be very odd and inappropriate for a country to try to get other countries to regulate their domestic economy by compulsion especially when the former is in favour of reducing public intervention in the marketplace. Such an attempt amounts to an intervention in the way the latter countries elect to operate their socio-economic systems and to handle their domestic affairs.

In addition to the criticism just made, the defences seem to be applied in a political rather than a legal context. Consequently they seem to be, in essence, discretionary 'politically oriented' devices. US courts appear to have the discretion to attach relative weights to every factor considered under each device and then weigh them against one another. To complicate matters even further, the US Department of Justice has insisted that US courts should refrain from the use of comity in order to dismiss antitrust actions brought by US antitrust authorities. According to the US Department of Justice's Antitrust Division, if the Department of Justice decides to pursue an antitrust action, it amounts to determination by itself that the interests of the USA should be given priority over the interests of any foreign country and that the challenged conduct is more harmful to the USA than any injury to foreign relations that might result from the antitrust action.[160] Thus, although it seems an attractive way to minimise conflicts of extraterritoriality, in practice, this 'conflict of laws' proposal seems to fall short of reaching the desirable end of avoiding or minimising such conflicts.

Schooner Exch. v. *M'Faddon*, 11 US (7 Cranch) 116 (1812). See also H. Pittney, 'Sovereign Compulsion and International Antitrust: Conflicting Laws and Separating Powers' (1987) 25 *Columbia Journal of Transnational Law* 403. In the USA, Congress enacted the Foreign Sovereign Immunities Act 1976, which gives US courts exclusive responsibility to decide when a foreign sovereign is entitled to immunity in US courts. Note that recently US Congress narrowed the immunity in 1976 by establishing that immunity does not extend to the commercial activity of foreign governments. See the Foreign Sovereign Immunities Act 1998.

For comments on the sovereign compulsion defence and comity see pp. 174–5 above.

[160] *Guidelines* (1995), note 167.

Respect for principles of public international law

Greater respect for principles of international law by US courts should enable them to resolve conflicts of extraterritoriality in a more objective manner without tipping the balance in favour of national interests and national firms at the expense of interests of other countries and their firms. Such respect therefore calls for a more careful balance of interests exercise to be undertaken by US courts.[161] Within this exercise, courts should take into account interests of foreign countries beyond the confines of national laws and policy goals.[162] As a result, it would be expected that fewer intrusions into the sovereignty of other countries would arise and this would ensure more respect for the principles of public international law, such as those aiming to safeguard non-intervention in the affairs of other countries by one country.[163]

Abandoning treble damages

The first thing to be said about the treble damages remedy is that it has been unique to US antitrust law. In some jurisdictions, injured parties may bring their own legal action but only after the country in question has condemned the conduct. The existence of this type of remedy under the US system of antitrust has given rise to a tension in the relationship between the USA and other countries.[164] The view held by several countries has been that it is not particularly appropriate for their national firms to be liable in treble damages in cases before US courts, especially since actions in these cases do not infringe their own antitrust laws.

Despite this protest, the USA considers the treble damages remedy to be a useful means of combating domestic and foreign anti-competitive behaviour and for this reason it has emphasised that there is no consideration of abandoning this remedy. ICPAC provided several reasons for this view. According to the Committee, US antitrust law makes no distinction between

---

[161] See generally E. Eric, 'The Use of Interest Analysis in the Extraterritorial Application of United States Antitrust Law' (1983) 16 *Cornell International Law Journal* 147.

[162] See the proposal suggested by some writers for the courts to substitute juridical factors of *forum non conveniens* for political decision-making in resolving extraterritorial antitrust cases. See Sandage, 'Forum', 1707–14.

[163] See the *Uranium* case and *U.S.* v. *General Electric Co.*, 170 F. Supp. 596 (SDNY 1959).

[164] Report of the American Bar Association Sections of Antitrust Law and International Law and Practice on *The Internationalization of Competition Law Rules: Coordination and Convergence*, December 1999, pp. 21–2.

US and foreign defendant firms. Furthermore, whilst it is recognised that removing the treble damages remedy in export restraint cases might result in fewer conflicts with the laws of other countries, such a move would also reward jurisdictions that have consistently been against the extraterritorial application of US antitrust laws. According to ICPAC, such an approach would result in foreign defendant firms gaining better treatment under US law than US defendants and could open floodgates regarding whether the offending conduct harmed 'imports' commerce or 'export' commerce. In ICPAC's view the case law record shows that a distinction between the two situations may itself be very difficult to make; most of the cases included claims involving both situations. The conclusion by ICPAC therefore was that in spite of the potential benefits from increased co-operation from foreign authorities and firms, it is not advisable to alter the treble damages remedy.[165]

Regardless of how compelling this explanation is, addressing foreign restraints that may impede access to markets through private litigation is problematic. For example, though the authorities in the USA have begun to consider principles of comity before applying their antitrust laws extraterritorially, there is no obligation on private firms to do so.

A question that is raised at present concerns whether abandoning the treble damages remedy would be considered a positive step forward. The answer suggested by some commentators has been in the positive.[166] One of the reasons why abandoning treble damages is considered to be important is that although actions brought to claim such damages seem to advance the public policies enshrined in antitrust policy, they actually represent personal interests as opposed to the public interest. These actions stand in complete contrast to public actions, which are brought in the name of the

---

[165] See ICPAC, pp. 247–8. Further reasons for retaining the remedy are that it underpins 95 per cent of antitrust litigation in the USA and is circumscribed by the antitrust injury requirement established in certain US cases which means that plaintiffs may only recover if they suffer losses flowing from the anti-competitive act itself. Hence, for example, if there was a firm thought to be failing but not in actual fact failing and a market leader merges with it, then another firm could not claim treble damages for subsequent losses arising from this merger as it had not suffered any antitrust injury as such.

[166] See Rosenthal and Knighton, *National*, p. 88. However, other writers are not particularly optimistic about abandoning private treble damages. See J. Davidow, 'Treble Damage Actions and US Foreign Relations: Taming the "Rouge Elephant"' (1985) *Fordham Corporate Law Institute* 37.

public interest. Hence, private parties have no responsibility to balance a broad range of public interest on whether they should initiate an action. It is not beyond logic to even suggest that private parties may intentionally contribute to widening the difference between their own country and other countries in antitrust policy in order to enhance their chances of receiving a favourable judgment. To this end, it seems that abandoning the treble damages remedy would be an effective way to minimise extraterritoriality conflicts. Nevertheless, it is difficult to force upon countries the elimination of treble damages, because public international law has no scope of application with regard to the way in which a country elects to organise its own economic, legal and political orders. It can only interfere in cases of antitrust conflicts between countries.

Developing a common approach

Surely at this point in the development of antitrust policy internationally, at a time when more and more countries are instituting systems of antitrust with laws aimed at similar types of conduct, the judiciary in all countries should acknowledge that the question of applying their domestic laws to conduct entered into outside their national territories by firms not located in that territory cannot be answered purely by an analysis of the national law. Just as anti-competitive conduct of foreign firms can have an effect in a country's territories, so too can judicial decisions in the country affect persons and conditions outside it.

Hence, though some US courts, including the Supreme Court, on occasions purported to take into account how the conduct in question would be regulated in the country where it took place, judges should also look at the relevant law in that country concerning extraterritorial jurisdiction in such matters.[167] This is not just to advocate an exercise in judicial reciprocity or an attempt to establish a lowest common denominator in extraterritoriality. Rather, it is to argue that the judiciary should develop common international standards and promote harmonisation in the extraterritorial application of antitrust laws. This would be an appropriate exercise of comity. This would also produce a positive influence on the practice of

---

[167] See J. Quinn, 'Sherman Gets Judicial Authority to Go Global: Extraterritorial Jurisdictional Reach of US Antitrust Laws Are Expanded' (1998) 32 *John Marshall Law Review* 141, 158.

antitrust authorities, and enhance consistency in decision-making as well as confine any exercise of discretion by those authorities.[168]

As an extension to this proposal, one could also encourage countries to strive to develop multilateral standards on the effect(s) of extraterritoriality. As an alternative, bilateral agreements between countries should be welcomed, in order to ensure reciprocity and international comity. There is no doubt that the disadvantages of extraterritoriality are one reason why considerable emphasis has been put in recent years on the development of mechanisms for bilateral, regional or even global co-operation between countries in the field of antitrust policy.[169]

Conclusion

Perhaps the main objection to extraterritoriality is that the techniques of the nineteenth century are not necessarily suitable or even sensitive to conditions and developments of the twenty-first century. Other objections seem to extend to the approaches adopted to minimise and solve conflicts arising as a result of extraterritoriality.

The above discussion makes it clear that aggressive use of extraterritoriality seems to be the primary source of tension between countries in antitrust policy. Nevertheless, there was an acknowledgement that in certain cases, extraterritoriality can be a valid basis for asserting jurisdiction, since traditional territoriality rules are inadequate to deal with acts of an economic nature. In light of this, a country asserting jurisdiction extraterritorially should not do so extensively, without regard to the legal, economic and political interests of other countries.

In any case, extraterritoriality, whether relied on expansively or in a limited manner, seems to have triggered various negative responses by countries. In an attempt to resolve the conflicts, which these responses have generated, the chapter examined several ways in which they may be avoided or minimised. An ideal situation would be to reach the stage where an international system of antitrust is effectively in place. However, this would require not only elimination of conflicts of extraterritoriality, but also uprooting the latter entirely. A 'second best' world would call for some action to be taken by the judiciary and domestic antitrust authorities, in order to

---

[168] See ch. 4.   [169] WTO Annual Report 1997, pp. 31–2.

foster harmonisation and co-operation in antitrust law and policy between different countries.

Finally, the chapter indicated that a great deal of extraterritoriality revolves around addressing anti-competitive conduct of domestic firms in one country which impedes the access of firms of another country to the markets of the former. This issue has quite frequently surfaced in antitrust policy debates in recent years. It is examined in the following chapter.

8

Antitrust and trade policies

This chapter is concerned with hindrances caused by the anti-competitive behaviour of domestic private firms to market access by foreign firms. In particular, the chapter examines the roles that antitrust and trade policies play in addressing this issue and the factors which may limit the role of either policy in this regard. The chapter considers the relationship between antitrust and trade policy, since, as will be seen, there are implications for both policies, especially in the case of hybrid practices. The purpose of the chapter, however, is not to give a detailed analysis of both policies independently, but rather to examine how antitrust policy interacts with trade policy in an increasingly integrated and liberalised global economy. In so doing, the chapter evaluates the implications and lessons which one policy holds for the other.

The chapter is structured as follows. The first part gives an overview of some important points. The second part describes the different restraints which may affect the access of foreign firms to domestic markets. The third part deals with the differing perspectives of antitrust and trade policy. The fourth part highlights the possible approaches currently available under antitrust and trade policy which can be used to address market access concerns involving anti-competitive behaviour of private firms. It also outlines the shortcomings of these approaches in both the short and long term. The fifth part advocates an alternative approach to deal with these practices. The sixth part gives an account of developments in the area during the course of the last decade. The seventh part contains some implications of the analysis and the eighth part gives a conclusion.

Overview

The efforts of the international community have, for many years, been primarily concentrated on removing hindrances to the flows of trade and investment erected by countries.[1] These efforts have been mainly in the form of agreements between countries. A good example is the General Agreement on Tariffs and Trade (GATT) which served as a tool to liberalise trade in the post-1950s era. Other efforts can be seen in the light of the events leading to the birth of the World Trade Organization (WTO). Whilst these efforts have contributed to the growth seen over the years in these flows, it seems that further growth can be achieved if hindrances caused by the anti-competitive behaviour of private firms are completely removed.[2] Indeed, as early as 1960, the GATT recognised that anti-competitive practices of firms may hinder the expansion of world trade and economic development in individual countries, frustrate the benefits of tariff reductions and removal of quantitative restrictions and undermine the aims and objectives of GATT.[3] The desirability of the removal of such hindrances is an issue to which attention has been turning, especially since governmental hindrances have decreased in significance.

The recognition that anti-competitive behaviour by private firms may affect the flows of trade and investment between countries that have been increasing, raises some important questions in the internationalisation of antitrust policy which need to be addressed.[4] Before dealing with these

---

[1] See C. Fedderson, 'Focusing on Substantive Law in International Economic Relations: the Public Morals of GATT's Article XX(a) and "Conventional Rules of Interpretation"' (1998) 7 *Minnesota Journal of Global Trade* 75, 79. Efforts have also taken root at the regional level, where different countries have concluded several agreements among themselves towards trade liberalisation, such as the European Community (EC), North American Free Trade Agreement (NAFTA) and the Asia Pacific Economic Co-operation Forum (APEC).

[2] See statement of J. Klein at the Hearings on Antitrust Enforcement Oversight, before the US House of Rep. Comm. on the Judiciary, 105th Cong., 1st Session, 5 November 1997, http://www.law.house.gov. Also, D. Wood, 'The Internationalization of Antitrust Laws', address at the DePaul Law Review Symposium, 3 February 1995.

[3] See S. Waller, 'Can US Antitrust Laws Open International Markets'? (2000) 20 *Northwestern Journal of International Law and Business* 207, 208–10; E. Fox, 'Foreword: Mergers, Market Access and the Millennium' (2000) 20 *Northwestern Journal of International Law and Business* 203, 203–4. See WTO Annual Report 1997 and 1998.

Interestingly enough, the International Chamber of Commerce does not believe that anti-competitive behaviour of private firms restraining market access necessarily presents a problem in the global economy, but rather such result may be explained by divergence in the international strategies of firms. See the ICC Joint Working Party on Competition and International Trade's replies to questions posed by the WTO Working Group, 6 October 1998, p. 2, http://www.iccwbo.org.

[4] See H. Applebaum, 'Antitrust and the Omnibus Trade and Competitiveness Act of 1998' (1989) 58 *Antitrust Law Journal* 557, 565; C. Ehlermann, 'The International Dimension of Competition Policy' (1994) 14 *Fordham International Law Journal* 833, 839.

questions however, it is desirable to cast some light on why restraints in general, and those caused by private firms in particular, are an issue of concern in the first place.

There are several ways in which concerns may arise. The most obvious way is when the access to domestic markets by foreign firms is impeded. Two important terms should be elucidated here. The first is 'hindrance',[5] which in the context of the market connotes anything that makes it difficult for a firm to enter a particular market. Nevertheless, it may not be easy in practice to draw a clear line between what amounts to hindrance and what does not. The second term is that of 'market access', which, though familiar, is a controversial issue in antitrust policy. Surprising as this may be, there is no universal consensus on the meaning of 'market access'.[6] In the present discussion, market access is taken to connote the conditions associated with the entry of firms into a particular market in order to sell goods and provide services. To an extent, this definition is similar to that given by the WTO. According to the WTO, market access describes the extent to which goods or services can compete with locally made products in another market. In the WTO framework the term stands for the totality of government-imposed conditions under which a product may enter a country under non-discriminatory conditions. It is essential to note, however, that this author's definition of market access is not intended to be comprehensive about what market access is in reality, but rather an explanation in order to facilitate a better understanding of the issues at hand.

Hindrance to market access can be caused by practices of firms, practices of countries and in some cases practices of both – known as 'hybrid' or 'mixed' practices.[7] If the hindrance is of the first type, one can expect it to

---

[5] A term that can be regarded as a synonym in antitrust policy is 'barriers to entry'. It may be of interest to observe the way different scholars have defined 'barriers to entry'. Chicago School scholars have given a very restrictive view on exclusionary practices. For example, Bork has argued that a barrier to entry is anything that makes entry more difficult. He believes that generally barriers to entry is a misunderstood concept. See R. Bork, *The Antitrust Paradox: a Policy at War with Itself* (Basic Books, New York, 1978), ch. 16. A more detailed account has been offered by Bain, whose work has done much to popularise the concept. He listed among barriers to entry such things as economy of scale, capital requirements and product differentiation, arguing that virtually any impediment to market entry should be regarded as a barrier. See J. Bain, *Barriers to New Competition* (Harvard University Press, Cambridge, 1956), pp. 114–15.

[6] See H. Hauser, 'Proposal for a Multilateral Agreement on Free Market Access (MAFMA)' (1991) 25 *Journal of World Trade Law* 77.

[7] Several complaints about private or hybrid practices have surfaced over the years. See, for example, claims by the American Electronics Association about restraining practices in the Japanese

be addressed under antitrust policy. If, on the other hand, the hindrance is of the second type, then one can expect that trade policy and its tools will become relevant. However, if the hindrance is of the third type, the position becomes less clear. In this case, one can expect there will be implications for both antitrust and trade policy. Using this division of types of hindrance, the responsibility for hindrance to market access may not always be easily apportioned between private firms or countries. There may be cases in which the responsibility may have to be attached to both firms and countries, since the restraints may be 'mixed' or 'hybrid' in nature.

The different restraints

Private anti-competitive behaviour

Horizontal agreements

Horizontal agreements – those entered into between firms operating at the same level of the market – amongst domestic firms can hinder access to domestic markets by foreign firms if the former, for example, agree to refrain from purchasing or distributing products imported by or from the latter, or to withhold from the latter materials, services, supplies or other necessary inputs. For example, if firms X, Y and Z in country A, which enjoy a position of economic strength, decide to stop importing a specific product of country B, the consequence of this agreement may prevent those domestic firms handling that product in country B from penetrating the domestic market of country A.

Vertical agreements

Agreements between domestic firms at different levels of the economy, for example, between a supplier and a distributor, may have the effect of hindering the ability of a foreign firm to develop a distribution network, which it needs in order to access the domestic market. Normally, this is the case in exclusive distribution agreements and exclusive purchasing agreements; such agreements can substantially raise barriers to entry by foreign firms.

electronics market (Submissions to the US Trade Representative (USTR) in 1991) and complaints from auto parts makers in Europe and the USA about similar practices in Indonesia and Korea. See http://www.ustr.gov.

Abuse of a dominant position

Hindrance to market access by foreign firms may occur in the case of dominant domestic firms which engage in abusive behaviour. Such behaviour can be in the form of refusal to supply or deal, and abuse of intellectual property rights,[8] predatory pricing and selective price-cutting which are all designed with the aim of excluding foreign firms from domestic markets.

Mergers

A merger between firms may generate anti-competitive spillover effects beyond the borders of the country or countries where the merger is taking place. The development of national champion firms through domestic mergers can harm markets beyond national boundaries, as well as hinder the ability of potential foreign firms to penetrate domestic markets.[9]

Practices of countries

There are several ways in which practices by countries may directly or indirectly impair market access by foreign firms.[10] The following two points illustrate how countries could be held accountable for hindering market access by foreign firms.

Exemptions from antitrust law

Countries may directly exempt the anti-competitive behaviour of domestic firms from the application of their domestic antitrust laws. This issue has for many years been subjected to close scrutiny[11] but is relevant to the present discussion on the effect of practices of countries on market access because exemptions from those countries' antitrust laws may have consequences beyond their domestic borders in general, and for firms aiming to access the market in those countries in particular. The concern about

---

[8] See generally S. Anderman, *EC Competition Law and Intellectual Property Rights* (Oxford University Press, Oxford, 1998).

[9] See D. Baker and W. Miller, 'Antitrust Enforcement and Non-Enforcement as a Barrier to Imports' (1996) 14 *International Business Law* 488, 490.

[10] Waller, 'Can US Antitrust Laws?', 208.

[11] See R. Inman and D. Rubinfeld, 'Making Sense of the Antitrust State Action Doctrine: Balancing Political Participation and Economic Efficiency in Regulatory Federalism' (1997) 75 *Texas Law Review* 1203.

exemptions in this case is a serious one, especially since there is no indication of willingness on the part of countries to unilaterally confine the scope and application of exemptions from their domestic antitrust laws. The reluctance of countries to abandon their existing exemptions and exclusions can be seen from the Organisation for Economic Cooperation and Development (OECD) Recommendations on Hard-Core Cartels (1998). Despite the willingness of participating countries, as expressed in the Recommendations, to co-operate on enforcement action against hard-core cartels, the Recommendations did not attempt to impose any binding rules on exemptions by countries.[12] As a result, an extensive use of exemptions could easily lead to a substantial amount of economic activity around the world avoiding the antitrust laws of different jurisdictions.[13] A study carried out by Hawk, commissioned by the OECD in 1996, found substantial exclusions from antitrust law in several sectors in eleven different jurisdictions, including employment-related activities, agriculture, energy and utilities, postal services, transport, communications, defence, financial services and media and publishing. There is no reason to believe that the position has substantially changed in the last six years since that study was carried out.

Strategic application of domestic antitrust law

Countries may indirectly strategically apply their domestic antitrust laws in order to promote 'national champions' at the expense of foreign firms. A country may undertake strategic measures for the protection of anti-competitive behaviour of domestic firms because it gains more from those measures than foreign countries. In a tactical application of its domestic antitrust law, a country may immunise private anti-competitive behaviour by virtue of different measures, such as the 'State Action' doctrine.[14]

Mixed or hybrid restraints

As outlined above, restraints on market access can be mixed or hybrid in nature. This is, for example, the case where the practices of a country

---

[12] See the OECD website at http://www.oecd.org.   [13] See below.

[14] See E. Fox, 'The Problem of State Action that Blesses Private Action that Harms "the Foreigners"' in R. Zach (ed.), *Towards WTO Competition Rules: Key Issues and Comments on the WTO Report (1998) on Trade and Competition* (Kluwer Law International, The Hague, 1999), p. 325. See further pp. 199–200 above.

facilitate the anti-competitive behaviour of private firms.[15] The following examples may be used to illustrate.

Limiting foreign direct investment

One way in which a foreign firm may access a market is through foreign direct investment. An action by a country to give an association of firms in a particular domestic industry the power to decide, for example, whether or not to grant licences to individual firms, can mean that the association may use this power in an exclusionary manner against foreign firms.

Standardisation

Standardisation in industries by standard-setting bodies, especially in the hi-tech sector, such as telecommunications and information technology, can offer considerable advantages to domestic firms. In a global market, the activities of standard-setting bodies will have an increasing impact on the flows of trade between countries. Firms and consumers will seek to use technological standards that can work easily abroad. A foreign standard that is not compatible with other technologies – mainly because of the decision of the domestic standard-setting body – can tilt the development of those technologies towards a domestically selected standard. As a result, the ability of a foreign firm, which does not have any presence in the standard-setting body, to access the domestic market may be hindered.

Lack of enforcement by antitrust authorities

Anti-competitive behaviour by private firms may also be encouraged by the lack of enforcement of antitrust policy by their domestic antitrust authorities. Such lack of enforcement may give tacit implication to those firms that

[15] An example of repeated allegations of hybrid restraints may be found in the history of the Japanese passenger vehicle industry. See generally J. Rill and C. Chambers, 'Antitrust Enforcement and Non-Enforcement as a Barrier to Import in the Japanese Automobile Industry' (1997) 24 *Empirica* 109.

A more recent allegation of hybrid restraint that was the subject of a proceeding under section 301 of the US Trade Law 1974, as amended, involves an alleged government-approved concerted refusal to deal in Mexico. In 1998, the US Corn Refiners Association complained to the US Trade Representative about the practices of the Mexican government, which was alleged to have supported a restrictive agreement between the Mexican sugar producers' association and the major Mexican soft drink bottling companies. The petition claimed that the parties agreed to limit the amount of high fructose corn syrup (HFCS) they would buy. See USTR Press Release 99–44, 14 May 1999, available at http://www.ustr.gov. Section 301 is discussed at pp. 225–7 below.

their anti-competitive conduct is permissible. Policy-makers in one country may even adopt a more active role by encouraging firms, for example, to divide markets, thinking that this will lead to stabilisation in a domestic industry in its early stage of development or infancy.[16]

Some remarks

In the case of hybrid restraints, anti-competitive behaviour by private firms may hinder market access because it may be facilitated by some supportive action by the country. The fact that this matter – mainly due to the involvement of public and private elements – cannot be addressed satisfactorily under antitrust or trade policy separately,[17] blurs the lines of accountability of countries and firms. As a result, one can expect that economic and political tensions will materialise between countries and between countries and firms.

The involvement of countries in hybrid restraints is a matter of legal significance when it comes to analysing these restraints under antitrust and trade policy. Interestingly, however, that legal significance differs under the two policies. As far as antitrust policy is concerned, the involvement of a country means that the behaviour of a private firm, which would otherwise be considered anti-competitive and possibly prohibited, may escape being caught by antitrust law.[18] Thus, a restrictive or anti-competitive behaviour of a firm may escape being caught by the provisions of antitrust law because it has been authorised by a country as part of a clearly formulated policy to displace competition with regulation and where the government of the country concerned supervises the behaviour in question.[19] Under trade policy, on the other hand, the involvement of a country in the manner just

---

[16] See generally M. Dabbah, 'Measuring the Success of a System of Competition Law: a Preliminary View' (2000) 21 *European Competition Law Review* 369.

[17] Current trade policy tools have not yet been tested with respect to hybrid restraints. For example, the Technical Barriers to Trade (TBT) agreement at the WTO prohibits the use of standard setting for the purpose of impeding market access. As yet, however, there has not been a WTO dispute settlement panel decision under the TBT concerning this problem. See ch. 10.

[18] See generally American Bar Association Antitrust Section, Antitrust Law Developments 1049 (1997), http://www.abanet.org. A good example is provided in the light of various doctrines such as the foreign sovereign compulsion doctrine, and the foreign sovereign immunity doctrine and the Act of state doctrine.

[19] See *Parker* v. *Brown*, 317 US 341 (1943) and *Southern Motor Carriers Rate Conference* v. *US* 471 US 48 (1985).

214 THE INTERNATIONALISATION OF ANTITRUST POLICY

described means that catching hybrid restraints is more possible.[20] Still, whereas active participation by a country in hybrid practices may be caught by trade policy, for example by the World Trade Organization (WTO) rules, there is less certainty whether a lesser role for countries – such as sanctioning or tolerating the private practice – can be caught.[21]

During the last decade or so, market access-restraining hybrid practices have become a major new element in the antitrust and trade policy debate. Whilst there has been no comprehensive empirical study with economic or statistical analyses in this important debate, there seems to be an increasing recognition and sufficient indication that the effect of private anti-competitive practices on trade and investment flows between countries can be as serious as hindrances solely caused by the behaviour of countries.[22] Equally, there seems to be a growing recognition that the anti-competitive behaviour of private firms may be blessed by actions of countries, policies and practices.[23] Under many of these factual patterns an important question raised is whether, and to what extent, the resulting antitrust policy problems from market access-restraining hybrid practices are attributable to the country as opposed to the private firms concerned.

Lastly, an important comment should be made about the place of the concept of 'market access' in antitrust and trade policy. Whilst the removal of artificial impediments to market access is perhaps the most obvious goal of trade policy, especially post-1945, it is not apparent that ensuring market access has been recognised as an appropriate goal for antitrust policy internationally. In order to understand these differing perspectives on the place

---

[20] The USA, for example, argued that the market access-restraining practices in the *Kodak/Fuji* case were orchestrated by the Japanese government. See pp. 219–21 below.

[21] See how the US Congress, for example, has attempted to reach such lesser government roles through the concept of 'toleration' within the meaning of section 301 Trade Act 1974. See pp. 225–7 below.

[22] It is interesting to observe that at present when access to proprietary technologies or to the facilities or services offered by dominant firms may be essential for other firms, especially foreign ones, as shown with respect to Internet-related areas, both antitrust policy and trade policy seem likely to focus increasingly on private access-denying practices.

[23] US firms in different industries have repeatedly argued that their access to Japanese markets is hindered by the behaviour of Japanese private firms. See http://www.ustr.gov. Hybrid market access restraints in trade in services have received particular attention in international trade negotiations. Articles VIII and IX of the General Agreement on Trade in Services (GATS) deal specifically with the obligations of Members to address the trade-restricting business practices of dominant firms and those which supply exclusive services as well as firms which offer other services.

of the concept of market access under both policies, one should consider their differences in general.

The perspectives of antitrust and trade policies

Antitrust and trade policies have different perspectives.[24] First, these policies address economic distortions of different kinds and origin. Antitrust policy is primarily concerned with the conduct of private firms[25] and is nationally determined and is centrally focused on protecting the operation of the market.[26] Trade policy, on the other hand, is internationally determined and is principally focused on the behaviour of countries, aiming to remove discriminatory acts by the latter that foreclose access to domestic markets for foreign firms.[27] Secondly, the legal basis of antitrust policy enforcement is wider than that of trade policy. According to some commentators, this is because trade policy is decided through more political than legal processes;[28] although it is arguable that the difference in politicisation of antitrust and trade policy is one of kind rather than degree.[29] Thirdly, trade policy has to be based on the political consent of those who win or lose from the expansion of trade and hence a greater weight is given to 'producer interests'.[30] Antitrust policy, on the other hand, tends to be more concerned with consumer interests than trade policy.[31] Fourthly, not all antitrust policy concerns are relevant to trade policy. For example, the procedural and

---

[24] For a general comparison of antitrust and trade policy, see H. Applebaum, 'The Interface of the Trade Laws and the Antitrust Laws' (1998) 6 *George Mason Law Review* 479; also, Draft Report of the International Chamber of Commerce Joint Working Party on Competition and International Trade, 'Competition and Trade in the Global Arena: an International Business Perspective' 12 February 1998. See http://www.iccwbo.org.

[25] Note, however, the existence of state aid rules in the antitrust policy chapter in the Treaty of Rome, such as Article 86 EC, under which the European Commission is able to control anticompetitive behaviour effected by governments.

[26] See R. Hudec, 'A WTO Perspective on Private Anti-Competitive Behavior in World Markets' (1999) 34 *New England Law Review* 79, 81–2.

[27] *Ibid.*

[28] See C. Doern, *Competition Policy Decision Processes in the European Community and United Kingdom* (Carleton University Press, Ottawa, 1992).

[29] C. Doern and S. Wilks, *Comparative Competition Policy* (Oxford University Press, Oxford, 1996), p. 336.

[30] See G. Feketekuty, 'Reflections on the Interaction between Trade Policy and Competition Policy: a Contribution to the Development of a Conceptual Framework' (OECD, Paris, 1993), p. 11.

[31] *Ibid.*, p. 15. See also J. Finger (ed.), *Antidumping: How It Works and Who Gets Hurt?* (University of Michigan Press, Michigan, 1993); T. Boddez and M. Trebilcock, *Unfinished Business: Reforming Trade Remedy Laws in North America* (C. D. Howe Institute, Toronto, 1993).

substantive features of multi-jurisdictional merger reviews are not matters customarily considered under trade policy. In addition, international cartels appear to be a serious problem for individual countries and the global economy, which provide serious antitrust policy issues but do not, directly at least, influence trade policy issues. Fifthly, when there is an overlap in antitrust and trade policy issues, different conclusions regarding the effects of a particular restraint may be reached. Judging a restraint from an antitrust policy perspective means that its effects have to be considered in terms of efficiency and consumer welfare and other goals mentioned in chapter 3 of the present book, whilst a trade policy perspective will mainly consider whether the restraint adversely impacts on the flows of trade and investment between countries and access to markets by keeping foreign firms out of those markets. Interestingly, from a trade policy perspective, the restraint can still be condemned even if it has positive effects on efficiency and the welfare of those participants in the domestic market.[32]

The different approaches

This part reviews the current approaches available under antitrust and trade policies which can be adopted to deal with restraints involving the anti-competitive behaviour of private firms.

Approaches under antitrust policy

Relying on extraterritoriality

If a country fails to address the anti-competitive behaviour of its domestic firms which hinders the entry of foreign firms to the domestic market, the home country of those foreign firms may wish to apply its antitrust law extraterritorially to open such a 'domestic' market.[33] Nevertheless, the efforts of the home country may be frustrated by several factors. This is a point that has emerged from the previous chapter, which showed that extraterritorial enforcement of domestic antitrust laws may not necessarily enjoy sufficient

---

[32] See WTO Annual Report 1997, p. 56.

[33] The use of extraterritoriality to open foreign markets is referred to in the USA as 'outbound' extraterritoriality. See *United States* v. *Pilkington plc*, 59 Fed. Reg. 30604 (1994), in which the US Department of Justice challenged restrictions imposed by Pilkington in the UK that prevented US firms from exporting to the UK. See further ch. 7.

impact to address antitrust concerns beyond domestic markets. To this, one can add the fact that reliance on the doctrine of extraterritoriality can aggravate conflicts between countries and disagreements over its application can lead to a serious friction in the interface between antitrust and trade policy.[34] To illustrate, the following hypothetical situation is used.

Suppose that country A and country B both have effective systems of antitrust. Imagine that the anti-competitive behaviour of firm X in country A does not harm either conditions of competition or other firms in the market in country A, but rather it is preventing firm Y of country B from penetrating that market. Of course, the primary concern of country A's antitrust authority would be to protect conditions of competition, and possibly competitors, in country A's market. The fact that no harm is done to conditions of competition and competitors may lead the antitrust authority to choose not to apply its domestic antitrust laws – even if harm is done to firm Y. However, country B's antitrust authority, being concerned about the lack of action on the part of country A's antitrust authority, may try to apply its antitrust laws extraterritorially in order to open the market in question for firm Y. The fact that more than one antitrust authority becomes involved and may reach different conclusions over one and the same matter will lead to conflicts between country A and country B and may trigger uncertainty.

Bilateral co-operation between antitrust authorities

Bilateral co-operation between antitrust authorities in the enforcement of their antitrust laws may be seen as a good alternative to the extraterritoriality option. Its effectiveness as a means to address anti-competitive behaviour restraining market access of private firms should be seen in light of the several problems associated with that option.[35] In particular, co-operation between antitrust authorities may eliminate conflicts between countries in practice and remove many problems associated with access to information and other evidentiary matters which frequently surface in antitrust cases.[36] The benefits of co-operation should also be seen against the backdrop of the fact that firms will be relieved from the burden of duplicated enforcement and inconsistent conclusions which may be reached by different antitrust

---

[34] D. Papakrivopoulos, 'The Role of Competition Law as an International Trade Remedy in the Context of the World Trade Organization' (1999) 22 *World Competition* 45, 59.
[35] See ch. 7.   [36] WTO Annual Report 1997, p. 31.

authorities.[37] In the context of practices of private firms restraining market access, co-operation is likely to enhance this access and promote the growth of flows of trade and investment in the global economy. This chapter identifies three different types of mechanism of bilateral co-operation between antitrust authorities.

Agreements with positive comity principle   Bilateral agreements using the positive comity principle are a positive mechanism through which co-operation between antitrust authorities can be facilitated. A report produced by the OECD in 1999 has identified six potential benefits of a positive comity approach to cross-border enforcement. The benefits include improved effectiveness in remedying illegal conduct, improved efficiency in investigations, reduced need for sharing confidential and other information, avoidance of jurisdictional conflict, prevention of damage to the requested country's interests and protection for other legitimate interests of the protected country. Under positive comity, one party to the agreement (known as the requesting party) can ask the other party (known as the requested party) to address anti-competitive behaviour within the latter's boundaries that has effect on the interests of the former. A good example of such an agreement with a positive comity principle is given by the 23 September 1991 agreement between the EC and the USA, which was extended by another agreement in 1998. Both of these agreements were discussed in chapter 5.[38]

The significance of positive comity has increased not only due to its incorporation into more formal agreements between antitrust authorities,[39] but also through the use of the principle in antitrust cases. However, it is of considerable interest to anticipate to what extent introducing a principle of positive comity in agreements between antitrust authorities may influence the natural tendency of those authorities not to take into account the effects

---

[37] See ch. 9.   [38] See pp. 112–16 above.

[39] For example, a co-operative enforcement agreement between Canada and the EC provides for reciprocal notification and cross-border requests for enforcement action. Under the agreement, each side is required to take the other's interests into consideration. In addition to placing a high degree of emphasis on traditional comity, the agreement provides protection for the confidentiality of information collected during the enforcement process. See http://www.europa.eu.int/comm/dg04/intern/multilateral. Another example is the agreement reached between the USA and Israel, which provides for enforcement co-operation and co-ordination, notification of enforcement action and confidentiality protections. See the US–Israel Agreement Regarding the Application of Their Competition Laws, 15 March 1999.

of their decisions on the interests of other countries. It would be sensible to suggest in this regard that the concept of comity should not be given an unduly restrictive interpretation, which would make it applicable only in cases of 'pure conflict' where a firm cannot comply with the requirements imposed by one jurisdiction without infringing the laws of another.

De facto use of positive comity   The second mechanism of co-operation that has arisen at times resides in what can be described as the de facto use of positive comity. In the absence of a formal agreement with a positive comity principle between domestic antitrust authorities, it may still be possible for one antitrust authority to make a positive comity type of referral to another authority. This was exactly what the USA did in the *Kodak/Fuji* case.[40]

Here, Kodak alleged that it was unable to penetrate the Japanese photographic and paper market because of hindrances caused by the Japanese authorities and Fuji Photo Film Co. In handling Kodak's claim, the US Trade Representative (USTR) lodged a complaint with the WTO, arguing that the practices of the Japanese authorities and Fuji amounted to unreasonable hindrances.[41] The USTR also referred the claims to the Japan Federal Trade Commission (JFTC). In its reference, the USTR expressed an interest in opening a dialogue under a GATT decision concerning consultations on restrictive business practices. The USTR also stated that the USA intended to discuss with Japan the significant evidence of anti-competitive activities that it had uncovered in this sector, and to ask the latter to take appropriate action.[42] The USTR confirmed the willingness of the USA to supply the JFTC with any necessary information that may assist the latter

[40] See WTO Report WT/DS44/R (98–0886) 'Japan – Measures Affecting Consumer Photographic Film and Paper', 31 March 1998, http://www.wto.org/wto/ddf/ep/public.htm.
[41] See press release, 'US Launches Broad WTO Case under GATT, GATS against Japan on Film' June 1996, http://www.wto.org/wto/ddf/ep/public.htm; Office of the USTR, 'Section 304 Determination: Barriers to Access to the Japanese Market for Consumer Photographic Film and Paper' 1996, http:www.ustr.gov. A WTO panel decided this case adversely to the US complaints. See J. Ramseyer, 'The Costs of the Consensual Myth: Antitrust Enforcement and Institutional Barriers to Litigation in Japan' (1985) 94 *Yale Law Journal* 604; J. Trachtman, 'International Regulatory Competition, Externalization, and Jurisdiction' (1993) 34 *Harvard Journal of International Law* 47, 54–5; H. First, 'Selling Antitrust in Japan' (1993) 7 *Antitrust* 34; W. Fugate, 'Antitrust Aspects of US–Japanese Trade' (1983) 15 *Case Western Reserve Journal of International Law* 505, 524.
[42] Office of the USTR, press release, 'Acting US Trade Representative Charlene Barshefsky Announces Action on Film', 13 June 1996.

in its investigation. The US Department of Justice, for its part, said it was willing to assist the JFTC in its analysis of anti-competitive behaviour in the relevant market.

The JFTC looked into the complaint, but determined that Fuji's behaviour was not contrary to the Anti-Monopoly Law. The JFTC said that access to the relevant market, including channels of distribution, was adequately available to all firms, whether foreign or domestic. This outcome was not received favourably by the USA, either at government level or the level of the industry. Several voices were heard within the USA expressing concerns about the co-operation between the USA and Japan in the field of antitrust policy, especially since at that time the USA was making good progress in its relationship with the EC under their co-operation agreements.[43] The reason for such concerns seems to go beyond the actual outcome of the case, and involves other factors, such as the US lack of confidence in Japan's commitment to combat anti-competitive behaviour and its enforcement of its antitrust laws. The fact that Japan relied on administrative guidance and informal enforcement rather than a formal decision-making process seems to be another factor, which seems to have given rise to this lack of confidence given the US commitment to the principles of transparency and due process.[44]

In 1999, the USA and Japan entered into a co-operation agreement for the enforcement of their antitrust laws. The agreement includes provisions on notification of enforcement and positive comity. Under this agreement, one party will inform the other of its enforcement activities and will consult with the other on matters arising under the agreement. However, the agreement does not strictly provide for a rigorous enforcement of the Japanese Anti-Monopoly Law. Instead, the agreement was expected to be implemented in accordance with the existing laws of each party, which means that its effect is surrounded by uncertainty.[45]

---

[43] See, for example, remarks by some members of the US Senate: 'Senate Sub-Committee Focuses on International Enforcement, Positive Comity', 6 May 1999. See http://www.senate. gov/-dewine.

[44] See, generally, J. Haley, 'Administrative Guidance Versus Formal Regulation: Resolving the Paradox of Industrial Policy' and I. Hiroshi, 'Antitrust and Industrial Policy in Japan: Competition and Cooperation in Law and Trade Issues of the Japanese Economy' in G. Saxonhouse and K. Yamamura (eds.), Law and Trade Issues of the Japanese Economy: American and Japanese Perspectives (University of Washington Press, Washington, 1986).

[45] See Agreement Concerning US–Japan Co-operation on Anti-Competitive Activities, 7 October 1999.

Co-operation agreements other than those with positive comity Agreements with positive comity are not the only type of formal co-operation that exists between antitrust authorities. There are other types of agreements, such as those aiming at co-ordination of enforcement efforts through non-confidential information sharing, which are likely to enhance the enforcement of antitrust policy globally. In addition, they have the potential to promote the flows of trade and investment between countries through enhancing market access.

Generally, these agreements provide that one party to the agreement should seek to take into account the important interests of the other party and notify the latter when its enforcement activities may have an impact on those important interests. This is widely known as 'negative comity'. Also, it is not uncommon for these agreements to provide for consultations on an annual basis between the officials of the enforcement authorities concerned which may address conditions under which the parties will offer assistance to each other and may further provide that, under appropriate circumstances, the parties may agree to co-ordinate enforcement activities.

Several such agreements have been entered into by several antitrust authorities over the years. As early as 1976, an agreement was entered into between the USA and Germany.[46] Other agreements were entered into by the USA with Australia in 1982[47] and with Canada in 1984.[48] It may be interesting to observe that these agreements seem to be reinforced by the OECD Recommendations of 1986,[49] last revised in 1995.[50]

---

[46] Agreement between the US and Germany Relating to Mutual Co-operation Regarding Restrictive Business Practices, 23 June 1976.

[47] Agreement between the US and Australia Relating to Co-operation on Antitrust Matters, 23 April 1997. This agreement was reinforced in 1999 by a mutual enforcement assistance agreement.

[48] Memorandum of Understanding between Canada and the US as to Notification, Consultation and Co-operation with Respect to the Application of National Antitrust Laws. This Memorandum of Understanding was superseded in 1995 by the Agreement between the US and Canada Regarding the Application of Their Competition and Deceptive Marketing Practices Laws, 23, April 1997.

[49] Recommendation of the Council for Co-operation between Member Countries in Areas of Potential Conflict between Competition and Trade Policies, OECD Doc. C(86)65(Final), 23 October 1986. The 1986 OECD Recommendation revised earlier versions issued on 5 October 1967 [C(678)53(Final)], 3 July 1983 [C(73)99(Final)], 25 September 1979 [C(79)154(Final)] and 21 May 1986 [C(86)44(Final)].

[50] Revised Recommendation of the Council Concerning Co-operation between Member Countries on Anti-Competitive Practices Affecting International Trade, OECD Doc. C(95)130(Final), 27–8 July 1995.

A comment

The above types of co-operation are certainly helpful in promoting greater consistency in antitrust policy enforcement outcomes globally. It is also possible that such consistent outcomes may, in conjunction with continued consultation amongst domestic antitrust authorities, facilitate substantive harmonisation and procedural convergence of domestic antitrust laws,[51] lead to more effective enforcement of antitrust policy and promote equal conditions of competition in all countries. Undoubtedly, all these factors are likely to foster the opening up of markets and enhance growth in trade and investment.

However, these types of co-operation suffer from certain limitations, mainly relating to the exclusion of provisions on the exchange of confidential information. Antitrust authorities are unable to share confidential business information amongst themselves without the consent of the firms involved.[52] This inability, in this author's view, makes it very difficult if not impossible for antitrust authorities to adequately address cross-border anti-competitive behaviour.[53] In 1994, the US Congress passed the International Antitrust Enforcement Assistance Act which permits the US antitrust authorities to obtain and exchange with foreign antitrust authorities, where relevant, investigative information otherwise protected by confidentiality provisions. The Act also provides that US authorities may open proceedings to obtain such information from nationals on behalf of foreign authorities, subject to them being satisfied that the latter will safeguard the confidentiality of the information and undertake to ensure reciprocity. In 1999, the USA entered into an agreement with Australia which was based on this Act. Nevertheless, it is thought that even with the removal of this confidentiality limitation not all the problems associated with these agreements will be resolved because these agreements are not vehicles of conflict resolution. It seems that, although as a result of the agreements the practices of antitrust

---

[51] See ch. 3.   [52] See WTO Annual Report 1997, p. 32.

[53] D. Rosenthal, 'Equipping the Multilateral Trading System with a Style and Principles to Increase Market Access' (1998) 6 George Mason Law Review 543, 568. Other, albeit more limited, agreements have been concluded by the USA with other states, including Canada. The latter, for example, has been confined to criminal investigations, including criminal antitrust law cases. See A. Bingaman, 'US Antitrust Policies in World Trade', address before the World Trade Center Chicago Seminar on GATT after Uruguay, Chicago, Illinois, 16 May 1994, available at http://www.usdoj.gov/atr/public/speeches/94-05-16.txt.

authorities are brought closer together, even with regard to national antitrust rules which may originally be far apart (e.g. those relating to vertical restraints), the agreements are unlikely to replace the need to agree on basic principles relating to their enforcement. It is very likely that commercial frictions may remain unresolved in the absence of a mechanism or procedure for dispute resolution to be based on a set of determined and collectively agreed antitrust rules. It is also difficult to imagine the emergence of a level playing field in the internationalisation of antitrust policy if this were to be founded only on a category of inevitably heterogeneous bilateral agreements. Furthermore, the scope of these types of co-operation is constrained by differences remaining in antitrust law and its enforcement in different jurisdictions. For example, in the light of the discussion in chapter 5, it is clear that the goals of EC antitrust law do not only aim to enhance consumer welfare and efficiency of firms, but also to further the integration of the single market. Consequently, in the USA the latter goal is neither recognised nor necessary under US antitrust law. Such differences are bound to lead to differences in approach between the two jurisdictions,[54] especially with respect to cases of vertical restraints, abuse of market dominance and possibly mergers.[55]

Other limitations also arise given the inherently long-term nature and cost of building a framework of co-operation between antitrust authorities and development of a globally comprehensive principle of positive comity. At present, the number of agreements with positive comity is very small. Hence, in the absence of a realistic possibility of adopting more preferable methods of addressing antitrust issues in the global economy – such as adopting a multilateral approach[56] – antitrust authorities should be encouraged to develop a network of such agreements, particularly one that would include countries other than those which most vigorously enforce their antitrust policy today. Adopting the EC–US agreement as a model, and building on the efforts of antitrust authorities which have entered

---

[54] See chs. 4 and 9.

[55] See, for example, how the EC antitrust rules in relation to vertical restraints have been reformed, with the enactment of Regulation 2790/99 EC. See R. Whish, 'Regulation 2790/99: the Commission's "New Style" Block Exemption for Vertical Agreements' (2000) 37 *Common Market Law Review* 887. Also, with regard to market dominance, Article 82 EC jurisprudence is admittedly far more substantial than section 2 Sherman Act 1890 case law.

[56] See chs. 9 and 10.

into similar agreements, seems to be a very appropriate step to take at present.

Approaches under trade policy

Rules within the WTO

The WTO rules do not cover the anti-competitive behaviour of private firms. Those rules are meant to address governmental practices as opposed to the practices of private firms. As things stand, no international rules directly address the anti-competitive behaviour of private firms. However, the possibility of extending the scope of some WTO rules to the latter is not ruled out completely.[57] A few possibilities may be identified through which the WTO rules may address the behaviour of private firms. There are several WTO provisions and mechanisms which are of possible relevance here: the consultation and co-operation arrangements under each of the main WTO agreements; the general rules of the WTO relating to non-discrimination and transparency; the areas where the WTO already provides for some minimum standards that governments are to follow in combating or regulating anti-competitive enterprise practices (notably in the area of basic telecommunications); the provisions which allow for remedies to enterprise practices, notably in the area of anti-dumping; and the WTO dispute-settlement mechanism. Furthermore, the number of areas where the multilateral trading system is already addressing antitrust policy issues has increased with the result of the Uruguay Round and the subsequent work of the WTO.[58]

One way in which the WTO can become involved is through the WTO addressing a request to each of its country members to create and enforce a system dealing with private anti-competitive practices. Arguably, the basis for doing so is already evident within the WTO. For example, under the Agreement on Technical Barriers to Trade, member countries are required to take such reasonable measures as may be available to them to

---

[57] The issues here regarding the role of the WTO in antitrust policy are highly controversial. See D. Papakrivopoulos, 'Role'; Report of the WTO Working Group on the Interaction between Trade and Competition Policy to the General Council, 8 December 1998, WT/WGTCP/2, http://www.wto.org; Waller, 'Can US Antitrust Laws?', 211.
   A fuller account of the role of the WTO can be found in ch. 9.
[58] WTO Annual Report 1997, at p. 32. See also the outcome of the WTO 4th Ministerial Conference held in Doha in November 2001, discussed at pp. 245–6 below.

ensure that non-governmental standard-setting bodies comply with the Agreement's Most-Favoured-Nation (MFN), national treatment and other requirements. The Agreement also provides that as to certain of its requirements, member countries shall formulate and implement positive measures and mechanisms in support of the observance by other than central government bodies.[59] The WTO's request towards each member country to address anti-competitive private practices could take one of several forms. One possibility could be for the WTO to insist on adopting general principles, such as those covered in the General Agreement on Trade in Services (GATS),[60] which the country concerned must follow. A second possibility would be for the WTO to lay down detailed substantive provisions, such as those provided in the Agreement on Trade-Related Aspects of Intellectual Property Rights (TRIPS).[61] A third possibility would be to introduce a requirement to set up and maintain a procedure in the domestic legal order for private firms to enforce their rights under domestic law.[62]

Domestic trade laws

The other way to reach private access-denying practices in foreign markets is by using the trade laws of individual countries. However, better success cannot be guaranteed here than with the previous option since no domestic trade law directly reaches such practices. However, in theory at least, such practices may be reached indirectly. One example is discussed below.

Case study: USA section 301, Trade Act of 1974   In the USA hindrance to market access by private practices may be considered 'unreasonable foreign practices' within the meaning of section 301 of the Trade Act 1974, as amended.[63] Section 301 tackles practices or policies of foreign countries that are 'unfair', 'unjustifiable', 'unreasonable' and 'burden or restrict US commerce'. This includes practices or policies that are contradictory to international norms and principles, such as the principle of MFN. Practices or policies which amount to 'toleration of systematic anti-competitive practices' are also considered to be unreasonable and therefore are addressed

[59] Marrakesh Agreement Establishing the WTO, Annex 1A, at Arts. 3.1, 3.5 and 8.1, 15 April 1994.
[60] *Ibid.*, Annex 1B, Article IX.   [61] *Ibid.*, Annex 1C.   [62] See ch. 9.
[63] The Act offers only limited application to governmental practices that tolerate anti-competitive private restraints. See A. Smith, 'Bringing Down Private Trade Barriers – an Assessment of the United States' Unilateral Options: Section 301 of the 1974 Trade Act and the Extraterritorial Application of US Antitrust Law' (1994) 16 *Michigan Journal of International Law* 241.

under the section.[64] For the purposes of the section, where the access by
US firms to the market of a foreign country is hindered by one or more
firms in the country behaving 'systematically' in an anti-competitive manner that 'burdens or restricts US commerce', then that country will be taken
to have tolerated that behaviour personally by failing to enforce its domestic
antitrust laws.

In practice, however, the effectiveness of section 301 is limited for three
main reasons. First, the Trade Act 1974, in general, and section 301, in particular, do not offer any definition of the terms 'toleration', 'anti-competitive'
or 'systematic'.[65] Secondly, the USTR – which is in charge of administering
the Act – enjoys full discretion regarding whether or not to initiate an action
in a given case. This is an important point to bear in mind in the context
of the present book, since as we saw in chapter 4 the use of discretion by
antitrust authorities can trigger difficulties in the internationalisation of
antitrust policy. Finally, a proceeding under the section does not involve
litigation, adjudication and ultimately a remedy. It is true that the Act refers
to initiation of action, an investigation, a hearing and possibly trade 'retaliation'. But, in practice it seems that all these elements do not always feature
in a section 301 proceeding. Hence, it would be more appropriate to regard section 301 as a medium for the USTR to negotiate with authorities
in foreign countries for the removal of an unfair trade practice. Even when
it comes to retaliation, it seems that in the majority of cases, section 301
proceedings lead to negotiated resolutions rather than trade retaliation.
Two fundamental reasons can be identified for this view.

First, retaliation as a last resort seems to be damaging to the US petitioning industry, except for rare cases in which there is two-way trade in the
product as to which market access problems exist. In those rare cases the
retaliatory trade restrictions would benefit the petitioner in the US market. Apart from those rare cases, however, the US industry does not gain
anything from trade retaliation. In most cases, the unfair practice in the
market of the foreign country, which is the petitioner's problem, remains
unresolved and the retaliatory action taken provides the petitioner with
no offsetting benefit. Secondly, in cases where the practice is considered

[64] See subsection 1(d)(3).
[65] In 1988, US trade law was brought closer to its antitrust law by making 'unreasonable' practices
or behaviour under section 301 also applicable to those governmental actions that constitute
systematic toleration of anti-competitive activities by foreign firms that restrict market access.
See Applebaum, 'Interface', 483.

'unreasonable', the USTR might run the risk of violating WTO rules if retaliatory measures are taken. One can expect a foreign country to take the matter to the WTO dispute resolution in response to the retaliation. This of course involves a high degree of probability that the USA will be ordered by the WTO to cease the retaliation.

A comment   It is not clear, however, that the USA will refrain from retaliation. For example, between 1992 and 2000, the Clinton administration's policy was that trade retaliation in section 301 proceedings would be adopted in certain cases even if this would trigger a strong reaction from the WTO. There is no reason however, why – now that the administration is no longer in power – one cannot doubt the validity of such statements. In the *Kodak/Fuji* dispute, for example, as was mentioned above, the USTR ultimately decided not to follow a section 301 route and instead referred the complaint to the WTO with regard to the claims of government unfair practices and turned to positive comity in dealing with the private anti-competitive practices. In light of this, it must be questioned whether future cases involving market access disputes will witness any use of the section. Nevertheless, it will be of some interest to observe how the current Republican administration under the presidency of George W. Bush will formulate its policies under section 301 and the US trade and antitrust laws more generally. After more than two years in office, the Bush Administration has not actually produced a coherent, consistent or sensible trade policy; although it has shown willingness to co-operate in the field of antitrust policy with major partners such as the EC at both bilateral and multilateral levels.[66]

Market access principle

The first thing that must be said is that the above options of antitrust and trade policy in terms of substance, especially the positive comity approach, may have the *potential* in the long run to be used as an effective means of combating market access-restraining private practices. However, this does not detract from the fact that currently each option suffers from certain limitations in respect of its approach. For example, the doctrine of extraterritoriality seems to raise more concerns than it actually solves. As far as the

---

[66] See pp. 218–21 above. Also see pp. 255–7 below on the discussion of the International Competition Network (ICN).

mechanisms of co-operation between antitrust authorities are concerned, these mechanisms suffer from an inherently prolonged process of developing an adequate global framework for them. The limitations facing trade policy options, on the other hand, are more obvious and primarily relate to the fact that these options do not directly address the anti-competitive behaviour of private firms. Yet the issue of market access-restraining private practices remains. To effectively address this concern, it is believed, requires the development of an adequate international approach to such practices in antitrust policy terms. This is an issue that goes to the heart of the internationalisation of antitrust policy;[67] it is important to note in this regard that the internationalisation of antitrust policy has been proposed in some countries as a response to claims by domestic firms that their ability to access foreign markets has been hindered by restrictive private and hybrid (public/private) practices.

Using domestic antitrust laws

Most domestic antitrust authorities – especially those in the USA – do not accept the view that the application of their domestic antitrust laws should consider the adverse effects on foreign firms or foreign economies. In the USA, for example – and this is a point that should be clear in light of the discussion in the previous chapter – the recent focus in antitrust law on allocative efficiency and consumer welfare addresses the role of foreign firms (as it does for domestic firms) from the standpoint of their contribution to the efficiency of the marketplace.[68] To this end, there does not seem to be any consideration of whether those foreign firms suffer adverse effects from the practices of domestic firms.[69] This means that quite often the anti-competitive behaviour of domestic firms will be exonerated where, on balance, it benefits domestic consumers and enhances market efficiency. It also means broader concepts of global welfare, including harm to foreign firms who are denied access to domestic markets, are ignored.[70] Furthermore, whilst domestic antitrust laws at best could contribute towards the

---

[67] See E. Fox, 'Toward World Antitrust and Market Access' (1997) 91 *American Journal of International Law* 1, at 1.

[68] See *Northern Pacific Railway* v. *United States*, 356 US 1, 4 (1958).

[69] See 'The EC Communication to the WTO Working Group on the Interaction between Trade and Competition Policy', 24 November 1997, http://www.wto.org.

[70] WTO Annual Report 1997, p. 31.

establishing of a liberal multilateral trading order, they fall short of fostering the exports of individual countries.[71]

At a time of relentless globalisation, this approach of domestic antitrust authorities in several countries does not seem to be suitable or satisfactory.[72] The OECD and the WTO, for example, have expressed certain reservations about this approach. A report produced within the OECD in 1995 stated:

> As trade policy should be made much more responsive to the interests of consumers, so should competition policy probably take international considerations and the interests of both producers and consumers beyond domestic jurisdictions greater into account.[73]

The WTO has expressed a similar view, arguing that:

> Even where the criteria of allocative efficiency are solely applicable, the fact that such criteria are generally applied in respect of efficiency and welfare within the jurisdiction in question and may not take into account adverse effects on the welfare of producers and consumers abroad may lead to situations where the enforcement of national competition law will not adequately take into account the interests of trading partners.[74]

Clearly, such views of important international organisations will contribute towards the internationalisation of antitrust policy by shifting the focus of domestic antitrust authorities from national to global welfare and efficiencies. It is less clear, however, whether there is a prospect in the foreseeable future that this can win the support of different countries and their domestic antitrust authorities, or at least of the USA and its antitrust authorities. Also, certain important organisations have expressed some scepticism in this regard. For example, the International Chamber of Commerce (ICC) has stated that it is not in favour of including antitrust policy on the multilateral trade agenda in the near future. The ICC has argued that sufficient progress has not been made in the understanding of the complex issues involved in antitrust and trade policy and their ramifications for this subject to be included on such an agenda.[75]

---

[71] See Waller, 'Can US Antitrust Laws?', 208.

[72] See D. Baker, 'Antitrust and World Trade: Tempest in an International Teapot?' (1974) 8 *Cornell International Law Journal* 16.

[73] *New Dimensions of Market Access in Globalizing World Economy* (OECD, Paris, 1995), p. 254.

[74] WTO Annual Report 1997, p. 75.

[75] See 'ICC Opposes Inclusion of Antitrust in Next Round of Trade Negotiations', June 1999, http://www.iccwbo.org. See also p. 263 below.

Market access principle under antitrust policy

It is this author's view that market access-restraining private practices can be effectively addressed through developing a universal antitrust market access principle – as a counterpart to the market access principle under trade policy. This principle would prohibit all forms of anti-competitive impediments – including all those involving private and public elements – to the ability of foreign firms to penetrate domestic markets. Including private and public practices avoids the difficulty associated with the existence of hybrid restraints. It is suggested that the principle could be introduced initially within the WTO, for the benefit of securing a wider agreement among countries on it.[76] When introduced, the principle could then be adopted in the domestic systems of different countries, who would assume the responsibility of this task. Countries would be required to provide effective enforcement mechanisms, tools for discovery, procedural enforcement and fair process with a principle of non-discrimination and sufficient remedies to countries and direct actions to firms within the national legal systems. The WTO would be responsible for monitoring whether countries are adopting and enforcing the principle.[77]

Developing the principle

Restraints covered

It would be over-ambitious, and possibly naive, to argue that a market access principle under antitrust policy should be adopted in the first instance regarding all types of restraints, including cartels, vertical restraints, abuses of dominance and mergers. Instead, it is suggested that the principle could be adopted first regarding certain types of restraints and then as it develops and its familiarity increases with time, it can be extended to cover other types of restraints. For example, it seems sensible to begin with hard-core cartels and mergers first, as opposed to vertical restraints and abuses of dominance. There is consensus internationally that cartels

---

[76] Note, however, that at present trade policy is well developed at the WTO. Thus it is essential, as the present chapter argues, to consider divergences between trade and antitrust policies.

[77] See Communication of the European Commission, submitted by L. Brittan and K. van Miert, COM (96) 296 Final, p. 11.

deserve immediate attention.[78] Furthermore, merger control also seems to be an issue of some urgency and importance. On the other hand, vertical restraints are an issue of some difficulty.[79] This point is clear in the light of the fact that there is hardly any evidence of consistency and clarity on how vertical restraints should be approached within one and the same jurisdiction, let alone in an international context. Hence it may be appropriate to recommend that the position with regard to the regulation of vertical restraints in individual jurisdictions must first be clarified and consolidated before examining the prospect of internationalisation in this area. Having said that, some jurisdictions have advocated a WTO market access rule that would address, *inter alia*, vertical restraints. The European Commission, for example, has been quite explicit in supporting a rule on vertical restraints that would condemn them for access-denying effects even where, taken individually, they are not inconsistent with or contrary to domestic antitrust laws; although pursuing this proposal has been opposed by the USA, especially within the WTO.[80] Finally, abuses of dominance do not seem to be a matter of considerable need for immediate attention, since there is not a large number of firms that enjoy such dominance in world markets.[81]

The use of Neofunctionalism

It is proposed that the development of a principle of market access under antitrust policy in the manner described above could be done through the use of the theory of *Neofunctionalism*.

The meaning of Neofunctionalism   Neofunctionalism is a political theory of how autonomous institutions can be formed and thereafter integrate

---

[78] See the OECD Report on Hard Core Cartels, introduced at the initiative of the USA, http://www.oecd.org/daf/clp/. Also see the view of the EC that priority attention should be given to cartels, including export cartels. *Ibid.*, p. 9. The OECD Recommendation was proposed to participants to ensure that hard-core cartels are addressed effectively under their domestic antitrust laws. The Recommendation is subject, however, to any exceptions and authorisation contained in the laws of participating countries. Nevertheless, it does provide that derogation by countries should be transparent and reviewed periodically to assess whether it is necessary and suitable to override policy objectives.

[79] See Fox, 'Toward World Antitrust', 18; P. Marsden, 'The Impropriety of WTO "Market Access" Rules on Vertical Restraints' (1998) 21 *World Competition* 5.

[80] See ch. 9.   [81] See below.

their own domain in an international system.[82] This approach explains how individual interests and players may be involved, with specific identities, motives and objectives in the creation of the system. Whilst this Neofunctionalist type of system construction has already been considered in certain areas,[83] it has never been applied to antitrust policy.

Neofunctionalism is generally concerned with explaining the methodology and reasons behind sovereign countries' decisions and actions to cease to be wholly sovereign. It explains how and why countries voluntarily mingle, merge or mix with each other so as to limit the factual attributes of sovereignty whilst acquiring new techniques for addressing different dimensions in their relationship, including any conflicts that may arise between them. In particular, the theory describes a process whereby political players in several distinct national settings are persuaded to shift their loyalties, expectations and political activities towards a new centre, where institutions enjoy jurisdiction over the pre-existing absolutely sovereign countries.[84]

Neofunctionalism is employed in the present context to explain several features of the internationalisation of antitrust policy. The author believes that the theory can help in advancing one's understanding of the process of internationalisation, and in particular the relationship between antitrust and trade policy. As we saw above, trade policy has international orientations and links, whereas antitrust policy seems to be more inward-looking and derives its validity from national origins.[85] Neofunctionalism can help to explain how spillover(s) arise from trade to antitrust policy, which consequently can help advance antitrust policy towards the international plane.

Neofunctionalism and market access   The theory of Neofunctionalism seems to be receiving an increasing support. For example, some scholars have argued that in present market circumstances – the scholars using globalisation as an example in point – any debate on the pros and cons of globalisation needs to be worked out on a sector-by-sector basis. Neither

---

[82] The term was borrowed from E. Haas, 'The Study of Legal Integration: Reflection on the Joy and Anguish of Pretheorising' (1970) 24 *International Organization* 607.

[83] See E. Haas, 'Technocracy, Pluralism and the New Europe' in S. Graubard (ed.), *A New Europe?* (Houghton Mifflin, Boston, 1964).

[84] E. Haas, 'International Integration: the European and the Universal Process' (1961) 15 *International Organization* 366.

[85] See Fox, 'Toward World Antitrust', 1.

those scholars nor other ones, however, have shown any awareness of the theory.

It was observed above that the thrust of Neofunctionalism revolves around the concept of spillover from one area to another.[86] It is essential to explain how this concept operates in the present discussion. The spillover in the case of developing a market access principle in antitrust policy, it is believed, will take place in two contexts. First, there will be a spillover from trade policy (which has an effective market access principle) to antitrust policy. The suggested approach is initially to adopt a general market access principle in relation to private anti-competitive behaviour. Secondly, once this is achieved, the principle could be adopted in relation to certain types of restraints, such as cartels and mergers, and then it could be expanded over time to cover other types of restraints, such as vertical agreements and abuses of dominance.

Neofunctionalism, different players and ideas　In addition to helping construct a market access principle in antitrust policy, Neofunctionalism will also help elucidate the role of different players in the internationalisation of antitrust policy. It is extremely important to realise that the players in the process are not only sovereign countries, but that forces above and below them also exist. Actors below include the individual and business interest groups and consumers etc. From above, there are existing regional and supranational orders, for example, those within the framework of the EC, the North American Free Trade Agreement (NAFTA), Australia–New Zealand Closer Economic Relations Trade Agreement (ANCESTRA), the OECD and the WTO.[87] These organisations promote integration, foster the development of interest groups and cultivate ties with them.

What role is there for sovereign countries within this setting of internationalisation? According to Neofunctionalism, a sovereign country's role is 'creatively responsive'.[88] As holders of the ultimate political power through their decisional authority, sovereign countries may accept, side-step, ignore

---

[86] See R. Kanbur's recent papers, available at http://www.people.cornell.edu/pages/sk145/papers.htm.

[87] For a review of these frameworks see R. Harmsen and M. Leidy, 'Regional Trading Arrangements' in S. Khemani (ed.), *International Trade Policies: the Uruguay Round and beyond* (IMF, Washington D.C., 1994).

[88] R. Harrison, *Europe in Question: Theories of Regional International Integration* (Allen & Unwin, London, 1974), p. 80.

or even sabotage decisions from above or below, which have been made regarding market conditions. The theory of Neofunctionalism on the other hand seems to have a great deal to offer in terms of propositions and ideas, which could be plausible to various interests and players when examining the process of internationalisation. The theory seems also to be able to accommodate the variety of goals that are claimed in the name of antitrust law. Hence, the use of the theory in the context of the internationalisation of antitrust policy is recommended.

Developments of some interest

Several efforts have been made at international, regional and national levels to consider the relationship between antitrust and trade policy, which are of some interest. This part reviews the different efforts witnessed in the last decade.

Work within the WTO

In 1996, due to the seriousness of market-access antitrust policy questions, a Working Group on the Interaction between Trade and Competition Policy was established within the WTO.[89] The mandate of this body, along with the Singapore Working Programme set up in December 1996, reflects the close relationship between antitrust and trade policy. These efforts have been aiming at regulatory reform in order to foster markets that are more open, contestable and competitive, to the benefit of foreign and domestic firms alike. At the same time, a discussion of antitrust policy within the WTO also reflects the long-standing recognition that private restraints can adversely affect the benefits of negotiated trade liberalisation measures, thereby reducing their benefits and potentially hindering the success that countries achieved in removing public hindrances to the flows of trade and investment.

Over the course of the last two years, a few reports have been produced within the WTO considering the intersection of antitrust and trade policy. Of particular importance is the WTO Annual Report (1997), which contains some interesting and useful examination of the relationship between antitrust and trade policy and the place of antitrust policy in the multilateral trading system more generally.

---

[89] See document WT/MIN (96)/Dec., para. 20, http://www.wto.org.

Work within the OECD

There have been several reports by the OECD over the last ten years dealing with the relationship between antitrust and trade policy.[90] The reports cover a wide range of topics concerning this relationship. Particular emphasis, however, has been placed on the consistencies and inconsistencies between the two policies. Some of these reports emphasised that differences between the two policies still remain, especially on both perspective and approach.[91] However, the reports have failed to identify how much differences between the two policies hinder the operation of one or the other policy.

Remarkably, the reports – despite realising the existence of important differences between the two policies – have reached the important conclusion that the two policies are broadly compatible. It has been said that the two policies are complementary with basically the same goals: free trade and free competition are mutually supportive.[92]

As far as the issue of market access is concerned, some of the reports – especially the Hawk report produced on behalf of the Trade Committee and the Competition Law and Policy Committee[93] – explained how market access is related to the enforcement of domestic antitrust rules. For example, the Hawk report argued that strengthening domestic antitrust laws in this respect would help minimise or alleviate trade policy disputes arising as a result of market access-restraining private anti-competitive behaviour. The report noted that this also would help reduce the need for extraterritoriality.

During the last two years, particular attention at the OECD has been paid to pursuing the following 'desirable and complementary' future options in furthering the internationalisation of antitrust policy: enhanced voluntary convergence in domestic antitrust laws; enhanced bilateral cooperation between antitrust authorities; fostering regional agreements containing antitrust policy provisions; building plurilateral antitrust policy agreements, and moving towards multilateral antitrust policy agreements.[94]

---

[90] Over the years, the OECD has established some important programmes. See, for example, the *Report on Competition and Trade Policy: Their Interaction* which was produced in 1984 by the Committee of Experts on Restrictive Business Practices. The Report examined the possible approaches to developing an improved international framework for dealing with problems arising at the frontier of antitrust and trade policy. See http://www.oecd.org.

[91] See *Consistencies and Inconsistencies between Trade and Competition Policies* (OECD, Paris, 1999).

[92] See *Trade and Competition Policy for Tomorrow* (OECD, Paris, 1999).

[93] See *Antitrust and Market Access* (OECD, Paris, 1996).

[94] See *International Options to Improve the Coherence between Trade and Competition Policies* (OECD, Paris, 2000).

These recent initiatives are important because, *inter alia*, they seek to engage non-member countries, academics and representatives of the business community. The initiatives are also important because they are *interdisciplinary* in nature.[95]

Work within the US Department of Justice, Antitrust Division

The International Competition Policy Advisory Committee (ICPAC) was formed in November 1997 by former US Attorney General J. Reno, and former Assistant Attorney General for Antitrust J. Klein, to examine what new tools and concepts were needed to address antitrust policy issues that are appearing on the horizon in the global economy. Part of ICPAC's efforts were devoted to the interface between antitrust and trade policies. A report was produced by ICPAC in February 2000 which covered a wide range of issues. It is beyond the scope of the present chapter to give an account of all these issues.

As far as antitrust and trade policies are concerned, ICPAC evaluated the current approaches to these practices. It concluded that no particular approach is appropriate to respond to all antitrust policy problems in the global economy, but without giving a particular set of proposals. It is argued that this is not satisfactory, and that there is a need for such a set of proposals.[96]

Work within the American Bar Association

In January 2000, the Antitrust and International Trade Sections Task Force of the American Bar Association produced a joint report concerning private anti-competitive practices as market access barriers. The report urged countries to take action against private anti-competitive practices that restrain market access by foreign firms in ways that substantially distort competition in the markets within an individual country's jurisdiction. The task force did not suggest that countries agree on the details of substantive antitrust law or procedure. Instead, it recommended that countries take actions consistent with the principles of national treatment and MFN, as well as provide a fair, transparent process, accessible to foreign firms where complaints

---

[95] See *Trade and Competition Policy: Exploring the Way Forward* (OECD, Paris, 1999).
[96] See ch. 10.

can be made of market access-denying practices and a resolution will be reached within a reasonable period of time. The American Bar Association took no position as to what, if any, dispute resolution mechanism should be established to deal with the situation where one country is aggrieved by another country's failure to take action against foreclosure by a private practice that distorts competition. Also, the report did not offer a view on the appropriate role of the WTO.

Implications of the analysis

Artificial barriers leading to market foreclosure cause trade tensions. Where entry to markets is restricted by a private act, rather than a public act, which amounts to antitrust violation then antitrust policy will be available – but not necessarily so – to dispel the tension. Yet, there are cases in which the restraint is not only implemented by firms. For example, a country may elect not to enforce its antitrust policy against market access-restraining private anti-competitive behaviour, which means that trade tensions may be triggered between countries as a result. In such a case, the problem of market access is not an easy one since it is hybrid in nature.

Substitutability of antitrust and trade policies

The above discussion illustrates how, at present, antitrust and trade policy approaches fall short of addressing hybrid restraints in general, and private restraints in particular, affecting market access. However, the discussion did not address the question of whether, in this case, one policy can be a substitute for the other. Of course, if trade policy can obviate the need for antitrust policy regarding impediments to market access involving, or arising as a result of, private anti-competitive behaviour, then there would be no need to consider the adoption of the market access principle under antitrust policy, or indeed any other principle.

Using trade policy instead of antitrust policy

However, it is possible to be sceptical about the claim in favour of trade policy rendering antitrust policy unnecessary, even if this result is achievable.[97] This is because while a free trade stance greatly reduces the scope of the task

---

[97] See ch. 7.

facing antitrust authorities, it does not imply that antitrust law and policy have no purpose to serve. Free trade must be complemented by the freedom of entry of firms, including the possibility to contest markets, in particular through foreign direct investment, especially in the services sector and as far as products confined to domestic markets are concerned.[98]

This view is in line with another on the potential role of antitrust policy in addressing private restraints that may arise in international trade. One of the driving forces of globalisation is liberalisation of trade and investment. Removing barriers to trade and investment does not necessarily ensure access to markets. A progress report produced within the OECD and submitted at its 1993 Ministerial Meeting argued that globalisation was expected to lead to more efficient production and marketing, lower prices and improved product quality and variety, but that it will fail to do so unless market access and competition can be preserved and enhanced.[99] As firms attempt to improve or maintain their competitive position in an increasingly more global environment, they may take actions aimed at effectively keeping foreign competitors out of their domestic market. While the dividing line between meeting competition and restricting or defeating it by hindering access can admittedly be a fine one, it nonetheless emphasises the potential contribution of antitrust policy to addressing problems of access to and presence in domestic markets encountered by foreign firms.[100] Thus the conclusion to be drawn from these points is that there is a need for antitrust policy in the global economy, and that the existence of trade policy does not affect this conclusion.

Using antitrust policy instead of trade policy

The flip-side of the debate just alluded to relates to whether antitrust policy obviates the need for trade policy, especially in the case of hybrid practices,

---

[98] B. Hoekman and P. Mavroidis, 'Linking Competition and Trade Policies in Central and East European Countries', Policy Research Working Paper 1346 (The World Bank, Washington, D.C., 1994), p. 3; W. Shughart, J. Silverman and R. Tollison, 'Antitrust Enforcement and Foreign Competition' in F. McChesney and W. Shughart (eds.), *The Causes and Consequences of Antitrust: the Public Choice Perspective* (Chicago University Press, Chicago, 1995), p. 180; M. Trebilcock, 'Reconciling Competition Laws and Trade Policies: a New Challenge to International Co-Operation' in Doern and Wilks, *Comparative*, p. 270.

[99] See Joint Progress Report on Trade and Competition Policies submitted by the Committee on Competition Law and Policy and the Trade, p. 2.

[100] A. B. Zampetti and P. Sauve, *New Dimensions of Market Access: an Overview* (OECD, Paris, 1995), p. 19. See also WTO Annual Report 1997, p 32.

and if so, what form antitrust policy should take in a liberal trade policy environment and moreover in a global economy. Of course, whilst trade policy tools remove public impediments to competition from foreign firms, such tools do not tackle private restrictions on competition within domestic markets, including competition from foreign firms.[101] In this way, inadequately framed or enforced domestic antitrust policy – to the extent that it permits anti-competitive behaviour which precludes effective market access or an effective market presence by foreign firms – may be an impediment to foreign competition and the flows of trade and investment between countries.

Using antitrust policy to combat private anti-competitive practices affecting international trade may be desirable. Nevertheless, its effectiveness as a remedy in this instance gives rise to several concerns. First, there is little awareness of the nature of similarities or differences between antitrust and trade policies with regard to market access. Secondly, it is not clear whether a commonly understood antitrust law which is applicable to market access-restraining practices exists. Thirdly, there is a risk that countries may be drawn into deep market access disputes of an antitrust nature. Countries do not often seem to have confidence in the ability of the institutions of one another to resolve such disputes, something that is likely to trigger differences between countries over dispute resolution.[102]

These concerns are mainly related to the scope and goals of antitrust law.[103] It was argued above that domestic antitrust law may be limited by the existence of exemptions.[104] A particular example of how exemptions can diminish the effectiveness of domestic antitrust law to address trade policy issues is the case of export cartels, for which all major trading countries provide some form of exemption.[105]

The scope of domestic antitrust law can also be limited in terms of its enforcement. The importance of the issue of enforcement may be observed in three different contexts. First, the extent to which foreign firms can have

---

[101] The WTO's website is rich with information on submissions by countries on this matter to the WTO Working Group on the Interaction between Trade and Competition Policy. See http://www.wto.org.

[102] E. Fox, 'Competition Law and the Agenda for the WTO: Forging the Links of Competition and Trade' (1995) 4 *Pacific-Rimely Law and Policy Journal* 1, 15.

[103] See WTO Annual Report 1997, pp. 46–8.   [104] See pp. 210–11 above.

[105] See U. Immenga, 'Export Cartels and Voluntary Export Restraints between Trade and Competition Policy' (1995) 4 *Pacific-Rimely Law and Policy Journal* 93, 96–107.

a private right of action to enforce the domestic antitrust laws of the host country. The position here rests on two factors: one factor is whether the relevant domestic system of antitrust provides for private actions generally and the second factor is whether firms have *locus standi* to institute actions in the host countries if they are neither incorporated nor have other legal presence therein.[106] Secondly, the extent to which domestic authorities responsible for the enforcement of antitrust policy will act in cases where foreign interests are involved.[107] The scope of national antitrust policy to respond to trade concerns of foreign countries can be limited by a possible non-enforcement of the antitrust rules of the host country. This issue triggers formidable difficulties, especially since enforcement of antitrust policy falls within the discretion of national antitrust authorities. Thirdly – and this is a point that arises due to the political nature of trade policy – the extent to which domestic antitrust authorities are immune from political pressures. The effectiveness of domestic antitrust law in resolving trade policy issues will depend upon the independence of domestic antitrust authorities. Ensuring such adequate independence is likely to encourage and enable antitrust authorities to initiate and deal with cases involving alleged anti-competitive practices that adversely affect foreign interests.[108]

Regarding the goals of antitrust law, reference should be made here to chapter 3, which contains a detailed discussion of this topic. Proceeding from that discussion, it is clear that domestic antitrust laws in different jurisdictions serve different goals. In the USA, the main objective of antitrust law generally accepted is economic efficiency and consumer welfare. In the EC, on the other hand, other goals have equal status such as furthering market integration. It seems that economic goals of efficiency and consumer welfare are regarded as more favourable to the use of antitrust law as a trade remedy, than those relating to fairness and political concepts. This is because the former goals are neutral, whilst the latter goals might be used to support domestic firms to the detriment of foreign firms and consumers. Wider political goals are likely to undermine the role of antitrust law and policy as an effective means to combat market access-restraining practices. It is interesting to observe in this regard the first recital of the WTO Agreement which sets out the objectives of the multilateral trading system. The recital refers to 'raising standards of living' and 'optimal use of the world's resources in accordance with the objectives of sustainable development' which seems

---

[106] See ch. 9.   [107] See further ch. 4.   [108] See pp. 62–3 above.

to indicate that promoting efficiency and welfare in a global economy are among such objectives.

Consistencies and inconsistencies between the policies

One caveat, however, is that even if economic efficiency and consumer welfare are recognised as appropriate goals of antitrust policy, it is not certain that antitrust and trade policies will coincide with how concerns relating to market access should be handled. This point can be explained with reference to the treatment of vertical restraints. It is arguable, however, that this should not present a problem provided that the issue is considered from a shared perspective, antitrust and trade policy.[109] Nevertheless, if there was a disagreement between the two policies, then it can be regarded as one of perspective rather than of principle, which can be justified by the traditional roles of both policies and the tension associated with them.[110] Antitrust and trade policies are compatible as far as concerns relating to market access are concerned. This can be seen in the context of the free movement and antitrust provisions in the EC, where the two sets of provisions have always been considered complementary in achieving the goals of the EC including promoting a continuous, harmonious and balanced development of economic activities.[111] The aim of both policies is to improve the efficient allocation of resources. Trade policy contributes to efficiency by removing barriers that impede the ability of foreign firms to access new markets. Antitrust policy contributes to efficiency by preventing firms from harming competition.[112] Under antitrust policy analysis, however, foreign or domestic competitors may be excluded from a market, so long as competition is not thereby harmed. In these cases, the objective of both policies is met and an efficient outcome is achieved.[113]

The above discussion indicated the extent to which anti-competitive or exclusionary practices restrict access to markets around the world and whether this is a problem which demands the immediate attention of policy-makers of the international community. It was argued that this type of restriction is a serious one, especially in the case of hybrid restraints. These restraints make the distinction between the application of antitrust and

---

[109] See Marsden, 'Impropriety', 9–10.   [110] Trebilcock, 'Reconciling', 269.
[111] See Articles 2, 3 and 4 EC. See further pp. 88–9 above.
[112] See generally Dabbah, 'Measuring'.   [113] Marsden, 'Impropriety', 9.

trade policies quite difficult to draw. Trade policy is sufficiently developed on the international plane, particularly within the auspices of the WTO. Antitrust policy, by way of contrast, is significantly less developed on the international plane. However, the need for international developments in this regard has been advocated throughout this book because this is where the central challenge facing the antitrust communities of the different countries lies.

Over the years, the interest in the relationship between antitrust and trade policies has grown, mainly due to the growing integration and expansion of the world economy. This development has revealed that anti-competitive behaviour of private firms increasingly may have wide cross-border dimensions. Furthermore, with the increase in flows of trade and investment in the global economy, foreign firms are concerned with whether domestic antitrust laws are fit and suitable for addressing the anti-competitive behaviour of domestic firms which hinders their entry to domestic markets.

At present, antitrust policy remains primarily national in outlook and there are neither rules which are enforceable on the international plane nor an international enforcement agency to enforce such rules. However, antitrust policy is addressed indirectly, albeit in limited aspects, in the main agreements that make up the WTO.[114] Outside the WTO, consultation and co-operation on how to deal with anti-competitive restraints are facilitated through a number of bilateral, regional and multilateral mechanisms and frameworks, such as the EC, NAFTA, ANCESTRA, UNCTAD, the World Bank, the OECD and more recently the International Competition Network (ICN).[115] For example, the OECD has adopted a series of recommendations and guidelines addressing anti-competitive behaviour of private firms. However, as the discussion in the following chapter will make clear, compliance with the majority of these rules is on a voluntary basis and so they are not legally binding.

Market access principle

In the absence of international antitrust rules, this chapter has proposed an effective application of antitrust policy through the development of a market access principle. It was seen that from a trade policy point of view, this is desirable. A country that has undertaken trade liberalisation measures

---

[114] See further ch. 9.   [115] See ch. 9 for a discussion on these organisations.

has every interest in ensuring that the welfare and efficiency benefits arising from such measures are not lost due to anti-competitive practices by firms. Avoiding the nullification or impairment of trade liberalisation commitments, as a result of such practices, is also a matter of legitimate concern for members of the global trading family. Antitrust law and policy do not normally have specific trade objectives, such as promoting market access. However, in pursuing the goals of promoting economic efficiency and consumer welfare, an effective application of antitrust law is essential for tackling barriers to entry set up by firms in the market or other anti-competitive practices, which affect both foreign and domestic firms.

Furthermore, adopting a market access principle under antitrust policy would not only lead to a growth in the flows of trade and investment, but also provide more consistency in the application of antitrust policy tools as a complement to trade policy. This can then be followed by the fostering of international co-operation, which seems to be desirable from a trade policy perspective: it seems that all countries would benefit from the effective application of antitrust law to anti-competitive practices which hinder access to markets. The substantial removal of hindrances to the flows of trade and investment globally erected by countries has greatly contributed to enhanced conditions of competition. At the same time, in the absence of an effective antitrust law framework, firms may have an incentive to engage in anti-competitive behaviour with a view to protecting the domestic market against foreign competition. The risk of conflicts of jurisdiction arising from the application of the antitrust laws of countries can also have repercussions for the global trading system. The scope for such conflicts is the greater if antitrust authorities pursue trade policy goals by seeking to apply domestic antitrust law to anti-competitive practices affecting exports and which do not have a substantial impact on the domestic market.[116] There is also a risk that, in the absence of effective remedial action under antitrust policy, pressure could grow for the unilateral use of trade sanctions or of such bilateral trade agreements that may run counter to the principles established and observed by the global trading family. Clearly in these instances the sensible thing to do would be for a country to apply its domestic antitrust law to practices which are both contrary to domestic welfare and the legitimate interests of other countries and to seek ways for co-operation with other countries. Enhanced international co-operation in antitrust policy would

[116] See ch. 7.

therefore lead to significant gains from both the antitrust and trade policy perspective.

Antitrust policy at the WTO

The dominant form of co-operation between antitrust authorities has taken the form of bilateral agreements. The inclusion of several important provisions, such as the principle of positive comity, has considerable potential for reducing the scope for conflict using close co-operation between antitrust authorities with the shared objective of protecting competition, including cases where foreign interests are involved. However, despite the actual and potential benefits of this form of co-operation, there is an increasing awareness of the need for an additional role by a multilateral framework. With 100 systems of antitrust worldwide and about thirty others in the process of being established it would be unrealistic to expect a single antitrust authority in one jurisdiction to build identical and intensive co-operation with all its counterparts around the world. Engaging in such a project is not mission difficult but mission impossible: the cost in terms of expenditure of very limited administrative resources would be extremely high, not to mention legitimate doubts about the efficiency and benefits of such a 'bilateral only' approach. The time is ripe therefore to intensify the search for finding multilateral solutions.

The WTO can be seen as a suitable forum for this task.[117] First, unlike other existing international organisations with actual or potential agenda for antitrust policy, the WTO comprises developing and developed countries and has established a tradition of enforcing binding rules. Secondly, it is capable of combining the establishment of binding disciplines with the flexibility required to take into account differences in antitrust law and practice and the particular concern of developing countries.[118] The possible development of such a multilateral framework using the WTO could substantially develop a market access principle under antitrust policy and complement trade policy tools as well as contribute towards the achievement of the objectives of a global economy. The WTO has argued that any stance on antitrust law or enforcement, including the decision not to have

---

[117] However, note the US resistance to pursuing antitrust policy programmes within the WTO generally. See further ch. 9.

[118] See chs. 9 and 10.

an antitrust law at all, or not to enforce the existing law, is a policy choice.[119]
This implies that it is often difficult to separate out private restraints from
public policy, since the fact that the private restraints exist might be attributable to the choice of countries not to intervene, or not to apply laws
under which they could intervene.

The future of establishing a multilateral framework for antitrust policy
within the WTO was part of the agenda during the WTO 4th Ministerial Conference held in Doha in November 2001. The issue triggered some
constructive and interesting debate at the event. This development is quite
remarkable because all parties who signed up to the Doha Declaration
recognised for the first time that there is a valid case for conducting negotiations and for concluding a multilateral agreement on antitrust and trade
policy at the WTO. Some of the parties are known for being sceptics when
it comes to proposing the inclusion of antitrust policy within the WTO,
such as developing countries. This development is also remarkable since
it has signalled a fundamental shift on the part of the USA with regard to
adopting a true multilateral approach to antitrust policy, especially at the
WTO. This shift in Washington's attitude has already been mentioned in
the course of the discussion in chapter 5. Indeed the shift should be given
a welcome since it has indicated that the USA is willing to adopt a positive
stance on the envisaged multilateral rules in the WTO and since the USA
also supported the text which was produced at the Doha Conference.

There is no doubt that any party in favour of including antitrust policy
within the WTO mandate should consider the Doha achievement as constructive, satisfactory and a step in the right direction. This should be so
since for many years the inclusion of a multilateral agreement on antitrust
policy at the WTO was highly controversial. Negotiating and concluding
such an agreement at the WTO will certainly underscore the huge progress
already made in lowering trade barriers and fostering liberalisation as witnessed in the past two decades. Such a development will also have positive
effects in terms of promoting and building domestic systems of antitrust;
spreading a competition culture, especially in developing countries; facilitating effective combating of anti-competitive practices worldwide; and
it will also lead to enhancing co-operation between different antitrust authorities. In sum, the Doha Conference has offered a great deal of incentive
in order to clarify the issues at stake at least until the 5th WTO Ministerial

---

[119] See WTO Annual Report 1997.

Conference, which will be convened during the course of 2003. Beyond that, the Conference has provided a great deal of optimism that soon formal negotiation of the envisaged agreement at the WTO will begin.

Conclusion

Foreclosure of domestic markets by restraints can involve private anti-competitive behaviour. This can be in the case of pure private restraints or in the case of hybrid restraints. In the former, antitrust policy tools are obviously relevant. However, it is not clear to what extent these tools are currently deployed to address such restraints effectively. The case of hybrid restraints, on the other hand, is a more difficult one because they involve issues of both antitrust and trade policy. It was argued that neither policy tool at present is a good fit to address the concerns arising from these restraints. Hence, the chapter proposed the development of an alternative approach to deal with hybrid restraints in general, and private restraints in particular. This, as we saw, supported the case for internationalising antitrust policy. The discussion concentrated on a particular aspect of the debate, namely the adoption of a market access principle under antitrust policy.

Whilst acknowledging that the WTO rules do not regulate the behaviour of private firms, the chapter suggested adopting the principle within the WTO. Indeed, the question whether the WTO should or should not address private restraints should not be raised. Rather, the fundamental question that seems to arise concerns the extent to which countries are willing to establish a global framework within antitrust policy in order to further trade liberalisation objectives. This particular aspect of the debate is examined in the following chapter, which gives a broader comparative overview of the internationalisation of antitrust policy.

9

Past, present and future: a comparative analysis

Previous chapters analysed and discussed important issues, concepts and ideas that are central components in any debate on the internationalisation of antitrust policy and the relationship between these components. Throughout all the chapters, the discussion and analysis were conducted at several levels. Often this was done from a past, present and, where appropriate, future perspective. This chapter complements that discussion and analysis by bringing together the different strands of past, present and some possible future developments of the internationalisation of antitrust policy.

The chapter is structured as follows. The first part looks at past developments. The discussion begins with past developments because in order to help understand where the internationalisation of antitrust policy should go, it is important to examine its past experience first. The second part constructs an institutional framework of the capabilities of international organisations to deal with international antitrust policy. The third part attempts to link present developments with the type of internationalisation of antitrust policy which seems to be emerging on the horizon. The fourth part deals with the issue of political power and the interests of business firms and countries. The fifth part gives an account of various model systems of antitrust. The sixth part examines the EC–US conflict in the internationalisation of antitrust policy. The seventh part sheds some light on the issue of convergence and harmonisation of antitrust law and policy of different countries. The eighth part considers some substantive issues. The ninth part offers some reflections and a summary.

Some important past developments

The first quarter of the twentieth century witnessed some general antipathy towards anti-competitive practices. This antipathy, which can be seen from the way the League of Nations considered international cartels as 'an enemy of world trade', was given a stronger impact in the early 1930s. During those years, cartels were employed by several countries, notably Germany, Italy and Japan, as a means for mobilising for what became World War II.[1] In an attempt to address international cartels and anti-competitive practices in general, the Draft Havana Charter was introduced. The Draft Charter aimed to, *inter alia*, establish an International Trade Organization (ITO) and introduce provisions dealing with restrictive business practices.[2] The Draft Charter imposed an obligation on member countries of the proposed ITO to prevent firms from engaging in activities which may 'restrain competition, limit access to markets or foster monopolistic control in international trade' where these restraints interfered with the trade-liberalising aims of the Charter.[3] The Charter stated that members could bring complaints about such restraints to the ITO. The latter would then be entitled, under Article 48 of the Charter, to investigate and recommend action to the home countries of the firms engaged in restrictive practices. However, due to US objection to this effort towards internationalisation of antitrust policy, the ITO never actually materialised and the Charter was deemed to fail.[4] This result may be considered to be surprising, particularly in light of the US' hostility at that time towards restrictive practices,[5] which can be seen from the following letter addressed to former Secretary of State, Cordell Hull by former President Franklin Roosevelt:

> During the past half century the United States has developed a tradition in opposition to private monopolies. The Sherman and Clayton Acts have become as much part of the American way of life as the due process clause of the Constitution. By protecting the consumer against monopoly these statutes guarantee him the benefits of competition.
>
> This policy goes hand in glove with the liberal principles of international trade for which you have stood through many years of public service. The trade agreement program has as its objective the elimination of barriers to the free flow of trade in international commerce; the antitrust statutes aim at

---

[1] See ch. 2 for a discussion on the historical perspective of antitrust law.

[2] See Havana Charter for an International Trade Organization, UN Doc. E/Conf. 2/78 1948. Printed in C. Wilcox, *A Charter for World Trade* (Macmillan, New York, 1949). See also P. Muchlinski, *Multinational Enterprises and the Law* (Blackwell, Oxford, 1995), p. 403.

[3] Havana Charter, Article 46.

[4] See A. Lowenfeld, *Public Controls on International Trade* (Matthew Bender, New York, 1983).

[5] See T. Arnold, *Bottlenecks of Business* (Reynal & Hitchcock, New York, 1973); C. Edwards, *Control of Cartels and Monopolies: an International Comparison* (Oceana Publications, Dobbs Ferry, 1967), at pp. 228–30; I. Bruce and E. Clubb, *United States Foreign Trade Law* (Little, Brown, Boston, 1991).

the elimination of monopolistic restraints of trade in interstate and foreign commerce.

Unfortunately, a number of foreign countries, particularly in continental Europe, do not possess such a tradition against cartels. On the contrary, cartels have received encouragement from some of these governments. Especially is this true with respect to Germany. Moreover, cartels were utilized by the Nazis as governmental instrumentalities to achieve political ends. The history of the use of the I.G. Farben trust by the Nazis reads like a detective story. The defeat of the Nazi armies will have to be followed by the eradication of these weapons of economic welfare. But more than the elimination of the political activities of German cartels will be required. Cartels practices which restrict the flow of goods in foreign commerce will have to be curbed. With international trade involved this end can be achieved only through collaborative action by the United Nations.

I hope that you will keep your eye on this whole subject of international cartels because we are approaching the time when discussions will almost certainly arise between us and other nations.[6]

Five years after the unsuccessful attempt of the Havana Charter, the United Nations Economic and Social Council (ECOSOC) recommended the inclusion of a draft convention that would have established a new international agency endowed with the responsibility to receive and investigate complaints of restrictive business practices. However, the USA rejected the draft convention because it felt that disparities in domestic policies and practices were so substantial that they would render an international organisation ineffective.[7] The USA also was not in favour of a provision in the draft under which each country enjoyed one vote, believing that this would have afforded certain countries the chance to abuse this provision.

Little progress was made in the internationalisation of antitrust policy until 1958, when a GATT Experts Group dealt with restrictive practices of private firms and made some recommendations that such practices of private firms should be excluded from dispute settlement review. It was thought that the absence of consensus and experience in this policy made it particularly difficult – and quite unrealistic – to try to reach any form of multilateral agreement on how to deal with restrictive business practices

---

[6] Obtained by the writer during a research visit to the Franklin Roosevelt Library, New York, File 277. See also Muchlinski, *Multinational*, p. 387.

[7] D. Wood, 'The Impossible Dream: Real International Antitrust' (1992) *University of Chicago Legal Forum* 277, 284–5.

with international components.[8] The group also stated that more internationalisation needed domestic antitrust laws and antitrust institutions. This was followed by a 1961 report in which the GATT recommended that parties to a dispute should engage in consultation with each other on the control of restrictive business practices.[9]

Institutional framework

The second half of the twentieth century saw an increase in the instituting of systems of antitrust around the world. However, it is obvious that differences still exist in experience with antitrust law and policy, as well as in the way that internationalisation thereof is conceived amongst the different jurisdictions where antitrust laws have been introduced. Until now, the international antitrust policy scene has not witnessed the conclusion of binding international agreements,[10] although various consultative mechanisms and procedures within different forums have been instituted.[11]

Despite this, it seems that the internationalisation of antitrust policy has gained renewed impetus and those in favour of internationalisation have not lost hope in pushing the project forward.[12] New or expanded international efforts must, however, be structured in a flexible and sensible manner to recognise remaining differences between countries in this highly important and topical area of law and policy. In light of this, the following discussion looks first at the institutional capabilities of existing international organisations. This will be complemented by the discussion in the following part, which considers the views of different interest groups with regard to the appropriate role of those organisations in antitrust policy.

---

[8] GATT Resolution 5 November 1958 cited in D. Furnish, 'A Transnational Approach to Restrictive Business Practices' (1970) 4 *International Lawyer* 317, 328. See also M. Janow, 'Competition Policy and the WTO' in J. Bhagwati and M. Hirsh (eds.), *The Uruguay Round and beyond* (University of Michigan Press, Michigan, 1998).

[9] GATT Resolution, BISD 28 (9th Supp., 1961).

[10] A. Fiebig, 'A Role for the WTO in International Merger Control' (2000) 20 *Northwestern Journal of International Law and Business* 233, 244.

[11] See generally S. Waller, 'The Internationalization of Antitrust Enforcement' (1997) 77 *Boston University Law Review* 343.

[12] See E. Fox, 'International Antitrust: Cosmopolitan Principles for an Open World' (1998) *Fordham Corporate Law Institute* 271; J. Halverson, 'Harmonization and Coordination of International Merger Procedures' (1991) 60 *Antitrust Law Journal* 531; E. Petersmann, 'International Competition Rules for the GATT–MTO World Trade and Legal System' (1993) 27 *Journal of World Trade Law* 35; Fiebig, 'Role', 233.

The World Trade Organization (WTO)

It has already been said in the previous chapter that the WTO is a unique international organisation and rule-making body. The WTO has a very wide membership base, which includes 144 developing and developed countries. It enjoys an advantage of having professional staff as well as centrality as a forum for negotiating binding rules governing the economic conduct of countries.[13] This uniqueness has been further enhanced with the increase of areas for convergence introduced in the Uruguay Round of multilateral trade negotiations as well as by the improved dispute settlement mechanisms within the WTO.

Like the GATT, the WTO deals principally with trade-distorting acts of governments. Thus, the WTO rules, except those on anti-dumping, have not been focused on the behaviour of private firms. Instead, the WTO has adopted a comprehensive set of rules obliging member governments to observe common non-discrimination principles and market-opening commitments included in different schedules.

Prior to the WTO, several GATT cases had come to light where countries claimed that other countries supported or fostered restrictive practices by firms that foreclosed access to markets. Neither the GATT nor the WTO has been a primary forum for resolving such disputes. Furthermore, save in circumstances such as those mentioned in the previous chapter, international trade rules have not held governments accountable for the actions of private firms. In this way, the WTO does not hold a multilateral set of rules that make governments responsible for market access-restraining practices of firms. Nevertheless, the WTO cannot be seen as lacking the features necessary to achieve antitrust policy objectives.[14] Indeed, the basic non-discrimination principles of national treatment, Most-Favoured-Nation (MFN) and transparency that underpin the WTO support the operation of impartial systems of antitrust at national level.[15] Furthermore, a domestic policy framework

---

[13] Fiebig, 'Role', 247.

[14] See P. Nicoliades, 'For a World Competition Authority' (1996) 30 *Journal of World Trade Law* 131; M. Matsushita, 'Reflections on Competition Policy/Law in the Framework of the WTO' (1997) *Fordham Corporate Law Institute* 31; F. Weiss, 'From World Trade Law to World Competition Law' (2000) 23 *Fordham International Law Journal* 250; E. Petersmann, 'Proposals for Negotiating International Competition Rules in the GATT–WTO World Trade and Legal System' (1994) 49 *Aussenwirtschaft* 231; P. Marsden, ' "Antitrust" at the WTO' (1998) 13 *Antitrust* 28; H. Arai, 'Global Competition Policy as a Basis for Borderless Market Economy', 22 July 1999, address, available at http://www.miti.go.jp/topic-e/eWTO0997e.html.

[15] See ch. 10.

that ensures that private firms do not, through private arrangements, re-strict the flow of trade and investment that countries worked hard towards achieving is equally important to support the international trading system. In these ways, the two policy frameworks are complementary.[16] As may be remembered, this conclusion was made very clear in the previous chapter. In addition, antitrust policy concepts appear in several WTO agreements such as: the Basic Telecommunications Agreement,[17] the General Agreement on Trade in Services,[18] Agreement on Trade-Related Investment Measures,[19] Trade-Related Aspects of Intellectual Property Rights[20] and the Accounting Disciplines Agreements.

The Organisation for Economic Cooperation and Development (OECD)

General

The OECD has been playing a leading role in looking at the internationalisa-tion of antitrust policy.[21] Through this role, the OECD has become not only an important consultative body for countries with systems of antitrust, but also a source of technical assistance to many countries introducing or aim-ing to introduce antitrust law and policy in their domestic legal systems.[22] In particular, the OECD has been helpful to national judges and officials in antitrust authorities in such countries who are keen on developing their decisional mechanisms and practices in antitrust cases.

At a more substantive level, the OECD has issued non-binding recom-mendations, such as a set of recommendations in 1986,[23] another in 1995

---

[16] See H. Applebaum, 'The Coexistence of Antitrust Law and Trade Law with Antitrust Policy' (1988) 9 *Cardozo Law Review* 1169; Petersmann, 'Proposals'.

[17] See Section 1.1 of the Fourth Protocol to the General Agreement on Trade in Services.

[18] See Articles VIII, IX and IX:2.

[19] See Article 9.   [20] See for example Article 41 of the TRIPS.

[21] In 1976, the Guidelines for Multinational Enterprises as revised were adopted, which deal with a variety of antitrust policy issues. See also OECD Declaration on *International Investment and Multinational Enterprises*, 21 June 1976.

[22] For a fuller description of the OECD's activities in antitrust policy, see P. Lloyd and K. Vautier, *Promoting Competition in Global Markets: a Multi-National Approach* (Edward Elgar, Cheltenham, 1999), pp. 131–8.

[23] Recommendation of the Council for Co-operation between Member Countries in Areas of Potential Conflict between Competition and Trade Policies [C(86)65(final)], printed in OECD, Competition Policy and International Trade (OECD Instruments of Co-operation, 1987), pp. 24–7. The Recommendation encouraged participating countries not to distort competition through abusing unfair trade laws, to take into account the effect of export/import restrictions on competition and trading partners when considering approval of such restrictions, ensure that their procedures are transparent and notify other countries of anti-competitive behaviour of their domestic firms.

on international co-operation amongst domestic antitrust authorities and most recently in 1998 another condemning hard-core cartels.[24]

The OECD has been particularly active in encouraging soft convergence amongst member countries. The OECD consists of most, if not all, of the world's developed countries, and as such one can expect that greater substantive convergence in antitrust policy matters could contribute towards the internationalisation of antitrust policy. Despite the OECD's contributions in this regard, it still suffers from certain institutional limitations, which constrain its ability to play a more expansive role in developing an international approach to antitrust policy. Moreover, many non-member countries regard the organisation as one for more developed countries. Such factors and other ones, such as the failure of the negotiations on a Multilateral Agreement on Investment (MAI) at the OECD have cast some doubt over the OECD's ability to serve as a forum for pursuing a form of internationalisation of antitrust policy that could lead to negotiating and concluding international agreements in the area. Notwithstanding these limitations, the OECD certainly enjoys strong experience in a wide range of antitrust and trade policy issues. Its contributions should be regarded as extremely valuable, especially in light of its current efforts towards designing collective antitrust projects with other international organisations, such as the World Bank.[25]

Committees

Several OECD committees are engaged in programmes dealing with antitrust policy. Two of these are worth mentioning.

The Competition Law and Policy Committee   The Competition Law and Policy Committee (CLP) consists of representatives from domestic antitrust authorities of the twenty-nine OECD members.[26] The aim of the CLP is primarily to promote common understanding and co-operation among antitrust authorities.[27] This is carried out through meetings of officials of domestic antitrust authorities. Such meetings have played a key role in facilitating greater convergence between the antitrust laws of the countries

---

[24] See http://www.oecd.org.

[25] More up-to-date information is available at http://www.worldbank.org and http://www.oecd.org.

[26] Known pre-1987 as the Committee of Experts on Restrictive Business Practices. The CERBP was established by the Organization for European Economic Cooperation (OEEC) in 1953.

[27] See http://www.oecd.org/daf/clp/COMMTE.htm.

concerned. Through publishing regular reports and holding discussion groups, the CLP has been offering the OECD family an opportunity to bring their understanding of antitrust policy principles closer together.

The Joint Group on Trade and Competition   The Joint Group on Trade and Competition (JGTC) has pursued a different strategy from the CLP. In particular, it has focused on fostering the understanding of member countries on issues relevant to the interface between antitrust and trade policy. To this end, it has published several reports,[28] which deal mainly with legal and regulatory exemptions under existing domestic antitrust laws and the relationship between the two policies. The JGTC has also facilitated meetings between officials of antitrust enforcement authorities and trade policy-makers to develop a common understanding about the framework for addressing matters of interest to both antitrust and trade policy communities.

UNCTAD Restrictive Business Practices Set

In 1973, the United Nations Conference on Trade and Development (UNCTAD) began negotiations on the control of restrictive business practices at the instigation of developing countries.[29] Eight years later, the United Nations General Assembly adopted UNCTAD's Set of Multilaterally Agreed Principles and Rules for the Control of Restrictive Business Practices ('Set').[30] The Set aims to ensure favourable treatment towards developing countries by offering them protection from the restrictive business practices of multinational firms. It provides that countries should improve and enforce their laws on restrictive business practices, and that they should consult and co-operate with competent authorities of countries adversely affected by restrictive business practices. It also requires multinational firms to respect the domestic laws on restrictive business practices of the countries in which they operate. It is indeed the case that today the Set is the only comprehensive multilateral agreement in the field of antitrust policy. However, despite being an important step forward, the Set is voluntary, is not binding, and has not been recognised as a source of public international

---

[28] See pp. 235–6 above.

[29] The negotiations took place within three different groups: Group B, made of industrialised countries; Group D, comprising principally socialist countries; and Group of 77, containing developing and less developed countries.

[30] See Muchlinski, *Multinational*, pp. 403–11.

law. Moreover, UNCTAD has yet to evolve into a dynamic body for the treatment of antitrust policy issues.

In September 2000, a Resolution in the field of antitrust policy was adopted by the 4th UN Conference which reviewed the Set. The Resolution deals specifically with the issue of co-operation between antitrust authorities. It recognises the importance of bilateral agreements in this regard. However, the Resolution states that there is a need to enhance regional as well as multilateral antitrust initiatives, especially as far as small and developing countries are concerned. The Resolution also asked the UNCTAD Secretariat to examine the possibility of formulating a model co-operation agreement on antitrust law and policy to be based on the Set.

The passing of the Resolution demonstrates that the time is ripe to move beyond bilateral co-operation between individual, and particular, antitrust authorities – a point that was demonstrated in the two previous chapters. It also shows that involving more antitrust authorities in the discussions on international antitrust issues will strengthen and complement both bilateral and multilateral initiatives. At the time of writing, a study dealing with the extent to which poor and developing countries suffer from anti-competitive practices, which hinder their opportunities to develop and become competitive, is in preparation within UNCTAD. This study has attracted the interest of several important antitrust authorities, including the European Commission. Among the issues the study is aiming to address are those concerning lack of consumer awareness about unfair and anti-competitive practices. The study strives to explore the various ways in which antitrust policy can help address some of the problems of developing and poor countries and make such countries less vulnerable to anti-competitive practices. It is understood that the study will attempt to argue that practices of this nature increase the costs for the economies of those countries, increase their inefficiencies and decrease their competitiveness in the global economy.

The International Competition Network (ICN)

The ICN is a multilateral initiative which was launched in October 2001.[31] The initiative was founded by several antitrust authorities, including key ones such as the US Department of Justice, the US Federal Trade Commission and the European Commission. In one way, it would be accurate to say that the initiation of the ICN was facilitated through the close and

---

[31] See http://www.internationalcompetitionnetwork.org.

positive co-operation between the USA and the EC in the area of antitrust policy which has come to be witnessed over the last decade or so. The ICN is an independent body with no structural links to any already existing international organisation dealing with antitrust policy.

The ICN is quite a unique organisation given the fact that it presents an imaginative response of antitrust authorities worldwide to the challenges posed in a globalised economy. It is a type of virtual network, which does not have a permanent secretariat, such as is the case with other international organisations. It does, however, have a steering group. The task of the steering group includes, *inter alia*, identifying projects and formulating work plans which will then be approved by all the members of the ICN which include developed and developing countries.

Membership of the ICN is open to any national or regional antitrust authority with responsibility for enforcing antitrust law. At the time of writing, at least sixty antitrust authorities have joined the organisation; this number will, if anything, increase in the future. The phenomenal increase in membership is an extremely remarkable development given that it occurred while the organisation was less than one year old and given the fact that such a large number of antitrust authorities have for the first time come together to discuss and share ideas on their difficulties and problems in addressing international antitrust issues. Both of these factors are capable of giving the ICN a global reach, especially since it is a 'project-oriented' body; but more importantly the factors will place the organisation in a good position to build a strong network between antitrust authorities from developed and developing countries.

The objectives and work of the ICN seem to be very promising. It has declared that it will work closely in co-ordinating its activities with international organisations involved in the field of antitrust policy, in particular the WTO, the OECD and UNCTAD as well as forces and figures from the private sectors, such as consumer organisations, practitioners in the field of antitrust law and academics.

Since its launch, the ICN has been focusing on two main issues: multi-jurisdictional merger control and competition advocacy.

Multi-jurisdictional merger control

There are three working groups within the ICN dealing with merger control issues, including merger notifications and procedures, the analytical framework of the assessment of merger cases and the relevant tools for merger investigations. Initial findings from the work of the three working groups reveal that there has been quite a fair amount of substantive and procedural convergence among most antitrust authorities. It is believed that this will contribute towards achieving legal security and predictability in cross-border mergers.

Competition advocacy

Competition advocacy was discussed in some detail in chapter 3. Hence, the concept should hardly require any further explanation at this point. Competition advocacy is dealt with by a separate working group within the ICN. The group's main work at the moment revolves around examining ways in which distortions to competition caused by public intervention in the marketplace can be addressed. The scope of the work of the group is expected to expand with time to cover other important areas.

Other matters

Merger control issues and competition advocacy are not the only items within the competence of the ICN. The organisation is also involved in the fight against international hard-core cartels. In particular, it is looking at the conduct and value of investigations by antitrust authorities into uncovering and punishing cartels. A special conference to be organised by the ICN, which will deal with this issue, is expected to take place before the end of 2003.

From present to the future

An important question confronting the antitrust communities of countries at present concerns what the next step should be, especially at the WTO, in the area of internationalisation of antitrust policy. The relevance of this question seems to be growing in light of attempts to build on the progress made at the 4th Ministerial Conference held in Doha in November 2001 and the preparations already underway for the 5th WTO Ministerial Conference to be held in Mexico in 2003. Thus, there is a question with regard to the extent to which in the short term antitrust policy should become part of any multilateral trade negotiations between countries at the WTO. Any view in favour of including antitrust policy issues must be clear on what should be considered in those negotiations. For example, should a set of rules subject to dispute settlement procedures be included? Should a framework for transparency and non-discrimination obligations to remove hindrances to market access be included? Or should the negotiations cover some other elements or aspects? More importantly, there is a need to determine the appropriate role for the WTO over the longer term on antitrust policy matters.

In discussing this vision for the future, it would be helpful to consider the views of different countries on establishing an international system of antitrust in general and on the appropriate role of the WTO in particular. The WTO Working Group has received various communications from many countries over the years. The discussion offers a description of some of these views.

The views of different countries

The USA

The position of the USA on the appropriateness of the WTO as a forum for negotiating antitrust rules has been inconsistent. Whilst the USA actively has supported efforts within the WTO's Working Group, for many years it expressed some reservation on the greater practical value of the WTO as a forum for negotiating any antitrust rules. The USA has raised several concerns with respect to the WTO venturing into the domain of antitrust policy. The main view held by antitrust officials in the USA is that the world antitrust community lacks the necessary knowledge on whether and to what extent key antitrust and trade policy issues may benefit from a binding international agreement, let alone the difficulty of developing a consensus on these issues. In particular, US antitrust officials believe that there is an inherent risk that the WTO would second-guess prosecutorial decision-making in complex evidentiary contexts – a task in which the WTO has no experience and for which it is not suited – and would inevitably 'politicise' international antitrust enforcement in ways that are not likely to improve either the economic rationality nor the legal neutrality of antitrust decision-making.[32] The main ingredient of US international antitrust policy has been to concentrate on the conclusion of bilateral agreements between different domestic antitrust authorities. Such agreements are considered to be crucial components of the internationalisation of antitrust policy. The USA

---

[32] J. Klein, 'A Reality Check on Antitrust Rules in the WTO, a Practical Way Forward on International Antitrust', address before the OECD Conference on Trade and Competition, 30 June 1999, available at http://www.usdoj.gov.

believes that countries need to develop a culture of sound and effective antitrust enforcement to be based on shared experience, bilateral co-operation and the provision of technical assistance to countries that are developing or about to develop antitrust law and policy within their domestic legal systems. Despite the US' emphasis on bilateral co-operation, however, it was said in the previous chapter that recently positive signals have been emerging from the attitude of the USA with regard to negotiating a multilateral agreement on antitrust policy within the WTO in light of the support the USA has given to the text produced at the Doha Conference in 2001.

The EC

Reference can be made at this stage to chapter 5, where it was argued that the EC has been in favour of a more internationalised antitrust policy. In particular, the European Commission has moved beyond placing a heavy emphasis on the importance and effectiveness of bilateral co-operative agreements between different antitrust authorities, the foundation tools in international antitrust policy issues. For the last decade or so, the Commission has been advocating and supporting the case for a multilateral agreement within antitrust policy. The Commission has recommended that preliminary negotiations look at restrictive business practices, provide adequate and transparent enforcement and provide for international co-operation through exchange of non-confidential information, notification and positive comity provisions. According to the Commission, a wider substantive convergence could be reached over time. The proposal suggests that these rules should be subject to dispute settlement, initially only for breaches of common principles or rules relating to the developing of systems of antitrust at the national level. Dispute settlement, according to the Commission, might also be used for alleged patterns of failure to enforce antitrust law in cases affecting the trade and investment of other WTO members.[33]

This position of the EC has won some support by a number of countries, including Australia, Canada and Japan, although each of these also has communicated its views to the WTO. For example, Japan appears in favour of developing international antitrust rules but also has concurred with developing countries, particularly from the Asia-Pacific region, by

---

[33] See the proposals of the EC Group of Experts 'Competition Policy in the New Trade Order: Strengthening International Co-operation and Rules' COM (95) 359, available at http://www.europa.eu.int. The proposals were discussed at pp. 130–1 above.

emphasising that multilateral negotiations on antitrust policy must include anti-dumping issues.[34]

Kenya

Kenya submitted its own views to the WTO, in which it noted that some developing countries view the creation of an international system of antitrust as a way of 'clipping the wings' of comparatively stronger firms of developing countries so that they are not able to compete with strong firms of the developed countries.[35] Therefore, Kenya proposed that any multilateral agreement on antitrust policy should include a code of conduct for multinational firms.[36] Kenya also contributed its views on behalf of the African Group, emphasising that the existence of domestic systems of antitrust, including effective authorities to enforce antitrust law and policy, was not common to all African countries. Kenya therefore recommended continuing with the educational, exploratory and analytical work of the WTO's Working Group with enhanced technical assistance offered to developing countries.[37]

South Africa

South Africa has recommended embarking on a thorough educational process that would incorporate huge analytical demands on developing countries regarding the preparations for future rounds of negotiations within the WTO.[38] According to South Africa, this educational process is a necessary condition for negotiating multilateral rules on antitrust policy within the WTO. It has called for the realisation that developing countries have not had the same opportunity to prepare for such negotiations, which means that developing countries are therefore not at a level playing field and cannot be expected to present a well-researched position. In particular, South Africa called for further analysis of the strengths and weaknesses of multilateral antitrust rules, and has made it clear that it would be desirable for UNCTAD and the World Bank to offer some assistance. According to South

[34] See Communications from Japan, WT/GC/W/308 25 August 1999, available at http://www.wto.org.
[35] See Communications from Kenya, WT/GC/W/233 5 July 1999, *ibid.*
[36] Note however, that efforts toward reaching consensus between developed and developing countries for such a code failed previously at the UN. See Muchlinski, *Multinational*, p. 10.
[37] See Communications from Kenya on behalf of the African Group, WT/GC/W/300 6 August 1999, available at http://www.wto.org.
[38] See Communications from the Republic of South Africa, WT/WGTCP/W/138 11 October 1999, *ibid.*

Africa, this technical assistance should extend beyond the traditional support offered to antitrust authorities in terms of development of antitrust
laws and their enforcement, and should include scrupulous assessment of
the expected outcomes and the implications for developing countries of
having international antitrust rules. To ensure fruitful results from this educational initiative, South Africa has suggested that process should extend
over a period of at least two years. It has also recommended that resources
be provided to developing countries in order to allow them to participate
in the formal negotiations on a multilateral agreement on antitrust policy
in a meaningful manner.

Korea

In its submission to the WTO, Korea has generally supported the creation of a multilateral framework in antitrust policy with an effective dispute settlement mechanism.[39] Korea has advocated the need for enhancing
international co-operation among antitrust authorities. According to the
submission, such enhanced co-operation will lead to better enforcement
of antitrust law and policy. Korea has encouraged opening a discussion
within the WTO on how to incorporate positive comity into a multilateral
framework to impose greater discipline on cross-border anti-competitive
behaviour. With regard to international mergers, however, Korea has cau-
tioned that it may not be feasible to harmonise substantive rules of
merger control in different jurisdictions; though it believes that it remains
worthwhile to examine possible means of enhancing co-operation among
antitrust authorities in areas such as common procedures for review of
mergers, harmonisation of filing formats and filing deadlines, and the establishment of a common filing office to deal with international mergers.
Korea issued a similar caution in the context of exchange of confidential
information, arguing that dealing with such exchange of information under a multilateral framework on antitrust policy is premature at this stage,
given the differences in the national antitrust laws governing the exchange
of information in member countries of the WTO.

  In supporting the case for a multilateral framework within antitrust policy, Korea has recommended, however, transitional periods for the application of the rules under the framework according to the level of economic
development in each country and other domestic conditions. It has recommended that, given the progressive liberalisation of trade worldwide and

---

[39] See Communications from Korea, WT/GC/W/298 6 August 1999, *ibid.*

the fact that as a result developing countries are no longer able to resort to the export-oriented economic growth policy through protection of domestic industries, antitrust policy should be introduced from the early stage of economic development. According to Korea, greater competition will lead to the best allocation of economic resources, help small and medium firms to grow and will enable the country in question to respond pro-actively and promptly to fast changing economic conditions within and outside national boundaries.

Norway

Norway has been in favour of negotiating and establishing a multilateral framework in antitrust policy within the WTO, covering conduct of a private and public nature, and containing, *inter alia*, a list of objectives, core principles, dispute settlement procedures as well as providing for international co-operation. Norway has also recommended that the negotiations should include an examination of the need to develop rules on anti-competitive conduct, including hard-core cartels. It has also advocated the proposition that the negotiations should take due account of the special needs of countries at different stages of development through implementation of transitional arrangements and the provision of technical assistance.[40]

Turkey

Turkey has taken the view that creating a multilateral framework within antitrust policy would be helpful to achieve the objectives of the WTO, and has proposed that future work should be fostered to reach a common understanding on the issue. In its opinion, which is very similar in content to that put forward by Norway as described above, a multilateral framework of antitrust rules should include provisions for transitional periods in order to allow members at different stages of development to observe and adhere to their commitments.[41]

Business firms

One of the most important issues to be considered as far as private firms are concerned, is how they view the role of international organisations, such as

---

[40] See Communications from Norway, WT/GC/W/310 7 September 1999, *ibid.*
[41] See Communications from Turkey, WT/GC/W/250 13 July 1999, *ibid.*

the WTO. In the USA, Business Roundtable has repeatedly voiced its anxiety about the necessity and productivity of antitrust policy negotiations at the WTO. According to Business Roundtable, international consensus on antitrust policy is a precondition to establishing any form of an international system of antitrust. In particular, Business Roundtable argued that consensus should be reached with regard to the WTO's institutional competence in antitrust policy matters. Concerns have also been expressed regarding the possibility that the multilateral balance struck in the WTO Antidumping Code might be disturbed by the involvement of developing countries in the negotiations. The Roundtable indicated that a more appropriate role for the WTO would be to establish a new work programme to assist countries in developing antitrust law and policy, to act as an 'information bank' and to provide technical assistance to different antitrust authorities on enforcement and related matters.[42] These views seem to be similar to those put forward by the International Chamber of Commerce, which believes that a basis for an international system of antitrust within the WTO has yet to be established.[43] Mirroring this view is another of the US Council for International Business, which has argued that it would be premature for the WTO Working Group to consider adopting dispute settlement mechanisms coupled with new international antitrust rules.[44] Instead, both groups are in favour of enhancing the educational tools in this area by using conventional methods of co-operation and offering technical assistance.[45]

Some analysis

The internationalisation of antitrust policy has been receiving increasing attention, within different groups and at different levels. The antitrust communities of countries around the world have been largely occupied with working out what the next step should be in this area. Thus far, their efforts have not been confined to a particular topic nor indeed any group of institutions. Clearly, it is advisable to further the internationalisation of antitrust policy through existing international organisations such as the WTO, the OECD and UNCTAD that have already instituted comprehensive programmes on antitrust policy. Some groups have even gone further by recommending that countries examine the prospect of building co-operation

---

[42] See http://www.wto.org.   [43] See http://www.iccwbo.org.
[44] See ICPAC, p. 268.   [45] See http://www.uscib.org.

between them and existing international organisations to forge a new initiative where government officials, private firms, non-governmental organisations and other interested parties can consult on matters of antitrust law and policy. This proposal was put forward in 2000 by the International Competition Policy Advisory Committee (ICPAC), which stated that this could be called a 'global antitrust initiative'. The Committee has recommended that this initiative should be open to developed and developing countries; be comprehensive or at least open to the possibility of breadth in its coverage of issue areas; and be accommodating to the private sector, non-governmental organisations and other interested parties.

Recommending the introduction of a 'global antitrust initiative' connotes the need for a change in the present direction of internationalisation of antitrust policy. Such a change is being considered due to the obvious limitations from which all existing international organisations dealing with issues of antitrust policy seem to suffer. Looking at the nature of the WTO and the OECD would explain why a change is crucial.

The WTO

Whilst the WTO is of crucial significance in developing international antitrust policy, it seems to be subject to certain limitations. Notably, the WTO is broadly inclusive in its membership, but is principally concerned with governmental trade-restraining practices. This gives rise to an important limitation because – in light of the discussion in the previous chapter – not all antitrust and trade policy problems overlap. Reflecting the general views of the USA, ICPAC has argued that first, the traditional mandate of the WTO – negotiation of rules, which are then made subject to dispute settlement – may be inappropriate for antitrust policy issues, which should rather be discussed broadly and in a consultative manner; secondly, only a limited range of antitrust matters, if any, are likely to be successfully enforced in any organisation that requires a binding commitment from countries; thus, in ICPAC's view it is inappropriate to add antitrust policy issues to the agenda within the WTO.[46]

Nevertheless, it is this author's view that the WTO should not be regarded as totally unsuitable to pursue antitrust policy issues. Whilst it is acknowledged that not all antitrust and trade policy issues overlap, the fact that there is a close nexus between the WTO objectives of trade liberalisation

---

[46] See the views of the USA, at pp. 258–9 above.

and the commitment of an increasing number of countries – most of whom are members of the WTO family – to instituting systems of antitrust and reinforcing existing ones is a factor in favour of developing an antitrust policy agenda at the WTO. Furthermore, the fact that the WTO is likely to receive support from other important organisations in the near future is another factor that is likely to enforce this argument. At the moment, there are real prospects that organisations such as the World Bank, UNCTAD and the recently established ICN will offer support to the WTO in the field of antitrust policy.[47] Nevertheless, it is acknowledged that certain institutional and policy limitations at the WTO have to (and can) be taken care of in the short term.[48]

The OECD

Like the WTO, the OECD constitutes an important forum for dealing with international antitrust policy issues, but equally is subject to its own limitations. As was seen above, discussions of international antitrust policy issues within the OECD have been conducted within the CLP and the JGTC, which have been particularly helpful in forging links between the domestic antitrust policies of the OECD's member countries, between antitrust and trade authorities and, to an extent, between the antitrust authorities of member countries and non-member countries. Amongst all existing international organisations, the OECD is the only organisation where countries have committed themselves to obligations on antitrust policy. This is evident from the analytical and policy-oriented studies undertaken within the various committees of the OECD concerning the internationalisation of antitrust policy. In this regard, the CLP deserves special mention due to the furthering of 'soft convergence' of antitrust policies among member countries of the OECD and its promotion of the technical assistance to certain non-member countries.[49]

However, little success has been achieved by the OECD in establishing rule-making or dispute settlement mechanisms. This is, of course, an obvious limitation to which the OECD is subject. Another obvious limitation concerns the fact that there are only twenty-nine country members within the OECD family. This means that several countries that either have systems of antitrust in place or are considering instituting such systems are

---

[47] See ch. 10.   [48] See ch. 10.
[49] For up-to-date information on the various programmes at the OECD, see http://www.oecd.org.

not members of the OECD. In addition, the current deliberations at the OECD do not seem to be particularly receptive to the particular needs of non-member countries with new systems of antitrust.

A comment

As a result of the limitations associated with the WTO and the OECD, it is understandable why a serious and a fresh consideration of antitrust policy and its place in the global economy should be undertaken. Undoubtedly, the work of these organisations has been extremely valuable – and continues to be so – in furthering the scope and idea of the internationalisation of antitrust policy.[50] Nevertheless, it is obvious that it is necessary at present to expand on the agenda, institutional capabilities and mechanisms of these organisations, if the process of internationalisation is to receive the adequate treatment and proper consideration it deserves.[51]

Political power and perspectives of countries, firms and consumer interests

Overview

Having looked at the role of existing international organisations which deal with the internationalisation of antitrust policy, the discussion now turns to analysing the issues from the perspective of the countries, firms and consumers. Previous chapters have already made it clear that in the internationalisation of antitrust policy, sovereign countries are not the only actors; there are also forces from above and below. From above, stand regional and international organisations, such as the EC, NAFTA, the WTO and the OECD. Examining these political forces in the internationalisation of antitrust policy, as chapters 6 and 8 explained, is important before one can complete an analysis of the internationalisation of antitrust policy. From below, on the other hand, there are equally important forces. One such force is business firms, which have gained increasing importance in the internationalisation of antitrust policy. On that basis, an examination of

---

[50] See J. Shelton, 'Competition Policy: What Chance for International Rules', speech delivered at the Wilton Park Conference, 24 November 1998, available at http://www.oecd.org/daf/clp/speeches/JS-WILTO.htm.
[51] See ch. 10.

future possible directions of more internationalised antitrust policy must be sensitive to the basic forces of international political power and the views of not only countries but also firms. Some commentators have noted that this variable has received little attention in the literature partly because the internationalisation of antitrust policy is a recent phenomenon, but more importantly because lawyers and economists do not tend to concern themselves with these issues.[52]

Countries on the international plane

If one categorises the different views on the role of countries on the international plane and on the creation of an international system of antitrust – following a process of internationalisation of antitrust policy – it may be possible to conclude that there are several schools of thought. Two main schools should be considered: *Realism* and *Neorationalism*.

Realism

From a Realist perspective, any form of internationalisation which will lead to the creation of an international system of antitrust with autonomous institutions will essentially be ineffectual by imposing rules and standards upon sovereign countries which do not conform to those countries' own interests and priorities.[53] Hence, to pursue this form of internationalisation is pointless and absurd. This view is explained on the basis of two Realist perspectives. At one end of the spectrum, it is thought to be unlikely that countries will co-operate towards the creation of an international system of antitrust, especially if this would mean that countries would have to limit their sovereignty in favour of the autonomous institutions in the system. At the other end of the spectrum, and assuming that countries would co-operate if they decide, for example, to limit the effect of rules and principles of an international system of antitrust, domestic courts and antitrust authorities would not apply that system's law due to reasons relating to sovereignty.[54]

---

[52] See C. Doern and S. Wilks, *Comparative Competition Policy* (Oxford University Press, Oxford, 1996), p. 306.

[53] For a detailed account on Realism see R. Wellek, *The Concept of Realism in Literary Scholarship* (J. B. Wolters, Groningen, 1961); M. Carré, *Realists and Normalists* (Oxford University Press, Oxford, 1964).

[54] See ch. 6.

Realism asserts the primacy of national politics over international antitrust law (the law from above) and emphasises the limits that sovereign
countries may impose upon their involvement in an international system
of antitrust, which will stop well short of any surrender of sovereignty to
autonomous institutions in such a system. Realism places no emphasis on
the importance of autonomous institutions in this system. From here, it
professes that such institutions have a very marginal role to play.

Neorationalism

This approach to the internationalisation of antitrust policy and the importance and effectiveness of autonomous institutions in an international system of antitrust,[55] proceeds from the basic Realist premise of the superiority
of sovereign countries, as described in the previous paragraph. However,
Neorationalists accept there is scope for co-operation among countries and
a role for such institutions based on rational choice made by sovereign countries towards some form of co-operation on the creation of an international
system of antitrust.

Neorationalists assert that autonomous institutions in an international
system of antitrust will in fact be unable to impose their rules and standards on sovereign countries and their domestic antitrust authorities or law
courts, which may even be part of such a system. Any scope for co-operation
between countries towards the creation of an international system of antitrust and the ability of autonomous institutions to play any role in such
a system do not result from an obligation of countries to co-operate or
from any autonomous power or discretion enjoyed by these institutions.
Sovereign countries' co-operation towards the creation of an international
system of antitrust with autonomous institutions, and their acceptance of
rules and standards enunciated by such institutions, indicate that sovereign
countries would act rationally. Sovereign countries in this case would opt
for the gain that could result from co-operating, and from complying with
those rules and standards, rather than the potential benefits from opting
for no systematic antitrust policy on the international plane. Neorationalism argues that it is in the sovereign countries' own interest to establish
an international system of antitrust and to transfer some competence to
its institutions. This will have the benefit of relieving countries, *inter alia*,

---

[55] See G. Garret, 'International Cooperation and Institutional Choice: the European Community's
Internal Market' (1992) 46 *International Organization* 533.

from having to enter into bilateral agreements that anticipate any disputes that may arise among them.

Other approaches

It may be appropriate to briefly mention in the present context one additional school of thought: public choice theorists. This school is keen to reverse assumptions made by Realist and Neorationalist scholars on the primacy of countries, with the result that domestic politics would dominate the international scene. However, the public choice approach does not pervade actual domestic decision-making institutions. In addition, it even plays down international organisations because sovereign countries are viewed as standing at the centre. For this reason, this approach does not seem to add anything in addition to what Realism and Neorationalism have already supplied. Nevertheless, the public choice approach is interesting because of its focus, unlike the latter schools of thought, on institutional dimensions.

Perspective of firms

Private economic power constitutes a central element in the study of international political economy and domestic policy formulation. On the one hand, firms exercise power in a profound functional sense simply and directly because they play a role in enhancing the economic prosperity of countries, especially developed ones. On the other hand, the lobbying capacity of firms affords them the opportunity to acquire political power.[56] The economic power of multinational firms can also be observed in light of market globalisation. Thus, multinational firms are a crucial variable in determining the extent to which antitrust policy is internationalised. Business firms have always played an important role in the developing of the antitrust laws of countries, but such laws contain provisions that may also limit the freedom of action of those firms, especially when competition in the marketplace is likely to be distorted.

At the moment, amidst relentless globalisation, it is not yet clear which particular industrial sectors or key multinational firms will support or resist the move towards greater internationalisation of antitrust policy. Business advisory groups are a part of the OECD and EC antitrust policy network,

---

[56] See M. Olson, *The Logic of Collective Action* (Harvard University Press, Cambridge, Mass., 1965); D. Mueller, *Public Choice* (Cambridge University Press, Cambridge, 1979).

and thus business views are often expressed – albeit in a limited manner – within these forums.[57] Moreover, among some sectors there is the
presumption that the electronic commerce sector, due to its nature, will
be especially interested in supporting the internationalisation of antitrust
policy.[58]

Perhaps what can be said is that much more needs to be known about
the views and needs of business firms in light of all efforts to further the
internationalisation of antitrust policy. This is a topic that has received insufficient attention by lawyers and economists alike. Having said that, it
is generally assumed that business firms are in favour of the internationalisation of antitrust policy and the creation of an international system of
antitrust. Several business concerns can be mentioned here in support of
this assumption.

Ensuring uniformity

Business firms prefer uniformity in the way antitrust cases are handled
and decided by antitrust authorities. As business operations increasingly
transcend national boundaries, such operations become subject to the jurisdiction of more than one domestic antitrust authority. As the number of
domestic systems of antitrust increases around the world, more and more
domestic antitrust authorities are likely to become involved in one and the
same business operation.[59] Equally likely is the possibility that these authorities may reach conflicting decisions – or at best different conclusions –
over the legality of the same practice.[60] The business community is not so
much concerned about the possibility of more than one domestic antitrust
authority asserting jurisdiction over a particular operation as much as they
are concerned about the possibility that these authorities may reach inconsistent decisions. Having said that, it would be advisable to bear in mind that
reaching conflicting decisions may be inevitable in some cases, mainly due
to the structure of the relevant market and the levels of its concentration.

---

[57] See http://www.oecd.org.
[58] For a good account of this issue see the ICPAC, pp. 287–92.
[59] The *Exxon/Mobile* operation was notified in no fewer than twenty jurisdictions. For a comment
on this issue see '*Exxon-Mobile*: Conquering the World' (1999) 13 *Antitrust* 16. Another operation, the *MCI/WorldCom* transaction in 1997, was reviewed by more than thirty antitrust
authorities in the world. See A. Frederickson, 'A Strategic Approach to Multi-Jurisdictional
Filings' (1999) 4 *European Counsel* 23.
[60] See *Shell/Montedison* Commission Decision, OJ 1994 No. L332/48; also *Boeing/McDonnell
Douglas*, OJ 1997 No. L336/16.

Also, differences in the legal standards employed by different antitrust authorities can give rise to inconsistencies.[61]

The possibility of conflicts between countries

The involvement of more than one antitrust authority and the reaching of inconsistent results by those authorities in a particular transaction may lead to international conflicts between the countries concerned, especially over industrial policy. Business firms are generally concerned about the prospect of being caught in such conflicts, where it is normal for industrial policy considerations and other considerations to override antitrust policy considerations.

Differences in procedures

Business firms are concerned by the length of time required for different antitrust authorities to reach a decision on a particular operation because delays in decision-making may be harmful to the interests of the former, especially in the case of mergers. It is therefore understandable that business firms seem to favour speedy decisions by antitrust authorities. One does not need to look beyond the examples provided by the EC and US merger review regimes to deduce the concern of firms in this context.[62] Surely, differences in procedure may subject firms to the burden and expense of having to comply with the laws of different countries.[63]

The use of confidential information

Business firms are generally concerned about situations in which one antitrust authority hands over confidential information about those firms to another one. The fear is that the latter may use this information for economic espionage. Also, there is an anxiety when information is handed over to a jurisdiction which allows private actions.[64] These actions are considered to be a 'rogue elephant' because private plaintiffs in these actions are not under the same constraints as antitrust authorities, for example, regarding

---

[61] See D. Wood and R. Whish, *Merger Cases in the Real World: a Study of Merger Control Procedures* (OECD, Paris, 1994). See further chs. 3 and 4.

[62] See J. Griffin, 'What Business People Want from a World Antitrust Code' (1999) 34 *New England Law Review* 39, at 42.

[63] See remarks by P. Condit, CEO of Boeing Corporation, about the conflicting results reached by the EC and the USA in the *Boeing/McDonnell Douglas* merger, press release 'Boeing Responds to European Commission Recommendation', 16 July 1997, available at http://www.boeing.com.

[64] See pp. 201–3 above.

breach of confidence. So, there may be a risk of confidential information being disclosed to other firms and individuals.

Consumer perspective

It is believed that the interests of consumers in a global economy would be maximised if antitrust rules as wide as markets were introduced. This view is based on the understanding that a global vision would better facilitate the appraisal of positive as well as negative impacts of international operations of firms. Important international organisations such as the OECD, World Bank, the WTO and Consumers International[65] have in recent years devoted special attention to consumer interests in global markets, as well as advocating ways to protect those interests. A clear consensus has been emerging, especially at the WTO and the OECD, that introducing global antitrust rules would enhance the welfare and interests of consumers in global markets. Both the OECD and WTO have called on countries to make antitrust and trade policy more responsive to the interests of consumers and to take those interests into account especially when consumers are located beyond national boundaries.[66]

The argument in favour of global antitrust rules aside, it seems that currently there is a heated debate on whether globalisation in general would benefit consumers.[67] It may be of interest to note the position of pro- and anti-globalisers. The former tend to assume markets are competitive, including markets in developing countries and those in transition. According to pro-globalisers, liberalisation will benefit consumers. Anti-globalisers, on the other hand, have adopted a different stance, arguing that liberalisation would have the opposite effect, namely leading to damaging monopolies.

However convincing the arguments of either camp are, it seems clear that this is another situation where a Neofunctionalist approach would be appropriate.[68] Thus, disagreements between anti- and pro-globalisation as far as the benefit to consumers is concerned should be worked out on a country-by-country basis and industry-by-industry basis. There is simply no room for misguided assumptions.

---

[65] See http://www.consumersinternational.org.
[66] See *New Dimensions of Market Access in Globalizing World Economy* (OECD, Paris, 1995), p. 254; WTO Annual Report 1997, p. 75.
[67] See ch. 1 for a discussion on the concept and process of globalisation.
[68] The theory of Neofunctionalism was discussed at pp. 231–4 above.

Model systems of antitrust

Several examples

This part is not intended to be an exhaustive study of different model systems of antitrust in the world. The aim is merely to provide an account of several models, as they represent important aspects of the debate on the internationalisation of antitrust policy.

The US model

The model served by the US system of antitrust is essentially one based on the principle of free market. The system, as evidenced in the interpretations and analyses applied to the US antitrust laws, mainly aims to combat anti-competitive behaviour that harms consumer welfare and reduces efficiency. The system is based on the ideology that, save for cases where a specific behaviour is seen as anti-competitive, public intervention in the market is unnecessary. Every firm is free to compete, including dominant firms, even if some harm might be caused to competitors of those firms during the process.[69]

The statutory language of the US antitrust laws as was seen in chapter 3 is generally very broad. Section 1 of the Sherman Act 1890, for example, states that every 'contract, combination ... conspiracy, in restraint of trade ... is declared illegal'. Congress did not provide an interpretation of the various terms mentioned in the section. As a result, US courts gave a common law interpretation to these terms. For example, the prohibition in the section refers to 'restraint of trade', which is not defined in the section itself. The US courts have held that only 'unreasonable restraints of trade' should be covered.[70] The jurisprudence of the courts in the USA has developed around two complementary modes of analysis: the *per se* and *rule of reason* approaches.[71] The former covers restraints that on their face appear to be of

---

[69] See *Spectrum Sports, Inc.* v. *McQuillan*, 506 US 447 (1993); *Brooke Group Ltd.* v. *Brown and Williamson Tobacco Corp.*, 509 US 209 (1993).

[70] See *Standard Oil Co.* v. *United States*, 221 US 1, 58 (1911); *Chicago Board of Trade* v. *United States*, 246 US 231, 238 (1918).

[71] The academic literature on this issue is abundant. See R. Bork, 'The Rule of Reason and Per Se Concept: Price Fixing and Market Division' (1965) 74 *Yale Law Journal* 775; T. Piraino, 'Reconciling the *Per Se* Rule and the *Rule of Reason* Approaches to Antitrust Analysis' (1991) 64 *Southern California Law Review* 685; 'Making Sense of the *Rule of Reason*: a New Standard for Section 1 of the Sherman Act' (1994) 47 *Vanderbilt Law Review* 1753; O. Black, '*Per Se Rule* and *Rule of Reason* : What Are They?' (1997) 18 *European Competition Law Review* 145; V. Korah,

the kind that would always or almost always tend to restrict competition and decrease output rather than ones designed to increase economic efficiency and render markets more competitive.[72] The latter approach on the other hand is an inquiry whether a restraint is one that promotes competition or one that suppresses competition, looking at the circumstances, details and logic of the restraint.[73]

There are several striking features about the US system of antitrust that must be mentioned. First, and this is a point that was made clear in chapter 4, under the system, the Department of Justice and the Federal Trade Commission – the antitrust authorities in charge of enforcement of US antitrust law – lack competence to grant exemptions to firms from the prohibitions of antitrust laws, and even to issue a binding decision on firms in the first place. Rather the authority in charge in a particular case is under an obligation to approach the judiciary to establish a violation before an injunction may be granted or a fine imposed. Secondly, serious violations of US antitrust laws can be prosecuted criminally by jailing executives of firms. An obvious example of such violations is price-fixing cartels. Thirdly, attorney generals in different states can bring actions to enforce US antitrust laws, even where the Department of Justice and the Federal Trade Commission have reviewed the matter and reached a different conclusion.[74] Fourthly, the US system of antitrust allows private injured parties to bring their own antitrust actions. Fifthly, the system includes a treble damages remedy and the 'Noerr' doctrine, dealing with antitrust petitioners' immunity.[75]

'The Rise and Fall of Provisional Validity – the Need for a Rule of Reason in EEC Antitrust' (1981) 3 *Northwestern Journal of International Law and Business* 320; R. Joliet, *The Rule of Reason in Antitrust Law: American, German and Common Market Laws in Comparative Perspective* (Faculté de Droit de l'Université de Liège, Liège, 1967); R. Whish and B. Sufrin, 'Art. 85 and the Rule of Reason' (1987) 7 *Yearbook of European Law* 1; V. Korah, 'EEC Competition Policy – Legal Form or Economic Efficiency' (1986) 39 *Current Legal Problems* 85.

[72] *Broadcast Music, Inc.* v. *CBS*, 441 US 1 (1979), at 19–20.

[73] *National Society of Professional Engineers* v. *United States*, 435 US 679 (1978), at 691. See also Muchlinski, *Multinational*, p. 392; S. Anderman, *EC Competition Law and Intellectual Property Rights* (Oxford University Press, Oxford, 1998), pp. 31–2.

[74] It may be interesting to compare this situation with those in Canada and Mexico, where provinces and states are not allowed to enforce national antitrust laws.

[75] See *Eastern Railroad Presidents Conference* v. *Noerr Motor Freight, Inc.*, 365 US 127 (1961) and *United Mine Workers* v. *Pennington*, 381 US 657 (1965). Under the doctrine, it is not unlawful to petition the government for anti-competitive restraints against competitors. Indeed, the right to petition is well founded under the US Constitution, First Amendment, Right to Petition. It may be of interest to note that in the Antitrust Enforcement Guidelines for International Operations 1995, it is stated that the Federal Trade Commission and Department of Justice stated they

The EC model

This model was extensively discussed in chapter 5.

The Federal German model

The German system of antitrust is based on social market principles, in particular on the significance of antitrust as a 'regulator' to protect against abuses of political as well as economic power, in part by safeguarding the freedom of private enterprise. The system shares several common features with the US system. Nevertheless, the following differences may be observed. First, the system is more interventionist than its US counterpart as far as abuse of dominance is concerned. Secondly, the system ascribes greater importance to the protection of competitors in merger cases than the US system.[76]

The Japanese model

The Japanese system of antitrust is based on the principle of industrial policy with competition and significant government intervention, a model also in existence in a few South-east Asian countries.[77] Japan believes that its economic dynamism has in fact been rooted in the robust market mechanisms created through competition among firms. According to Japan, industrial policy and antitrust policy co-ordinated mutually and developed an environment that allowed firms to engage in free and fair competition. Japan believes that the introduction of antitrust policy early in Japan's economic reconstruction, as well as the subsequent evolution of this in response to economic development, was a great factor in Japan's rapid economic growth in the past.

The origins of the Japanese system date back to the 1940s when the USA attempted to export its antitrust tradition into Japan. Following World War II, Japan carried out a wide reform of its economic system. It also sought to foster the starting of a new era of liberalisation through abolishing economic control legislation with the aim of ensuring wide-ranging and equitable income distribution. This included the 1947 formulation

would apply the 'Noerr' doctrine to the petitioning of foreign governments in the same manner they treat attempts to petition the US Government.

[76] See the German Cartel Office's website http://www.bundeskartellamt.de/english.html.

[77] One such country is Korea. For a good examination of the system see D. Sakong, *Korea in the World Economy* (Institute for International Economics, Washington D.C., 1993).

of an Anti-Monopoly Law based on US antitrust law, with the Fair Trade Commission established to enforce the new law.

Some common features can be identified between the Japanese Anti-Monopoly Law and the US Sherman Act. However, differences can be deduced in the case of vertical restraints. Under the Japanese Anti-Monopoly Law, vertical restraints are covered under the section on unfair business practices. The section covers, *inter alia*, passing-off and all conducts considered unfair, which in the USA are not considered as antitrust law issues as such.[78]

Initially, the Japanese Ministry of International Trade and Industry enjoyed extensive powers in controlling the national economy. It adopted a regulatory policy, based on its regulatory law, encouraging firms to co-operate between themselves and with the government. This co-operation took the shape of the creation of associations of firms which shared common directors, ownership of shares and suppliers and customers. These were called *kieretsu*.[79] The integration of Japan into world trade has, however, somewhat undermined the position of *kieretsu* and the regulatory barriers which these often erected. Nevertheless, complaints from Japan's trading partners are sometimes made about market access barriers, which seem to indicate that the idea of *kieretsu* has not been entirely extinguished.[80]

A comment

The introduction to the book stated that nearly 100 countries have introduced systems of antitrust in the world. The flip-side of this means that many others do not have such systems. Some countries have free-market principles but have not yet adopted antitrust laws. For example, Hong Kong and Singapore have relied on the market itself to provide the forces of competition, choosing free trade as their antitrust policy. Other countries have laws against restrictive business practices such as several African and Southeast Asian countries, a number of which have some reservations regarding

---

[78] Note that in the USA, fair trading laws have been repealed.

[79] See J. Davidow, 'The Application of US Antitrust Laws to *Kieretsu* Practices' (1994) 18 *World Competition* 5; Muchlinski, *Multinational*, pp. 69–70.

[80] See pp. 219–20 above. For more information about the Japanese system of antitrust law see the Japan Fair Trade Commission's website http://www.jftc.admix.go.jp.

capitalism.[81] The fact that many countries do not have antitrust laws may affect the role of antitrust policy in the global economy as an effective means to address anti-competitive behaviour that impedes and distorts the flows of trade and investment worldwide. These countries are at a disadvantage in combating certain anti-competitive behaviour with international compo- nents, both because multinational firms are likely to adhere to the antitrust authorities of the major economies where such behaviour is concerned and because of their greater need for accessing information outside the ju- risdictions. This highlights the importance of international co-operation for them. But these countries generally do not participate in such forms of co-operation. They sometimes do not have antitrust authorities and, where they do, they may be constrained due to lack of resources, whether financial or human.[82] Undoubtedly, most of these disadvantages should disappear if these countries are encouraged, or actually seek, to adopt antitrust laws in their national legal orders, and if they are encouraged to seek international co-operation with other countries.

Another comment should be made on the fact that the above-mentioned model systems of antitrust differ in many ways. The fact that this is so is bound to affect the internationalisation of antitrust policy, especially if strong models are likely to impose their standards on the weaker models. In addition, differences may lead to conflicts between the different models, especially between the stronger ones, as the discussion in the following part shows.

The EC–US conflict

Previous chapters put forward several reasons why attention has been turning to the internationalisation of antitrust policy. Those reasons are

---

[81] Arguably, the collapse of many Asian economies in 1998 seems to have increased the fear of these countries about capitalism. See W. Kovacic, 'Capitalism, Socialism and Competition Pol- icy in Vietnam' (1999) 13 *Antitrust* 57; 'Merger Enforcement in Transition: Antitrust Controls on Acquisitions in Emerging Economies' (1998) 66 *University of Cincinnati Law Review* 1075; 'Getting Started: Creating New Competition Policy Institutions in Transition Economies' (1997) 23 *Brooklyn Journal of International Law* 403; N. Pakaphan, 'Indonesia: Enactment of Compe- tition Law' (1999) 27 *International Business Lawyer* 491; W. Cho, 'Korea's Economic Crisis: the Role of Competition Policy' (1999) 27 IBL 495; S. Supanit, 'Thailand: Implementation of Competition Law' (1999) 27 *International Business Lawyer* 491.
[82] WTO Annual Report 1997, p. 32.

important. However, one can find at least one additional reason, which seems to be of considerable importance. The reason concerns the conflict between the EC and the USA in this area. As was said before, the EC has been in favour of more internationalised antitrust policy. It has proposed developing antitrust rules within the WTO. The USA, on the other hand, has been very sceptical about this, and has rejected any move to that effect. Equally, however, the conflict between the EC and the USA is caused by differences in the substantive laws and procedures of the two jurisdictions. The present chapter so far as well as chapters 4 and 7 have spelt out these differences and how they impact on the internationalisation of antitrust policy. The fact that the economic policies prevalent in the two jurisdictions also differ makes this impact all the greater.

As the discussion in chapter 5 demonstrated, the EC has given the world community a conception in respect of the internationalisation of antitrust policy, which in some way has been based on the challenge to build a single integrated market. This conception seems to have been strengthened by the fact that Member States have been converging their domestic antitrust laws towards EC antitrust law, with the result that major business operations in the EC will be relieved from the burden of multiple application of different antitrust laws with different standards. This strength has also been enhanced by the fact that Central and Eastern European countries have been taking steps to approximate their antitrust laws towards EC antitrust law.

It may well be anticipated that the internationalisation of antitrust policy and the creation of an international system of antitrust will eventually depend on the respective positions of the EC and the USA. The above discussion made it clear that the systems of antitrust in both jurisdictions have grown in significance and this ensured the influence of both systems on the international plane, perhaps with the balance tilted towards the EC system of antitrust.[83] Both the EC and the USA have been particularly active in encouraging countries to introduce systems of antitrust, especially ones based on the EC and US models, in their legal orders. Some countries have responded by basing their antitrust laws exclusively on EC antitrust

---

[83] See K. van Miert, 'Competition Policy in Relation to the Central and Eastern European Countries – Achievements and Challenges' (1998) 2 *European Community Competition Policy NewsLetter* 1; K. McDermott, 'US Officials Provide Competition Counseling to Eastern Europe' (1991) 5 *Antitrust* 4; S. Singham, 'US and European Models Shaping Latin American Competition Law' (1998) 1 *Global Competition Review* 15.

law. These include most Central and Eastern European countries.[84] Other countries seem to have turned to the US model and not to the EC when adopting antitrust laws. One such country is Mexico[85] whose adoption of antitrust law formed part of the country's opening of the national economy in anticipation of NAFTA, under which participating countries are required to adopt and maintain measures prohibiting and combating anticompetitive behaviour of firms.[86] Between these two ends, a few countries have adopted combined aspects of EC and the US antitrust laws. For example, Canadian antitrust law on abuse of market dominance is similar to that of the EC, while provisions on mergers, horizontal and vertical agreements are similar to US antitrust law.[87] Other countries that could be mentioned here include Australia,[88] New Zealand,[89] Argentina,[90] Columbia,[91] Venezuela[92] and Brazil.[93]

Against these categories stands an independent category of countries – normally developing ones – who have opted for neither the EC nor the US type of antitrust laws because they fear that antitrust law is a tool for developed countries to exploit the economy of less developing countries. This is an interesting situation, because it seems that these countries are keen on ensuring adequate control on anti-competitive behaviour,[94] especially

---

[84] M. Ojala, *The Competition Law of Central and Eastern Europe* (Sweet & Maxwell, London, 1999); M. Cowie & M. Novotria, 'Pre-Merger Notification in Central and Eastern Europe' (1998) 12 *Antitrust* 19; C. Brzezinski, 'Competition and Antitrust Law in Central Europe: Poland, the Czech Republic, Slovakia and Hungary' (1994) 15 *Michigan Journal of International Law* 1129; G. Oprescue and E. Rohlck, 'Competition Policy in Transition Economies: the Case of Romania' (1999) 3 *European Community Competition Policy NewsLetter* 62.

[85] See G. Castañeda and F. Ugarte, 'Mexico Still Setting the Pace for Latin America' (1998) 1 *Global Competition Review* 12. More information can be found on the Mexican antitrust authority's website http://www.cfc.gob.mx.

[86] See Article 1501(1) of NAFTA.

[87] See the Canada Competition Bureau's website, http://www.strategis.ic.gc.ca/competition.

[88] See the Australian Competition and Consumer Authority's website, http://www.accc.gov.au.

[89] See the New Zealand Commerce Commission's website, http://www.comcom.govt.nz and New Zealand Ministry of Commerce's website, http://www.moc.govt.nz.

[90] See Argentina Antitrust Authority, Comisión Nacional de Defensa de la Competencia's website, http://www.mecon.gov.ar.

[91] See the Superintendencia Brancia's website, http://www.superbancaria.gov.co and the Superintendencia de industria y comercio's website http://www.sic.gov.co.

[92] See the Procompetencia's website, http://www.procompetencia.gov.ve.

[93] See the Brazilian Competition Tribunal's website, http://www.mj.gov.br/cade.

[94] I. Kyvelidis, 'State Isomorphism in the Post-Socialist Tradition' (2000) 4 *European Integration Online Papers*, available at http://www.eiop.or.at/eiop/texte/2000-002.htm; J. Hellman, 'Constitutions and Economic Reform in the Post-Communist Traditions' (1996) 5 *East European Constitutional Review* 46.

since they may be subject to the risks of such behaviour in light of the dismantling of state barriers to the flows of trade and investment in the global economy and since they may be subject to the extraterritorial application of antitrust laws of other countries.

Convergence and harmonisation

During the last ten years or so, domestic antitrust laws have been converging, which has been facilitated by several factors. Perhaps the most obvious one is the informal process of bilateral co-operation between domestic antitrust authorities. Domestic antitrust authorities have, albeit to a limited extent,[95] increasingly engaged in informal consultations among themselves in enforcement matters in cross-border antitrust cases. Co-operation has been particularly common in merger cases. For example, Canadian, EC and US antitrust authorities quite frequently exchange views on their analytical approaches on issues such as market definition and economic analysis in general in these cases. Furthermore, these antitrust authorities have offered valuable technical assistance to countries with economies in transition and others with infant experience using the concept of competition and antitrust law. This process of technical assistance has generated many benefits, perhaps the most important of which is the fact that the very process of exchange of information-sharing has clarified differences between the EC and US systems as well as differences between what mature systems offer and what developing countries think is appropriate for their economic and political conditions. By the same token, co-operation helps identify the areas of agreement among countries, promote convergence and further common understanding. The benefits of co-operation and technical assistance can be observed in the case of South Africa and Israel, where antitrust authorities have relied heavily on information from other jurisdictions when interpreting, applying and enforcing their laws.[96]

Convergence of antitrust laws may be observed in different forums, including in the EC,[97] in the USA and even in the OECD. Some commentators have argued that convergence is a prerequisite to any move towards comprehensive internationalisation of antitrust policy, including the creation of an international antitrust code.[98] Whether this is a valid argument or

---

[95] For example, limitations of confidentiality restrictions in national laws.
[96] See Israel's antitrust authority's website, http://www.antitrust.gov.il.
[97] See ch. 5.   [98] See further ch. 10.

not depends on certain factors, which will be alluded to in the following chapter, as well as on the advantages and disadvantages associated with such convergence that are important to highlight.

Advantages

Sovereignty and related considerations

An obvious argument that can be advanced in favour of convergence, especially soft convergence, is that this form of internationalisation of antitrust policy is preferable to the form that will lead to the creation of an international system of antitrust with autonomous institutions or an international antitrust code. This is because, unlike the latter, it hardly threatens the sovereignty of countries and the enforcement prerogatives of different national antitrust authorities.

The needs of countries with no antitrust laws

Another argument in favour is that the creation of an international system of antitrust is quite ambitious for the moment, so for this reason one must focus on important intermediate steps. Convergence, in this regard, is seen as such an important step, which can help countries with no antitrust laws to develop them.

Relief for firms from dealing with multiple systems

Convergence of domestic antitrust laws offers substantial benefits to firms operating in international markets. In particular, firms would be offered relief from the burden of having to deal with systems of antitrust that are different in both substantive law and the procedures used. The net result would be that the cost of their operations and compliance would be substantially reduced as well as enhancing efficiency in the market. Moreover, it is guaranteed that, with convergence, uniformity of approach by different antitrust authorities will be more likely than otherwise. This is especially so in merger review cases.[99]

Removing hindrances to market access

Convergence is likely to enhance the flows of trade and investment between countries by removing market access-restraining private anti-competitive

---

[99] See pp. 270–1 above.

behaviour. This is especially valuable in the case of those countries which have not been tough enough on private anti-competitive behaviour within their own boundaries and thus have impaired the entry to domestic markets by foreign firms and in the case of countries with no antitrust laws.

Disadvantages

Offsetting these advantages are some disadvantages associated with convergence of domestic antitrust laws which must be mentioned.

The long process inherent in convergence

It would not be difficult, in the light of the discussion in chapters 3 and 5, to point out the fact that convergence of domestic antitrust laws is a very slow process, and as a matter of fact its success cannot be guaranteed. In the EC, despite the strength of the EC system of antitrust and its influence on Member States' domestic systems of antitrust, convergence has been developing for more than forty-five years without reaching its full maturity. On the basis of this situation, it is difficult to imagine that better progress, or even an equal one, will be made in the convergence of domestic antitrust laws in the world. Countries do not share common antitrust traditions. Furthermore, their seriousness in enforcing their antitrust laws differs, not to mention the fact that many countries do not even have antitrust laws in place at the moment.

The different goals of antitrust law

Those countries with antitrust laws differ with regards to what the goals of antitrust law should be. Whilst some countries have opted for economic goals, others have used their antitrust laws to further social and even political goals.[100] Of course, an attempt to converge antitrust laws with different goals risks collision between them. In addition, it is very likely that some goals advocated by strong countries will override competing ones advocated by weaker countries.

Defining 'competition'

It is not clear whether countries agree on how the concept of 'competition' should be defined and understood.[101] Moreover, there does not seem to be full consensus on whether antitrust law should be used to protect

---

[100] See pp. 52–7 above.   [101] See ch. 2. for a comprehensive examination of the concept.

competition. As was said earlier in the chapter, some countries have opted for systems based on the principle of restrictive business practices as opposed to competition, a fact that will undoubtedly widen the differences between countries.[102]

Substantive issues

In 1993, a Multilateral Antitrust Code with substantive principles to be enforced by an autonomous antitrust authority was proposed by the Munich Group, a private group made of twelve scholars and experts.[103] A proposal was put forward by the Group to establish minimum standards, which could then be incorporated into the WTO. Those standards would be enforceable by domestic antitrust authorities in their jurisdictions. In case of disputes, the Group suggested that they should be heard by a permanent international antitrust panel, forming part of a wider dispute settlement mechanism. The areas which were proposed to be covered under the standards included specific principles of antitrust law, national treatment, supervision of enforcement by an independent authority empowered to request domestic courts and antitrust authorities to initiate investigations and intergovernmental dispute settlement procedures.

At a supranational level, several similar proposals have been made. One is to establish an international variant of the domestic systems of antitrust. The idea here is to develop through the support of the WTO structural features of systems of antitrust. Within such a framework, the WTO would create a set of rules with a dispute settlement mechanism, which would require countries to introduce antitrust laws in their jurisdictions. Another proposal put forward for involving the WTO has been to develop general principles, both procedural and substantive, of antitrust law.[104] The OECD and the World Bank have been seeking for the last three years to develop a 'Global Corporate Governance Forum'.[105] The OECD has also developed a set of 'best practices' principles on corporate governance, which complement its joint projects with the World Bank. The joint initiative has been hosting meetings and workshops attended by representatives of the business community and governments of countries.

---

[102] See ch. 1.
[103] International Antitrust Code Working Group, Draft International Code as a GATT–MTO Plurilateral Trade Agreement, 10 July 1993.
[104] See the suggestion by J. Shelton, former Deputy Secretary-General of the OECD, made in 1999, http://www.oecd.org.
[105] See http://www.gcgf.org.

There seems to be a recognition that countries may be prepared to co-operate in meaningful ways on the internationalisation of antitrust policy, but are not necessarily prepared to be legally bound by substantive provisions under public international law. The Asia-Pacific Economic Co-operation Forum (APEC) has been built on this recognition, that it is possible to advance some liberalisation and harmonisation of practices outside a framework of binding legal instruments. The proposed global antitrust initiative by ICPAC, which was mentioned above,[106] is built on the premise that countries can usefully explore areas of co-operation in the field of global antitrust policy and facilitate further convergence and harmonisation. Countries do not seem to be prepared to be bound in all areas of restrictive business practices. In some cases, countries seem to prefer developing a common understanding through consultations and non-binding principles.

Reflections and summary

It should be obvious from the above discussion that the internationalisation of antitrust policy has evolved into a topic of great contemporary importance and debate. Over the last eighty years or so, considerable efforts have been made to address this topic and these continue to be of crucial significance. The chapter analysed these efforts, drawing comparative analyses where appropriate. It seems that one can expect this topic to be subjected to heated debate in the years to come. At present, antitrust policy varies in terms of its development and understanding, whether within individual countries or within existing international organisations. The fact that this is so leaves a general consensus on how to go about expanding the way into the jungle of internationalisation of antitrust policy – whether leading eventually to the creation of an international system of antitrust, or even substantive harmonisation amongst different systems of antitrust – far from appearing on the horizon in the near future.[107]

It seems that the success in making consensus more imminent, and even going beyond this, depends in large part on the position of the EC and the

---

[106] See pp. 263–4 above.
[107] G. Drauz and T. Lingos, 'The Treatment of Trans-Border Mergers in the 1990s: a European Perspective' in *Policy Directions for Global Merger Review*, a special report by the Global Forum for Competition and Trade Policy (1999), 58; D. Melamed, 'Antitrust Enforcement in a Global Economy' (1998) *Fordham Corporate Law Institute* 1; W. Baer, 'International Antitrust Policy' (1998) *Fordham Corporate Law Institute* 247; A. Schaub, '*Boeing/MDD*' (1998) 1 *European Community Competition Policy NewsLetter* 2, 4.

USA, and the extent to which it is possible to create a common ground between these two forces in relation to the internationalisation of antitrust policy.[108] The EC has expressed very positive views in favour of internationalising antitrust policy and the creation of an international system of antitrust in order to better address transnational antitrust issues and tackle political conflicts resulting from the overlap in application of different antitrust laws.[109] Conversely, the USA remains doubtful about the need and desirability for such a system.[110] The fact that the EC has been active in the area of international antitrust policy and that the EC system of antitrust has developed into a strong system has meant that the US system of antitrust has lost the dominant position that it held for many years. At present, perhaps the EC and US systems of antitrust stand in the position of equals. Within the EC, the antitrust laws of several Member States, most notably Germany, and to a lesser extent the UK, play an important role in regulating many business operations with international components. Moreover, the antitrust laws of countries outside the EC and the USA, such as Japan, have gained greatly in significance and impact in recent years, and even in Latin America, the African continent and the Middle East, antitrust law, and the need for it in the domestic legal system, is being taken more seriously.

Reaching some form of consensus on the internationalisation of antitrust policy is subject also to other challenges. However, perhaps the greatest challenge in this instance is to convince national politicians and antitrust regulators that fostering greater internationalisation of antitrust policy culminating in the creation of an international system of antitrust is in their domestic interests,[111] as well as in their overall best interest. As a matter of fact, this proposition is applicable not only to the USA, but also to many other countries, whether developing or developed; though the task is much harder in the case of the former. Politicians are not generally in favour of surrendering power, even to a limited extent, to autonomous institutions

---

[108] See D. Gerber, 'Afterword: Antitrust and American Business Abroad Revisited' (2000) 20 *Northwestern Journal of International Law and Business* 307, 310.

[109] See K. van Miert, 'The WTO and Competition Policy: the Need to Consider Negotiations', address before ambassadors to the WTO, 12 April 1998, available at http://www.insidetrade.com/sec-cgi.

[110] See D. Valentine, 'Building a Cooperative Framework for Oversight in Mergers – the Answer to Extraterritorial Issues in Merger Review' (1998) 6 *George Mason Law Review* 525, 529; D. Wood, 'Caution Necessary Concerning WTO Agenda on Competition Rules: Justice Officials Warn' (1996) 13 *International Trade Representative* 1856.

[111] See generally A. Guzman, 'Is International Antitrust Possible?' (1998) 73 *New York University Law Review* 1501.

in an international system of antitrust.[112] This point can be illustrated with reference to merger control.

Decisions in merger cases often have important political value because they can be employed to impose costs on foreign firms or prevent unemployment, which normally accrue from rationalisation following mergers.[113] One does not need to go beyond the *Boeing/MDD* and *GE/Honeywell* cases to be able to deduce the political value of mergers approval decisions.[114] Due to the importance of the attitude of politicians and antitrust regulators, a study on the internationalisation of antitrust policy and an attempt to create an international system of antitrust must be sensitive to *political realities*. In this sense, one can trace the failure of efforts towards internationalisation thus far to the fact that those efforts have been over-ambitious and have neglected to give adequate and proper consideration to *political realities*.

The whole project of the internationalisation of antitrust policy may be reduced to the reaching of consensus on the issue. Whether one is dealing with the definition of the concept of competition; the issue of goals of antitrust law; the proper institutional approach that must be adopted when applying antitrust laws and the use of discretion by antitrust authorities; and other issues such as those relating to the doctrine of sovereignty and extraterritoriality, one has to accept that all these issues concern the need to reach consensus. Of course, it is not sufficient to recognise that the project involves reaching such consensus. One has to go further to determine the need, and moreover the urgency, for this consensus. In light of the above discussion, it would appear that despite the fact that the case for the internationalisation of antitrust policy does not appear to be an extremely urgent one, there seems to be a measure of consensus that countries should move forward, albeit slowly, in addressing antitrust law and policy and their place in the global economy.[115]

---

[112] Ch. 5 also demonstrated how the role of politicians in Member States is influential with regard to the success of the EC system of antitrust.

[113] M Coate, 'Bureaucracy and Politics in FTC Merger Challenges' in F. McChesney and W. Shughart (eds.), *The Causes and Consequences of Antitrust: the Public Choice Perspective* (Chicago University Press, Chicago, 1995), p. 229; W. Shughart and R. Tollison, 'The Employment Consequences of the Sherman and Clayton Acts' (1991) 147 *Journal of Institutional and Theoretical Economy* 38.

[114] E. Fox, 'Antitrust Regulation across National Borders: the United States Boeing Versus European Union of Airbus' (1998) 16 *Brookings Law Review* 30.

[115] C. Bellamy, 'How Can We Harmonize?' (1999) 34 *New England Law Review* 134.

10

Conclusions: the way forward

The purpose of this book has been to examine the internationalisation of antitrust policy and to furnish an account of the law, economics and politics thereof. Each of the previous chapters dealt with a specific set of issues and each chapter was closed with a specific set of conclusions. This chapter presents a summary of the analysis as a whole and offers a glimpse of the future.

The internationalisation of antitrust policy has developed with alacrity. With the various developments witnessed throughout the twentieth century, it has become essential to bring this topic under close scrutiny. In particular, the relentless process of globalisation has increased the number of antitrust cases with international components. This can be observed in light of how transnational cartels and international merger cases have come to form an increasingly significant part of the work of antitrust authorities worldwide. Not infrequently, such cases involve firms and information located in several jurisdictions. This may present hurdles when antitrust authorities seek to enforce their antitrust laws in those cases as well as trigger difficulties when they actually do so. Very often, international antitrust issues can only be effectively addressed through enhanced international co-operation between different antitrust authorities. Such co-operation also provides relief for business firms, which may in some cases face excessive costs, in time and money, caused by concurrent antitrust investigations initiated in different jurisdictions.

Effective co-ordination of enforcement between antitrust authorities cannot, however, be expected to deliver fruitful results unless the antitrust laws of countries are aimed at addressing practices of firms, whether private or hybrid (public/private), which may have an anti-competitive effect, especially one capable of preventing foreign firms from penetrating domestic markets. Nor can the extraterritorial application of domestic antitrust laws be considered appropriate, if at all effective, in dealing with such behaviour. Extraterritoriality can give rise to disputes between countries as well as prove ineffective where vital information and evidence is located in foreign jurisdictions.

International antitrust issues in general and those with market access dimension in particular can only be addressed satisfactorily if countries recognise the value of competition and adopt effective antitrust law and policy and enforce them vigorously. The last few decades witnessed an impressive record of removing governmental restrictions to the flows of trade and investment in the global economy. This has helped identify the extent to which market access by foreign firms to domestic markets can be hindered by the private anti-competitive behaviour of domestic firms. Such situations generate great concern, especially since such behaviour may not only harm the welfare of the country where it occurs, but also threaten the legitimate interests of other countries. The fact that anti-competitive practices by private firms may be blessed by governmental ones – thus creating hybrid practices – complicates the situation further. In this case, there is no substitute for an effective enforcement by the country concerned of its antitrust law. Antitrust policy in this way complements trade policy. It is important both to acknowledge and support this conclusion.

Recent years have witnessed an interesting move on the part of many countries with regard to the role of governments in the global economy. In parallel with the move on the part of many countries away from monopolisation and exerting strict control and planning over their domestic economies, systems of antitrust have been introduced as well as reinforced in many countries at all levels of development. With nearly 100 systems of antitrust worldwide and more than thirty countries actively engaged at present in adopting some form of antitrust law, a clear international consensus, despite certain differences subsisting between countries, has been emerging on the need for antitrust law as a vital instrument to protect competition and as an integral part of the domestic reform countries usually undertake in order to integrate in the global economy. This development is important for developed and developing countries alike. It shows that antitrust law has become an issue of vital interest for all countries at different levels of development. Hence, international co-operation in the field of antitrust policy should involve developed as well as developing countries, especially in providing technical assistance by countries with strong systems of antitrust to others where antitrust law is a very young phenomenon, exchange of information and co-ordination in enforcement practices. By the same token, this development also shows how business firms have become important players in the global economy. In light of this, there is a need to devote special attention to the concerns and needs of business firms as well as their relationships with sovereign countries in the context of the internationalisation of antitrust policy.

There is no doubt that these factors enhance the proposal towards the internationalisation of antitrust policy and facilitate a vigorous antitrust law enforcement with regard to anti-competitive behaviour with an adverse effect on the flows of trade and investment between countries. However, it is essential to shed light on all the elements necessary in order to pursue this and to offer an insightful account on the way forward.

The efforts of countries and their antitrust communities towards the internationalisation of antitrust policy thus far have been channelled mainly through the conclusion of bilateral co-operation agreements; convergence and harmonisation; proposals for an international antitrust code; and suggestions regarding a multilateral antitrust agreement as a means to develop an international system of antitrust. These four 'examples' of the internationalisation have been discussed in previous chapters. There is no reason to believe that these examples, inspite of their differences, are not fully consistent. It is very true that they differ greatly in terms of how ambitious, realistic and possible the achievement of each example independently is. Nevertheless, they are complementary. This can be observed, for example, in the case of bilateral co-operation and the pluralist approach, furnished by the proposal to create an international system of antitrust.

A pluralist approach towards the internationalisation of antitrust policy would strengthen antitrust law enforcement by all participating countries in the global trading system. It would also foster the conclusion of bilateral agreements among the antitrust authorities in those countries which are willing to engage in closer enforcement co-operation. This has been the experience within the Organisation for Economic Cooperation and Development (OECD), where the Organisation's recommendations on co-operation produced over the years, have provided a solid ground for the conclusion of bilateral agreements between member countries. With over 100 antitrust authorities in the world, it is legitimate to anticipate that building a comprehensive network of bilateral agreements is bound to be a very expensive, complicated and slow process. This may render the process neither realistic nor effective. There is the possibility that not all antitrust authorities of countries will be able to participate in this network, with the inevitable result that an adequate account would not be taken of the interests and needs of those countries. In this way, at least, a pluralist approach can be expected to complement efforts under bilateral co-operation.

That the bilateral and pluralist approaches are consistent and complement each other can also be observed in the case of EC antitrust law experience. Chapter 5 demonstrated beyond doubt the commitment of the EC to both regional integration and the development of an international system of antitrust. A great part of the EC's efforts towards co-operation in antitrust policy revolves around strengthening EC antitrust law and fostering a consistent, effective application of its provisions in Member States, developing a framework of regional agreements such as Partnership and Co-operation Agreements and Association Agreements with Central and Eastern European countries and to a certain extent agreements with some Mediterranean countries. The European Commission has also sought to expand and deepen its bilateral co-operation with partners beyond Europe. Agreements have been entered into with several countries such as the USA, Canada and South Africa. In parallel to these efforts, the Commission has supported the case for reaching a multilateral agreement in antitrust policy. Over the years, the Commission has made it clear that it is convinced that bilateral agreements, however, are not sufficient to meet all the concerns and challenges raised by globalisation, adding that a comprehensive multilateral agreement is vital if countries are to reap the benefits of greater trade liberalisation.

Nevertheless, it ought to be acknowledged that a transformation of a pluralist approach – which the EC and several countries support – from a proposal on paper to one put into practice is bound to face severe objections from some countries, especially the USA. The view held on the other side of the Atlantic is that it is not desirable at present to pursue any pluralist approach which may lead to the creation of an international system of antitrust. There is a particular US objection to concluding a multilateral agreement within the World Trade Organization (WTO); although as was said in previous chapters, there are some indications that this objection was somehow relaxed at the WTO 4th Ministerial Conference, which was held in Doha in November 2001. According to the USA, the WTO option suffers from both institutional and policy difficulties. The USA is sceptical over whether countries enjoy the necessary experience and knowledge. Furthermore, the USA is against any proposal which would threaten its sovereignty and usurp its prerogatives in antitrust policy. Instead, it has proposed that countries work on consensus-building, through encouraging links between antitrust authorities where views can be exchanged and technical assistance can be offered to countries at an early stage of developing antitrust law. The USA seems to be in favour of pursuing this within a forum similar to that of the OECD.

It is important to be aware that this scepticism is likely to affect efforts towards the internationalisation of antitrust policy. However, this does not mean that one should not attempt to support these efforts, especially reaching a multilateral agreement within the WTO. The WTO is very inclusive in its membership, combining both developed and developing countries. The fact that there is a close nexus between the WTO objectives of trade liberalisation and the commitment of an increasing number of countries – most of whom are WTO participants – to effective antitrust law enforcement is another factor in favour of developing such an agreement under the auspices of the WTO. This is especially so in light of the existence of persuasive precedents at the WTO such as that of Trade-Related Aspects of Intellectual Property (TRIPS). By incorporating intellectual property provisions within the WTO, there is no reason in principle why the WTO should be viewed as a trade-only organisation. Furthermore, when analysing GATT Article I on Most-Favoured-Nation (MFN) principle and Article III on National Treatment, when assessing the likeness or substitutability or interchangeability of products, the WTO panels and Appellate Body (AB) are already adept at using issues such as market definition and cross-price elasticity analysis. Hence, they should be competent to handle the application of antitrust rules. In addition, it seems that currently there are bright prospects for other important international organisations to support the WTO. One such organisation is the World Bank, which it is believed could provide 'firepower' to the WTO. This is especially important since the World Bank is willing to devote its research capabilities to supporting the WTO. Recently, it has become apparent that support can be expected from younger and less-developed, though important, organisations, such as the International Competition Network (ICN).

It is crucial to warn however that such an agreement within the WTO should be based on realistic aims. Policy-makers, economists and lawyers – judges, practitioners and academics – should remain aware of the *sensitivity* of this area, where a delicate balance needs to be struck between diverse forces: countries and firms, developed and developing countries, countries and international organisations and to an extent between antitrust authorities and law courts.

292   THE INTERNATIONALISATION OF ANTITRUST POLICY

With these thoughts in mind, it may be appropriate to offer some recommendations on how countries should proceed in the internationalisation of antitrust policy. The recommendations offered here are fundamentally different from various recommendations produced by different bodies over the years.[1] The recommendations can be used as guidelines by countries, international organisations working in the field of antitrust policy and other interested groups in order to further the process of internationalisation of antitrust policy in a manner that would be fair and sensitive to the interests and needs of all parties. It is very important to note that the recommendations are not intended to serve as a draft multilateral agreement. As was demonstrated in previous chapters, the debate and the inevitable negotiations for such an agreement are bound to take a very long time before any draft of such an agreement may materialise. However, it is believed the recommendations are capable of enhancing the efforts towards the internationalisation of antitrust policy.

1. It is recommended that countries create a Global Antitrust Framework (GAF), preferably under the auspices of the WTO.
2. It is recommended that GAF should include a principle on the binding commitment of countries to introduce antitrust law in their domestic legal systems. In this way, countries, especially those with economies in transition, will be able to develop antitrust laws to suit their own legal, economic and political conditions, as opposed to parachuting-in antitrust laws. Countries with strong systems of antitrust have an important role to play, where they can provide technical assistance on how systems of antitrust can be developed. It is essential that transitional periods be introduced, in order to cater for the needs of countries at different levels of development.
3. Once the previous task has been completed, countries should then be required under GAF to adapt their domestic antitrust laws and enforcement mechanisms to the agreed rules under GAF which will emerge at some point within the framework. It is recommended that private firms do not have a direct right of action before the body responsible under GAF.
4. It is essential to include principles of non-discrimination and transparency under GAF. The first principle has become of central significance

---

[1] See ch. 9 for a discussion on these recommendations.

in the global trading system. The principle can be useful in antitrust policy, in so far as there would be a commitment to extend antitrust law
progressively to all sectors of domestic economies and apply the law in
the same manner to all firms, public and private, domestic and foreign.
The transparency principle, on the other hand, is useful to ensure that antitrust enforcement is effective and non-discriminatory. It ensures both
openness in the decision-making of antitrust authorities and adequate
control of the exercise of discretion by those authorities. To this end,
there is a need for the availability of direct actions by interested parties
against antitrust authorities before the courts. By the same token, there
is a need for a guarantee that firms enjoy a protection of confidential
information submitted by them to antitrust authorities.

5. GAF should facilitate co-operation procedures among antitrust authorities. It is recommended that it enhance the use of principles of 'positive
comity', 'traditional comity' and information-sharing in general. The
inclusion of such principles, on a non-binding basis, is bound to lead to
market access issues being addressed effectively.[2]

6. GAF should not aim to force on countries the convergence and harmonisation of their antitrust laws. Convergence of the substantive provisions
of the antitrust laws of countries may not be very effective, or realistic. Furthermore, convergence of the goals of antitrust law can lead to
goals advocated by some countries prevailing over goals advocated by
other countries. However, convergence can be used in order to identify those issues that require immediate attention and build consensus
among countries with respect to how these can be addressed. To this
end, it is recommended that countries should consider building a process of regular meetings bringing together individuals responsible for
the development and management of antitrust policy worldwide. Such
meetings will facilitate constructive dialogues and exchange of experiences between domestic antitrust authorities on enforcement policy and

---

[2] Support for this can be found in the case law of the Appellate Body (AB) of the WTO.
The AB insists on the least restrictive trade measures being adopted and accordingly
on the primacy of multilateral negotiations and co-operation. See the *Gasoline* (available
at http://www.wto.org/english/tratop_e/envir_e/edis07_e.htm) and *Shrimp-turtle* (available at
http://www.wto.org/english/tratop_e/dispu_e/distab_e.htm) cases.
  Also, the case law of the AB has introduced an unarticulated doctrine of proportionality, which
would be an important 'selling-point' for advocating GAF since it would maximise market access
and ensure unnecessary burdens on trade and competition are avoided.

practice. Holding such meetings will also help reach consensus on fundamental issues such as the substance and economics of antitrust policy.

7. It is recommended that GAF include – following a period of five to ten years after its creation – a dispute settlement procedure in order to address differences which may arise between countries individually. However, the procedure should not extend to a review of antitrust cases on a case-by-case basis.[3]

8. Within GAF, countries should be encouraged to substitute the use of extraterritoriality with the offer of technical assistance to one another and reliance on co-operation.

In this respect, at least, building such a framework on antitrust policy is both desirable and possible. A framework based on these recommendations cannot be regarded as a real threat to the sovereignty of countries. It is true that the framework would call for some limitation on the sovereignty of countries. However, this should be regarded as understandable and acceptable in light of the benefits which countries will be able to reap through opting for building the framework. Building the framework within the WTO in particular can ensure a wider consensus among countries as well as complement trade policy objectives, which are already pursued within the WTO. This will enhance the flows of trade and investment in the global economy as well as expand the way forward by facilitating more and better globalisation while supporting the desirability of continuing the process of internationalisation of antitrust policy.

---

[3] If GAF is adopted within the WTO, then it would be desirable to introduce an amendment to The Understanding on Rules and Procedures Governing the Settlement of Disputes (DSU), which is covered under Annex 2 to the WTO Agreement, to allow antitrust lawyers to sit on panels and on the AB, in addition to international trade lawyers.

BIBLIOGRAPHY

Books

Akopova, I., Bothe, M., Dabbah, M., Entin, L. and Vodolgin, S. (eds.), *The Russian Federation and European Law* (Hopma, Moscow, 2001)

Amato, G., *Antitrust and the Bounds of Power* (Hart Publishing, Oxford, 1997)

Anderman, S., *EC Competition Law and Intellectual Property Rights* (Oxford University Press, Oxford, 1998)

Anderson, J. (ed.), *The Rise of the Modern State* (Wheatsheaf Books, Brighton 1986)

Areeda, P. and Kaplow, L., *Antitrust Analysis: Problems Text, Cases* (Little, Brown, Boston, 1988)

Arnold, T., *The Bottlenecks of Business* (Reynal & Hitchcock, New York, 1973)

Atwood, J., *Antitrust and American Business Abroad* (McGraw-Hill, New York, 1981)

Auerbach, P., *Competition: the Economics of Industrial Change* (Blackwell, Oxford, 1988)

Bain, J., *Barriers to New Competition* (Harvard University Press, Cambridge, 1956)

Baumol, W., Panzar, J. and Willig, D., *Contestable Markets and the Theory of Industry Structure* (Harcourt Brace Jovanovich, New York, 1988)

Bengoetxea, J., *The Legal Reasoning of the European Court of Justice* (Oxford University Press, Oxford, 1993)

Bhagwati, J. and Hirsh, M. (eds.), *The Uruguay Round and beyond* (University of Michigan Press, Michigan, 1998)

Bishop, J. and Kay, M., *European Mergers and Merger Policy* (Oxford University Press, Oxford, 1993)

Boddez, T. and Trebilcock, M., *Unfinished Business: Reforming Trade Remedy Laws in North America* (C. D. Howe Institute, Toronto, 1993)

Bork, R., *The Antitrust Paradox: a Policy at War with Itself* (Basic Books, New York, 1978)

The Tempting of America (Sinclair-Stevenson, London, 1990)

Brewster, K., *Antitrust and American Business Abroad* (McGraw-Hill, New York, 1958)

Brierly, J., *The Law of Nations* (Oxford University Press, Oxford, 1963)

Brittan, L., *Competition Policy and Merger Control in the Single European Market* (Grotius, Cambridge, 1991)

Brownlie, I., *Principles of Public International Law* (Oxford University Press, Oxford, 1998)

Bruce, I. and Clubb, E., *United States Foreign Trade Law* (Little, Brown, Boston, 1991)

Buchanan, J., Tollison, R. and Tullock, G. (eds.), *Toward a Theory of the Rent Seeking Society* (Texas A and M University, Houston, 1980)

Camilleri, J. and Falk, J., *The End of Sovereignty?: the Politics of a Shrinking and Fragmenting World* (Edward Elgar, Aldershot, 1992)

Carré, M., *Realists and Normalists* (Oxford University Press, Oxford, 1964)

Charleston, M., *Rudiments of Law and Governments Deducted from the Law of Nature* (Library of Congress, Washington D.C., 1783)

Clark, J., *Competition as a Dynamic Process* (Brookings Institution, Washington D.C., 1961)

Claude, I., *Swords into Plow Shares* (Random House, New York, 1977)

Coretesi, H. (ed.), *Unilateral Application of Antitrust and Trade Laws: toward a New Economic Relationship between the United States and Japan* (The Institute, New York, 1994)

Craig, P. and De Burca, G., *EU Law* (3rd edn, Oxford University Press, Oxford, 2002)

Davis, K., *Discretionary Justice* (Louisiana State University Press, Louisiana, 1969)

De Visscher, C., *Théorie et réalité en droit international public* (Paris, 1953), translated into English by P. E. Corbett, *Theory and Reality in Public International Law* (Princeton University Press, Princeton, 1968)

Doern, C., *Competition Policy Decision Processes in the European Community and United Kingdom* (Carleton University Press, Ottawa, 1992)

Doern, C. and Wilks, S., *Comparative Competition Policy* (Oxford University Press, Oxford, 1996)

Duguit, L., *Traité de droit constitutionnel* (Paris, 1927)

Dunning, J., *The Globalization of Business: the Challenges of the 1990s* (Routledge, London, 1993)

Dworkin, R., *Law's Empire* (Harvard University Press, Cambridge, Mass., 1986)

Eden, L. and Potter, E. (eds.), *Multinationals in Global Political Economy* (Macmillan, New York, 1993)

Edwards, C., *Control of Cartels and Monopolies: an International Comparison* (Oceana Publications, Dobbs Ferry, 1967)

Eeckes, A., *Opening America's Market: US Foreign Trade Policy since 1776* (University of North Carolina Press, North Carolina, 1995)

Ehlermann, C. and Laudati, L. (eds.), *European Competition Law Annual 1997: Objectives of Competition Policy* (Hart Publishing, Oxford, 1998)

Finger, J. (ed.), *Antidumping: How It Works and Who Gets Hurt?* (University of Michigan Press, Michigan, 1993)

Fingleton, J., Fox, E., Neven, D. and Seabright, P., *Competition Policy and the Transformation of Central Europe* (CEPR, London, 1995)

Freeman, P. and Whish, R., *A Guide to the Competition Act 1998* (Butterworths, London, 1999)

Friedmann, W., *The Changing Structure of International Law* (Columbia University Press, New York, 1964)

Fugate, W., *Foreign Commerce and Antitrust Laws* (Little, Brown, Boston, 1958)

Gerber, D., *Law and Competition in Twentieth Century Europe* (Oxford University Press, Oxford, 1998)

Gilpin, R., *The Political Economy of International Relations* (Princeton University Press, Princeton, Guilford, 1987)

Goyder, D., *EC Competition Law* (4th edn, Oxford University Press, Oxford, 2002)

Granovetter, M. and Swedberg, R. (eds.), *The Sociology of Economic Life* (Westview Press, Boulder, 1992)

Graubard, S. (ed.), *A New Europe?* (Houghton Mifflin, Boston, 1964)

Green, A., *Political Integration by Jurisprudence: the Work of the Court of Justice of the European Communities in European Political Integration* (Sijthoff, Leiden, 1969)

Griffin, J. (ed.), *Perspectives on the Extraterritorial Application of US Antitrust and Other Laws* (ABA, Section of International Law, New York, 1979)

Haas, E., *Beyond the Nation-State* (Stanford University Press, Stanford, 1964)
  The Uniting of Europe (Stanford University Press, Stanford, 1958)

Haas, E. and Lindberg, L., *The Political Dynamics of European Economic Integration* (Stanford University Press, Stanford, 1963)

Harrison, R., *Europe in Question: Theories of Regional International Integration* (Allen & Unwin, London, 1974)

Haucher, L. and Moran, M., *Capitalism, Culture and Economic Regulation* (Oxford University Press, Oxford, 1989)

Hawk, B., *United States, Common Market and International Antitrust: a Comparative Guide* (Prentice-Hall Law and Business, New York, 1993)

Hayek, F., *The Road to Serfdom* (Chicago University Press, Chicago, 1944)

Hermann, A., *Conflicts of National Laws with International Business Activity: Issues of Extraterritoriality* (Howe Institute, London, 1982)

Hinsley, F., *Sovereignty* (C. A. Watts, London, 1966)

Hodgson, G., *Economics and Institutions* (Polity, Cambridge, 1988)

Jackson, J., *The Jurisprudence of GATT and the WTO* (Cambridge University Press, Cambridge, 2000)

Jenks, C., *A New World of Law: a Study of the Creative Imagination in International Law* (Longman, Harlow, 1969)

Jennings, R. and Watts, A., *Oppenheim's International Law* (Longman, London, 1996)

Joliet, R., *The Rule of Reason in Antitrust Law: American, German and Common Market Laws in Comparative Perspective* (Faculté de Droit de l'Université de Liège, Liège, 1967)

Kelsen, H., *Principles of International Law* (Rinehart & Winton, New York, 1996)

Kerse, C., *EC Antitrust Procedure* (Sweet & Maxwell, London, 1994)

Khemani, S. (ed.), *International Trade Policies: the Uruguay Round and beyond* (IMF, Washington D.C., 1994)

Kintner, E., *An Antitrust Primer* (Macmillan, London, 1973)

Kitzinger, U., *The Politics and Economics of European Integration: Britain, Europe, and the United States* (Basic Books, New York, 1963)

Korah, V., *An Introductory Guide to EC Competition Law and Practice* (Sweet & Maxwell, London, 1994)

Lasok, D. and Bridge, J., *An Introduction to the Law and Institutions of the European Communities* (Butterworths, London, 1982)

Lerner, M. (ed.), *The Mind and Faith of Justice Holmes: His Speeches, Essays, Letters, and Judicial Opinion* (Random House, New York, 1943)

Lipsey, R. and Chrystal, K., *An Introduction to Positive Economics* (Oxford University Press, Oxford, 1995)

Principles of Economic Law (Oxford University Press, Oxford, 1999)

Lloyd, P. and Vautier, K., *Promoting Competition in Global Markets: a Multi-National Approach* (Edward Elgar, Cheltenham, 1999)

Locke, J., *Two Treatises of Government* (Cambridge University Press, Cambridge, 1988)

Lowe, A., *Extraterritorial Jurisdiction: an Annotated Collection of Legal Materials* (Grotius Publications, Cambridge, 1983)

Lowenfeld, A., *Public Controls on International Trade* (Matthew Bender, New York, 1983)

Lutz, H., *American Legal Writing during the Founding Era* (Liberty Press, London, 1983)

Maine, H., *Ancient Law: Its Connection with the Early History of Society and Its Relation to Modern Ideas* (University of Arizona, Arizona, 1985)

McChesney, F. and Shughart, W. (eds.), *The Causes and Consequences of Antitrust: the Public Choice Perspective* (Chicago University Press, Chicago, 1995)

Mendes, M., *Antitrust in a World of Interrelated Economies: the Interplay between Antitrust and Trade Policies in the US and the EEC* (Editions de l'Université de Bruxelles, Brussels, 1991)

Morrison, A. (ed.), *Fundamentals of American Law* (Oxford University Press, Oxford, 1996)

Muchlinski, P., *Multinational Enterprises and the Law* (Blackwell, Oxford, 1995)

Mueller, D., *Public Choice* (Cambridge University Press, Cambridge, 1979)

Neale, A. and Goyder, D., *The Antitrust Laws of the United States of America: a Study of Competition Enforced by Law* (Cambridge University Press, Cambridge, 1980)

Neven, D., Nuttall, R. and Seabright, P., *Merger in Daylight* (Centre for Economic Research, London, 1993)

North, D., *Institutions, Institutional Change and Economic Performance* (Cambridge University Press, Cambridge, 1990)

Ohmae, K., *The Borderless World: Power and Strategy in the Interlinked Economy* (HarperCollins, London, 1994)

Ojala, M., *The Competition Law of Central and Eastern Europe* (Sweet & Maxwell, London, 1999)

Olmstead, C., *International Law Association, Extraterritorial Application of the Laws and Responses Thereto* (Oxford University Press, Oxford, 1984)

Olson, M., *The Logic of Collective Action* (Harvard University Press, Cambridge, Mass., 1965)

Pocock, J., *Politics, Language and Time: Essays on Political Thought and History* (Atheneum, New York, 1972)

Porter, M., *The Competitive Advantage of Nations* (Macmillan, London, 1989)

Posner, R., *Antitrust Law: an Economic Perspective* (University of Chicago Press, Chicago, 1976)

Pryce, R., *The Politics of the European Community* (Butterworths, London, 1973)

Rittler, L., *EEC Competition Law – a Practitioner's Guide* (Kluwer, Deventor, 1991)

Rodger, B. and MacCulloch, A. (eds.), *The UK Competition Act* (Hart Publishing, Oxford, 2000)

Rosenthal, D. and Knighton, W., *National Laws and International Commerce: the Problem of Extra-Territoriality* (Routledge, London, 1982)

Roth, P. (ed.), *Common Market Law of Competition* (5th edn, Sweet & Maxwell, London, 2001)

Sakong, D., *Korea in the World Economy* (Institute for International Economics, Washington DC, 1993)

Saxonhouse, G. and Yamamura, K. (eds.), *Law and Trade Issues of the Japanese Economy: American and Japanese Perspectives* (University of Washington Press, Washington D.C., 1986)

Scherer, F. and Ross, D., *Industrial Market Structure and Economic Performance* (Houghton Mifflin, Boston, 1990)

Schumpeter, J., *Capitalism, Socialism and Democracy* (Allen and Unwin, London, 1976)

Simons, H., *A Positive Program for Laissez Faire: Some Proposals for a Liberal Economic Policy* (Chicago University Press, Chicago, 1934)

Singleton, S., *Blackstone's Guide to the Competition Act 1998* (Blackstone, London, 1999)

Slot, P. and McDonnell, A. (eds.), *Procedure and Enforcement in EC and US Competition Law* (Sweet & Maxwell, London, 1993)

Staniland, M., *What Is Political Economy?: A Study of Social Theory and Underdevelopment* (Yale University Press, New Haven, 1985)

Stopford, J. and Strange, S., *Rival States, Rival Firms* (Cambridge University Press, Cambridge, 1991)

Sullivan, E. (ed.), *The Political Economy of the Sherman Act* (Oxford University Press, Oxford, 1991)

Swann, D., *Competition and Consumer Protection* (Penguin, Harmondsworth, 1979)

Thorelli, H., *The Federal Antitrust Policy: Origination of an Antitrust Tradition* (Johns Hopkin Press, Baltimore, 1954)

Vernon, R., *Sovereignty at Bay: the Multinational Spread of US Enterprises* (Longman, London, 1971)

Walker, R. and Mendlovitz, S. (eds.), *Contending Sovereignties: Redefining Political Community* (Boulder, Co., Lynne Rienner, London, 1990)

Waller, S., *Antitrust and American Business Abroad* (Clark Boardman Callaghan, New York, 1997)

Walters, M., *Globalization* (Routledge, New York, 1995)

Wellek, R., *The Concept of Realism in Literary Scholarship* (J. B. Wolters, Groningen, 1961)

Whish, R., *Competition Law* (4th edn, Butterworths, London, 2001)

Wilcox, C., *A Charter for World Trade* (Macmillan, New York, 1949)

Williamson, O., *Antitrust Economics* (Blackwell, Oxford, 1987)

Zach, R. (ed.), *Towards WTO Competition Rules: Key Issues and Comments on the WTO Report (1998) Trade and Competition* (Kluwer Law International, The Hague, 1999)

Articles

Akehurst, M., 'Jurisdiction in International Law' (1972–3) 46 BYBIL 145

Alford, R., 'The Extraterritorial Application of Antitrust Laws: the United States and the European Community Approaches' (1992) 33 VJIL 1

'Subsidiarity and Competition: Decentralized Enforcement of EU Competition Laws' (1994) 27 CILJ 275

Anderson, T., 'Extraterritorial Application of National Antitrust Laws: the Need for More Uniform Regulation' (1992) 38 WLR 1579

Applebaum, H., 'Antitrust and the Omnibus Trade and Competitiveness Act of 1998' (1989) 58 ALJ 557

'The Coexistence of Antitrust Law and Trade Law with Antitrust Policy' (1988) 9 CLR 1169

'The Interface of the Trade Laws and the Antitrust Laws' (1998) 6 GMLR 479

Ashley, R., 'Untying the Sovereign State: a Double Reading of the Anarchy Problematique' (1988) 17 JIS 231

Averitt, N. and Lande, R., 'Consumer Sovereignty: a United Theory of Antitrust and Consumer Protection Law' (1997) 65 ALJ 713

Azcuenaga, M., 'The Evolution of International Competition Policy: a FTC Perspective' (1992) FCLI 1

Baer, W., 'International Antitrust Policy' (1998) FCLI 247

Bailey, T., 'Contestability and the Design of Regulatory and Antitrust Policy' (1981) 71 AER 178

Baker, D., 'Antitrust and World Trade: Tempest in an International Teapot?' (1974) 8 CILJ 16

Baker, D. and Miller, W., 'Antitrust Enforcement and Non-Enforcement as a Barrier to Imports' (1996) 14 IBL 488

Bator, F., 'The Autonomy of Market Failure' (1958) 72 QJE 358

Bechtold, R., 'Antitrust Law in the European Community and Germany – an Uncoordinated Co-Existence?' (1992) FCLI 343

Bellamy, C., 'How Can we Harmonize?' (1999) 34 NELR 134
  'Some Reflections on Competition Law in the Global Market' (1999) 34 NELR 15

Bellis, J., 'International Trade and the Competition Law of the European Economic Community' (1979) 16 CMLRev 647

Benyon, 'Les "accords européens" avec la Hongrie, la Pologne et la Tchécoslovaquie' (1992) RMCLUE 25

Bishop, B. and Bishop, S., 'Reforming Competition Policy: Bundeskartellamt – Model or Muddle' (1996) 17 ECLR 207

Black, O., '*Per se Rule* and *Rule of Reason*: What Are They?' (1997) 18 ECLR 145

Blässar, M. and Stragier, J., 'Enlargement' (1999) 1 ECCPNL 58

Bork, R., 'Legislative Intent and the Policy of the Sherman Act' (1966) 9 JLE 7
  'The Role of the Courts in Applying Economics' (1985) 54 ALJ 2
  'The Rule of Reason and Per Se Concept: Price Fixing and Market Division' (1965) 74 YLJ 775

Born, G., 'Recent British Responses to the Extraterritorial Application of United States Law: the *Midland Bank* Decision and Retaliatory Legislation Involving Unitary Taxation' (1985) 26 VJIL 91

Bos, P., 'Towards a Clear Distribution of Competence between EC and National Competition Authorities' (1995) 16 ECLR 410

Bourgeois, J., 'EC Competition Law and Member States Courts' (1993) 17 FILJ 331

Bowett, D., 'Jurisdiction: Changing Patterns of Authority over Activities and Resources' (1982) 53 BYBIL 1

Bridge, J., 'The Law and Politics of United States Foreign Policy Export Controls' (1984) 4 LS 2

Brodley, J., 'The Economic Goals of Antitrust: Efficiency, Consumer Welfare, and Technological Progress' (1987) 62 NYULR 1020

Brown, P., 'The Codification of International Law' (1935) 29 AJIL 25

Brzezinski, C., 'Competition and Antitrust Law in Central Europe: Poland, the Czech Republic, Slovakia and Hungary' (1994) 15 MJIL 1129

Burr, S., 'The Application of US Antitrust Law to Foreign Conduct: Has *Hartford Fire* Extinguished Considerations of Comity?' (1994) 15 UPJIBL 221

Calkins, S., 'The October 1992 Supreme Court Term and Antitrust: More Objectivity than Ever' (1994) 62 ALJ 327

Carroll, A., 'The Extraterritorial Enforcement of US Antitrust Laws and Retaliatory Legislation in the United Kingdom and Australia' (1984) 13 DJILP 377

Carstensen, P., 'Antitrust Law and the Paradigm of Industrial Organization' (1983) 16 UCDLR 487

Castañeda, G. and Ugarte, F., 'Mexico Still Setting the Pace for Latin America' (1998) 1 GCR 12

Chang, S., 'Extraterritorial Application of US Antitrust Laws to Other Pacific Countries: Proposed Bilateral Agreements for Resolving International Conflicts within the Pacific Community' (1993) 16 HICLR 295

Cho, W., 'Korea's Economic Crisis: the Role of Competition Policy' (1999) 27 IBL 495

Christoforou, T. and Rockwell, D., 'European Economic Community Law: the Territorial Scope of Application of EEC Antitrust Law' (1989) 30 HILJ 195

Collins, W., 'The Coming of Age of EC Competition Policy' (1992) 17 YJIL 249

Conn, D., 'Assessing the Impact of Preferential Trade Agreements and New Rules of Origin on the Extraterritorial Application of Antitrust Law to International Mergers' (1993) 93 ColLR 119

Cova, B. and Fine, F., 'The New Italian Antitrust Act *vis-à-vis* EC Competition Law' (1991) 12 ECLR 20

Cowie, M. and Novotria, M., 'Pre-Merger Notification in Central and Eastern Europe' (1998) 12 *Antitrust* 19

Craig, E., 'Extraterritorial Application of the Sherman Act: the Search for a Jurisdictional Standard' (1983) 7 STLJ 295

Crampton, P., 'Alternative Approaches to Competition Law: Consumer's Surplus, Total Welfare and Non-Efficiency Goals' (1994) 17 WC 55

Cumming, G., 'Assessors, Judicial Notice and Domestic Enforcement of Articles 85 and 86' (1997) 18 ECLR 370

Dabbah, M., 'Conduct, Dominance and Abuse in "Market Relationship": Analysis of Some Conceptual Issues under Article 82 EC' (2000) 21 ECLR 45

'The Dilemma of Keck – the Nature of the Ruling and the Ramifications of the Judgment' (1999) IJEL 84

'Measuring the Success of a System of Competition Law: a Preliminary View' (2000) 21 ECLR 369

Dam, K., 'Extraterritoriality in an Age of Globalization: the *Hartford Fire* Case' (1993) SCR 289

Davidow, J., 'Antitrust and Trade Policy in the United States and the European Community' (1986) FCLI 45

'The Application of US Antitrust Laws to *Kieretsu* Practices' (1994) 18 WC 5

'Extraterritorial Antitrust and the Concept of Comity' (1981) 15 JWTL 500

'Treble Damage Actions and US Foreign Relations: Taming the "Rouge Elephant"' (1985) FCLI 37

Deringer, A., 'The Distribution of Powers in the Enforcement of the Rules of Competition and the Rome Treaty' (1963) 1 CMLRev 30

Dewey, D., 'The Economic Theory of Antitrust: Science or Religion?' (1964) 50 VirLR 413

Dunfee, T. and Friedman, A., 'The Extraterritorial Application of United States Antitrust Laws: a Proposal for an Interim Solution' (1984) 45 OSLJ 883

Easterbrook, F., 'The Limits of Antitrust' (1984) 63 TLR 1

Ehlermann, C., 'The Contribution of the EC Competition Policy to the Single Market' (1992) 29 CMLRev 257

'The European Community, Its Law and Lawyers' (1992) 29 CMLRev 213

'Implementation of EC Competition Law by National Antitrust Authorities' (1996) 17 ECLR 88

'The International Dimension of Competition Policy' (1994) 17 FILJ 833

'Reflections on a European Cartel Office' (1995) 32 CMLRev 471

Ehrenzweig, A., 'The *lex fori* – Basic Rule in the Conflict of Laws' (1960) 58 MicLR 637

Elzinga, K., 'The Goals of Antitrust: Other than Competition and Efficiency, What Else Counts?' (1977) 125 UPLR 1191

Engzelius, F., 'The Norwegian Competition Act 1983' (1996) 15 ECLR 384

Eric, E., 'The Use of Interest Analysis in the Extraterritorial Application of United States Antitrust Law' (1983) 16 CILJ 147

Farlow, J., 'Ego or Equity? Examining United States Extension of the Sherman Act' (1998) 11 TL 175

Farmer, S., 'Altering the Balance between Sovereignty and Competition: the Impact of *Seminole Tribe* on the Antitrust State Action Immunity Doctrine' (1997) 23 ONULR 1403

'Balancing State Sovereignty and Competition: an Analysis of the Impact of *Seminole Tribe* on the Antitrust State Action Immunity Doctrine' (1997) 42 VillR 111

Faucompert, E., Konings, J. and Vandenbussche, H., 'The Integration of Central and Eastern Europe in the European Union – Trade and Labour Market Adjustment' (1999) 33 JWTL 121

Faull, J., 'Effect on Trade between Member States and Community: Member States Jurisdiction' (1989) FCLI 485

Fedderson, C., 'Focusing on Substantive Law in International Economic Relations: the Public Morals of GATT's Article XX(a) and "Conventional Rules of Interpretation" ' (1998) 7 MJGT 75

Feinberg, R., 'Economic Coercion and Economic Sanctions: the Expansion of United States' Extraterritorial Jurisdiction' (1981) 30 AULR 323

Fernandez Ordonez, M., 'Enforcement by National Authority of EC and Member States' Antitrust Law' (1993) FCLI 629

Fidler, D., 'Competition Law and International Relations' (1992) 41 ICLQ 563

Fiebig, A., 'A Role for the WTO in International Merger Control' (2000) 20 NJILB 233

Fine, F., 'The New Italian Antitrust Act *vis-à-vis* EC Competition Law' (1991) 12 ECLR 87

First, H., 'Selling Antitrust in Japan' (1993) 7 *Antitrust* 34

Flynn, J., 'Antitrust Jurisprudence: a Symposium on Economics, Political and Social Goals of Antitrust Policy' (1977) 125 UPLR 1182
  'The Reagan Administration's Antitrust Policy, "Original Intent" and the Legislative History of the Sherman Act' (1988) 83 AB 259

Forrester, I. and Norall, C., 'The Laicization of Community Law: Self-Help and the Rule of Reason: How Competition Law Is and Could Be Applied' (1984) 21 CMLRev 11

Fox, E., 'Antitrust Regulation across National Borders: the United States Boeing Versus European Union of Airbus' (1998) 16 BLR 30
  'Competition Law and the Agenda for the WTO: Forging the Links of Competition and Trade' (1995) 4 PRLPJ 1
  'Extraterritoriality and Antitrust – Is Reasonableness the Answer?' (1986) FCLI 49
  'Foreword: Mergers, Market Access and the Millennium' (2000) 20 NJILB 203
  'Global Problems in a World of National Law' (1999) 34 NELR 11
  'Harnessing the Multinational Corporation to Enhance 3rd World Development – the Rise and Fall and Future of Antitrust as a Regulator' (1989) 10 CLR 1981
  'International Antitrust: Cosmopolitan Principles for an Open World' (1998) FCLI 271
  'The Merger Regulation and Its Territorial Reach: *Gencor Ltd. v. Commission*' (1999) ECLR 334
  'The Modernization of Antitrust: a New Equilibrium' (1981) 66 CorLR 1140

'The Politics of Law and Economics in Judicial Decision Making: Antitrust as a Window' (1986) 61 NYULR 554

'Toward World Antitrust and Market Access' (1997) 91 AJIL 1

'Trade, Competition and Intellectual Property – TRIPS and Its Antitrust Counterparts' (1996) 29 VJTL 481

'US Law and Global Competition and Trade – Jurisdiction and Comity' (1993) AR 3

Fox, E. and Sullivan, E., 'Antitrust – Retrospective and Prospective: Where Are We Coming From? Where Are We Going?' (1987) 62 NYULR 936

Francis, B., 'Subsidiarity and Antitrust: the Enforcement of European Competition Law in the National Courts of Member States' (1995) 27 LPIB 247

Frazer, T., 'Competition Policy after 1992: the Next Step' (1990) 53 MLR 609

Frederickson, A., 'A Strategic Approach to Multi-Jurisdictional Filings' (1999) 4 EC 23

Friedberg, J., 'The Convergence of Law in an Era of Political Integration: the *Wood Pulp* Case and *Alcoa* Effects Doctrine' (1991) 52 UPLR 289

Fugate, W., 'Antitrust Aspects of US – Japanese Trade' (1983) 15 CWRJIL 505

Furnish, D., 'A Transnational Approach to Restrictive Business Practices' (1970) 4 IL 317

Garret, G., 'International Cooperation and Institutional Choice: the European Community's Internal Market' (1992) 46 IO 533

Gerber, D., 'Afterword: Antitrust and American Business Abroad Revisited' (2000) 20 NJILB 307

'The Extraterritorial Application of German Antitrust Law' (1983) 77 AJIL 756

'The Transformation of European Community Competition Law' (1994) 35 HILJ 97

'The US–European Conflict over the Globalisation of Antitrust Law' (1999) 34 NELR 123

Gill, D., 'Two Cheers for *Timberlane*' (1980) 10 SRICL 7

Gluck, A., 'Preserving *Per Se*' (1999) 108 YLJ 913

Griffin, J., 'EC/US Antitrust Cooperation Agreement: Impact on Transnational Business' (1993) 24 LPIB 1051

'EC and US Extraterritoriality: Activism and Cooperation' (1994) 17 FILJ 353

'Extraterritorial Application of US Antitrust Law Clarified by United States Supreme Court' (1993) 40 FBNJ 564

'Extraterritoriality in US and EU Antitrust Enforcement' (1999) 67 ALJ 159

'Foreign Governmental Reactions to US Assertion of Extraterritorial Jurisdiction' (1998) 6 GMLR 505

'International Antitrust Guidelines Send Mixed Message of Robust Enforcement and Comity' (1995) 19 WC 5

'Possible Resolutions of International Disputes over Enforcement of US Antitrust Law' (1982) 18 SJIL 279

'What Business People Want from a World Antitrust Code' (1999) 34 NELR 39

'When Sovereignties May Collide in the Antitrust Area?' (1994) 20 CUSLJ 91

'United States Antitrust Laws and Transnational Transactions: an Introduction' (1987) 21 IL 307

Grippando, J., 'Declining to Exercise Extraterritorial Jurisdiction on Grounds of International Comity: an Illegitimate Extension of the Judicial Abstention Doctrine' (1983) 23 VJIL 395

Grossfield, B. and Rogers, P., 'A Shared Values Approach to Jurisdictional Conflicts in International Economic Law' (1983) 32 ICLQ 931

Gupta, V., 'After Hartford Fire: Antitrust and Comity' (1996) 84 GLJ 2287

Guzman, A., 'Is International Antitrust Possible?' (1998) 73 NYULR 1501

Haas, E., 'International Integration: the European and the Universal Process' (1961) 15 IO 366

'The Study of Legal Integration: Reflection on the Joy and Anguish of Pretheorising' (1970) 24 IO 607

Haight, G., 'International Law and Extraterritorial Application of the Antitrust Laws' (1954) 63 YLJ 639

Halliday, F., 'State and Society in International Relations: a Second Agenda' (1987) 16 JIS 218

Halverson, J., 'Harmonization and Coordination of International Merger Procedures' (1991) 60 ALJ 531

Ham, D., 'International Cooperation in the Antitrust Field and in Particular the Agreement between the United States and the Commission of the European Communities' (1992) 30 CMLRev 571

Hannay, W., 'Transnational Competition Law Aspects of Mergers and Acquisitions' (2000) 20 NJILB 287

Harvers, M., 'Good Fences Make Good Neighbours: a Discussion of Problems Concerning the Exercise of Jurisdiction' (1983) 17 IL 784

Hauser, H., 'Proposal for a Multilateral Agreement on Free Market Access (MAFMA)' (1991) 25 JWTL 77

Hawk, B., 'Antitrust in the EEC – the First Decade' (1972) 41 FLR 229

'International Antitrust Policy and the 1982 Acts: the Continuing Need for Reassessment' (1982) 51 FLR 201

Hay, D., 'The Assessment: Competition Policy' (1993) 9/2 OREP 1

'Competition Policy' (1986) 2 OREP 1

Held, S., 'German Antitrust Law and Policy' (1992) FCLI 311

Hellman, J., 'Constitutions and Economic Reform in the Post-Communist Traditions' (1996) 5 EECR 46

Hiljemark, L., 'Enforcement of EC Competition Law in National Courts – the Perspective of Judicial Protection' (1997) 17 YEL 83

Himmelfarb, A., 'International Language of Convergence: Reviving Antitrust Dialogue between the United States and the European Union with a Uniform Understanding of "Extraterritoriality" ' (1996) 17 UPJIEL 909

Hudec, R., 'A WTO Perspective on Private Anti-Competitive Behavior in World Markets' (1999) 34 NELR 79

Huntley, A., 'The Protection of Trading Interests Act 1980: Some Jurisdictional Aspects of Enforcement of Antitrust Laws' (1981) 30 ICLQ 213

Hutchings, M. and Levitt, M., 'Concurrent Jurisdiction' (1994) 15 ECLR 123

Immenga, U., 'Export Cartels and Voluntary Export Restraints between Trade and Competition Policy' (1995) 4 PRLPJ 93

Inman, R. and Rubinfeld, D., 'Making Sense of the Antitrust State Action Doctrine: Balancing Political Participation and Economic Efficiency in Regulatory Federalism' (1997) 75 TLR 1203

Jacquemin, J., 'The International Dimension of European Competition Policy' (1993) 31 JCMS 91

Jaffe, L., 'Standing to Secure Judicial Review: Public Actions' (1961) 74 HLR 1265

Jakob, T., 'EEA and Eastern Europe Agreements with the European Community' (1992) FCLI 403

Jenny, F., 'French Competition Law Update: 1987–1994' (1995) FCLI 203

Joelson, M., 'International Antitrust: Problems and Defences' (1983) 15 LPIB 1121

Katzenbach, N., 'Conflicts on an Unruly Horse: Reciprocal Claims and Tolerance in Interstate and International Law' (1956) 65 YLJ 1087

Kelsen, H., 'The Principles of Sovereign Equality of States as a Basis for International Organization' (1944) 53 YLJ 207

Kennedy, D. and Webb, D., 'The Limits of Integration: Eastern Europe and the European Communities' (1993) 30 CMLRev 1095

Kerse, C., 'The Complainant in Competition Cases: a Progress Report' (1997) 34 CMLRev 230

Khan-Freund, O., 'English Contracts and American Antitrust Law: the Nylon Patent Case' (1955) 18 MLR 65

Khemani, S., 'Competition Policy: an Engine for Growth' (1997) 1 GCR 20

Kirchner, C., 'Competence Catalogues and the Principle of Subsidiarity in a European Constitution' (1997) 8 CPE 71

Korah, V., 'EEC Competition Policy – Legal Form or Economic Efficiency' (1986) 39 CLP 85

'The Rise and Fall of Provisional Validity – the Need for a Rule of Reason in EEC Antitrust' (1981) NJILB 320

'Tetra Pak II – Lack of Reasoning in Court's Judgment' (1997) 18 ECLR 98

Korowicz, M., 'Some Present Aspects of Sovereignty in International Law' (1961) 102 RDC 1

Kovacic, W., 'Capitalism, Socialism and Competition Policy in Vietnam' (1999) 13 *Antitrust* 57

'Getting Started: Creating New Competition Policy Institutions in Transition Economies' (1997) 23 BJIL 403

'Merger Enforcement in Transition: Antitrust Controls on Acquisitions in Emerging Economies' (1998) 66 UCinLR 1075

Kramer, L., 'Extraterritorial Application of American Law after the Insurance Antitrust Case: a Reply to Professors Lowenfeld and Trimble' (1995) 89 AJIL 750

Krueger, A., 'The Political Economy of Rent-Seeking Society' (1974) 64 AER 291

Lande, R., 'Wealth Transfers as the Original and Primary Concern of Antitrust: the Efficiency Interpretations Challenged' (1982) 34 HLJ 65

Lao, M., 'Jurisdictional Reach of the US Antitrust Laws: Yokosuka and Yokota, and "Footnote 159" Scenarios' (1994) 46 RLR 821

Leidig, J., 'The Uncertain Status of the Defence of Foreign Sovereign Compulsion: Two Proposals for Change' (1991) 31 VJIL 321

Liakopoulos, T., 'New Rules on Competition Law in Greece' (1992) 16 WC 17

Lowe, A., 'Blocking Extraterritorial Jurisdiction: the British Protection of Trading Interests Act 1980' (1981) 75 AJIL 257

'The Problems of Extraterritorial Jurisdiction: Economic Sovereignty and a Search for a Solution' (1985) 34 ICLQ 727

Lowenfeld, A., 'Conflict, Balancing of Interests and the Exercise of Jurisdiction to Prescribe: Reflections on the Insurance Antitrust Case' (1995) 89 AJIL 42

Lucron, C., 'Contenu et portée des accords entre la Communauté et la Hongrie, la Pologne et la Tchécoslovaquie' (1992) RMCLUE 293

Lytle, C., 'A Hegemonic Interpretation of Extraterritorial Jurisdiction in Antitrust: from *American Banana* to *Hartford Fire*' (1997) 24 SJILC 41

Maher, I., 'Alignment of Competition Laws in the European Community' (1996) 16 YEL 223

Maier, H., 'Extraterritorial Jurisdiction at a Crossroads: an Intersection between Public and Private International Law' (1982) 76 AJIL 280

'Interest Balancing and Extra-Territorial Jurisdiction' (1983) 31 AJCL 579

Mann, F., 'The Doctrine of Jurisdiction in International Law' (1964) 111 RDC 9

'The *Dyestuffs* Case in the Court of Justice of the European Communities' (1973) 22 ICLQ 35

Marceau, G., 'The Full Potential of the Europe Agreements: Trade and Competition Issues: the Case of Poland' (1995) WC 44

Marenco, G., 'The Uneasy Enforcement of Article 85 E.E.C. as between Community and National Levels' (1993) FCLI 605

Maresceau, M. and Montaguti, E., 'The Relations between the European Union and Central and Eastern Europe: a Legal Appraisal' (1995) 32 CMLRev 1327

Marsden, P., ' "Antitrust" at the WTO' (1998) 13 *Antitrust* 28

'The Impropriety of WTO "Market Access" Rules on Vertical Restraints' (1998) 21 WC 5

Martinzez Lage, S., 'Significant Developments in Spanish Antitrust Law' (1996) 17 ECLR 194

Mason, E., 'Monopoly in Law and Economics' (1937) 47 YLJ 34

Massey, P., 'Reform of EC Competition Law: Substance, Procedure and Institutions' (1996) FCLI 91

Matsushita, M., 'Reflections on Competition Policy/Law in the Framework of the WTO' (1997) FCLI 31

May, J., 'Antitrust Practices in the Formative Era: the Constitutional and Conceptual Reach of State Antitrust Laws, 1880–1918' (1987) 135 UPLR 495

McDermott, K., 'US Officials Provide Competition Counselling to Eastern Europe' (1991) 5 *Antitrust* 4

McGowan, L. and Wilks, S., 'The First Supranational Policy in the European Union: Competition Policy' (1995) 28 EJPR 141

McNeill, J., 'Extraterritorial Antitrust Jurisdiction: Continuing the Confusion in Policy, Law, and Jurisdiction' (1998) 28 CWILJ 425

Meade, J., 'Decentralisation in the Implementation of EEC Competition Law – a Challenge for the Lawyers' (1986) 37 NILQ 101

Melamed, D., 'Antitrust Enforcement in a Global Economy' (1998) FCLI 1

Messen, K., 'Antitrust Jurisdiction under Customary International Law' (1984) 78 AJIL 783

Millon, D., 'The Sherman Act and the Balance of Power' (1988) 61 SCLR 1219

Mirabito, J. and Friedler, W., 'The Commission on the International Application of the US Antitrust Laws: Pulling in the Reins' (1982) 6 STLJ 1

Muchlinski, P., 'A Case of Czech Beer: Competition and Competitiveness in the Traditional Economies' (1996) 59 MLR 658

Murphy, D., 'Moderating Antitrust Subject Matter Jurisdiction: the Foreign Trade Antitrust Improvements Act and the Restatement of Foreign Relations Law (Revised)' (1986) 54 UCinLR 779

Newman, G., 'Potential Havens from American Jurisdiction and Discovery Laws in International Antitrust Enforcement' (1981) 33 UFLR 240

Nicoliades, P., 'For a World Competition Authority' (1996) 30 JWTL 131

Norberg, S., 'The EEA Agreement: Institutional Solutions for a Dynamic and Homogeneous EEA in the Area of Competition' (1992) FCLI 437

Novicoff, M., 'Blocking and Clawing Back in the Name of Public Policy: the United Kingdom's Protection of Private Economic Interests against Adverse Foreign Adjudications' (1985) 7 NJILB 12

Ongman, J., '"Be No Longer Chaos": Constructing a Normative Theory of the Sherman Act's Extraterritorial Jurisdictional Scope' (1977) 71 NULR 733

Oprescue, G. and Rohlck, E., 'Competition Policy in Transition Economies: the Case of Romania' (1999) 3 ECCPNL 62

Orland, L., 'The Paradox in Bork's Antitrust Paradox' (1987) 9 CLR 115

Pakaphan, N., 'Indonesia: Enactment of Competition Law' (1999) 27 IBL 491

Palim, M., 'The World Wide Growth of Competition Law: an Empirical Analysis' (1998) 43 AB 105

Papakrivopoulos, D., 'The Role of Competition Law as an International Trade Remedy in the Context of the World Trade Organization' (1999) 22 WC 45

Pearce, B., 'The Comity Doctrine as a Barrier to Judicial Jurisdiction: a US–EU Comparison' (1994) 30 SJIL 525

Pera, A. and Todino, M., 'Enforcement of EC Competition Rules: a Need for Reform?' (1996) FCLI 125

Petersmann, E., 'International Competition Rules for the GATT–MTO World Trade and Legal System' (1993) 27 JWTL 35

'Legal, Economic and Political Objectives of National and International Competition Policies: Constitutional Functions of WTO "Linking Principles for Trade and Competition"' (1999) 34 NELR 145

'Proposals for Negotiating International Competition Rules in the GATT–WTO World Trade and Legal System' (1994) 49 *Aussenwirtschaft* 231

Pettit, P. and Styles, C., 'The International Response to the Extraterritorial Application of United States Antitrust Laws' (1982) 37 BL 697

Piraino, T., 'Making Sense of the *Rule of Reason*: a New Standard for Section 1 of the Sherman Act' (1994) 47 VanLR 1753

'Reconciling the *Per Se* Rule and the *Rule of Reason* Approaches to Antitrust Analysis' (1991) 64 SCLR 685

Pitofsky, R., 'The Political Content of Antitrust' (1979) 127 UPLR 1051

Pittney, H., 'Sovereign Compulsion and International Antitrust: Conflicting Laws and Separating Powers' (1987) 25 CJTL 403

Posner, R., 'The Federal Trade Commission' (1969) 64 CKLR 48

Quinn, J., 'Sherman Gets Judicial Authority to Go Global: Extraterritorial Jurisdictional Reach of US Antitrust Laws Are Expanded' (1998) 32 JMLR 141

Ramsey, L., 'The Implications of the Europe Agreements for an Expanded European Union' (1995) 44 ICLQ 161

Ramseyer, J., 'The Costs of the Consensual Myth: Antitrust Enforcement and Institutional Barriers to Litigation in Japan' (1985) 94 YLJ 604

Rapsenau, J., 'Muddling, Meddling and Modelling: Alternative Approaches to the Study of World Politics in an Era of Rapid Change' (1979) 8 JIS 130

Ratliff, J. and Wright, E., 'Belgian Competition Law: the Advent of Free Market Principles' (1992) 16 WC 33

Reynolds, M. and Mansfield, P., 'Complaining to the Commission' (1997) 2 EC 34

Rholl, E., 'Inconsistent Application of the Extraterritorial Provisions of the Sherman Act: a Judicial Response Based upon the Much Maligned "Effects" Test' (1990) 73 MarLR 435

Riley, A., 'More Radicalism, Please: the Notice on Co-operation between National Courts and the Commission in Applying Articles 85 and 86 of the EEC Treaty' (1993) 14 ECLR 93

Rill, J. and Chambers, C., 'Antitrust Enforcement and Non-Enforcement as a Barrier to Import in the Japanese Automobile Industry' (1997) 24 *Empirica* 109

Rishikesh, D., 'Extraterritoriality Versus Sovereignty in International Antitrust Jurisdiction' (1991) WC 33

Romani, F., 'The New Italian Antitrust Law' (1991) FCLI 479

Rosenthal, D., 'Equipping the Multilateral Trading System with a Style and Principles to Increase Market Access' (1998) 6 GMLR 543

'Relationship of US Antitrust Laws to the Formulation of Foreign Economic Policy, Particularly Export and Overseas Investment Policy' (1980) 49 ALJ 1189

'What Should Be the Agenda of a Presidential Commission to Study the International Application of US Antitrust Law?' (1980) 2 NJILB 372

Roth, P. (ed.), 'Jurisdiction, British Public Policy and the Supreme Court' (1994) 110 LQR 194

Rowe, F., 'The Decline of Antitrust and the Dilution of Models: the Faustian Pact of Law and Economics' (1984) 72 GLJ 1511

Sabalot, D., 'Shortening the Long Arm of American Antitrust Jurisdiction: Extraterritoriality and the Foreign Blocking Statutes' (1982) 28 LLR 213

Sandage, J., 'Extraterritorial Application of United States Antitrust Law' (1985) 94 YLJ 1693

'Forum Non Conveniens and the Extraterritorial Application of United States Antitrust Laws' (1985) 94 YLJ 1693

Santos, J., 'The Territorial Scope of Article 85 of the EEC Treaty' (1989) FCLI 571

Schaub, A., '*Boeing/MDD*' (1998) 1 ECCPNL 2

Schwartz, L., ' "Justice" and Other Non-Economic Goals of Antitrust' (1979) 127 UPLR 1076

Sennett, M. and Gavil, A., 'Antitrust Jurisdiction, Extraterritorial Conduct and Interest Balancing' (1985) 19 IL 185

Sharma, V., 'Approaches to the Issue of Extra-Territorial Jurisdiction' (1995) 5 AJCorpL 45

Shenefield, J., 'Extraterritoriality in Antitrust' (1983) 15 LPIB 1109

'Thoughts on Extraterritorial Application of the United States Antitrust Laws' (1983) 52 FLR 350

Shughart, W. and Tollison, R., 'The Employment Consequences of the Sherman and Clayton Acts' (1991) 147 JITE 38

Singham, S., 'US and European Models Shaping Latin American Competition Law' (1998) 1 GCR 15

Siragusa, M. and Scassellati-Sforztine G., 'Italian and EC Competition Law: a New Relationship – Reciprocal Exclusivity and Common Principles' (1993) 29 CMLRev 93

Smith, A., 'Bringing Down Private Trade Barriers – an Assessment of the United States' Unilateral Options: Section 301 of the 1974 Trade Act and the Extraterritorial Application of US Antitrust Law' (1994) 16 MJIL 241

Snell, S., 'Controlling Restrictive Business Practices in Global Markets: Reflections on the Concepts of Sovereignty, Fairness and Comity' (1997) 33 SJIL 215

Snyder, J., 'International Competition: towards a Normative Theory of United States Antitrust Law and Policy' (1985) 3 BUILJ 257

Stanford, J., 'The Application of the Sherman Act to Conduct Outside the United States: a View from Abroad' (1978) 11 CILJ 195

Stockmann, K., 'Foreign Application of European Antitrust Laws' (1985) FCLI 251
'Trends and Developments in European Antitrust Laws' (1991) FCLI 441

Stragier, J., 'The Competition Rules of the EEA Agreement and Their Implementation' (1993) 14 ECLR 30

Sullivan, E., 'Economics and More Humanistic Disciplines: What Are the Sources of Wisdom for Antitrust?' (1977) 125 UPLR 1214

Supanit, S., 'Thailand: Implementation of Competition Law' (1999) 27 IBL 497

Tarullo, D., 'Norms and Institutions in Global Competition Policy' (2000) 94 AJIL 478

Temple Lang, J., 'European Community Constitutional Law and the Enforcement of Community Antitrust Law' (1993) FCLI 525

Torremans, P., 'Extraterritorial Application of EU and US Competition Law' (1996) 21 ELR 280

Trachtman, J., 'International Regulatory Competition, Externalization, and Jurisdiction' (1993) 34 HILJ 47
'L'Etat, c'est nous: Sovereignty, Economic Integration and Subsidiarity' (1992) 33 HILJ 459

Trentor, J., 'Jurisdiction and the Extraterritorial Application of Antitrust Laws after *Hartford Fire*' (1995) 62 UCLR 1583

Trimble, P., 'The Supreme Court and International Law: the Demise of Restatement Section 403' (1995) 89 AJIL 53

Turner, D., 'Application of Competition Laws to Foreign Conduct: Appropriate Resolution of Jurisdictional Issues' (1985) FCLI 231

Ullrich, H., 'Harmonisation Within the European Union' (1996) 17 ECLR 178

Valentine, D., 'Building a Cooperative Framework for Oversight in Mergers – the Answer to Extraterritorial Issues in Merger Review' (1998) 6 GMLR 525

van Bael, I., 'Insufficient Judicial Control of EC Competition Law Enforcement' (1992) FCLI 733

 'The Role of National Courts' (1994) 15 ECLR 6

van der Esch, B., 'The Principles of Interpretation Applied by the Court of Justice of the European Communities and Their Relevance for the Scope of the EEC Competition Rules' (1991) FCLI 223

van Gerven, W., 'EC Jurisdiction in Antitrust Matters: the *Wood Pulp* Judgment' (1989) FCLI 451

van Miert, K., 'Competition Policy in Relation to the Central and Eastern European Countries – Achievements and Challenges' (1998) 2 ECCPNL 1

 'Global Forces Affecting Competition Policy in a Post-Recessionary Environment' (1993) 17 WC 135

 'International Cooperation in the Field of Competition: a View from the EC' (1997) FCLI 13

Vardady, T., 'The Emergence of Competition Law in (Former) Socialist Countries' (1999) 47 AJCL 229

Vernon, R., 'Sovereignty at Bay: Ten Years after' (1981) 35 IO 517

Vissi, F., 'Challenges and Questions around Competition Policy: the Hungarian Experience' (1995) 18 FILJ 1230

Waller, S., 'Can US Antitrust Laws Open International Markets?' (2000) 20 NJILB 207

 'The Internationalization of Antitrust Enforcement' (1997) 77 BULR 343

Weiler, J., 'Community, Member States and European Integration: Is the Law Relevant?' (1982) 21 JCMS 39

Weiner, M., 'Remedies in International Transactions: a Case for Flexibility' (1996) 65 ALJ 261

Weintraub, R., 'Globalization Effect on Antitrust Law' (1999) 34 NELR 27

Weiss, F., 'From World Trade Law to World Competition Law' (2000) 23 FILJ 250

Wesseling, R., 'The Commission Notices on Decentralisation of EC Antitrust Law: in for a Penny, Not for a Pound' (1997) 18 ECLR 94

 'Subsidiarity in Community Law: Setting the Right Agenda' (1997) 22 ELR 35

Wessman, P., 'Competition Sharpens in Sweden' (1993) 17 WC 113

Whatstein, L., 'Extraterritorial Application of EU Competition Law – Comments and Reflections' (1992) 26 ILR 195

Whish, R., 'Enforcement of EC Competition Law in the Domestic Courts of Member States' (1994) 15 ECLR 60

'Regulation 2790/99: the Commission's "New Style" Block Exemption for Vertical Agreements' (2000) 37 CMLRev 887

Whish, R. and Sufrin, B., 'Art. 85 and the Rule of Reason' (1987) 7 YEL 1

Widegren, M., 'Competition Law in Sweden – a Brief Introduction to the New Legislation' (1995) FCLI 241

Wood, D., 'Caution Necessary Concerning WTO Agenda on Competition Rules: Justice Officials Warn' (1996) 13 ITR 1856

'The Impossible Dream: Real International Antitrust' (1992) UCLF 277

Yntema, H., 'The Comity Doctrine' (1966) 65 MicLR 1

Yu, T., 'An Anti-Unfair Competition Law without a Core: an Introductory Comparison between US Antitrust Law and the New Law of the People's Republic of China' (1994) 4 IICLR 315

INDEX

Antitrust law
  competition advocacy *see*
    competition advocacy
  concept of, 46
  consumer protection, 21, 52
  decision-making, 59–60
  developing countries, 48, 260
  domestic antitrust laws
    differences, 2–4
    similarities, 2
  exemptions, 75
  extraterritoriality *see*
    extraterritoriality
  framework of, 48
  generally, 46
  goals of, 49
    classification, 52: economic, 52;
      political, 53; social, 53
  historical perspective of, 28
  independence of antitrust
    authorities, 62
  legislative intent, 51
  nature of, 46
  political perspective of, 58
  principles of liberal democracy, 58
  procedural differences, 75–6
  protection of competition and
    competitors, 63
  public intervention, 60
  system of antitrust, 10–11
Asia-Pacific Economic Cooperation
  Forum (APEC), 284
Association Agreements (Europe)
  antitrust law
    role of, 122
  approximation of laws, 122, 126–9

background of, 121
contents of, 122
EC secondary legislation
  place of, 125
jurisdictional matters, 123–5
negotiation with the European
  Commission, 128, 129–30
parties to, 121
suitability of EC antitrust law for
  Associated Countries, 127
Australia–New Zealand Closer
  Economic Relations Trade
  Agreement (ANCESTRA), 233,
  242
Austria, 28–30

Bilateral agreements
  comity *see* comity
  EC/Canada Agreement, 290
  EC/Common Market for East and
    Southern Africa (COMESA)
    co-operation project, 132
  EC/South Africa Agreement, 290
  EC/US co-operation agreements,
    112–16
  limitations of, 222–4, 290
  relationship with multilateral
    approach, 289–90
  types of, 218, 291
  US/Australia Agreement, 222
  US/Japan Agreement, 220

Comity
  negative comity agreements, 221
  positive comity agreements, 218–19,
    291

Competition
  allocative efficiency, 22
  Chicago School, 24
  concept of, 17
  contestable market theory, 24
  conventional economic analysis, 23
  dynamic competition, 20
  economics
    contextual, 25
  function of, 19
  invisible hand, 19
  law see antitrust law
  meaning of, 17
  means and end debate, 27
  perfect competition, 22–4
  policy consideration, 26
  productive efficiency, 22
  public choice approach, 25
  total welfare approach, 20
  trade policy and competition policy
    see market access
  workable competition, 24
Competition advocacy
  enforcement of antitrust law, 64
  generally, 63
  necessity of, 63
  public awareness, 66
  work at the International
    Competition Network (ICN),
    257
Convergence and harmonisation of
    domestic antitrust laws, 280

Discretion
  checking discretion, 79
  confining discretion, 77
  dealing with, 77
  discretion as a matter of choice, 83
  informal settlements and interim
    decisions, 74
  instances of, 72
    adoption of binding decisions, 73
    case selection, 73
    exemptions, 75
    initiation of proceedings, 73
  law courts
    role of, 79, 192
  meaning of, 71

  policy considerations, 83
  political factors, 83
  rule-making
    relationship with, 72
  structuring of, 77
Draft Havana Charter, 248

EC antitrust law
  antitrust chapter, 88–9
  Article 2, 89
  Article 3(g), 89
  Article 4, 89
  Article 81, 88
  Article 82, 88
  Article 234, 94
  Association Agreements see
    Association Agreements
    (Europe)
  bilateral co-operation see bilateral
    agreements
  centralisation, 98
  characteristics of, 86–8
  conflict with US antitrust law,
    277–80
  convergence of domestic antitrust
    laws, 105–8 see also convergence
    and harmonisation of domestic
    antitrust laws
  co-operation with national
    competition authorities
    1996 Notice on Co-operation with
    the Commission, 102
  co-operation with national courts
    1993 Notice on Co-operation with
    the Commission, 100–1
  decentralisation, 98–105
  enlargement of the EC see also
    Association Agreements
    (Europe)
  European Commission
    efforts towards
      internationalisation, 136–8
    generally, 91–3
    provision of technical assistance
      to third countries, 131–2
    use of discretion see discretion
  European Court of First Instance
    (CFI), 81–3

European Court of Justice (ECJ),
  79–81, 93–4
European Economic Area (EEA) *see*
  European Economic Area EEA
horizontal co-operation between
  domestic systems of antitrust,
  108
judicial review of Commission
  decisions *see* discretion
Merger Regulation
  Gencor v. Commission, 177–9
  GE/Honeywell International,
    179–81
modernisation, 109–12
  new Regulation 1/2003 to replace
    Regulation 17/62, 111
national courts, 94–5
nature of, 89–91
Partnership and Co-operation
  Agreement (PCA) with Russian
  Federation, 122
relationship with domestic antitrust
  laws, 95
reliance on domestic antitrust laws,
  103–5
single market goal, 87
two barrier theory, 95
value of, 132–4
European Economic Area (EEA)
  agreement, 116–17
  antitrust chapter, 119
  institutions
    court, 119
    surveillance authority, 118–19
Extraterritoriality
  Act of state doctrine, 199
  bilateral co-operation *see* bilateral
    agreements
  conflicts of extraterritoriality,
    196–204
  definition of, 164–5
  developing a common approach,
    203–4
  economic conduct, 161
  EC antitrust law *see* EC antitrust law
  effects doctrine
    Alcoa, 162
    justification for, 163–4

  Hartford Fire Insurance, 171–2
  Nippon Paper Industries, 175
  reluctance of ECJ to endorse the
    doctrine, 182
extraterritoriality in exceptional
  circumstances, 1, 199–200
foreign sovereign compulsion
  defence, 174, 199
implementation doctrine, 176–7
international comity *see* comity
judicial aggression, 191–2
law courts
  role of, 192–5
links with internationalisation of
  antitrust policy, 165–7
Lowenfeld, 173
political dimension of, 167
principles of public international
  law
  respect for, 201
problem of, 195
responses to, 187
  blocking through legislation,
    188–9
  blocking through case law,
    189–90
  diplomatic protest, 188
shortcomings of, 217
territoriality principle
  exceptions to, 159–61
treble damages *see* US antitrust law
Wood Pulp, 176

General Agreement on Trade in
  Services (GATS) *see* World
  Trade Organization (WTO)
General Agreement on Tariffs and
  Trade (GATT), 207
Germany, 30–2
Global Antitrust Framework (GAF),
  292–4
Globalisation, 1, 12–15, 199–200

International Antitrust Code, 9, 283–4
International Competition Network
  (ICN), 255–7
International Trade Organization
  (ITO), 248

Internationalisation
  business firms, 269–72
  confidential information, 271
  conflicts between countries, 271–6
  examples of, 9
  extraterritoriality see
    extraterritoriality
  globalisation see globalisation
  International Competition Network
    (ICN) see International
    Competition Network (ICN)
  international system of antitrust, 11
  making of important commercial
    decisions, 59–60
  model systems of antitrust, 273
  Organization for Economic
    Cooperation and Development
    (OECD) see Organization for
    Economic Cooperation and
    Development (OECD)
  past developments, 247–50
  reaching consensus on, 284
  role of politicians, 285
  sovereignty see sovereignty
  United Nations Conference on Trade
    and Development (UNCTAD)
    see United Nations Conference
    on Trade and Development
    (UNCTAD)
  views of different countries on
  World Trade Organization (WTO)
    see World Trade Organization
    (WTO)

Japan, 275–6

Kenya, 260
Korea, 261–2

Market access
  development of principle under
    antitrust policy, 230–4, 242–4
  different bodies
    work of: American Bar
      Association (ABA) 236–7;
      Organization for Economic
      Cooperation and Development
      (OECD) see Organization for

    Economic Cooperation and
      Development (OECD); US
      Department of Justice, 236;
      World Trade Organization
      (WTO) see World Trade
      Organization
  domestic trade laws, 225
    section 301 US Trade Act 1974 see
      US antitrust law
  extraterritoriality see
    extraterritoriality
  hindrances to, 206–9
    hybrid hindrances, 211–13:
      limiting foreign direct
      investment, 212;
      standardisation, 212
    private hindrances, 209–10: abuse
      of a dominant position, 210;
      horizontal agreements, 209;
      mergers, 210; vertical
      agreements, 209
    public hindrances, 209–11:
      exemptions see antitrust law;
      strategic application of
      domestic antitrust laws, 211
  meaning of, 208
  Neofunctionalism see
    Neofunctionalism
  perspectives of antitrust and trade
    policy, 215–16
  principle of, 227–8
  shortcomings of domestic antitrust
    laws, 228–9
  substitutability of antitrust and trade
    policies, 237–41
Market definition
  basic principles, 37–40
  internationalisation of antitrust
    policy see internationalisation
  Notice on market definition, 37
  potential competition, 39
  purpose of, 35
  relevant geographic market,
    39–40
    evidence relied on to define
      relevant market: customer
      habits, 38; past evidence of
      diversion to other areas, 39;

trade flows, 39; transport costs, 39; views of customers and competitors, 41
relevant product market, 37
demand substitutability, 37–9: SSNIP test, 38, 39
intended use, 38
physical characteristics, 38
supply substitutability, 38
significance of, 36–7
Mexico, 279

Neofunctionalism
different players, 233–4
meaning of, 231–2
Neorationalism, 268–9
North American Free Trade Agreement (NAFTA), 262, 279
Norway, 262, 279

Organization for Economic Cooperation and Development (OECD)
committees, 253–4
generally, 252–3
Hawk report, 211, 235
limitations on, 265–6
Multinational Agreement on Investment (MAI), 253
provision of technical assistance, 265
Recommendations, 252
work on relationship between antitrust and trade policy, 235–6

Realism, 267–8

South Africa, 260–1
Sovereignty
acquisition of, 145
business power, 155–7
content of, 143
dimensions
national, 149–50
international, 150–1
relationship with internationalisation of antitrust policy, 149

relinquishment of, 145, 147
roles of, 142–3
significance of, 142
substance of, 148–9
transfer of competence, 141
types of, 152–3

Trade-Related Aspects of Intellectual Property Rights (TRIPS) see World Trade Organization (WTO)
Turkey, 262

United Kingdom, 32–3
United Nations Conference on Trade and Development (UNCTAD), 254–5
US antitrust law
adoption of binding decisions, 73
bilateral co-operation
EC/US agreements, 112–16
characteristics of, 273–4
Clayton Act 1914, 34
Enforcement Guidelines for International Operations 1995
extraterritorial application see extraterritoriality
Foreign Trade Antitrust Improvements Act (FTAIA) 1982, 169
goals, 273
guidelines, 169–71
historical perspective, 33–4
ICPAC, 198, 264
influence of, 279
International Antitrust Enforcement Assistance Act 1994, 222
per se approach, 273
procedure, 76
rule of reason approach, 273
Sherman Act 1890, 273
Trade Act 1974, 225–7
treble damages, 201–3, 274
views on internationalisation, 258–9

World Trade Organization (WTO),
        251–2
    Appellate Body (AB), 291
    development of antitrust policy,
        234
    4th Ministerial Conference, 257
    goals of antitrust law, 54

    limitations on, 264–5
    Most-Favoured-Nation (MFN)
        principle, 225, 291
    support by other organisations, 291
    Trade-Related Aspects of Intellectual
        Property Rights (TRIPS), 225,
        291

LIST OF WEBSITES

1. Asia-Pacific Economic Cooperation (APEC), Competition Law Aspects
http://www.apecsec.org
2. Australia National Competition Council
http://www.ncc.gov.au
3. Australian Competition and Consumer Commission
http://www.accc.gov.au
4. Canada Competition Bureau
http://strategis.ic.gc.ca
5. Canadian Bar Association, Competition
http://www.algonquinc.on.ca/cba
6. Consumer International
http://www.consumerinternational.org
7. EC Commission, the Competition Directorate
http://europa.eu.int/comm/competition
8. EFTA Surveillance Authority
http://www.efta.int/structure/SURV/efta-srv.cfm
9. International Competition Network (ICN)
http://www.internationalcompetitionnetwork.org
10. Japanese Fair Trade Commission
http://www.jftc.admix.go.jp
11. New Zealand Commerce Commission
http://www.comcom.govt.nz
12. New Zealand Ministry of Commerce, Competition and Enterprise Branch
http://www.med.govt.nz/cae
13. OECD, Competition Policy
http://www.oecd.org/daf/clp
14. UK Competition Commission
http://www.competition-commission.org.uk
15. UK Department of Trade and Industry
http://www.dti.gov.uk

16. UK Office of Fair Trading
http://www.oft.gov.uk
17. US American Antitrust Institute
http://www.antitrustinstitute.org
18. US American Bar Association, Antitrust Section
http://www.abanet.org/antitrust
19. US Antitrust Law and Economics Review
http://home.mpinet.net/cmueller
20. US Department of Justice, Antitrust Division
http://www.usdoj.gov
21. US Fair Trade Commission
http://www.ftc.gov
22. World Bank
http://www.worldbank.org
23. World Biggest Antitrust Sites
http://www.clubi.ie/competition
24. WTO
http://www.wto.org